D1370698

Course III ■ Volume 1

21Book

Credits and acknowledgments appear on pages 344–346, which constitute an extension of this copyright page.

ISBN-13: 978-0-545-31466-4
ISBN-10: 0-545-31466-6

1 2 3 4 5 6 7 8 9 10　　09　　19 18 17 16 15 14 13 12 11 10

 Text pages printed on 10% PCW recycled paper.

Salen w... **Game Designer**

Subject: Welcome to the *21Book!*
To: Expert 21 Students
From: Expert 21 Editors (expert21@scholastic.com)

reply ▼

Dear Reader,

Are you ready to read, explore, learn, and master the skills you need to succeed in the 21st Century? This book is a good place to start. You'll complete four workshops on exciting topics, focused on questions that only you can answer.

Is college on your horizon? Many careers and jobs require some education beyond high school. Plus, the further you go in school, the more money you're likely to make. College graduates, on average, earn almost twice as much over a lifetime as workers who only graduate from high school. Now is the time to sign up for **Workshop 1, "College 101,"** and start planning for life after high school. Discover your own answer to the question: **How can I get ready for the future I want?**

Personal computers are just a few decades old, but it's hard to imagine life before them. What new inventions will come along—and make us wonder how we lived without them—over the next several decades? See for yourself in **Workshop 2, "Designing the Future."** Along with the excitement of new inventions comes the fear that technology will affect our lives in ways that aren't so desirable! Get ready to weigh the answers to this question: **What are the costs and benefits of technology?**

There are places on this planet where temperatures average well below freezing; then, there are desert regions where daytime temperatures can soar as high as 120 degrees Fahrenheit. **How do people survive in extreme environments?** That's the question you'll explore in **Workshop 3, "Life at the Edges."**

Hey, we can't hear you! Find inspiration to be loud, be proud, and stand up for your beliefs as you read about the outspoken young people of the 1960s. In **Workshop 4, "1960s: Stand Up, Be Heard,"** you'll meet youth and adults who spoke out for equal rights for all Americans, protested a war, and made their voices heard on the national stage. You'll discover a variety of answers to the question: **How can we be heard?**

Let the Expert 21 Team know what you think! Email us at:
Expert21@scholastic.com

Sincerely,
The Editors

LEDGE
"THE TEACHER"

LA VIDA ROB

By Lydia Okutoro

1962

In August, **Spider Man** makes his **first appearance** when Marvel Comics publishes *Amazing Fantasy (#15).*

In September, **Rachel Carson** publishes *Silent Spring,* which becomes a best seller and sparks the **environmental movement**. Chemical companies threaten to sue her to keep her quiet.

AMAZING FANTASY
SPIDER MAN

DE TO EMBE

Reading 1   SHORT STORY

THE STORY OF KEESH

By Susan
Lieberma
Adapted
The Rea

COLLEGE 101

Expert Question:
How can I get ready for the future I want?

Inquiry 1: Choosing a Path

Skills & Strategies

Inquiry 2: Getting There

2

DESIGNING THE FUTURE

Inquiry 1: Human Versus Machine

Skills & Strategies

Inquiry 2: Technology to the Rescue

Life at the Edges

Inquiry 1: Lands of Ice and Snow

Skills & Strategies

Inquiry 2: Desert Zones

1960s: STAND UP, BE HEARD

Inquiry 1: The Power of Free Speech

Skills & Strategies

Inquiry 2: Changing Times

[21] Questions

▶ **Answer these questions to get ready for the 21 Book.**

1 **Prioritize.** What do you want to get out of life—and give to the world? Check the top three goals you hope to achieve.

- ☐ earning a high salary
- ☐ helping people
- ☐ doing creative work
- ☐ helping the environment
- ☐ learning new things
- ☐ serving your country
- ☐ other: _____
- ☐ other: _____

2 **Plan.** What are you doing now to prepare for your future? Check ✓ all that apply.

_____ developing good relationships with adults who can connect you with jobs or other opportunities

_____ saving money for education after high school

_____ taking summer courses or finding jobs in topics that interest you

_____ practicing skills (drawing, fixing things, or other activities) you hope to use in your adult life

3 **Evaluate.** Put a **T** (true) next to the statements you believe to be true. Put an **F** (false) next to the statements you think are false.

_____ Your eighth grade grades will be important for college admissions.

_____ You can apply for scholarships that will pay for college tuition—and even your living expenses—while in college.

_____ After-school activities like band, sports, and volunteering may help you get into the school you want.

_____ Taking summer courses or getting an internship can help prepare you for college.

4 **Synthesize.** Think about people you know who have jobs (teachers, family, adults in your neighborhood, older relatives). Who seems to enjoy his or her job the most? What do you think he or she enjoys about it?

_____

_____

_____

_____

5 **Question.** Which of the following do you think is the most popular college major so far in the 21st Century? Check one.

- ☐ Computer and Information Science
- ☐ Psychology
- ☐ Business
- ☐ Nursing and other health-related majors

6 **Evaluate.** Put a **T** (true) next to the statements you think are true. Put an **F** (false) next to the statements you think are false.

_____ Only your friends can see what you post online.

_____ You should never publish your full name on a social networking site.

_____ Future employers may look at what you have posted online.

_____ You should add as many friends as possible on a social networking site.

_____ It is safe to put your address online.

7 **Solve.** What would you do with your own personal robot? If you could design and program a robot to perform an everyday task, what would you like a robot to do for you? Explain.

_____

_____

_____

_____

_____

_____

8 **Justify.** Do you know anyone who spends too much time playing video games? (It's not you, right?) What is a reasonable amount of time to play video games? _____ hour(s) a week

Explain your response.

_____

_____

_____

_____

_____

9 **Predict.** Most people would agree that life today is better than it was 100 years ago. What about 100 years from now? Do you think the future will be a better time to live in than the time you live in today? Explain your response.

_____

_____

_____

_____

_____

_____

10 **Evaluate.** What should designers who invent new technology consider in their plans? Rate these factors from **1** (least important) to **3** (most important).

RATING

_____ the cost of using the new technology

_____ how many people the technology will benefit

_____ the number of people who will have access to the technology

11

Personalize. Put an **X** next to the actions you would be willing to take to help reduce global warming.

_____ Unplug any electrical device that you are not using.

_____ Limit how often you use an air conditioner during the summer.

_____ Wait until you have a full load of clothes to do laundry.

_____ Ride a bike or walk whenever possible, instead of riding in a car.

12

Decide. Warmer global temperatures are causing polar ice caps to melt. Polar bears are threatened as their hunting grounds shrink. What should we do to help the bears?

☐ Move all polar bears to zoos.

☐ Nothing; polar bears are not our problem.

☐ Do what we can to stop temperatures from rising.

☐ Other _____

_____

Explain why you chose this response.

_____

_____

13

Prioritize. What would a community need to survive in a vast desert? Rate each item below from **1** (least important) to **4** (most important).

RATING

_____ water

_____ a vehicle

_____ a strong leader

_____ shelter

_____ livestock such as camels or goats

14

Decide. How big do you think the Sahara Desert in Africa is? Check your best guess.

☐ the size of Texas

☐ the size of the lower 48 U.S. states

☐ the size of California

☐ the size of Illinois, Iowa, and Wisconsin

15

Decide. Which way of life sounds most interesting to you? Circle one.

Living in a polar region so bitterly cold that it has no native human inhabitants.

Living in a vast desert with scorching temperatures, and relying on camels for transportation.

Explain your response.

_____

_____

_____

_____

_____

16

Evaluate. What is the best way to deal with a law you think is unfair? Check the courses of action that would be effective.

☐ Talk to the mayor of your town or city.

☐ Organize a protest.

☐ Write a letter to the local paper.

☐ Hold a school-wide meeting.

17

Empathize. One of your family members has joined the military and is leaving to fight a war in another country. What do you say to this person before he or she leaves?

_____

_____

_____

_____

18

Evaluate. Dr. Martin Luther King, Jr. said, "I have a dream that my four little children will one day live in a nation where they will not be judged by the color of their skin but by the content of their character." Do you think people are now judged mostly by the content of their character—meaning how they act and the kind of person they are? Explain.

_____

_____

_____

_____

_____

19

Describe. What is your generation like? Mark three words that describe what you think people will say about you and your peers 50 years from now.

☐ cared about the environment

☐ cared about justice for all

☐ materialistic (cared about money and possessions)

☐ ambitious

☐ self-centered

☐ generous

☐ other _____

_____

20

Decide. Circle the issue or issues that you think Americans care the most about.

Ending poverty　　　Fighting for equal rights

Stopping wars　　　Protecting the environment

21

Be an Expert. Look through the Table of Contents on pages IV–VII. Which article or topic looks most interesting to you? Why does it interest you?

_____

_____

_____

_____

After you read the workshops, come back and see if you feel the same way!

21st Century Learning in Action

▶ **Rate your 21st Century Skills—and show how you apply these skills to school and life.**

Intellectual

C

Content Area

SCHOLASTIC

expert **21**
™

Inquiry

Personal

Social

Global

Communication and Collaboration

1 I always **ask** the **five Ws** (who, what, when, where, why) when I'm trying to understand a situation or event. [RATING _____]

2 I know some of the **roles and rules** of being on a **team**. When I'm on a team, I always remember to: _____

_____

_____

_____

_____

Critical Thinking and Problem Solving

3 When **considering** a decision, I always weigh the **risks** and **rewards** of my options. [RATING _____]

4 When I make a mistake on something, I go back and **evaluate the error**. An example of a mistake that I was able to correct is: _____

_____

_____

_____

_____

Creativity and Innovation

5 I'm good at keeping **ideas flowing** during a **brainstorming** session. [**RATING** _____]

6 I'm able to use my **creativity** in my daily life. I use creativity to: _____

_____

_____

_____

_____

Information and Media Literacy

9 When I am **gathering data** for a project, I make sure I use up-to-date information and trustworthy source material. [**RATING** _____]

10 I know the steps in the **research process**. Some of the steps are: _____

_____

_____

_____

_____

_____

College, Workplace, and Life Skills

7 For each of my long-term **goals**, like graduating high school, I also have short-term goals that I keep track of, like passing my classes this year. [**RATING** _____]

8 I know my **work habits** and I try to plan how much **time** I need to do each assignment. For example, an assignment that takes me about two hours would be:

_____

_____

_____

_____

ICT Literacy

Information and Communication Technology

11 I use the **help function** and search for troubleshooting guides on the Internet to solve any problems I encounter while using software. [**RATING** _____]

12 I use **RSS feeds** and **bookmarking** to keep up to date on my favorite topics on the Web. One way I use the Web to keep up to date is:

_____

_____

_____

_____

My [21] Page

▶ Fill in the section for each workshop as you complete it.
Keep track of your interests and goals, as well.

Name | ▼ _____   Age | ▼ ____

Hometown | ▼ _____   State | ▼ ____

🌐 My World

Places I'd Like to Explore

- _____
- _____
- _____
- _____

People (Dead or Alive) I'd Like to Meet

- _____
- _____
- _____
- _____

📖 My Media

Media I Like (Books and Movies)

- _____
- _____
- _____

Video Games I'm Playing

- _____
- _____
- _____

Web Sites I'm Visiting

- _____
- _____
- _____

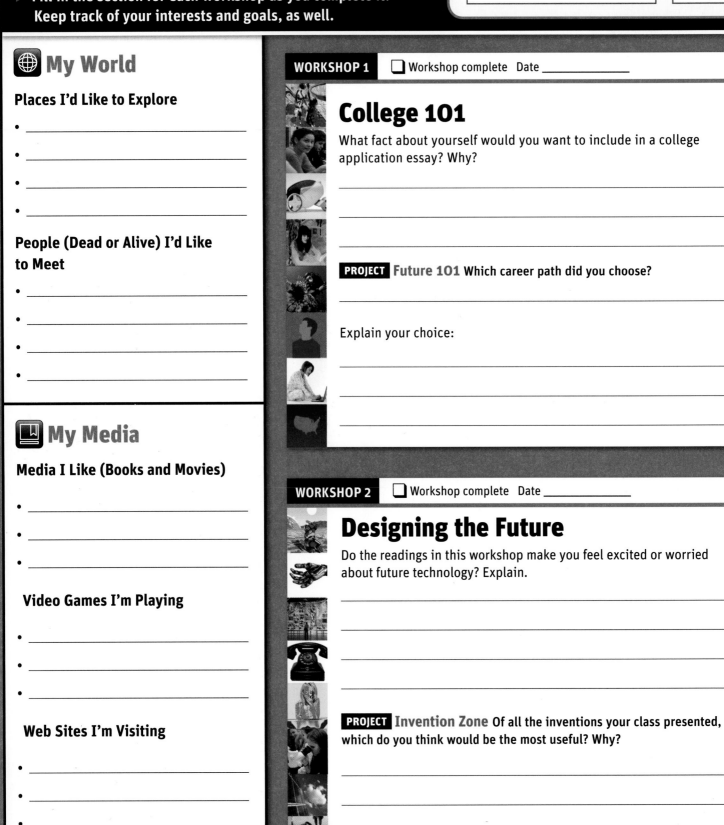

WORKSHOP 1   ☐ Workshop complete   Date _____

College 101

What fact about yourself would you want to include in a college application essay? Why?

_____
_____
_____

PROJECT Future 101 Which career path did you choose?

_____

Explain your choice:

_____
_____
_____

WORKSHOP 2   ☐ Workshop complete   Date _____

Designing the Future

Do the readings in this workshop make you feel excited or worried about future technology? Explain.

_____
_____
_____

PROJECT Invention Zone Of all the inventions your class presented, which do you think would be the most useful? Why?

_____
_____

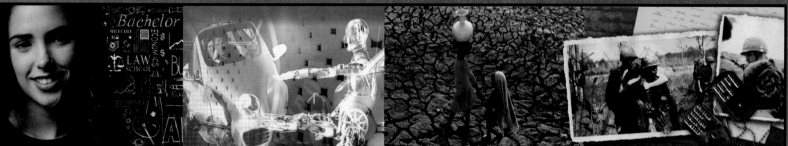

Life at the Edges

Do you think it would be more challenging to live in a polar region or a desert zone? Why?

_____

_____

_____

_____

PROJECT **Extreme Habitat** Who might adapt most easily to life at the South Pole station? List four qualities you think people should have to survive in this extreme environment.

_____

_____

_____

1960s: Stand Up, Be Heard

If you were going to write a song about your generation, what would you call it? Why?

_____

_____

PROJECT **Rally for a Cause** The most challenging part of holding the rally you and your group planned would be:

_____

_____

Explain your choice:

_____

_____

★ My Skills

Topics I'm an Expert In

- _____
- _____
- _____
- _____

Skills I'm an Expert In

- _____
- _____
- _____
- _____

🏹 My Goals

Jobs That I Know About

- _____
- _____
- _____

Jobs I Want to Know More About

- _____
- _____
- _____

Skills That I Want to Learn

- _____
- _____
- _____

COLLEGE 101

? Expert Question:
How can I get ready for the future I want?

Explore the Expert Question

[21] Expert Knowledge

Watch the Anchor Media!

PAGE 4
An audiovisual introduction to **College 101.**

Explore Expert Space

PAGE 5 **expert space**
See **College 101** online at
www.expert21.com/student.

[21] Meet the Expert

Veronica Rivera Savage: Social Worker

PAGE 6   Savage helps students find their dreams and reach their goals.

Read and Synthesize

Inquiry 1   Choosing a Path

 **L** **Reading 1**
NOVEL EXCERPT

Playing the Game

AWARD WINNER

By Walter Dean Myers

Drew and his team have been playing hard and winning all season. Now with the final playoff game approaching and college on the line, Drew's game is more important than ever.

PAGE 10

i **Reading 2**
PROFILES

Finding Their Futures

By Karen Fanning

There are many paths to success after high school—no two look exactly the same. Follow four students as they make their way down different roads toward their futures. Whose path appeals to you?

PAGE 22

 **i** **Reading 3**
INFOGRAPHIC

Options, Options, and More Options

You've made it through high school. Now what? This infographic gives facts about some of the many options you have.

i *infographic*
FAST FACTS

PAGE 28

[21] 21st Century Skills

Analyze Data

PAGE 34

MY COLLEGE OPTIONS CHART

	A	B	C	D	E
1		Allied Tech University	Breck School of Business and Technology	Western States Community College	ANALYSIS
2	LOCATION	Bakersfield, California (100 miles from home)	Los Angeles, California (220 miles from home)	Fresno, California (30-minute bus ride)	I could live at home and commute to Western States Community College.
3	SPECIALTY	Liberal arts college with nationally ranked programs in computer technology	Business courses; computer technology; both on-site and online classes	computer technology; preparation for 4-year college	A degree from Allied Tech would look good on my resume.
		$7,000 per	$325 per on-site class (12 weeks) $255 per online	$300 per class	Breck's classes are reasonable, but I

NewsWIRE

College Students Face Growing Debt
Susan Whitehall, Media News Service.

January 15, 2009 –As the economy stagnates, students are facing mountains of debt when they graduate from college, and also worries about how to pay the debt.

College graduates, on average, earn almost twice as much as those who only finish high school. College grads also have the opportunity to pursue fields that interest them, because a B.A. or B.S. is often a prerequisite for many jobs.

However, the economy is not getting better very fast. As of December 2008, the unemployment rate was 7.6% and growing, a figure that does not include recent graduates who have not yet found work, or people who have given up on looking for work. Students may be stuck with debt, and no way to pay it back.

a secret. I'm stage
to the theater has al
l experience for me.
go down, I feel like
er world. I was even
e a Broadway musical
om of the Opera. Ou
e very last row, but
n't really see a futu
though. My dad is an
ad always hoped I mig
trical engineering. He
d job. I've looked up
know he's right.
s year, I went to a j
hool. When I first go
rvous. Then, the wom
ngineering table asked
joy science and math

21 How can I get ready for the future I want?

What do you want to become? A doctor? An athlete? An artist? Now is the time to take your goals seriously and become the best at what you most love to do.

▶ Anchor Your Knowledge

Watch the Anchor Media, "College 101," and meet Veronica Rivera Savage, a social worker who helps teens work toward their career and college goals every day.

▶ Concept Web

Create a concept web of your thoughts about the pros, cons, and challenges of going to college. Use ideas from the Anchor Media to get started.

College

WORKSHOP GOALS

To gain expert knowledge about career goals, you will

- study **informational texts** about teens who found their own unique paths to college and careers.

- read **literature** about teens exploring where they want to go in life.

- learn **important skills and strategies** to help you understand what you read.

- develop **21st Century Skills** to **solve problems** and **analyze data.**

- write a **personal narrative** to use as a college admissions essay.

- complete an **Expert Project** to create a career action plan.

▶ Preview the Expert Project

At the end of this workshop, you'll decide on a career path you would like to explore and create a plan to reach your goals. Preview the **Expert Project** on pages 76–79.

Career Profiles

Sha-Ella Shelton, *Hairstylist*

What she does: "I help clients look their best. I cut hair and create new styles. I also help clients keep their hair healthy."

How she got here: "I studied cosmetology in high school. My first job was at a top New York City salon. I started as a shampoo girl. Within months, I was a stylist. Now, I am the head stylist."

Advice for others interested in this career: "Make sure you love it. Some hairstylists just do their work, and others have a passion for their gift. To succeed in this business, you really have

Gina Riley, *Dolphin Trainer*

What she does: "My job is to care for 14 dolphins at Discovery Cove, an animal theme park in Orlando, Florida. I also train dolphins to respond to my signals. For example, I'll swing my arm to get them to do a jump. If the dolphin does it, I'll give it a rub or a fish as a reward."

How she got here: "I started by getting a college degree in marine biology. During college, I worked as a summer intern at Sea World. I fell in love with the park and got a job at Discovery Cove after I graduated."

Advice for others interested in this career: "Try volunteering at an animal shelter or an animal hospital. Also, try to swim as much as you can. Trainers must swim well."

▶ What will you need to know or do to complete the Expert Project?

_____

_____

_____

_____

▶ Explore Expert Space

 Go to **www.expert21.com/student** to learn more about the topics in this workshop.

DISCOVER ONLINE

- Slideshow of 12 Major Career Paths
- Colleges and Universities
- Vocational Education

READ ONLINE

- College Sports
- Summer Search
- The Peace Corps
- College Visits

RESEARCH ONLINE

- The College Curriculum
- Financial Aid
- Internships

▶ Personal Inquiry

Explore the topic of college and careers by asking your own questions. Return to add questions as you continue reading Workshop 1. Plan to revisit your questions.

21

Veronica Rivera Savage: Social Worker

Savage helps students find their dreams and reach their goals.

Veronica Rivera Savage believes that learning by doing is powerful. At City-As-School, the high school where Savage works, students "spend half their week in classes and the other half doing internships." As a social worker, Savage helps students succeed in both worlds by answering the key questions "Who am I?" and "What do I want to do with my life?" Find out how she does it.

"Having a sense of your strengths and what you enjoy will serve you well."

FACTS AND STATS

NAME: Veronica Rivera Savage

HOMETOWN: New York City, New York

JOB: Social Worker at City-As-School High School, New York City

EDUCATION: Bachelor of Science; Master of Social Work

PROUD MOMENT: "I was the first in my family to graduate from college. That's an important accomplishment."

WORKPLACE SKILLS: Interviews, solves problems; makes decisions

PAY: Social workers start at about $30,000 a year; with experience, they can earn up to $60,000 a year.

CAREER CONNECTION Human Services
www.careerclusters.org

Go to **21 Tool**Kit **Expert File 6.25** to learn more about careers in Human Services.

RELATED JOBS: Guidance counselor, career counselor

MONDAY MORNING — Communicating and Troubleshooting

Savage starts her workday at 8 a.m. For two hours every morning, she **communicates** with parents and caregivers—updating them on students' progress. "Family involvement is a powerful way to communicate to young people that they are important."

Next, Savage and her team begin **collaborating** to **solve particular problems** that students may be having. One young woman fears interning out in "the real world." What should she do? The team decides to modify her program. "The student will have a complete in-house schedule now. We will revisit the internship next term." In the meantime, the team will work on building up the young woman's social skills and self-confidence.

MONDAY AFTERNOON — Teaching Life Skills

After a quick thirty-minute lunch break, Savage **teaches** a class. Today the class focuses on living a healthy lifestyle. They also work on **goal setting** and learn about volunteering, civic responsibility, and how to handle conflict.

TUESDAY Focusing on Special Situations

Today, as well as having regular meetings and classes, Savage works with special-needs students. They may have learning disabilities, physical limitations, or medical issues. She also makes sure that on test days, these students "receive testing accommodations that include extended test time, use of calculators, or having instructions read aloud to them."

WEDNESDAY AND THURSDAY Being an Advisor

Savage often attends afternoon sessions that teachers hold with their students. She's there to help students think about questions like "What am I enjoying?" and "What am I having trouble with?" On Thursdays, she also gives a talk to students. This week's topic is "Holiday Stress Busters"—ways to cope with the pressures the holidays can bring.

FRIDAY Discovering What's Right

Part of Savage's job is reaching out to students who have dropped out or missed a lot of school. Today she discovers that one student has dropped out to get a job to help support the family. Savage sets up a meeting with the family to figure out a way for the student to return to the classroom. In the afternoon, she and her team discuss offering classes in dealing with anxiety and building confidence.

The **ultimate goal** of Savage's work is to help students reach their full potential and be prepared to meet the challenges of life. That begins with "knowing yourself."

ANALYZE EXPERT SKILLS

1. Solve Problems
How does Savage help students solve problems?

_____

_____

2. Set Goals
In working with students, what are two goals Savage wants to achieve?

_____

_____

_____

3. Communicate
With whom does Savage communicate during a typical week? Complete the chart below.

| Person/Group: |
| Topic: |
| Person/Group: |
| Topic: |
| Person/Group: |
| Topic: |

DISCOVER ONLINE

expert space
Go to **www.expert21.com/student** to learn more about Slideshow of 12 Major Career Paths; Colleges and Universities; Vocational Education.

Novel Excerpt

PLAYING THE GAME

For a very few students, an athletic scholarship opens the door to college. In this story, you'll meet a basketball player who knows he's playing to win more than just a game.

 **QuickWrite**

For many teens, basketball and football are more than just games. These activities are closely linked to their dreams for the future. Write a paragraph about an activity you do now that is related to your dreams for the future.

Character and Motivation LITERARY ANALYSIS

Motivation is the reason a character acts a certain way. When you analyze a story character, you think about his or her motivation.

Writers do not always directly tell you a character's motivation. You have to **infer** it using clues in the text—such as what a character says, does, or thinks—as well as what you know from your own experiences.

▶ Read this passage from "Playing the Game." Then complete the chart.

> In the locker room Sky was sobbing in the corner. Nobody thought it was his fault; nobody thought that he had lost the game or even that his mistake had cost us the game. But nobody had the emotional energy to console him. I was numb; all my tears were inside.

Who?	Action/Feelings	Motivation
Narrator	Does not console Sky	Feels too sad to cheer someone up
Sky		

Summarize COMPREHENSION

A summary is a brief restating of the main ideas, steps, or events in a piece of writing.

When you summarize, use your own words and focus only on the most important characters, events, and details.

▶ Write one sentence that summarizes the passage below.

> I had sent regular applications to a number of schools, as my guidance counselor had advised me. My first letter back was from Arizona. It was a straight letter turning me down and asking me to reconsider for my sophomore year. Then I was turned down by Howard, in D.C., Charleston Southern, Virginia Union, the University of Washington, and Louisiana State University.

_____

_____

_____

_____

_____

_____

_____

Academic Language VOCABULARY

▶ Rate your knowledge of each word. Then write its meaning and an example sentence.

Word	Meaning	Example
EXPERT WORDS *Use these words to write and talk about the workshop topic.*		
advise *ad•vise (verb)* ① ② ③ ④	to guide; to suggest something	I asked the school counselor to advise me on what classes to take.
recruit *re•cruit (noun)* ① ② ③ ④		
scholarship *schol•ar•ship (noun)* ① ② ③ ④		I just got a scholarship to attend Indiana University!
ACADEMIC WORDS *Use these words in all your subject classes.*		
transit *tran•sit (adjective)* ① ② ③ ④	related to a system of buses or trains that moves people or goods	
violation *vi•o•la•tion (noun)* ① ② ③ ④		
SELECTION WORDS *These words are key to understanding this selection.*		
adore *a•dore (verb)* ① ② ③ ④		
console *con•sole (verb)* ① ② ③ ④		
represent *rep•re•sent (verb)* ① ② ③ ④		

Rating Scale ① I don't know the word. ② I've seen it or heard it. ③ I know its meaning. ④ I know it and use it.

Context Clues: General WORD ANALYSIS

Context clues are words or phrases in a text that can help you figure out the meaning of an unfamiliar or confusing term.

The context of an unfamiliar term is the phrase or sentence in which it appears.

▶ **Read the sentence below.**

My mother got all choked up and needed a tissue after the principal announced that I had won a college scholarship.

What does *choked up* mean?

_____

Underline the context clues that helped you figure out the meaning of *choked up*.

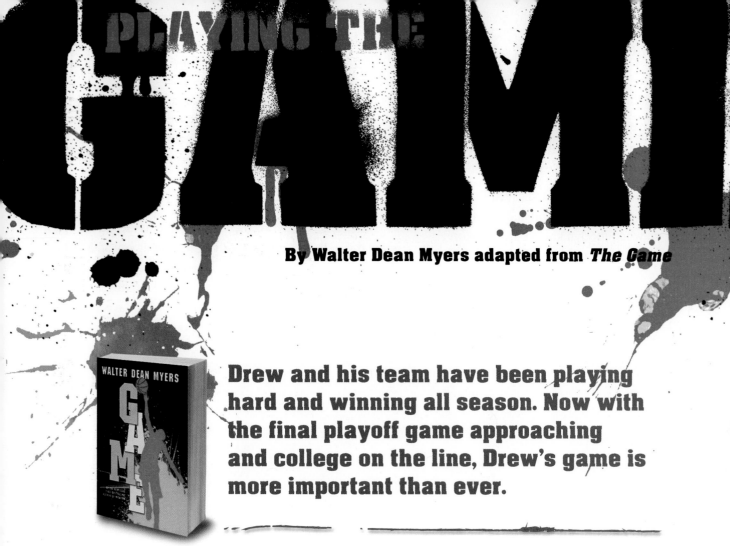

PLAYING THE GAME

By Walter Dean Myers adapted from *The Game*

Drew and his team have been playing hard and winning all season. Now with the final playoff game approaching and college on the line, Drew's game is more important than ever.

Mom had floured some chicken in the morning, and when we got home, she deep-fried it and we had it along with some homemade French fries and green peas.

"Everybody was just looking at you and hanging on everything you did!" Mom said. "You don't know how proud of you I was. A woman I didn't even know was saying how good you were playing."

"Didn't I tell you that Drew is the man?" Jocelyn had a chicken wing in her hand as she talked. "When he came out on the court for the second half, I could see he was going to take care of business. What did you think, Pops?"

"Drew, I don't know much about ball playing," Pops said. "But I was sitting in the stands and watching all the people watching you, and it was like … a real good feeling. You know, I never had nothing like that in my life. People cheering. What you were doing was important. I was thinking about you going to college and all, and it means a lot to me. You being my boy and all."

"How about me?" Jocelyn asked. "I don't count because I'm a girl?"

"No, you count, honey," Pops said. "But—you know, you're smart and everything."

"Yo, you mean I'm not smart enough to go to college?" I put on a mean face.

Pops looked at me and started to say something, but then he got choked up and just gave my arm a little push.

After supper I went to my room and called Ruffy. His mom said he was in the bathroom and he'd call me back. I had just hung up when Jocelyn knocked and, before I could tell her to come in, had framed herself in the doorway.

"You want me to stand here and **adore** you or anything?" she asked.

"I feel like going outside and telling everybody about the game."

"So why don't you?" Jocelyn's eyebrows came together. "They need to hear some good news in this neighborhood."

I felt a little stupid taking the elevator downstairs just to tell somebody how good I felt, but I did anyway. There were two guys on the stoop, but I didn't know them. One of them looked sleepy. Just seeing him started me coming down off my good feeling.

What I wished was that they were all into playing ball and wanted to hear about how Baldwin had won the game and how well I thought I had done. But that wasn't what was going down. What they were doing was getting on with their lives, dealing with the corner business, dealing with whatever they had to sell or buy on their market to get money for whatever they needed to be doing, or thought they needed to be doing, with their lives.

In a way it was like a bunch of guys in a game. They were falling behind every minute that passed, but they had lost interest in the score. It was as if they were just a ton behind and had given up on the win. And maybe deep inside they didn't want to peep the score, maybe they knew what was happening but just didn't want to think

"Give it up, fool! Give it up!"

about it anymore. I could understand that. I had played enough ball in my life, and was deep enough into my game to know I had to be in the hunt for a win or I could lose who I was. And once I lost who I was, my inner me, then there wasn't anything in the world that was going to make it right.

The strange thing was that everybody was feeling the same thing, that there was a huge game going on, and that the game was going to decide who was a winner and who lost. But so many of the brothers on the corner didn't have a play. They were out buying their uniforms, their gold chains, and the fancy clothes like they were real players, but they knew better. Even when they angled into their best gangster lean, it was just a pose. There was never going to be a jump ball. I could feel for them because they were just like me in most ways, thinking that everybody should have a number, everybody should have the same playing time, and knowing it wasn't going to happen.

When we got to the arena the next day for the final playoff game, I was about as nervous as I could get. To make it worse, there was a television crew there and a whole section of photographers. Across from the television cameras there was a big banner that spelled out L-A-N-E.

Everybody knew Franklin K. Lane High School. Little kids in Brooklyn who wanted to play ball would hang around their school yard to show off their stuff. You had to play good team ball to stay with their squad, and you always had to look over your shoulder to see who was sneaking up on your position.

"There aren't any dragons on their team," House, our coach, said. "Nobody who's going to eat us up. But every player on their team has talent, and we're going to have to play both ways—offense and defense—if we're going to

---

angled (*v.*) shifted position

offense (*n.*) players who try to score points

walk away with the championship. Nobody brought us here but our own efforts. Hard work and talent got us here, and it can take us to the next level. So let's get it done!"

Clarify
What does House mean by "dragons"?

When the teams came out, the refs had us all shake hands. The dude I was up against had fat clammy hands. He was younger than me, but he was big.

The Lane players were flat-out good. They played like they were going to business. All they needed were some attaché cases.

At the quarter they were ahead 19–14. Fletch, the assistant coach, said they had used nine guys in the first quarter.

"They're outhustling us on offense," House said. "They're bringing the ball down faster than any team we've faced. On defense they're solid, but nothing special. We need to tighten up our defense and keep them off the boards."

I hadn't thought much about the boards, but we were only getting one shot most of the time.

Ernie hit a trey to start the second quarter, and when they got a backcourt **violation,** he hit another one. We were up by a point, but they came back and started the same routine.

"Come on, let's get it going! Let's get it going!" my teammate Abdul said. He was trying to pump things up.

I went after my man hard on D, ragging him wherever he went. I pushed him when I caught him standing still, and talked to him whenever he got the ball.

"Give it up, fool! Give it up!"

He looked at me like I was crazy, and one of their players, a forward, told me to keep my mouth shut.

"Why don't you come and shut it?"

When we stepped up our game, we were playing them just about even. We took away the little bump-and-run pick they were using and hustled back on defense fast enough to keep them from setting up easy plays. They only had one fast break the whole second quarter. But at the end of the half they were still ahead, 36–29.

"Right now it's anybody's game," House was saying in the locker room. "Whoever wants it the most is going to get it. How much you guys want it? How much you guys want it?"

> **off the boards** (adj.) slang for not in a position to make a rebound
> **trey** (n.) slang for a basket worth three points

LITERARY ANALYSIS

Character and Motivation

Underline what Drew says about his own attitude toward winning and losing.

- What is Drew's motivation for trying so hard to win?

_____

_____

_____

_____

VOCABULARY/WORD ANALYSIS

Context Clues

Review paragraph 2 on page 13.

- What are attaché cases? Check one.
  ☐ cases carried by businesspeople
  ☐ diseases carried by travelers
- Circle the context clue that helped you figure this out.
- Why does Drew say that all the Lane players needed were attaché cases?

_____

_____

COMPREHENSION

Summarize

Draw a box around the paragraphs that describe the second quarter of the basketball game.

- Check ✓ the events that should be included in a summary of the quarter.
- Write a brief summary of the second quarter.

_____

_____

_____

_____

_____

_____

We all said we wanted it more than Lane did, and we meant it. Seven points can disappear in a heartbeat, and I knew it and everybody on both teams knew it.

We came out and started our warm-ups for the second half. When a television reporter started talking to the two coaches, I went over to where Fletch was standing.

"What you thinking?" I asked him.

"They're not turning the ball over," he said. "We got to take it on defense and get the ball inside more on offense. Their guards keep double-teaming the ball, and that boy on you is holding you so tight, I thought he was part of your jersey."

The third quarter was all them. They didn't do anything special, but they made plays and all we could get were a few humbles and some lucky bounces. At the end of the quarter they were up by nine.

"Tomas, can you do anything inside, man?" I asked him as we went out for the last quarter.

"Get me the ball," he said.

He didn't say it with a lot of confidence, but I saw that me and Ernie weren't killing their guards. House wanted to win too bad to bring Colin in, and Ricky was too small to deal with their big guards. Sky's man was tall, and he had this little twelve-foot jumper that he hit anytime Sky gave him an inch. Sky could keep him away from that shot, but he was keeping Sky off the boards. Tomas couldn't jump with their forwards, so that left all the rebounding to Ruffy and whatever came out to me and Ernie.

Lane hardly ever made mistakes, but they started the fourth quarter with a carrying call. I brought the ball down as fast as I could, made a big move at the top of the key, and brought the ball in hard to Tomas sliding across the lane. He got the ball and went up in one motion, made the deuce, and got the foul.

I looked up at the clock. Six seconds. Their ball.

Time was flying, and when the ref stopped play to wipe some sweat off the court, I checked the clock. There were less than two minutes to play and we were actually up by a point. House called a time-out. He told us what the deal was.

"We need to score a deuce and then be aggressive to get the ball back," he said. "What they need to do is get the ball now. They know that and you know that, so hang on to the ball and look for a good shot. Sky, get more active. See if you can shake your man without the ball, then look for the backdoor. Drew, Ernie, if you see Sky break loose, see what it creates. It could end up with a backdoor or the two play, with both of you coming in and crossing at the foul line. Stay alert. It's our game if we want it!"

> **Clarify**
> Why does the coach say "It's our game if we want it"?

Time was back in and the game was on. This was my game. I felt it, I could almost taste it as Ernie passed to me.

I put the ball on the floor and went hard to my right. As I moved toward the key, I saw Sky's man chasing him. Tomas blocked out Sky's man, and I let the pass go. Sky made the deuce and we were up by three. I looked up and there were thirty seconds to go.

House was waving us into a full-court press. I found my man and got on him as their center inbounded a full-court pass. I looked downcourt and saw Ernie chasing his man. The ball landed in the lane, and the dude who got it swooped it up and made a perfect layup. They had scored in one second.

We were still up by one, and now it was Lane who was in the full-court press. We got the ball across the ten-second line and they weren't sure what to do. They made a few attempts at the ball but they didn't want to foul us.

---

deuce (n.) slang for a basket worth two points

full-court press (n.) defensive play in which a team tries to stop the other team from moving down the court

LITERARY ANALYSIS

Character and Motivation

Why does House call a time-out?

_____

_____

CRITICAL THINKING

Evaluate

 Is Drew a team player, or does he just focus on himself?

_____

- (Circle) details on these pages that support your answer.

VOCABULARY/WORD ANALYSIS

Context Clues

Review paragraph 5 on page 14. Find the phrases *a few humbles* and *some lucky bounces*.

- **Underline** the context clues that helped you determine that these are not things Drews feels proud of.

- What do you think *humbles* and *lucky bounces* are?

_____

_____

_____

21 | **SMALL GROUPS/INDEPENDENT**

COLLABORATE

Invent Create a glossary of basketball terms and phrases, such as *deuce* and *full-court press*.

COMMUNICATE

React and Write Write a brief article for Baldwin's school newspaper about the basketball game. Take notes about the most important events before you begin writing.

W

I didn't want to look at the clock but I did. Fifteen seconds.

"Foul him! Foul him!" their coach was screaming.

My man came toward me, and so did Ernie's man. I passed the ball to Ernie, who was open. They both ran toward him and he passed it to Sky, who started in one direction, then changed his mind and walked with the ball.

The ref blew his whistle as he signaled the walking violation.

I looked up at the clock. Six seconds. Their ball.

We lined up close. It was jersey on jersey, sweat on sweat. They were in a tight line when the ref threw the ball to them. Their center backed off, and their two guards took off down the court. Me and Ernie chased them and caught them before they turned. We turned with them and saw one of their forwards with the ball. My man came out and took a bounce pass, with me reaching for the ball. He started falling forward. I brought my hands back and saw him push the ball back to the guy who had brought the ball down. Sky was still on him when he faked a move at the foul line and went straight up. Sky went up with him and they seemed to go up forever. The ball left the dude's fingertips, and I turned and looked for somebody to block out. I saw their center move toward the basket and I stepped in front of him. I felt him on my back as the ball came down, rattled in the rim, and fell through as the buzzer sounded.

My head went crazy. I looked around for the scoreboard. At first I couldn't find it high above the stands. Then I saw it, but by that time I didn't need it. All the Lane players were screaming and shouting around me. We had lost.

Was the game too important in my life?

In the locker room Sky was sobbing in the corner. Nobody thought it was his fault, nobody thought that he had lost the game or even that his mistake had cost us the game. But nobody had the emotional energy to **console** him. I was numb; all my tears were inside.

The world stopped. It just stopped. Noises stopped. Movement stopped. Reasons stopped happening. Someone was trying to get us to go back out onto the floor for some kind of ceremony. People were patting us on the back. Words were coming at us. But my world had stopped.

Was the game too important in my life? Did it weigh too much for me to carry any farther? I didn't know. I just knew I felt so miserable. It was as if standing in the locker room, trying to get up the courage to go through the doors into the corridor and onto the gym floor again, was the moment that summed up my whole life.

We stood in a line on the floor and were given watches. There were photos and congratulations. Then we were back in the locker room and changing our clothes.

Jocelyn and Mom were in the parking lot. Jocelyn's eyes were red despite her smile. Mom was patting me on the shoulder, her lips saying something I couldn't hear or maybe couldn't understand.

> **Clarify**
> Why can't Drew hear what his mother is saying?

How quiet can a bus be?

House was cool. He went to each guy on the team, even the ones who had sat on the bench for the whole game, and said something about how the year had gone or what he hoped for next year.

---

corridor (n.) hallway

Monday came, and there was a special assembly to thank us.

"We need to thank the team for their athletic performances," Principal Barker said. "But we also need to thank them for how they **represented** Baldwin. They were gentlemen in their wins, and gentlemen in their one defeat. I was proud of all of them, and proud of the school they come from."

The team still hung together. Tomas was the first one to get college offers. He got an offer from New Mexico, one from West Virginia, and one from Winona State. We helped him look up Winona and found it was in Minnesota. They were a Division II school. I congratulated Tomas, but I felt bad that it was him and not me. I didn't think it was right for me to feel bad, but I did. He said he would talk it over with House to see where he would go.

"The school that is cheapest is the one I will love," he said. "What school are you going to go to?"

"I'm not even sure," I lied, not wanting to say that I hadn't received any offers. "I might even play pro ball in Italy for a while."

Ernie got two offers, one from a university in Puerto Rico and one from Monroe Community College. He took the one at Monroe because he didn't know anything about Puerto Rico.

"If I go to Puerto Rico, they're going to expect me to speak good Spanish, man," he said.

All I could think was that at least he had two offers.

Sky got an offer from Providence, which had a smoking basketball program, and I hadn't figured him to get even a sniff from a Division I school. He said he had been hoping to play ball in the Midwest, but that Providence was okay.

"All the fine mamas go to the Midwest schools," he said.

I had sent regular applications to a number of schools, as my guidance counselor had **advised** me. My first letter back was from Arizona. It was a straight letter turning me down and asking me to reconsider for my sophomore year. Then I was turned down by Howard, in D.C., Charleston Southern, Virginia Union, the University of Washington, and Louisiana State University.

Ruffy didn't get any offers either, and he was talking about working for the **Transit** Authority.

---

assembly (n.) a group of people gathered together

reconsider (v.) to think about a decision again

Read and Synthesize

VOCABULARY/WORD ANALYSIS

Context Clues

 Locate the word *numb* in paragraph 8 on page 16.

- What does *numb* mean here?

_____

- <u>Underline</u> the context clues that helped you determine the word's meaning.

COMPREHENSION

Summarize

Complete the sentences to summarize what happened after Baldwin lost.

In the locker room _____

_____ .

Back on the gym floor _____

_____ .

In the parking lot _____

_____ .

On the bus _____

_____ .

LITERARY ANALYSIS

Character and Motivation

 Check ✓ the sentences that describe the offers Drew's teammates receive.

- Ⓒircle what Drew says and feels in response to each offer.
- Complete the chart below to show what Drew says and does, and why.

Action	
Motivation	
Action	
Motivation	

"Or maybe I'll open a store," he said.

I knew Ruffy's mom didn't have any money to open a store, but I let it slide.

It wasn't that I just felt bad. I could deal with bad. But I felt ordinary. All my dreams of playing pro ball and being a star looked as if they were gone, and I was going to be just another brother standing on a Harlem street corner, leaning in a ghetto doorway, pretending the street hustle wasn't about me.

Clarify
Why does Drew think his life is going to be ordinary now?

Saturday morning I went to play ball but just sat on the bench and watched some kids. When I got home, Jocelyn met me at the door.

"There's a priest here to see you," she said. "What did you do this time?"

The priest was sitting in the living room, a cup of tea in front of him, looking cool in his priest outfit and white hair. There was a man with him. Mom was sitting in the chair near the window. I couldn't figure what was going down, but Jocelyn hadn't given me a heads-up, which she would have if there was something I needed to know.

They stood up when I walked into the room.

"Hello, Drew. I'm Father Gabaccia, and this is Coach Mickey Burns." The priest extended his hand and I shook it.

Burns stood up and looked me up and down. "You're a solid six-five, maybe six-six," he said. "So many kids put down six-something on their résumés and they're really five-something."

"We've come by to leave you with some information about our basketball program at DePaul University," the priest said. "We think you'd fit into our program nicely and we're offering you a full **scholarship** if you commit to

I knew I could represent. I would do it for Mom.

us. We had some other players in mind along with you, some quite good, but we can't get them all. We've brought along a ton of paper for you to go over, but I just want to add two things. One is that we can offer smaller class sizes than most schools and you'll get all the help you need to succeed academically, and second, we really want you out in Chicago."

I didn't want to grin. I wanted to be so cool, so calm and laid-back, and I almost pulled it off. Then I looked over and saw Mom sitting on the edge of her seat and Jocelyn sitting at the table.

"I've seen you play a number of times," Coach Burns said. "I saw the way you handled yourself against Bryant, and I particularly liked the way you played against Lane. That was a tough team. I thought you could have worked the boards more in the first half. What do you think?"

"They were tough on the boards," I said. "But I should have been in there banging with them."

What DePaul had to offer was a full ride. Coach Burns started telling me about the program, who all they played, and who had played for them in the past.

"If you decide on our program, you're going to have some competition for the starting guard slot," Father Gabaccia said. "But you certainly have size and character going for you."

They left me with some booklets about the school. All I had to do was to write a letter of intent and I was set. I told them I would talk it over with my family and let them know as soon as possible.

When they left, me and Mom and Jocelyn were jumping up and down that apartment and hugging each other big-time. I had my tears coming again and couldn't stop them.

extended (v.) reached out
résumés (n.) lists of people's experiences and achievements; used to get jobs or other positions

House congratulated me, and so did Fletch. When I got a moment with Fletch alone, I apologized for some of the things I had said along the way.

"Drew, your enemies can mess your life up," he said. "Or they can make it easy for you to do it yourself. You need to congratulate yourself for not blowing your chances. Go on to college, represent the way you're supposed to, and then maybe we can talk about it again one day."

I knew I could represent. I would do it for Mom and Jocelyn, who were going to be in my corner no matter what. I would do it for Pops and all the dreams he had looked at from a distance. And somewhere, in a dark part of my mind, I was representing for Coach Burns's list of **recruits.** He told me I was number three, but how many guys had been on the list and couldn't deal with the SAT or had messed up their averages? How many would spend the next ten years busting butt on a hundred playgrounds around the country and not getting squat out of it? If I hadn't made it through high school, how many more dudes with serious game could have taken my place? It was something to think about, something to deal with. My moment had come, but I knew that what mattered was what I did with it. ■

Walter Dean Myers

BORN August 12, 1937, in Martinsburg, West Virginia

URBAN LIFE Myers moved to Harlem (a predominantly African American neighborhood in New York City) when he was three. He lived there until he joined the army at age 17. Many of his poems, stories, and novels are set in Harlem.

AUTHOR FILE

FINDING TIME TO WRITE After Myers finished his military service, he worked during the day and wrote at night. He wrote stories and articles for magazines. He even wrote advertisements for cemeteries!

HOOP DREAMS If Myers could be anything he wanted, he would still be a writer, but he would also be a star player in the NBA.

AWARDS Myers has published more than 85 books. He has won two Newbery Honors and five Coretta Scott King awards.

squat *(n.)* slang for a worthless amount

CRITICAL THINKING

Analyze

Coach Burns tells Drew he could have worked the boards more in the first half of the game against Lane. Draw a **box** around Drew's response. What does his response say about his character?

_____

_____

_____

_____

LITERARY ANALYSIS

Character and Motivation

Why does Drew want to succeed in college?

_____

_____

_____

21 **SMALL GROUPS/INDEPENDENT**

COLLABORATE

Debate Is it a bad idea for young people to pin their hopes on playing a professional sport? Have a class debate about it.

COMMUNICATE

Discuss and Write With a partner, go back through the story and underline the different things Drew says about basketball being a way out of the ghetto. Discuss whether you think Drew would find a different way out if he couldn't play basketball. Write about it.

W

READ ONLINE

expert space
Go to **www.expert21.com/student** to learn more about College Sports; Brooklyn; Walter Dean Myers.

Profiles

FINDING THEIR FUTURES

For many high school students, going on to college isn't easy. That doesn't mean you should give up your hopes and dreams. There are ways around all kinds of obstacles, as the four students in this reading have proved.

Main Idea and Details   COMPREHENSION

The **main idea** is the most important idea in a piece of writing.

Details are pieces of information that tell more about the main idea.

There are different kinds of supporting details.

- **Examples** explain the main idea by providing real-world occurrences of it.

- **Sensory details** describe how things look, sound, feel, taste, or smell.

- **Anecdotes** are stories used to make a point that supports the main idea.

▶ Read the main idea and supporting details. Write *example, sensory details,* or *anecdote* under each detail.

Main Idea: Cooking is a very demanding job.

Detail: Professional chefs endure long days, crowded kitchens, and constant stress.

Detail: Imagine the stifling heat of the kitchen, the clatter of pots and pans, and the intense mix of smells.

Detail: One chef says, "I cooked 200 omelets on Sunday. I never want to look at another egg!"

Text Structure   NAVIGATING TEXT

Some common text structures include

- chronological (time) order.
- main idea and details.
- cause and effect.
- compare and contrast.
- problem and solution.

▶ Read the summaries below. Draw a line to match each article with the type of text structure it is most likely to have.

"So You Want to Be a Doctor": This article gives a step-by-step description of the things a person must do to become a doctor.

"Ten Reasons to Go to Business School": This article uses examples and anecdotes to prove that business school is a good option for many.

"How to Improve Your Grades": This article lists the top five reasons why students struggle in school and gives tips on how to address each problem.

Main Idea and Details

Problem and Solution

Chronological Order

Academic Language   VOCABULARY

▶ Rate your knowledge of each word. Then write its meaning and an example sentence.

Word	Meaning	Example
EXPERT WORDS *Use these words to write and talk about the workshop topic.*		
advantage ad•van•tage (noun) ① ② ③ ④	a benefit; something that helps you get ahead	The free tutoring sessions I got gave me an advantage on the math test.
internship in•tern•ship (noun) ① ② ③ ④		
semester se•mes•ter (noun) ① ② ③ ④		
CONTENT AREA WORDS *Use these words to talk and write about social studies.*		
coordination co•or•di•na•tion (noun) ① ② ③ ④	the act of working together smoothly	
income in•come (noun) ① ② ③ ④		
SELECTION WORDS *These words are key to understanding this selection.*		
grueling gru•el•ing (adjective) ① ② ③ ④		The last part of the hike was grueling because we had to climb up a slippery, muddy mountain.
prefer pre•fer (verb) ① ② ③ ④		
supportive sup•port•ive (adjective) ① ② ③ ④		

Rating Scale ① I don't know the word.   ② I've seen it or heard it.   ③ I know its meaning.   ④ I know it and use it.

Context Clues: Examples and Definitions   WORD ANALYSIS

When you come across an unfamiliar word, look for definitions or examples that can help you figure out its meaning.

Definitions and examples can usually be found immediately after the new or unfamiliar term.

▶ One sentence below gives a definition of *internships*. The other sentence gives examples of *internships*. Write *example* or *definition* next to each sentence. Then underline the context clues in the sentence itself.

Many college students have internships, jobs that give students professional experience. _____

Some students get internships working at offices, labs, or national parks. _____

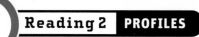
FINDING THEIR FUTURES

By Karen Fanning

It's never too early to think about your future and start making plans for life after high school. No matter which professional path you choose, furthering your education will open up a world of career opportunities (and better salaries) to you.

On the following pages, you'll meet four students who, like many people, struggled on their way toward success. Today, all four are thriving in school. They hope their stories inspire others to follow in their footsteps.

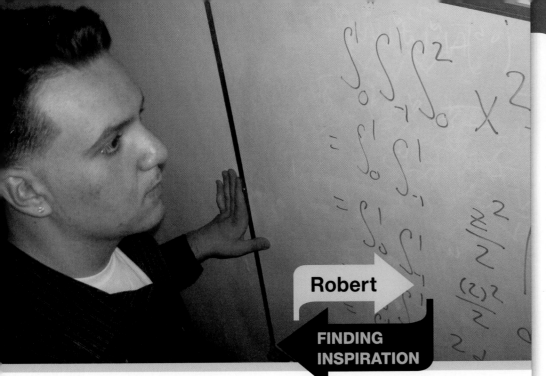

Robert

FINDING INSPIRATION

Robert Santos always hated math—until one day during his junior year at Herbert H. Lehman High School in the Bronx, New York.

"I walked into my math classroom, and I had this sudden urge to answer my teacher's question," says the 18-year-old. "I kept answering more questions. My teacher, Mr. Lifrieri, said, 'Robert, you're on fire today.' He kept saying that. I liked that feeling. I wanted to keep that fire going. I didn't want it to burn out."

So Robert buckled down and studied hard, finishing the year with a 99 average in math. As a senior, he regularly stayed at school past 8 p.m. to help his math teacher grade tests. When his assistant principal offered him a job tutoring other students, Robert jumped at the chance, working 15 hours a week.

While Robert had the grades to get into college, he knew he would need assistance with tuition, so he applied to the *New York Times* College Scholarship Program. With 1,400 applicants, the competition was fierce. But after a **grueling** application process, Robert was one of twenty New York City high school seniors awarded a scholarship. When he was accepted to New York University—his first choice—tears of joy followed.

"I am the first one from my family to ever go to college, so it's kind of a big deal," he says. "When I found out I got in, it was really crazy. I was so excited. My mom cried."

Now a freshman at NYU, Robert is majoring in math and hopes to someday teach. He says he has his math teacher, Mr. Lifrieri, to thank for his success.

"If I didn't have that motivation of having someone push me and tell me I can do it, I don't think I would have accomplished what I have," says Robert. "It was his motivation and my decision to focus that led me to succeed."

---

applicants *(n.)* people who have applied for something
majoring *(v.)* concentrating in a specific subject

COMPREHENSION

Main Idea and Details
Based on the introduction, what do you think will be the main idea of the article?

_____

_____

_____

_____

_____

_____

_____

_____

What details will be used to support this idea?

_____

_____

_____

_____

_____

_____

_____

COMPREHENSION

Main Idea and Details
What kind of details does the author use to support the main idea "One day in high school, Robert Santos started liking math"?

   anecdote   example   sensory

• **Check** ✓ the paragraph that helped you figure out your answer.

Sharhea

SAVING FOR THE FUTURE

Sharhea Wade grew up with her grandmother on the Caribbean island of Montserrat. Her mother had moved to the United States to work when Sharhea was just five years old. She never knew her father—he left the family before she was born.

Sharhea was finally reunited with her mother when she moved to Boston, MA, at age 12. Her new neighborhood was plagued by crime. Few local kids attended college. But from the beginning, Sharhea stayed focused.

"The whole purpose of me coming to America was to get an education," she says.

Sharhea got involved with several after-school programs that provided homework help and tutoring. She graduated from middle school with a 4.0 grade-point average (GPA). After acing her high school entrance exam, she was accepted to the prestigious Boston Latin Academy.

But just as Sharhea was set to begin her freshman year, her home life started to unravel. Her mother fell behind in the rent, and she and Sharhea were evicted from their apartment. When her mother had a nervous breakdown, Sharhea's grandmother came to Boston to care for her. But it was Sharhea who ended up being the caretaker when her grandmother's health failed.

Sharhea missed dozens of school days of while she shuttled her grandmother back and forth to doctors. Despite the setbacks, Sharhea remained determined to become the first person in her family to go to college.

"One thing that really kept me going was that I strongly believe education is the key to success," says Sharhea, now 21. "Despite everything that was going on, I knew I had to get through school. There was no other option in order to get beyond the life of my parents and grandparents. They didn't graduate from high school."

Make Inferences
How will getting an education help Sharhea move beyond the life of her parents and grandparents?

Shortly after moving in with her aunt, Sharhea got involved with Summer Search, a national program designed to help low-**income** students attend college. During her two years with Summer Search, Sharhea went on a month-long wilderness trip to the southern United States and participated in a language study program in Costa Rica. Her experience with Summer Search gave her the confidence to further her education, she says.

Sharhea graduated from Boston Latin Academy with a 3.6 GPA and won a scholarship to attend Bryn Mawr College in Pennsylvania. While the scholarship covered her tuition, she still had to come up with money to pay for room and board and other school fees. So she worked six days a week, ten hours a day.

"I would pay myself every week by putting $100 into my savings account," Sharhea says. "By the end of the summer, I had enough money to pay for the fees for my first **semester**, as well as my books."

Now a junior, Sharhea is thriving at Bryn Mawr. But she insists she's just getting started. "I've always had high hopes for a lot of things," she says. "This is just the first step. There are a million more steps to go."

prestigious *(adj.)* having a good reputation
shuttled *(v.)* transported

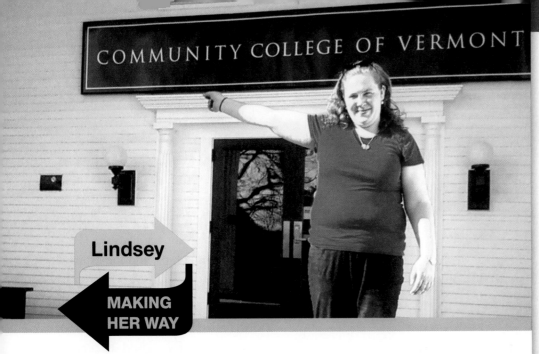

COMMUNITY COLLEGE OF VERMONT

Lindsey

MAKING HER WAY

When Lindsey Cote-Abel began making plans to go to college, her family worried whether she would be able to make the grade.

Lindsey was born with cerebral palsy (CP), a series of disorders of the developing brain that affect body movement and muscle **coordination.** Individuals with CP may also have learning disabilities. While Lindsey's physical limitations are mild, school has always been a challenge for her.

"I don't test well, and understanding reading material is difficult and stressful," says the 21-year-old from Brattleboro, Vermont. "I knew it was going to be a struggle, but I was always determined to go to college."

In high school, Lindsey took **advantage** of the extra help that was available to her, and through hard work and perseverance, she earned all As and Bs. While she initially considered going to a state college, community college was more affordable. Academically, it was also more flexible.

"At community college," Lindsey says, "I could take as little as one class or as many as four classes."

> **Make Inferences**
> In what ways could academic flexibility be helpful for many students?

Since enrolling at the Community College of Vermont three years ago, Lindsey has been taking two classes a semester. With a lighter workload, Lindsey has not only been able to study at her own pace, she's also been able to hold down a full-time job.

Lindsey works as a nanny 50, sometimes 60 hours a week and is paying her own way through college. She expects to complete her associate's degree by the spring of 2011. Then she hopes to transfer to a four-year college, where she will major in special education or elementary education.

"I decided I wanted to be a teacher when I learned how difficult some things were for me in school," she says. "I would love to make learning a great experience for kids instead of a stressful one."

perseverance *(n.)* the quality of not giving up easily

Read and Synthesize

VOCABULARY/WORD ANALYSIS

Context Clues: Examples and Definitions

 Review paragraph 5 on page 24. What does the word *unravel* mean?

_____

_____

• <u>Underline</u> examples of how Sharhea's life unraveled.

NAVIGATING TEXT

Text Structure

Review the last two paragraphs on page 24. How are they organized? Put a check mark by your answer.

☐ cause and effect

☐ chronological order

☐ main idea and details

CRITICAL THINKING

Synthesize

Name something that both Sharhea Wade and Robert Santos did to succeed.

_____

_____

_____

How was this action important for success?

_____

_____

_____

_____

NAVIGATING TEXT

Text Structure

 What is the text structure of Lindsey's profile?

problem/solution   compare/contrast

• Check ✓ the paragraphs that helped you find your answer.

Alec

FINDING A UNIQUE PATH

Alec set his sights on culinary school, but coming up with the tuition money would be a challenge. After all, his mother, a former flight attendant, was on disability after injuring her back. But then Alec learned that the Professional Culinary Institute (PCI) offered scholarships, and the aspiring chef decided to try his luck.

He, along with the nine other candidates, were given a list of ingredients and asked to create their own dish. Alec spent two months preparing for the cooking competition, which would be judged by three of PCI's chefs. In the end, his hard work paid off. Alec's chicken roulade won first place, and he took home a $15,000 scholarship.

When Alec isn't in class, he's got his nose in a cookbook or is watching cooking shows. What is his favorite program? The Food Network's *Good Eats* with Alton Brown.

While he would like someday to open up his own place, Alec is happy to kick off his culinary career

> **Make Inferences**
> **Why does Alec read cookbooks and watch cooking shows?**

Alec Hunter admits he was just an average student in high school.

"I was bored," says the 18-year-old from Cupertino, California. "I never really enjoyed sitting down and listening to lectures all day. I **prefer** to do something with my hands."

During his senior year at Cupertino High, Alec finally discovered something he could wrap his hands around. At the suggestion of one of his teachers, he enrolled in an **internship** program and ended up assisting the chef at a local seafood and steak restaurant. After a few days in the kitchen, Alec was hooked.

"You are on your feet for a long time," says Alec. "It can get crazy, but I liked being able to work really hard and actually see the rewards from it."

at someone else's restaurant. But no burger joints, please.

"I'm really interested in fine dining," he says. "It's artwork. I like the creativity and the different kinds of flavors. It's just such a unique experience when you taste your not-so-average food."

> **candidates** *(n.)* people who are applying for a job or running for election
> **culinary** *(adj.)* related to cooking

Beating the Odds

Robert Santos, Sharhea Wade, Lindsey Cote-Abel, and Alec Hunter are four people who refused to quit.

They stayed focused on their goals. They took advantage of the academic services made available to them. They found **supportive** mentors. They worked hard and saved money.

They followed their passions. They found schools that fit their academic interests and needs. They beat the odds.

Today, Sharhea, Robert, Lindsey, and Alec are busy pursuing their individual dreams. But they remain united in their shared belief that getting an education is key to having a successful future. ■

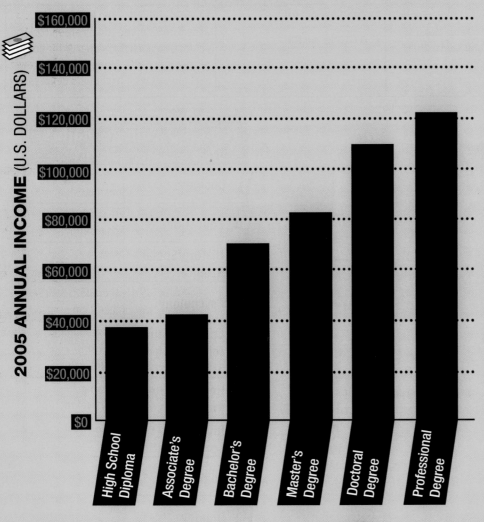

Earnings in 2005 by Educational Attainment of the Population 25 Years and Over

2005 ANNUAL INCOME (U.S. DOLLARS)

$160,000
$140,000
$120,000
$100,000
$80,000
$60,000
$40,000
$20,000
$0

High School Diploma
Associate's Degree
Bachelor's Degree
Master's Degree
Doctoral Degree
Professional Degree

EDUCATION LEVEL

COMPREHENSION

Main Idea and Details

Review the section titled "Beating the Odds."

- Draw a box around the paragraph that gives examples of successful behaviors.
- What main idea do these details support? Underline it in the text.

NAVIGATING TEXT

Text Structure

Why did the author present the information about average salary as a chart rather than as text?

_____

_____

_____

_____

_____

_____

21 SMALL GROUPS/INDEPENDENT

COLLABORATE

 Brainstorm List ten tips for getting into and succeeding in college.

COMMUNICATE

 Discuss and Write Choose one of the four students and discuss what might have happened if he or she had done one critical thing differently. Then write an alternate ending for that story.

W

READ ONLINE

 expert space
Go to **www.expert21.com/student** to learn more about Summer Search; Culinary School; Junior and Community Colleges.

OPTIONS, OPTIONS, AND MORE OPTIONS

You've made it through high school. Now what? This infographic gives facts about some of the many options you have.

Q: What Surprised You Most About College?

A: "I had no one telling me what to do. I could stay out every night if I wanted. It was exciting, but I had to take care of myself. My life was my responsibility." *—Ryan Parker, Miami University, OH*

HOT Field in the 21st Century

	This Is for You If	**What Does It Pay?**	**What Do I Need?**
Nursing	• you are interested in helping people. • you like science and health classes. • you want an in-demand career that pays well.	$37,940 for an LPN $60,010 for an RN	1-year training for an LPN. An associate's degree (takes around 2 years) or a bachelor's degree for an RN, plus certification. Many hospitals now seek nurses with bachelor's degrees.

ENROLLMENT ON THE RISE IN THE LAST 30 YEARS

Total college enrollment has more than doubled in the last 30 years (from 7.3 million students to **15.1 million** students).

The number of women attending college has almost tripled (from 3.1 million students to **8.6 million** students).

30 years

GETTING TECHNICAL

• Vocational schools (also known as trade schools or technical schools) offer career education in a variety of fields, from art and design to cooking, automotive technology, and real estate.

• Programs can be as short as a few weeks or months to as long as a few years.

• Vocational schools offer an alternative to colleges for students who know exactly what they want to do and want specific training.

• Vocational schools aren't the best option for students who want to explore different career options.

Top **10** College Majors
(and some possible career paths)

#	Major	Career paths
1	Business	advertising, management
2	Education	teaching, counseling
3	History/Social Science	law, archeology
4	Psychology	therapy, medicine
5	Computer and Information Science	programming, network engineering
6	Health-related Professions	nursing, physical therapy
7	Journalism/Communication	news reporter, public relations
8	Engineering	technology, architecture
9	Biology	medicine, medical research
10	English	journalism, writing, teaching

NOT YOUR PARENTS' SCHOOL

Can you imagine taking a class in your pajamas? Now you can! Half of colleges and universities now offer classes online—and the number is increasing every year. Some schools even offer virtual classrooms, learning environments created in virtual space.

Increasing Diversity

Today, a greater percentage of college students are Asian American and Latino than ever before.

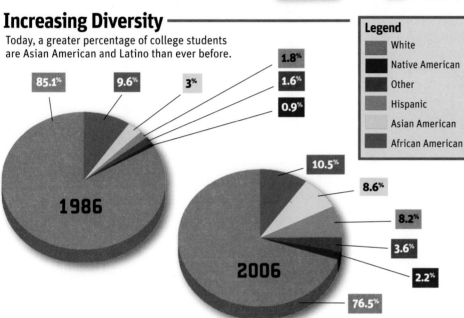

Legend

■	White
■	Native American
■	Other
■	Hispanic
■	Asian American
■	African American

1986: 85.1% 9.6% 3% 1.8% 1.6% 0.9%

2006: 76.5% 10.5% 8.6% 8.2% 3.6% 2.2%

HOT Field in the 21st Century

Computer Information Technology	This Is for You if	What Does it Pay?	What Do I Need?
1 = 6 x 43 + 2.5	• You are interested in how technology works. • You want to develop your own software and video games. • You enjoy math class and solving puzzles.	$68,220 for a network architect $83,130 for a software developer	Bachelor's degree

IS COMMUNITY COLLEGE FOR YOU?

- Community colleges offer a variety of associate's degrees (which can be completed in two years of full-time enrollment). Some community colleges even offer bachelor's degrees.

- Community-college students make up 46 percent of all undergraduates in the U.S.

- The average annual tuition at a community college is $2,361, versus $6,185 at a public four-year institution and $23,712 at a private four-year institution.

- Many students go to community college to take specific courses that they are interested in. Others go to get credits they eventually will transfer to a four-year school.

NAVIGATING TEXT

Infographic

An infographic presents great amounts of information using visuals, labels, and captions. Each block of text is independent, so blocks can be read in any order.

🖊 Find and (circle) the headings that introduce the nursing and computer information technology careers.

• What information do these two features give about each career?

_____

_____

_____

_____

_____

_____

_____

_____

_____

COMPREHENSION

Summarize

🖊 Draw a box around the section that gives information about changes in college enrollment.

• Summarize this section below.

_____

_____

_____

_____

_____

_____

_____

_____

_____

_____

_____

Money Matter$

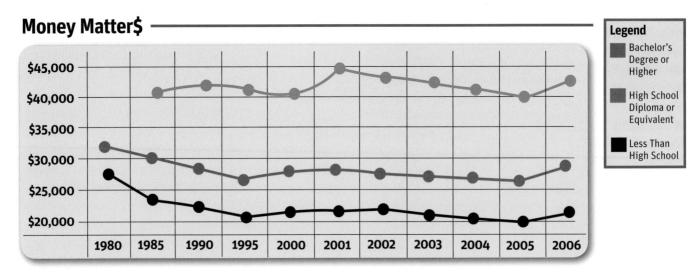

Legend
- ■ Bachelor's Degree or Higher
- ■ High School Diploma or Equivalent
- ■ Less Than High School

Since 1980, the average income of students with only a high school diploma has gone down, while the average income of students with a bachelor's degree or higher has increased.

HOT Field in the 21st Century

Environmental Science	This Is for You if	What Does it Pay?	What Do I Need?
Environmental Science	• You are interested in protecting the environment. • You like earth science or biology. • You want to make a difference by solving environmental problems.	$56,100 for an environmental scientist $66,260 for a hydrologist (scientist who studies water)	Bachelor's degree in environmental science. Many jobs require a specialized master's degree.

CONSIDERING THE MILITARY? THINK ABOUT BECOMING AN OFFICER!*

- The starting salary for an enlisted soldier is $16,794. The starting salary for a military officer is **$49,870.**
- The top salary for a high-ranking officer is **$215,894.80** after twenty years of service. The top salary for a high-ranking enlisted soldier is less than half that ($101,227.51) for the same length of service.
- Only officers can perform certain jobs, such as flying planes in the air force.

Officers usually have a four-year degree and military training.

CHANGING THE WORLD

Thinking about the Peace Corps? Some jobs in the Peace Corps, like teaching, require a college degree. Most volunteers have college degrees, but some can qualify with three or more years of work experience. Looking to help in your own community? Become a social entrepreneur! Social entrepreneurs start businesses that help their communities solve social problems, such as pollution or poverty.

COLLEGE + FOCUS = FREEDOM

"You have to learn to adapt to a completely different schedule and way of life than you're used to in high school. You need to take responsibility for making sure your days are productive, because no one is making sure everything is falling into place on its own anymore."

—Alissa Valiante, Colgate University, NY

HOT Field in the 21st Century

	This Is for You if	What Does it Pay?	What Do I Need?
Skin Care Specialists	• You like working with your hands. • You like cosmetology. • You like making others look and feel their best.	$29,910 if you work in a salon. $36,260 if you work in a doctor's office.	A high school diploma or a GED plus certification from a cosmetology school

NAVIGATING TEXT

Infographic

Check ✓ the graphic that helps explain the section titled "Money Matters."

• What information does it tell you?

_____

_____

_____

_____

_____

_____

_____

COMPREHENSION

Summarize

Draw a box around the statements made by college student Alissa Valiente. Summarize his viewpoint below.

_____

_____

_____

_____

_____

_____

READ ONLINE

expert space
Go to **www.expert21.com/student** to learn more about The Peace Corps; ROTC; Nursing.

Think Across Texts

Organize and Synthesize ···

1. The students in "Playing the Game" and "Finding Their Futures" all had educational goals beyond high school. Complete the web below, showing the paths that Drew, Robert, Sharhea, Lindsey, and Alec took to meet their goals.

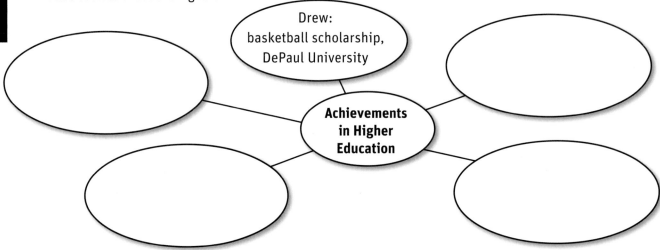

Drew: basketball scholarship, DePaul University

Achievements in Higher Education

Compare and Evaluate ···

2. Compare "Finding Their Futures" and "Options, Options, and More Options." Name two ways in which the selections are alike and two ways in which they are different.

Alike: _____

_____

_____

_____

Different: _____

_____

_____

_____

3. "Options, Options, and More Options" has the fewest pages of the three selections. Do you think it contains the least information? Explain your answer using evidence from the text.

_____

_____

_____

_____

4. Of all the paths you read about, which one are you most likely to follow? Explain your answer using information from the text.

_____

_____

_____

_____

_____

_____

_____

_____

_____

_____

_____

Discuss and Write ·····················

5. With a partner, discuss how the three readings in "Choosing a Path" helped you understand the options available to you after high school. Take notes as you talk. Then use your notes to write a response to the question: *Where do I go after high school?*

Apply Word Knowledge

Word Lab

1. **Decide.** For each pair of college majors, circle the one you would **prefer.**

Business	Education
English	Biology
Engineering	History

2. **Complete.** Use the information in the selections to complete these sentences with the following words: **semester, internship, scholarship, recruit.**

- Drew was a basketball _____ at DePaul University.

- During his senior year in high school, Alec enrolled in a(n) _____ program.

- Lindsey went to the Community College of Vermont and took two classes a(n) _____.

- Sharhea won a(n) _____ to Bryn Mawr College.

3. **Order these.** Which would you like to do to earn **income** for your education? Rank them, with 1 being what you'd most like and 3 what you'd least like to do.

___ be a nanny

___ work at a bookstore

___ work at a restaurant

4. **Think about it.** Identify three activities that you think are **grueling.**

_____

_____

_____

_____

5. **Name them.** In each situation, name a person you would ask to **advise** you.

- You need to plan your schedule for freshman year in high school: _____

- You are having trouble with your math homework: _____

- You're stressed out about a problem with a friend: _____

Word Analysis

6. Use context clues to help you complete the passage with three words from the box.

recruit	internships
transit	violations

I didn't have any _____ in the last game, so a major university wants me to be a _____. I'll use the _____ system to get to my interview.

7. Read the passage below, and underline context clues that help you determine the meaning of the boldface words. Then write which type of context clue it is—example or definition.

> Dancers need **coordination,** or the ability to control the movement of their muscles. Trying out for shows can be stressful. Fortunately, my friends do really **supportive** things, such as telling me I'm a great dancer and cheering me up when I have a bad day.

coordination: _____

supportive: _____

21 Analyze Data

CAREER CONNECTION Science, Technology, Engineering & Mathematics www.careerclusters.org

Go to **21** ToolKit **Expert File 6.30** to learn more about careers in science and technology.

When you're faced with a decision—like what to do after high school—gathering and analyzing data can help you make the right choice.

Data about College Technology Programs

▶ Read the chart below to see how one student analyzed information about his college options.

MY COLLEGE OPTIONS CHART

	A	B Allied Tech University	C Breck School of Business and Technology	D Western States Community College	E ANALYSIS
2	**LOCATION**	Bakersfield, California (100 miles from home)	Los Angeles, California (220 miles from home)	Fresno, California (30-minute bus ride)	I could live at home and commute to Western States Community College.
3	**SPECIALTY**	Liberal arts college with nationally ranked programs in computer technology	Business courses; computer technology; both on-site and online classes	computer technology; preparation for 4-year college	A degree from Allied Tech would look good on my resume.
4	**TUITION**	$7,000 per semester plus room and board	$325 per on-site class (12 weeks) $255 per online class (14 weeks) (no dorms on campus)	$300 per class $1,350 per semester	Breck's classes are reasonable, but I would have to rent an apartment. The community college is more affordable.
5	**DEGREE**	Bachelor's Degree (4 years)	Certificate Programs (1–2 years)	Associate Degree (2 years)	I need to find out what kinds of jobs require what kind of degree.

MARK IT

Identify the Purpose. Underline the student's purpose for analyzing this data.

Analyze the Data. Underline the data the student compares to conclude that commuting from home is a possible option.

Record Your Analysis. You may need additional data. (Circle) the additional information the student wants to find out.

Here's How ▶ Follow these steps to learn how to analyze data:

Step 1 Identify your purpose. What do you want to decide? A clear purpose will help you gather the most relevant information.

Step 2 Create an organizer. After you gather information, decide how to best organize your data. You may want a list, a pro-and-con chart, a graph, an outline, or a flow chart. A well-planned organizer will allow you to quickly read and process information.

Step 3 Analyze the data. Compare the data you have collected. Look for any patterns or relationships and make connections. Record your analysis either as part of your data organization or separately.

Apply: Analyze Data About Jobs

▶ **Follow these steps to analyze data about careers that interest you. Refer to Reading 3 on pp. 28–33 to gather information, or search the Internet.**

1. **Identify your purpose.** For example, you could analyze the education and pay of several careers that interest you. What do you want to analyze?

_____

2. **Create an organizer.** Create a graph or chart below that organizes data. For example, if you are comparing several factors of several careers, a chart is probably your best option. What is the best way to organize your information?

_____

3. **Analyze the data.** Record your analysis of each line or row of data you have collected, or in your Expert Journal.

Procedural Text

How To Survive, Thrive, and Prepare for What's Next

Life doesn't come with a set of instructions. But if you follow the steps outlined in this guide, you will be off to a good start!

QuickWrite

List three problems students might have that would keep them from doing well in school. For each one, come up with two possible solutions.

Summarize   COMPREHENSION

In a **summary**, you briefly restate the main ideas, steps, or events in a piece of writing in your own words.

To **summarize** an informational text, look for

- headings and subheadings
- topic sentences that tell main ideas
- important details
- key words and boldface text

▶ **Read the following passage from the reading. Underline the most important ideas. Then write a summary of the passage.**

Pick a destination—a college, a career path, a consuming interest, or a specific goal (graduating with honors, for example), the military, or becoming certified in a technical skill. But don't stop there! Find out exactly what you need to get to that place—don't guess. Once you know what path will lead you toward your goal, then start, one step at a time, moving along it. *You* are the driver on this journey—decide where you want to go. You can change goals along the way, but don't drift, waiting for the goal to appear suddenly. Also, remember that you can pursue college and career goals at the same time.

Summary:

_____

_____

_____

Steps in a Process   NAVIGATING TEXT

By breaking down a complex activity and identifying the **steps in a process**, writers can make complicated activities easier to understand.

How-to articles are often organized around the presentation of a step-by-step process.

Step-by-step explanations are especially useful when the steps must be done in a specific order.

▶ **Select an activity from the list on the left. Write out four steps necessary to complete the activity. Make sure to list the steps in the proper order.**

- Writing a paper for a class
- Painting a picture
- Cooking a favorite food
- Getting to school from home
- Using a browser to search the Internet
- Shooting a free throw

Activity: _____

Step 1: _____

_____

Step 2: _____

_____

Step 3: _____

_____

Step 4: _____

_____

Academic Language VOCABULARY

▶ Rate each word. Then write its meaning and an example sentence.

Word	Meaning	Example
EXPERT WORDS *Use these words to write and talk about the workshop topic.*		
course *course (noun)* ① ② ③ ④	a class or series of classes in a subject	The science course I took made me want to become a marine biologist.
extracurricular *ex•tra•cur•ric•u•lar (adjective)* ① ② ③ ④		
ACADEMIC WORDS *Use these words in all your subject classes.*		
efficiently *ef•fi•cient•ly (adverb)* ① ② ③ ④	in a way that gets the best results with the least waste of time or effort	
pursue *pur•sue (verb)* ① ② ③ ④		
requirement *re•quire•ment (noun)* ① ② ③ ④		
strategy *strat•e•gy (noun)* ① ② ③ ④		
SELECTION WORDS *These words are key to understanding this selection.*		
memorize *mem•o•rize (verb)* ① ② ③ ④		
varsity *var•si•ty (adjective)* ① ② ③ ④		I tried out for the varsity tennis team because all my friends from school were on it.

Rating Scale ① I don't know the word. ② I've seen it or heard it. ③ I know its meaning. ④ I know it and use it.

Base Words and Affixes WORD ANALYSIS

A **base word** is the part of a word to which affixes may be added.

An **affix** is a **prefix, suffix,** or **ending** that changes the meaning or part of speech of a base word. For example:

inform (base word, verb) + *-ation* (affix) = *information* (noun)

▶ Circle the base word and underline the affix in each word below.

truthful   inefficient

spitefully   amoral

How To Survive, Thrive, and Prepare for What's Next

By Susan Abel Lieberman, Ph.D.

Adapted from *The Real High School Handbook*

In a few simple steps, lay the foundation for the rest of your life.

There are two things you need to do well in school: desire and determination. First you have to have the desire to do better, and then you have to have the determination to make it happen. Determination turns desire into reality.

Success in school is about more than your ability to do well in classes. School also shows you how well you manage your life situations. If you can make school work for you, it's likely that you will make the rest of your life work for you as well. But how can you make school work for you? It's easier than you think!

Step One:
Know Your Goal

Pick a destination—a college, a career path, a consuming interest or a specific goal (graduating with honors, for example), the military, or becoming certified in a technical skill. But don't stop there! Find out exactly what you need to get to that place—don't guess. Once you know what path will lead you toward your goal, then start, one step at a time, moving along it. *You* are the driver on this journey—decide where to go. You can change goals along the way, but don't drift, waiting for the goal suddenly to appear. Also, remember that you can **pursue** college and career goals at the same time.

High school offers a variety of classes, sports, and activities. The more you discover and the more you try, the more you learn about yourself and the world. Use this information to help you make decisions about your future. You don't need to graduate from high school

with every question about your life answered. However, high school can help you answer specific questions, like: Do I need college to pursue my career goals? Am I interested in pursuing a career in art? Am I happier working with my hands? How can I use this information to develop a career plan?

consuming *(adj.)* very interesting
certified *(adj.)* having a certificate that shows mastery

NAVIGATING TEXT

Steps in a Process
Draw a box around the text that names the first step the author suggests.
- What process does the author refer to?

_____
_____
_____
_____
_____
_____

CRITICAL THINKING

Synthesize
Do you think Drew from "Playing the Game" would agree with the author about the importance of setting a goal? Why or why not?

_____
_____
_____
_____
_____
_____

COMPREHENSION

Summarize
<u>Underline</u> the most important ideas on page 39 to include in a summary.
- How might this summary help you to form an opinion about what you read?

_____
_____
_____
_____
_____

Step Two:
Choose Your Course(s)

From the end of eighth grade, every student needs a plan for meeting **course requirements,** for getting all the necessary credits for graduation, and for leaving high school headed toward success. It's fine to change your plan as you learn more about yourself. It's *not* fine to be without a plan.

Sit down with your parents, look over all the possibilities, and talk about what seems right for you. Your parents may have ideas and suggestions. If you disagree with them, explain and defend your choices (but don't make excuses to take easier classes than you can handle). If your parents don't understand the system, teach them how your high school works. Involving your parents in your planning will help them and yourself—they will have fewer anxieties about your school life and can support you in your goals (instead of nagging you to get some).

Since you are running your own show, you should always know how many credits you have completed, how many more you need, and in what subjects (without always going to the office to look it up). In the spring of each year, sit down and review what you have done in school against what you know you must accomplish to graduate. Do this with a parent, an adviser, a mentor, or an adult you respect. Review what you've taken, what you still plan to take, and whether you want to make changes.

> **Question**
> **What questions do you have about choosing courses?**

Step Three:
Study Smart

Do you find yourself struggling to study? Don't worry, most students have this problem. It has nothing to do with how smart they are, and everything to do with how they study. Before you think, "I don't want to spend all my time studying," remember that it's not how long you study, it's how *well* you study. If you study **efficiently,** you don't have to spend hours in your books. Here are a few tried-and-true study **strategies:**

1. **Be truthful.** Don't lie to yourself. You know when you are studying and when you're just pretending to study.

2. **Set small goals.** Don't say, "I will work harder in science class." Instead say, "I will **memorize** the steps of photosynthesis by Tuesday at 7 p.m."

3. **Be organized.** Keep class notes and past tests where you can find them. Figure out a system that works for you. If you're not using a school planner or date book, give it a try.

4. **Review.** Go over old homework and do practice problems or exercises. Focus on things that gave you trouble the first time around.

5. **Use flash cards.** Make flash cards for all your subjects. Quiz yourself or get a parent or friend to use your cards to quiz you.

6. **Start early.** Cramming doesn't work. The more nights your brain has to process information, the better you will remember it.

7. **Look at headings.** Begin reviewing assigned chapters by scanning the headings and captions first. To prepare for a final exam, make an outline of the material from these headings.

8. **Use memory tricks.** Make up songs, sayings, poems, pictures, equations, or silly words that help you remember.

Step Four:
Get Involved

There are clubs, teams, groups, and organizations for every kind of interest. For example, if you love sports but aren't good enough for a **varsity** team, find a club team, a church team, or a community league and play for the fun of it. If you don't like football, try soccer. Sing in a chorus, play in a band, or learn an instrument. Act in plays, help paint the backdrop, collect the props, or make the costumes. Repair cars, race cars, or make models.

There are plenty of good reasons to get involved in **extracurricular** activities (besides the fact that they're fun): you become a more interesting person, you make new friends, and you learn new skills (skills that can help you in the job world or even lead you to a career). Extracurricular activities also appeal to employers, scholarship committees, and college admissions committees. However, people are more impressed with long-term dedication to two or three activities. Joining every activity for a short period of time—just to say you did—doesn't fool anyone.

> **cramming** *(v.)* studying a lot of material in a short time
> **process** *(v.)* make sense of

Step Five:
Get the Help You Need

In four years of high school, you won't like every teacher or every class. But do the work, figure out something in the class that you find interesting, learn something useful from the experience, and get on with it. You don't have to like it. You just have to *do* it. If you find yourself doing poorly in a class, take steps to improve. For example, make an appointment to talk with your teacher and explain your situation, listen to what your teacher has to say, and follow his or her advice. You can also find a tutor, a study group, or a study guide. Most important, don't expect that excuses will be enough—it's up to you to pass, not up to your teachers to pass you.

Step Six:
Stay True to Yourself

Decide what *you* want from high school, then set out to get it. Learn what you need to know to accomplish your personal goals. If your school can't provide you with everything you need, look for summer courses, private tutorials, or work experiences. If you're wise enough to use your education to prepare for life after high school, you're way ahead of the crowd. ∎

CAREER CONNECTION **Human Services**
www.careerclusters.org

Go to ToolKit **Expert File 6.25** to learn more about careers in human services.

study guide *(n.)* a written review of a subject or book
tutorials *(n.)* tutoring sessions

Read and Synthesize

COMPREHENSION

Summarize

 Review Step Three. (Circle) the most important ideas.

• Write a brief summary below.

_____

_____

_____

_____

_____

VOCABULARY/WORD ANALYSIS

Base Words and Affixes

 Review Step Six. <u>Underline</u> the word *tutorials*.

• What is the base word and affix in *tutorials*?

_____

• How does the affix change the meaning of the base word?

_____

_____

_____

21 SMALL GROUPS/INDEPENDENT

COLLABORATE

Represent Create a poster that conveys the most important information in the selection.

COMMUNICATE

React and Write Write about your plans for high school and the future. Begin by listing your main goals in life.

W

READ ONLINE

 expert space
Go to **www.expert21.com/student** to learn more about SATs; How to Study; Vocational Guidance.

Short Story

My People

Lindley, a teen from a poor Appalachian family, is proud and excited when she is chosen to attend a summer program at a college several hours from home. But can she afford to go? And will she feel like an outsider among the other students attending?

 QuickWrite

Most people have felt out of place at one time or another. Describe a time when you felt like an outsider.

Narrator's Point of View LITERARY ANALYSIS

If a story is told by one of the characters, it is told from the **first-person point of view**. The narrator—the person telling the story—refers to himself or herself as *I* and *me*.

When the narrator is not a character in the story, the story is told from the **third-person point of view**. The narrator refers to all the story characters using the pronouns *he*, *she*, and *they*.

▶ **Read these sentences from the reading. Identify each sentence as first-person point of view or third-person point of view.**

• Should I mention right here that nobody in my family had ever gone to college?

_____

• The whole tableful of kids began comparing all the different camps and summer programs they'd gone to in their lives.

_____

• Tears began dripping down my face before I even passed the serving line.

_____

Main Idea and Details COMPREHENSION

The **main idea** of a paragraph or passage is the most important point the author is making.

To find a **stated main idea,** ask yourself, "What big, important idea does the author state?"

Sometimes the main idea is not stated directly. This is called an **implied main idea.** To find an implied main idea, ask yourself, "What main point do all the details support?"

▶ **Read the paragraph below. Then write the implied main idea of the paragraph.**

> But before very long the scenery changed. The land flattened out, and I could see from horizon to horizon. It made me nervous, being able to see so far ahead of me. I missed the mountains protecting me.

Implied Main Idea: _____

_____

_____

_____

Academic Language VOCABULARY

▶ **Rate each word. Then write its meaning and an example sentence.**

Word	Meaning	Example
ACADEMIC WORDS *Use these words in all your subject classes.*		
alternate al•ter•nate (adjective) ① ② ③ ④	every second time	Twice a month, on alternate Saturdays, I volunteer at the local animal shelter.
orientation o•ri•en•ta•tion (noun) ① ② ③ ④		
evaluate e•val•u•ate (verb) ① ② ③ ④		
CONTENT AREA WORDS *Use these words to talk and write about social studies and science.*		
administration ad•min•is•tra•tion (noun) ① ② ③ ④	the people in the executive branch of government during a certain president's term	
satellite sat•el•lite (noun) ① ② ③ ④		
SELECTION WORDS *These words are key to understanding this selection.*		
aptitude ap•ti•tude (adjective) ① ② ③ ④		You must score well on an aptitude test to get accepted into that school.
maneuver ma•neu•ver (verb) ① ② ③ ④		
ruefully rue•ful•ly (adverb) ① ② ③ ④		

Rating Scale ① I don't know the word. ② I've seen it or heard it. ③ I know its meaning. ④ I know it and use it.

Roots and Affixes WORD ANALYSIS

A **root** is a word part that comes from another language, such as Latin or Greek.

Knowing common roots can help you figure out the meanings of unfamiliar English words.

Affixes are word parts attached to the beginning or end of a word that change its meaning or part of speech.

▶ The word *administrate* comes from the Latin root *ministrare*, which means "to manage."

Write the word's affix and its meaning.

_____

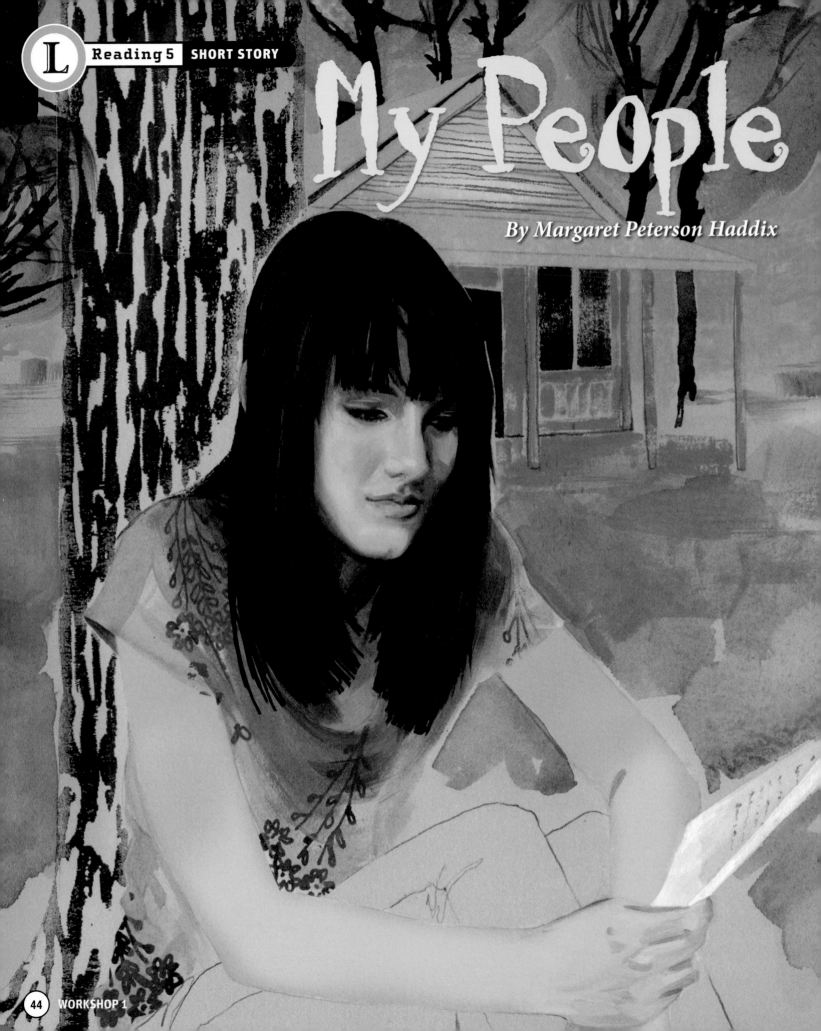

My People

By Margaret Peterson Haddix

A young woman learns that growing up means knowing where you want to go and remembering where you come from.

The people in my family aren't the kind who ever go anywhere. So when that letter came in the fall, I knew it didn't make any sense to go getting my hopes up.

But as Granny always says, hope and sense aren't exactly kissing cousins. My hopes went shooting up like a firecracker on the Fourth of July. I read that letter again and again, near fifty times, until I could close my eyes and see the words in my head.

Dear Ms. Havens:

Congratulations! As the top scorer in your region on the state **aptitude** *test, you are cordially invited to participate in the College for High Schoolers at Mercer University, July 12–19. Join in college-level seminars with the best and brightest in the state. Learn from Mercer's world-class faculty. Experience the finest in Mercer's state-of-the-art facilities. …*

The rest of the letter got into specifics, like what kind of sleeping bag to bring. I thought it was fascinating reading, the way *Soap Opera Digest* was for my aunt Eugenia.

Should I just mention right here that nobody in my family had ever gone to college? We heard tell that one of my third cousins, Bobby Ray Brighton, stepped foot on a community college campus once, but he was just lost. Should I mention that Mercer University was four, maybe five hours away, and I'd never been any farther from home than the discount store over in Spikesville?

If you know those couple of facts, you'll know why I hid that letter in the bottom of my underwear drawer for a week. I took it out every morning to read, just in case the words might have changed in the night. But I never showed it to anyone. Who was I going to show it to?

My parents would have said, "Well, that's real nice, honey," and gone back to watching reruns of *The Price Is*

Right. It never would have occurred to them that I might want to go to this College for High Schoolers.

My teachers would have been proud enough, but they would have held the letter up for the whole school to see. "Look, you all, and see what Lindley went and did! See what you can accomplish with a little studying and hard work?" And all the other kids would have looked at me like I'd grown an extra head, like I belonged with the bearded lady and the miniature man at the county fair.

If I'd shown my friends—well, see above.

But there was Granny…

Granny had dropped out of school in about fifth grade. Still, if there was any sort of degree out there in listening, she would have deserved one.

So on a Sunday afternoon when everyone else in my house seemed to be taking naps, I sneaked down the hill to Granny's. I wanted to thrust the letter at her and let her read it for herself, but between her bad eyes, her bad glasses the welfare office never gets around to replacing, and that dropping out of school all those years ago, she's not much for reading. So I read the letter out loud. I read her everything, even the part about sleeping bags.

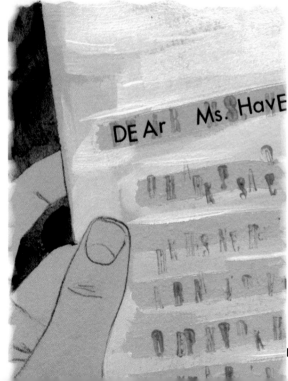

---

cordially *(adv.)* warmly; sincerely
facilities *(n.)* buildings created for a specific purpose

"Always knew you were smart," she said when I was done.

"I'm good at taking tests," I said. "Daddy'll tell you that's not the same thing."

"The state thinks you're smart," Granny said, like that settled the question. She rocked a little bit, staring out her living room window at the mountain that rose up smack in front of her driveway. "So you gonna frame this letter and hang it on the wall, or you gonna do something about it?"

That's Granny. She's good at getting right to the point.

I squirmed on Granny's sunk-in couch, which I can remember sitting on as far back as when I was two.

"Well, I *want* to," I said. "I'd give anything to go to College for High Schoolers. I reckon it'd be like—like heaven. But how am I going to get there? How am I going to pay for it? I mean, I don't even own a sleeping bag!"

"Seems like one of my cousins has a sleeping bag," Granny said. "Now, if I could just remember which one. … And you've got nine months to raise the money. As for getting you there—why, I'll take you. I always did want to see a little bit more of the world before I die."

I stared at Granny. She had a beat-up pickup truck sitting in her driveway—well, who didn't, around here. But I'd never seen her drive it. If she ever needed anything down at the store, we'd pick it up for her, or we'd take her along with us.

"But, but—" I kind of sputtered.

"Now, don't you worry," Granny said. "I can drive fine. Just never had a reason to do much of it before. What do you say?"

What I wanted to say was, "But I didn't tell you about the biggest obstacle of all. How can *I* go to that big fancy university? How can I pull up a chair beside all those really smart kids from all over the state? Don't you know I'm scared out of my shoes of making a fool of myself?" But how could I mention a little thing like terror when

Granny was willing to drive for the first time in years?

THOSE NINE MONTHS I spent waiting for the College for High Schoolers couldn't seem to decide whether to drag or fly by. I'd read the letter again and get excited all over again, and it'd seem like all the clocks in the world had just plain stopped. Then I'd get hit with a fit of nerves, and it'd seem like two or three days would zip by while I was just standing there, telling my heart to quit pounding.

When I got excited, I'd beg for extra hours working at the hamburger stand or I'd go help Granny tinker on her truck. We had it running pretty strong by January, but we kept having to fine-tune it.

When I got nervous, I'd walk down to the library to study so I'd be ready for Mercer University. I read or reread every book there that might be the slightest bit educational. And I read the library's *Time* magazine from cover to cover every week. You wouldn't believe all the things that were going on in the world outside Pine Hollow.

> **Summarize**
> **What did Lindley do to prepare for the program?**

And then suddenly it was July.

On July 12, all my relatives came by to tell Granny and me goodbye. I think some of them thought they'd never see us again. And I think some of my uncles had a little bet going about whether or not we'd go through with our plum fool plan. Still, it was quite a sight, all those arms waving at us as we drove away. It made me think of people seeing the *Titanic* off, cheering and yelling, and no one knowing an iceberg lay right ahead.

I tried not to think about it.

Granny and I were both quiet for a long while, chugging down the mountain. I hugged the sleeping bag I'd borrowed from my cousin Edna, once removed. My feet rested on the suitcase I'd borrowed from my uncle Floyd. Suddenly it seemed like I was bringing my family with me, not just their things. I felt a little better.

> **squirmed** *(v.)* fidgeted; wriggled about uncomfortably
> **reckon** *(v.)* to have an opinion

"Look," Granny said softly.

It was the "Leaving Spikesville" sign, right at the edge of the discount store parking lot. The road curved ahead, leading to places I'd never been.

"New territory," I breathed. I thought of Christopher Columbus, Ferdinand Magellan, Vasco da Gama—any one of those explorers we studied in school. I wished I'd never learned that some of them came to a bad end. Was it Sir Francis Drake or Sir Walter Raleigh who got beheaded by his own people?

We drove around the curve.

"Doesn't look much different," Granny said, sounding a little disappointed. I felt relieved. Every tuft of familiar-looking weeds, every rock-faced mountain, and every falling-down tobacco barn we drove past reminded me I wasn't *that* far from home.

But before very long the scenery changed. The land flattened out, and I could see from horizon to horizon. It made me nervous, being able to see so far ahead of me. I missed the mountains protecting me.

But mostly it was just cornfields around me. I knew about cornfields.

In the next hour, we drove through Chalmersburg, Mitchell, Good Egg, Peeveysville, and Silo. I collected places like beads on a string. I planned to remember always the little kid who waved at me in Good Egg, the crooked sidewalks in Silo, the stately dome on the courthouse in Peeveysville. Would I dare talk about any of those with the other kids at Mercer University? Could I mention casually, "Well, when I was driving through Chalmersburg …"?

No. Probably all the other kids had been to New York, Los Angeles, London, Paris—real places. Places *Time* magazine mentioned all the time.

What did I think I was doing?

An hour later, Granny dropped me off in front of Mercer Hall at Mercer University and departed in a belch of smoke. Then I turned around and faced Mercer Hall.

"They invited me," I whispered to myself. "They want me here."

Still, I was kind of glad that Granny wasn't standing right there with me. If there'd been something behind me to go back to, I couldn't have made my feet go forward.

---

beheaded *(n.)* had his head cut off
stately *(adj.)* impressive in size

LITERARY ANALYSIS

Narrator's Point of View

Who is the narrator of this story?

_____

- Is the narrator inside or outside the story?

_____
_____
_____
_____
_____

- From what point of view is this story written?

_____
_____
_____
_____
_____
_____
_____

- Circle two pronouns that help you identify the story's point of view.

CRITICAL THINKING

Analyze

Underline the things Lindley thinks during the drive to Mercer that show her small-town upbringing.

- What do these thoughts tell you about Lindley?

_____
_____
_____
_____
_____
_____
_____
_____

Or—maybe I couldn't make my feet go forward, anyway. I stood there, staring up at the stern brick building, until someone pushed open the door.

"Hey!" a girl yelled. "Are you here for the College for High Schoolers program?"

"Y-yes," I stammered.

"Well, come on in," she said heartily. "You have just enough time to take your luggage to your room before **orientation**."

That was the push I needed. The girl, who introduced herself as Claire, **maneuvered** me through a registration form, a trip to a dorm room I'd be sharing with someone else, and a return to Mercer Hall. I stepped into a living room of sorts filled with other kids.

"Hey there, everyone!" Claire announced. "This is Lindley."

"Everyone" turned and looked. I looked back. I felt like I'd stepped onto the set of *Dawson's Creek.* Everyone had beautiful skin, beautiful hair, beautiful teeth. I decided I was thinking too much like my uncle Lester, who's a horse trader and sometimes takes to **evaluating** humans the same way as animals. I switched my attention to everyone's clothes. The boys were mostly wearing T-shirts and shorts; the girls were wearing skintight tanks or T's and shorts.

I was wearing a dress.

Furthermore, my suitcase back in the dorm room was full of folded-up dresses, brand-new from the discount store. Oops. Why had I relied on *The Bell Jar* to know what kids wore to college? I should have remembered that Sylvia Plath went to college in the 1950s. Years and years and years ago.

"Where are you from?" the girl in the tightest tank and the skimpiest shorts asked me.

"Oh, I'm an exchange student from Appalachia," I said **ruefully.**

I felt so out of place in that dress, I was ready to offer

"Oh, I'm an exchange student from Appalachia," I said ruefully.

up myself and my home for comic relief. As Granny always says, sometimes it pays to laugh at yourself before anyone else has a chance to. But nobody laughed. Looking at the blank look on tight-tank girl's face, I decided *Time* magazine was right, and American teens nowadays were woefully ignorant of geography.

"Well," tight-tank girl said, "you certainly speak English beautifully. There's just a trace of an accent."

I sat down.

Claire started in on the program, telling us what a wonderful week we were going to have. We were all supposed to introduce ourselves and tell what we wanted to major in when we got to college for real. The tight-tank girl's name was Daphne, and she planned to get a doctorate in engineering.

"You?" a haughty boy with dark, curly hair said. He'd introduced himself as "Justin—political science with an economics minor."

Daphne flipped her long blond hair over her shoulder.

"Hello?" she said. "I've won the state science fair the past three years. A doctorate in engineering is just the *beginning* of my plans."

That shut Justin up, though as we all learned later, he wasn't one to keep his mouth closed for long.

When it was my turn, I said my name loud and proud, then kind of mumbled, "I don't know what I want to major in." I didn't add, "I probably won't get to go to college for real." Everyone else seemed to be taking it for granted.

"That's okay," Daphne said comfortingly. "You're an exchange student. The university system probably isn't the same in your country."

The others must not have heard what I'd said earlier, because now there was a little flurry of whispers around the circle. I heard, "Oh, an exchange student. That explains it," and "Where's she from?" and an overconfident,

---

exchange student *(n.)* a student from a different country
haughty *(adj.)* very proud and boastful

too-loud answer from Justin, "I think it's one of those poor, formerly Communist countries in Eastern Europe. See how bad her teeth are?"

I should have corrected them once and for all, said, "Hello? Don't you know that Appalachia starts right at the eastern edge of your state?" But I was too busy trying to make sure my lips hid my bad teeth.

And as the days passed, I discovered it was right handy having everyone think I was a foreigner. Because of that, nobody was surprised that I was the only person who hadn't taken an eighth-grade trip to Washington, D.C., who couldn't brag, as Justin did, "Well, when I saw the Constitution and the Declaration of Independence at the National Archives, I was not impressed. ..." Nobody minded explaining to me that college cafeterias are in different buildings than the classrooms, not like high school at all. Nobody seemed concerned that I mostly sat silently in the back of the group, just listening.

> **Summarize**
> **What is Lindley ashamed of?**

Still, I decided that thirty-year-old textbooks, the Pine Hollow library, *Time* magazine—and teachers who sometimes slipped and said "ain't" themselves—hadn't given me *that* bad of an education. Once, I was the only person who could name all the Cabinet officials of the current **administration,** even more than Justin could.

"I got everyone but the Secretary of the Interior," Justin sulked at lunch that day. "It's not my fault that one changed last week. I was at computer camp then."

"You?" Daphne teased. Justin had made it clear all along that he had nothing but contempt for computer experts—or "techno-drones," as he called them.

Justin blushed.

"My dad thinks that's where the money is," he muttered. "He just doesn't take a long-term view. Sure, when I'm president, I won't be making that much—but then there'll be hefty speaking fees for years after that, and fame and honor. ..."

"*When* you're president?" Daphne asked. "When, not *if*?"

"Of course," Justin said. "You're not the only one who's got everything planned."

I thought about my own future plans, which were—nothing. I wasn't even sure I could count on Granny being there at the end of the week to pick me up.

---

contempt (*n.*) a total lack of respect

LITERARY ANALYSIS

Narrator's Point of View

Review the scene in which Lindley introduces herself to the other students. How would it be different if it were told from Daphne's point of view?

_____

_____

_____

_____

_____

_____

VOCABULARY/WORD ANALYSIS

Roots and Affixes

 Review paragraph 5 on page 48.

- The Latin word *dormire* means "to sleep." <u>Underline</u> a word that comes from this root.
- Explain how the meaning of this word is related to sleeping.

_____

_____

[21] SMALL GROUPS/INDEPENDENT

COLLABORATE

Represent Create a poster that shows five pieces of "basic summer clothing" that an American eighth-grader needs in order to fit in.

COMMUNICATE

Discuss and Write Discuss strategies for dealing with unkind comments about your appearance. Then write a paragraph stating an alternate strategy Lindley could have used instead of keeping quiet.

When I tuned back in to the conversation, Justin and Daphne were arguing about the whole point of College for High Schoolers.

"It's such a joke, really," Justin was saying. "We all know it's a marketing ploy on the university's part, to try to get the state's smartest kids to come here, when everyone knows we belong at Harvard or Yale."

"Or M.I.T.," Daphne added.

"Whatever," Justin said. "Do they really think *any* of us would settle for a second-rate institution like this?"

I hadn't known Mercer was second-rate. I'd thought it was world-class. State-of-the-art.

The pizza I was chewing started tasting like cardboard. I swallowed carefully.

"Then why are you here now?" I asked Justin quietly.

He shrugged. "It got me away from my dad for another week," he said.

"And he didn't get into Harvard's summer program," a pimply-faced boy named Ryan said from down the table.

"That's not true!" Justin said, gripping the table like he was ready to spring up and start throwing punches.

"Hey, hey, I was just joking," Ryan said. "Sheesh."

Then the whole tableful of kids began comparing all the different camps and summer programs they'd gone to in their lives, dating back to first grade. Soccer camp, ballet camp, young inventors' camp, discovery camp, math camp, writers' camp. … I got quieter and quieter, and I wondered why nobody else noticed. What was I going to say? *Back in Pine Hollow, we'uns have a summer reading program at the library. Kids go there and the librarian reads them books?* Once upon a time, I'd been mighty impressed with that program.

"Know what I did last month?" Ryan said. "I had work camp with my church youth group. We went to South Carolina and put roofs on poor people's houses."

"Oh, that sounds thrilling," Justin said. I think he was still mad about Ryan's Harvard comment.

"Well, it was kind of interesting," Ryan said. "I want to be a sociologist, you know? And the people down there, you just can't figure them out. They live in these old, falling-down shacks in the mountains—or maybe, maybe, a rusty old trailer—but they've all got these huge **satellite** dishes and big-screen TVs. Things my dad would say *we* couldn't afford."

"Maybe they just like TV," I said in such a small voice I was surprised anyone else heard me. Or maybe everyone else heard better than I did. My ears had started ringing. I went on. "Maybe they just care more about what their TVs look like than what their houses look like. And in the mountains, maybe they wouldn't get any reception at all without that satellite dish. It's not like there's cable wires strung out everywhere in the country."

Suddenly everyone was staring at me.

"You don't understand," Ryan said. "These people are on *welfare*. They're taking *charity*."

"So they don't have a right to watch *Oprah?*" I said fiercely. "Or soap operas or game shows or Saturday morning cartoons?"

"Ah, a good question has been raised here," Justin interjected, sounding like one of those pompous moderators on political talk shows. "Do Americans have a basic right to TV? Even poor people? Even at taxpayers' expense?"

"It's not at taxpayers' expense," I said. "Welfare doesn't pay for televisions."

"But if these people can't afford to feed their families, how can they afford TVs? Top-of-the-line, big-screen TVs?" Ryan asked.

"They work for them," I said. "They work *hard*." My eyes blurred then, to go along with my ringing ears. I was going to cry. I shoved myself away from the table and ran away. Tears began dripping down my face before I even passed the serving line.

> **Summarize**
> In one sentence, summarize the problem Lindley is having.

---

second-rate *(adj.)* not very good
pompous *(adj.)* arrogant

Narrator's Point of View

Review the second paragraph on page 50. Rewrite the first sentence as though Justin were the narrator of the story.

_____

_____

_____

_____

_____

COMPREHENSION

Main Idea and Details

Draw a box around paragraph 12 on page 50. What is the implied main idea of this paragraph?

_____

_____

_____

_____

_____

- Underline the details that helped you figure out this implied main idea.

VOCABULARY/WORD ANALYSIS

Roots and Affixes

The Latin word *servire* means "to serve." Circle a word in the last paragraph on page 50 that comes from this root.

- What is the affix in this word? _____

CRITICAL THINKING

Evaluate

Review the last three paragraphs on page 50. Do you agree or disagree with Lindley? Explain why.

_____

_____

_____

_____

One of the cooks saw me and called out, "Are you all right, honey?" I shrugged and kept going, though the cook probably would have understood better than the whole cafeteria full of smart-alecky, know-it-all, too-big-for-their-pants rich kids. I ducked out a side door, into a clump of trees. Hidden by a huge shrub, I crouched down and let myself sob.

If I hadn't started crying, I could have flung all sorts of arguments out at Ryan. *My mother's been working at a fast-food restaurant for twenty years, and she still makes the same as me: minimum wage. You want to tell me we don't deserve food stamps? Ever been in a coal mine? That's where my granddad worked. Days went by when he never saw the sun. And then he died of the black lung. And my granny? Want to know why she had to drop out of school? Eleven years old, she had to go to work in a tomato-canning factory to support her family.* But no—I couldn't have said any of that without exposing myself, exposing my family.

> **Summarize**
> **Sum up Lindley's argument.**

The shrubbery around me started moving, and the next thing I knew, Justin and Daphne were peeking through the leaves at me.

"Go away," I growled.

"We just wanted to—" Daphne began.

"Apologize," Justin finished. "That Ryan can be such a jerk."

That struck me as truly ridiculous—like the pot calling the kettle a little shady.

"It was just an academic discussion," Justin said. "Nothing personal."

"I live in a trailer," I said. "We have a satellite dish. And a big-screen TV."

"Oh," Daphne said weakly. "But in your country; probably—"

"Look at a map," I said. "Appalachia's part of Ohio."

They both blinked at me a few times. Then Justin said, "I knew that. I just thought you said you were from somewhere else."

I gave him such a scornful look he actually took a step backward.

"I don't belong here," I said. "I just want to go home. And you know what's really stupid? I can't. Any of the rest of you, you could just call Mommy or Daddy, and they'd be right here, 'Was that big bad university mean to my little sweet-ums?' Not me. I'm stuck here the rest of the week, everybody thinking … everybody knowing …"

"Doesn't your family have a phone?" Daphne said gently.

"Of course we have a phone," I snarled. Explaining about Granny's truck, everyone else's immobility, was too complicated. I just repeated, "I don't belong here. I shouldn't have come."

I pushed past them in search of a better place to hide.

BY DINNERTIME I'd resorted to hiding out in my room, lying facedown on my bed. I'd skipped all the afternoon sessions, and I'd pretended to be asleep when my roommate tiptoed in to dump her books before dinner.

"I think she's sick," I heard her report to someone in the hall as she slipped back out.

Good, I thought. *Maybe they'll feel sorry for me now.*

Good, I thought. Maybe they'll feel sorry for me now

But wasn't that the point—that I didn't want anyone feeling sorry for me? To be honest, I was starting to feel a little foolish. Did I really think I was going to lie here on this bed for the next four days? I was already getting bored.

Someone knocked on my door.

"Lindley?" It was Daphne. "I know you're in there. I have something to show you. I'll slide it under the door."

> **scornful** *(adj.)* full of disapproval
> **immobility** *(n.)* the inability to move

I wanted to keep lying there, stubborn and still, but my curiosity got the better of me. Very quietly, I got up and inched over to the door.

A thin square of paper was on the floor, half in my room, half out. Maybe Daphne hadn't fully made up her mind that she wanted me to see it. I picked it up. It was a picture—a school picture of a girl with painful-looking braces and glasses as thick as canning jars and stringy hair the color of a grocery sack.

"That's me," Daphne said from the other side of the door.

"No way," I said aloud.

"Yes it is," Daphne said. "Open the door and you'll see."

I opened the door and there was Daphne, looking as much like an MTV *Spring Break* contestant as ever. Justin was standing right behind her.

"That's how I looked until a month ago," Daphne said. "So now you know a secret about me, too. I brought that picture with me—I don't know, just to remind myself."

I looked again, back and forth between the picture and Daphne. There was something familiar about the cheekbones of the girl in the picture. Still, I couldn't make my eyes see her as Daphne.

"So?" I said rudely. "You're blond and beautiful now."

"And you know what? I'm not sure I like it," Daphne said. She glanced back at Justin, but he didn't say anything. She kept talking. "I don't like people expecting me to be dumb. When I was ditsy before, it was like, 'Oh, absent-minded genius. Einstein never learned how to tie his shoes either.' Now it's, 'Dumb blond. Of course.' It's awful. I probably couldn't even win a local science fair looking like this."

"Oh," I said weakly.

Daphne nudged Justin in the ribs. "Your turn," she said.

Justin looked jolted, like he'd just intended to come along as an observer.

"For what?" he said.

"To tell us a secret," Daphne said. "So we'll all be even."

I thought he was going to refuse—probably on the grounds that it might hurt his future presidential campaign. But he took a deep breath and said, rapid-fire, "I really didn't get into the Harvard summer program.

jolted *(adj.)* surprised
intended *(v.)* meant to

COMPREHENSION

Main Idea and Details

Review Daphne's response after Lindley tells her, "You're blond and beautiful now." What is the main point of her response in paragraph 10 on page 53?

_____

_____

_____

Is this main idea stated or implied?

_____

LITERARY ANALYSIS

Narrator's Point of View

Draw a box around a paragraph on page 53 that does not contain dialogue.

- Rewrite this paragraph from a third-person point of view.

_____

_____

_____

_____

_____

And my dad said it didn't matter, because I don't have the social skills to be a politician, anyway. That's the real reason he wants me to go into computers."

"Your own father said that? Ouch," I said.

"See? None of the rest of us know who we are either," Daphne said.

I leaned against the doorway. Maybe I should have let her comment go, accepted the secrets she and Justin were telling me, and pretended to get along for the rest of the week. But I couldn't.

"You don't understand," I said. "I *do* know who I am. That's the problem. I'm bologna on white bread. Casseroles made with processed cheese. Old cars rusting up on cinder blocks for decades on end. Nasty old shacks with satellite dishes behind them. I'm not—my people aren't—we're not *college material.*"

Daphne seemed to be trying very hard to accept that people actually ate processed cheese. I looked over at Justin, expecting to see him trying out a (failed) politician's smile. But he was shaking his head.

"Maybe you are all that," he said. "But you're also one of us. You do belong here. Think about it. You *memorized* all the Cabinet positions."

"Dating back five administrations," I said shakily.

"Really?" Justin said. "I only know four."

"I was scared there'd be a test," I admitted.

"Glory be," Daphne said, in an imitation of what she probably thought was an Appalachian accent. "You're an even bigger geek than the rest of us!"

GRANNY SHOWED UP at the end of the week, just like she'd promised. The truck's engine was positively purring.

I gave Mercer one last look around. Justin was getting into a silver Saab. Daphne was climbing into a blue minivan that seemed to be filled with younger girls in varying sizes, all wearing glasses. I noticed that Daphne was wearing glasses now, too. I felt like I was seeing the beginnings of a makeover in reverse. Several other kids were staring at Granny and me. And the truck. I just

smiled and waved and held my shoulders high. Then I slipped onto the seat beside Granny.

"So. You get your fill of college?" she asked as we drove down the street, lofty academic buildings whizzing past.

"No," I said. "I think I'll probably be back next year. In the fall. To stay for good."

Granny kind of gasped and said, "What for?"

I just shrugged. "Why not?" I said. There were too many answers to go into. *Because Justin and Daphne are seriously considering Mercer now, too ... Because Claire says I have a good shot at a full scholarship ... Because I belong at Mercer as much as I belong in Pine Hollow ... Because now I know who my people are. The rest of them.*

I wasn't sure how that was going to work, me being two different kinds of people at the same time. Would I start eating Belgian endive on my bologna sandwiches? Would I write papers quoting Dolly Parton and Plato in **alternate** sentences?

> **Summarize**
> **What decision has Lindley come to?**

I didn't care. I'd been somewhere now. And it didn't look like there were any limits at all anymore on where else I could go. ■

Margaret Peterson Haddix

WHO Margaret Peterson Haddix

BORN April 9, 1964, Washington Court House, Ohio

ADVICE TO YOUNG WRITERS *"Read a lot. Write a lot. Think a lot. Enjoy what you read, write, and think about it."*

AUTHOR FILE

LEAVING HOME Peterson Haddix comes from a long line of farmers, but even as a child she knew she wanted to travel and be an author. Like Peterson Haddix, Lindley also wants to see the world outside her hometown.

OTHER WORKS Peterson Haddix has written more than 20 books, including exciting and suspenseful novels about futuristic cities, secret villages, and other fantasy worlds.

---

endive (n.) a lettuce-like vegetable
Plato (n.) an ancient Greek philosopher

Read and Synthesize

LITERARY ANALYSIS

Narrator's Point of View
Why might Margaret Peterson Haddix told Lindley's story from the first-person point of view? What might that add to the story?

_____
_____
_____
_____
_____
_____
_____
_____
_____

COMPREHENSION

Main Idea and Details
Review page 55. **Check** ✓ the paragraph that states the main idea of this part of the story.

21 SMALL GROUPS/INDEPENDENT

COLLABORATE

Examine Perspectives Discuss places you would like to visit in order to broaden your view of the world. Present your chosen destinations, and explain why you want to travel there.

COMMUNICATE

React and Write Imagine that Lindley graduates from Mercer. Write a letter from Lindley to the kids back home encouraging them to strive for college. Take notes to help you organize your thoughts.

READ ONLINE

expert space
Go to **www.expert21.com/student** to learn more about College Visits; Appalachia; Margaret Peterson Haddix.

ESSAYS
That Make a
DIFFERENCE

Writing an admissions essay for college can be a scary process. The goal of this kind of essay is to show a college admissions committee that you're an individual—that you're more than just grades, test scores, sports, and activities.

What does a successful college essay really look like? Two of the essays that follow are real examples of exactly what a great college admissions essay should be. The writers present themselves in a positive way and find something unique about themselves or their lives to write about. The third essay is a satire of an admissions essay that portrays its author in a superhuman way.

CHRISTINA

"I couldn't imagine wanting to dye my hair blond to feel better about myself. I absolutely love being different and not walking the same path as everyone else."

This essay shows that the writer is mature and self-aware—the kind of student every school wants.

JAMES

"I have the persistence of the little glob of peanut butter that sticks to the roof of your mouth. This drive has enabled me to achieve academic success."

This writer found an interesting way to describe himself that everyone can relate to.

HUGH

"I have won bullfights in San Juan, cliff-diving competitions in Sri Lanka, and spelling bees at the Kremlin."

This satire expresses the writer's frustration with the college essay-writing process. He entered into the Scholastic Art & Writing competition—and won!

I Couldn't Imagine Wanting to Dye My Hair Blond

By **Christina Mendoza**

Growing up in a small, conservative community, it's easy to be shoved into your own category if you don't look or act like everyone else. My hair and eyes, instead of being blond and blue like all of my Czech classmates', were chocolate and espresso. My last name had a "z" in it, and my grandmother called me "mija." By the time I was in grade school, the teasing began, and I was hurt and confused. Didn't all grandmothers call their grandchildren "mija"? Why did everyone except me have blue eyes?

After an afternoon of teasing and tormenting from my classmates, I asked these questions to my mother, between sobs. By this time, she had become extremely good at giving me the "you're unique and beautiful" speech, but it was hard for her to truly empathize with me because neither she nor my father knew how I felt. She was a Caucasian who grew up in California; he was a Mexican American who grew up as the majority in San Antonio. I was the product of the two—the "half-breed" daughter who was raised in the small town of Seymour, population 2,800.

My other family members didn't seem to have any trouble fitting in. My father's ethnicity is well respected. He is the only doctor within a fifty-mile radius who can speak Spanish. My sister was the beauty queen of our town—her sleek, glossy hair and olive complexion were the envy of every girl. My little brother received the recessive genes (fair skin, blue eyes), so he looks like everyone else in Seymour. I felt I was stuck somewhere in the middle of my siblings, stuck in the middle of two cultures, and not accepted by either.

Time does have a way of healing things. I didn't just wake up one morning and think, "I'm proud to be Hispanic," but as I have matured, I have learned not to be ashamed of my ethnicity. Instead of hiding who I really am, I have embraced my Mexican heritage and have become proud of it. Finding out about the many opportunities that are available to students of Hispanic descent has motivated me even more to delve deeper into my culture.

Looking back, I couldn't imagine wanting to dye my hair blond to feel better about myself. The blond girls are unique in their own way, but diversity makes the world go round. I absolutely love being different and not walking the same path as everyone else. The last racist comment I received was after I was named a National Hispanic Scholar. My assailant said in a mocking tone, "I wish I could be a smart Mexican." Feeling sorry for his cultural ignorance, I smiled and replied, "Yeah, I bet you do."

---

conservative *(adj.)* disliking difference and change
empathize *(v.)* to understand and share someone else's feelings

---

COMPREHENSION

Main Idea and Details

 Underline the sentence that states the main idea of Christina Mendoza's essay.

- List two details that help support this main idea.

_____

_____

_____

_____

_____

_____

_____

NAVIGATING TEXT

Text Structure

Describe how the author of "I Couldn't Imagine Wanting to Dye My Hair Blond" uses the problem-and-solution structure in her essay.

_____

_____

_____

_____

_____

_____

_____

_____

VOCABULARY/WORD ANALYSIS

Context Clues

 Find the word *assailant* in the last paragraph.

- **Circle** the words and phrases that give you clues to its meaning.

- What is the meaning of *assailant*?

_____

Chunky Peanut Butter

By James Gregory

To really understand who I am, remember your childhood. Remember the pleasure that eating a great big peanut butter and jelly sandwich delivered? How it seemed to just slide down your throat and ease into your stomach? That sandwich is the result of the perfect combination of ingredients, all working together to create a satisfying experience. If any one ingredient were missing, the whole sandwich would fall apart. In fact, I would argue that the world is very much like one large PB&J, filled with many different ingredients. People can be classified according to their personality and similarity to these ingredients. I am like the chunky peanut butter. Although I may not be as showy as the jelly or as visible as the bread, I am the heart of the sandwich. I am essential to the sandwich's success. I work behind the scenes, holding it all together, keeping all the ingredients organized and focused on their task. I lead through example, but I am flexible. I am able to work with any kind of jelly. I am slightly shy, so I do not need to be at the center of attention; I am content in leading without recognition. However, you always know I am there. You taste all my chunks, all the little quirks that set me apart from the rest. Whether it is my dry sense of humor, my volunteer work at a summer day camp for kids, or my fervent school spirit, each unique piece guarantees that your experience will not be mundane or bland. With every bite you take, you taste more of me: my excellent grades, my size 15 feet, and my dedication to Student Council. I am more fun than creamy peanut butter; you never know what to expect, but you know that it is going to be good. However, my most important attribute is my willingness to sacrifice to help others. I have unselfishly stepped aside on the basketball court to let the team as a whole shine, and I enthusiastically devote time to service projects through Junior Civitans that help the community. This desire to help is ingrained in my personality, and drives my plan to become a physician and continue my service to others. I refuse to give up before I attain this dream; I have the persistence of the little glob of peanut butter that sticks to the roof of your mouth. No matter how many times you smack your mouth, I will not go away. This drive has enabled me to achieve academic success, success that I will continue into my higher education, and into my life. I am fun, I am good for you, and I am more than the sum of my pieces. I am the chunky peanut butter.

> **Summarize**
> **What is the main point of James's essay?**

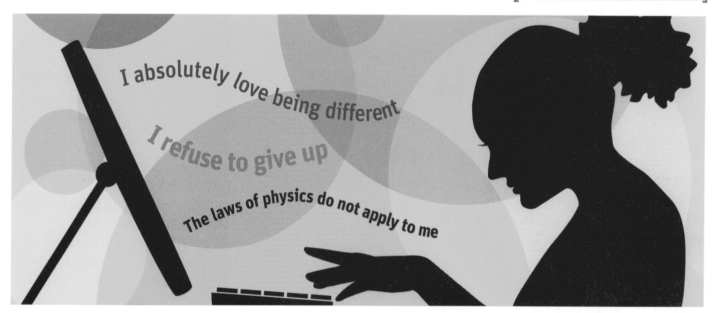

I absolutely love being different

I refuse to give up

The laws of physics do not apply to me

> **fervent** *(adj.)* passionate
> **mundane** *(adj.)* everyday and boring

Essay 3A

By Hugh Gallagher

I am a dynamic figure, often seen scaling walls and crushing ice. I have been known to remodel train stations on my lunch breaks, making them more efficient in the area of heat retention. I write award-winning operas. I manage time efficiently. Occasionally, I tread water for three days in a row.

I woo women with my sensuous and godlike trombone playing. I can pilot bicycles up severe inclines with unflagging speed. And I cook Thirty-Minute Brownies in twenty minutes. I am an expert in stucco, a veteran in love, and an outlaw in Peru.

Using only a hoe and a large glass of water, I once single-handedly defended a small village in the Amazon Basin from a horde of ferocious army ants. I play bluegrass cello. I was scouted by the Mets. I am the subject of numerous documentaries. When I'm bored, I build large suspension bridges in my yard. I enjoy urban hang gliding. On Wednesdays, after school, I repair electrical appliances free of charge.

I am an abstract artist, a concrete analyst, and a ruthless bookie. Critics worldwide swoon over my original line of corduroy eveningwear. I don't perspire. I am a private citizen, yet I receive fan mail. I have been caller number nine and have won the weekend passes. I bat 400. My deft floral arrangements have earned me fame in international botany circles. Children trust me.

I can hurl tennis rackets at small moving objects with deadly accuracy. I once read *Paradise Lost, Moby Dick*, and *David Copperfield* in one day and still had time to refurbish an entire dining room that evening. I know the exact location of every food item in the supermarket. I have performed several covert operations for the CIA. I sleep once a week; when I do sleep, I sleep in a chair. While on vacation in Canada, I successfully negotiated with a group of terrorists who had seized a small bakery. The laws of physics do not apply to me.

I balance, I weave, I dodge, I frolic, and my bills are all paid. On weekends, to let off steam, I participate in full-contact origami. Years ago I discovered the meaning of life but forgot to write it down. I have made extraordinary four-course meals using only a mouli [food grater] and a toaster oven. I breed prizewinning clams. I have won bullfights in San Juan, cliff-diving competitions in Sri Lanka, and spelling bees at the Kremlin. I have played Hamlet. I have performed open-heart surgery. And I have spoken with Elvis.

But I have not yet gone to college. ■

dynamic *(adj.)* exciting
heat retention *(n.)* the ability to trap heat

Context Clues

Find the word *quirks* in the second column of James Gregory's essay.

- <u>Underline</u> a context clue that helps you determine the meaning of *quirks*.
- Circle the type of context clue it is.

    example   definition

Author's Style

Review "Chunky Peanut Butter," and check each feature that is true of James Gregory's style.

- [ ] rhythmic repetition
- [ ] straightforward reporting
- [ ] humorous exaggeration
- [ ] absolute honesty

- (Circle) an example of each feature in the essay itself.

Main Idea and Details

What unstated main idea do all of the details in Hugh Gallagher's "Essay 3A" add up to? State the main idea using the first-person voice.

_____

_____

_____

_____

expert space
Go to **www.expert21.com/student** to learn more about The College Application Process; Satire.

Think Across Texts

Organize and Synthesize

1. Complete this chart using information from "How to Survive, Thrive, and Prepare for What's Next"; "My People"; and "Essays That Make a Difference."

	What do students need to do or learn in order to get a good education?
"How to Survive, Thrive, and Prepare for What's Next"	
"My People"	
"Essays That Make a Difference"	

Compare and Evaluate

2. What things did Lindley from "My People" do that are suggested in "How to Survive, Thrive, and Prepare for What's Next"?

_____

_____

_____

_____

_____

3. "My People" and "Essays That Make a Difference" seem to agree that going to college should be a goal for high school students. Do you agree? Why or why not?

_____

_____

_____

_____

_____

4. Which writer made college seem most reachable? How did the writer do this? Use examples from the text.

_____

_____

_____

_____

_____

_____

_____

_____

_____

Discuss and Write

5. With a partner, discuss how the three readings in "Getting There" helped you understand the strategies you need to follow to meet your future goals. Take notes as you talk. Then use your notes to write a response to the question: *What do I need to reach my goals?*

Apply Word Knowledge

Word Lab

1. **Decide.** Which of these things would you do **ruefully**? Check all that apply.

☐ ask a friend to come over

☐ apologize for an accident

☐ announce, "Dinner is ready!"

☐ say, "I burned the pie."

2. **Order them.** Which of these things do you have the most **aptitude** for? Number them from 1 to 4, with 1 being the least aptitude and 4 being the most aptitude.

__ learning a new sport

__ solving problems

__ making new friends

__ remembering facts

3. **Complete.** Complete the sentence below with the words **pursue** and **maneuver**.

In order to _____ the suspect, the police had to _____ their car around several parked trucks.

4. **Think about it.** How can you **efficiently memorize** new words?

_____

_____

5. **Decide.** What would you learn in an **orientation**? Fill in the circle next to the correct answer.

Ⓐ how to use a compass

Ⓑ the layout of a summer camp

Ⓒ the address of your senator

Ⓓ how to construct a birdhouse

6. **Match.** Draw a line from each **strategy** to its goal.

study every evening   save money on lunch

pack lunch for school   keep family ties strong

talk often to your parents   do well in school

Word Analysis

7. The Latin word *extra* means "outside" or "beyond." Below are English words that contain this root. Write the meaning of each word.

extracurricular (adj.): _____

extraordinary (adj.):_____

8. Write the base word for each entry in the chart.

Word	Base Word
requirement	
displace	
rueful	rue
internship	

21 Analyze Risk

CAREER CONNECTION Law, Public Safety, Corrections & Security
www.careerclusters.org

Go to 21 ToolKit **Expert File 6.27** to learn more about careers in the military.

Your future is full of great opportunities. However, there are also great risks to consider. Find out how to use risk analysis to make up your mind.

Risking Debt for an Education

www.schools.com

ABOUT US   NEWS   EVENTS

College Students Face Growing Debt

Susan Whitehall, Media News Service,

January 15, 2009–As the economy stagnates, students are facing mountains of debt when they graduate from college, and also worries about how to pay the debt.

College graduates, on average, earn almost twice as much as those who only finish high school. College grads also have the opportunity to pursue fields that interest them, because a B.A. or B.S. is often a prerequisite for many jobs.

However, the economy is not getting better very fast. As of December 2008, the unemployment rate was 7.6% and growing, a figure that does not include recent graduates who have not yet found work, or people who have given up on looking for work. Students may be stuck with debt, and no way to pay it back.

One student, Terrell Jones, is graduating from Virginia State University $30,000 in debt. He'll face monthly payments of $300 for the next 10 years. "It's going to be harder to make opportunities for yourself," Jones said. "But you shouldn't let that hold you back from your dreams and your aspirations."

MARK IT

Underline two rewards of a college education.

Check ✔ two risks of taking on debt for an education.

[Here's How] ▶ **Follow these steps to analyze risk.**

Step 1 **Identify the risks.** How dangerous is each one? What might happen as a result? Draw a table listing the risks. Rank them on a scale of 1 (low risk) to 10 (high risk).

Step 2 **Evaluate the rewards.** List the rewards in a column next to the risks. Rank the rewards on a scale of 1 (low reward) to 10 (high reward).

Step 3 **Compare the risks and rewards.** Look especially at the risks and rewards that you ranked 7 or higher. Do the rewards outweigh the risks? Is the risk worth taking? Why?

Apply: Army and Education

▶ Do a risk analysis to decide whether or not to join the army and receive an education benefit.

Trina's Life

The Military—A Rewarding Career

Posted by Trina A. March 5, 2009

I joined the military for a lot of reasons. The military provides medical, dental, and vision benefits, a paycheck, free room and board, and training in a career field while you decide what you want to do. Plus, you can get up to $81,756 to help pay for college.

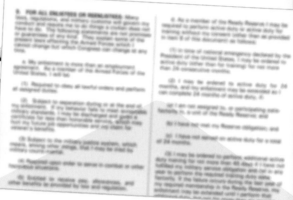

a. FOR ALL ENLISTEES: If this is my initial enlistment, I must serve a total of eight (8) years, unless I am sooner discharged or otherwise extended by the appropriate authority. ...

b. I understand that I can be ordered to active duty at any time.

… In a time of war, my enlistment may be extended without my consent for the duration of the war and for six months after its end (10 U.S.C. 506, 12103(c)).

1. **Identify the risks** and rank them on a scale of 1 (low risk) to 10 (high risk).

2. **Identify the rewards** and rank them on a scale of 1 (low reward) to 10 (high reward).

RISKS	Rank	REWARDS	Rank

3. **Compare** the risks and rewards. Based on this information and whatever else you know about serving in the military would you join? Explain your choice.

_____

_____

Personal Narrative

Personal narratives relate an experience from the author's life. They can be used in essays, histories, college applications, and in many other places.

In this writing workshop, you will write a personal narrative about an experience for a college admissions essay.

Example: Columnists, bloggers, and TV show hosts often write personal narratives with a message. This TV show host writes about meeting someone special.

> Last week, as I was walking up my street, I saw a pile of broken boxes under a tree. Angrily, I went over to pick them up, so that I could bring them to the recycling bin. "Those litterbugs," I thought. Then, I saw a pair of shoes—attached to a pair of feet. I leaned down, and realized that a man was huddled under the boxes. His name was Jim, and we began to talk.

Traits of Writing

Traits of Writing is a model for assessing and teaching. The traits work within the writing process to support revision and editing.

Each puzzle piece below represents one of the **traits** that define good writing.

Each trait is made up of four **key qualities**. The trait that you will focus on in this lesson is Sentence Fluency.

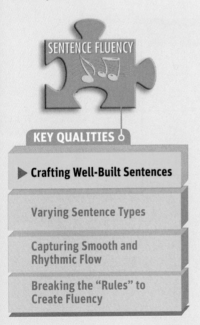

KEY QUALITIES

▶ **Crafting Well-Built Sentences**

Varying Sentence Types

Capturing Smooth and Rhythmic Flow

Breaking the "Rules" to Create Fluency

▶ **Analyze Features** A strong personal narrative has the following features.

FEATURE	🖊 MARK IT
Look for these features in the Student Model on the next page.	Mark the features as you read the Student Model.
1. An **introduction** that catches the readers' attention and leads into the experience. (Organization)	<u>Underline</u> the sentence that leads into the experience.
2. Details and **feelings** that help the reader picture the experience, including a problem. (Ideas)	Circle the problem that was resolved in this narrative.
3. Focus Trait: Sentence Fluency Craft well-built sentences that make the essay read fluently.	Check ✓ well-built sentences that make the essay read fluently.
4. A clear telling of **events** in order so the reader can follow what happened. (Organization)	Star ★ each event in the experience.
5. A strong **conclusion** that tells why the experience was important. (Organization)	Draw a box around the sentence that sums up the experience.

► **Read Gina's personal narrative about a career that interests her.**

STUDENT MODEL

Engineering My Future
By Gina Spinelli

I have a secret. I'm stage struck. Going to the theater has always been a magical experience for me. When the lights go down, I feel like I'm in another world. I was even lucky enough to see a Broadway musical once, *Phantom of the Opera*. Our seats were in the very last row, but I didn't care. I didn't really see a future in it for me, though. My dad is an electrician, and he had always hoped I might go into electrical engineering. He's says it's a good job. I've looked up the salary, and I know he's right.

This year, I went to a job fair at my school. When I first got there, I felt nervous. Then, the woman at the engineering table asked me "Do you enjoy science and math?" I said I did, but I didn't always find it easy. She laughed and said she knew what I meant. It felt good to know that professional people are not always perfect at everything. Other people were waiting, so I took her card and left.

That could have been the end of the story, but it wasn't. The next day, my English teacher wanted us to interview someone about their job as a writing assignment. "Boring!" I thought, and I figured I would just interview my dad. But I decided to challenge myself. I dug through my backpack to find the card of the woman I met at the engineering table. She seemed nice. I typed in her email address and sent her a short note asking if I could interview her.

I never would have expected it, but the interview with that woman changed my life. I talked to her about engineering for over an hour. She told me that electrical engineering was more than just wiring lights into buildings. She said that electrical engineers are responsible for light and sound systems for concert halls and theaters. That's when it hit me. I could be in the theater and still be an engineer. Acting was not the only job that would keep me close to the bright lights. Broadway, here I come!

► **Read Gina's notes about how she worked on her personal narrative.**

ORGANIZATION

My first draft was about going to work with my dad. I realized that a reader would learn more about me if I wrote about something I really cared about—my dream of working on Broadway.

SENTENCE FLUENCY

In my first draft, almost every sentence began with the word "I." When I revised, I made a point of beginning my sentences in different ways, not only with different subjects, but with clauses, like "The next day."

► **Analyze how Gina developed and organized her ideas. Fill in the missing parts of the outline.**

Event 1

Meaningful Event: went to a Broadway play
Feelings: It was magic.

Event 2

Related Event: went to a job fair
Feelings: _____

Event 3

My Challenge: _____
_____
Feelings: _____

Event 4

Realization: _____
_____
Feelings: _____

 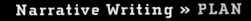

How Do I Get Started?

Assignment: Personal Narrative

Purpose: to tell about a personal experience for a college admissions essay

Audience: college admissions

Ideas: Finding a Topic

Finding a topic you care about makes writing easier and more fun. Use these Think-Abouts as you work on your ideas:

- Have I chosen a topic that I really like?
- Do I have something new to say about this topic?
- Am I writing about what I know and care about? *In the Student Model, the author tells us she is "stage struck" by theater.*
- Have I gathered enough information so that I'm ready to write?

IDEAS

○ KEY QUALITIES

▶ **Finding a Topic**

Focusing the Topic

Developing the Topic

Using Details

▶ **Model** Go back to Reading 5, "My People," in this workshop. Find language that shows this author cares about her topic.

▶ **Practice** To come up with a topic that interests you, think about a personal experience when you solved a problem.

The problem: _____

How I solved it: _____

_____

▶ **Plan Your Narrative** Use the organizer below to help you think about your personal narrative.

Event 1

Meaningful Event: _____

_____

Feelings: _____

Event 2

Related Events: _____

_____

Feelings: _____

Event 3

My Challenge: _____

_____

Feelings: _____

Event 4

Realization: _____

_____

Feelings: _____

How Do I Get Organized?

Organization: Creating the Lead

Good writers think about how to order and chunk their ideas. Ask yourself these Think-Abouts as you work on your organization.

- Did I give the reader something interesting to think about right from the start?
- Will the reader want to keep reading?
- Have I tried to get the reader's attention? *For example, in the Student Model, the author begins with, "I have a secret."*
- Did I let the reader know what is coming?

ORGANIZATION

KEY QUALITIES

▶ **Creating the Lead**

Using Sequence Words and Transition Words

Structuring the Body

Ending With a Sense of Resolution

▶ **Model** Go back to Reading 4, "How to Survive, Thrive, and Prepare for What's Next," and think about how the first sentence leads you into the article.

▶ **Practice** Think up a new powerful and engaging opening for the Student Model.

_____

_____

_____

_____

_____

▶ **Write a Paragraph** Practice using sequence and transition words as you write a first draft of one of your paragraphs here.

_____

_____

_____

_____

_____

▶ **Draft Your Personal Narrative** Write a first draft.

Quick Check

▶ Check how well you found a topic for your personal narrative. Have a writing partner rate it, too.

6 = Expert   **3** = Making Strides

5 = Well Done   **2** = On The Way

4 = Almost There **1** = Getting Started

Ideas

1. Have I chosen a topic that I really like?

Self   ① ② ③ ④ ⑤ ⑥
Partner ① ② ③ ④ ⑤ ⑥

2. Do I have something new to say about this topic?

Self   ① ② ③ ④ ⑤ ⑥
Partner ① ② ③ ④ ⑤ ⑥

3. Am I writing about what I know and care about?

Self   ① ② ③ ④ ⑤ ⑥
Partner ① ② ③ ④ ⑤ ⑥

4. Have I gathered enough information so that I'm ready to write?

Self   ① ② ③ ④ ⑤ ⑥
Partner ① ② ③ ④ ⑤ ⑥

How Do I Craft Well-Built Sentences to Make My Writing More Fluent?

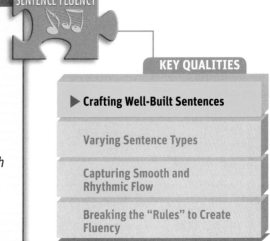

FOCUS TRAIT

Sentence Fluency: Crafting Well-Built Sentences

Good writers make sure that sentences are strong on their own and as a group within paragraphs. Use these Think-Abouts to make sure you craft well-built sentences in your essay.

- Do my sentences begin in different ways?
- Are my sentences different lengths? *Look at the first paragraph of the Student Model for sentences of different lengths.*
- Are my sentences built with sturdy construction?
- Have I used transitions (*but, and, so*) to connect parts of sentences?

KEY QUALITIES

▶ **Crafting Well-Built Sentences**

Varying Sentence Types

Capturing Smooth and Rhythmic Flow

Breaking the "Rules" to Create Fluency

▶ **Model** Go back to Reading 6, "Essays That Make a Difference," and describe Christina Mendoza's sentences.

▶ Read Ruth Culham's writing blog below to get advice on improving your writing.

Ask the Expert: Ruth Culham

Ruth Culham, an award-winning teacher, is the author of *6+1 Traits of Writing: The Complete Guide for Middle School* and other books on writing.

Q & A: Sentence Fluency: Crafting Well-Built Sentences

Rambling Ruby Writes:

"Oh my gosh! My day was the best because first we had a substitute so I didn't need to have my history paper finished and there was an assembly with a guy who talked about bullying which is a really important topic because there are lots of bullies in our school. It was an awesome day."

Rambling Ruby, you've created three sentences that should be at least five or six. You've begun those three differently—which is great. But your main sentence is so long, even using those words doesn't let the reader take a breath. Try making three new stunning sentences from your longer one—and see if you can vary their lengths and beginnings, too.

Posted by: Ruth Culham | December 22 at 04:30 P.M.

▶ **Practice** Read the sample paragraphs and think about which sentences are well built.

<u>Underline</u> the sentences that are too similar.

(Circle) the sentences that are well-built.

Star ★ the sample that shows the best example of well-built sentences.

Sample 1: A Helping Hand

I could see him falling in slow motion. The next thing I knew, my friend and his bike were in a tangled heap on the ground. He had some cuts on his hands and a bad one on his chin. It was lucky he was wearing a helmet and pads. Everyone was freaking out! I alone stood calmly. I never thought of myself as much of a leader, but that day changed me.

Sample 2: A Helping Hand

I could see him falling in slow motion. I could see my friend and his bike in a tangled heap. I could see him on the ground with cuts on his hand. I could see he was wearing a helmet and pad, luckily! I could see everyone freaking out. I could not really see myself as a leader before. Now I can.

▶ **Revise** Now craft well-built sentences to make your writing more fluent. Choose a paragraph from your first draft and revise it below. Remember to keep your sentences sturdy but unique.

_____

_____

_____

_____

_____

_____

_____

_____

_____

_____

Quick Check

▶ Check your personal narrative for how well you crafted your sentences. Then have a writing partner rate it, too.

6 = Expert   **3** = Making Strides

5 = Well Done   **2** = On The Way

4 = Almost There   **1** = Getting Started

Sentence Fluency

1. Do my sentences begin in different ways?
Self ① ② ③ ④ ⑤ ⑥
Partner ① ② ③ ④ ⑤ ⑥

2. Are my sentences different lengths?
Self ① ② ③ ④ ⑤ ⑥
Partner ① ② ③ ④ ⑤ ⑥

3. Are my sentences built with sturdy construction?
Self ① ② ③ ④ ⑤ ⑥
Partner ① ② ③ ④ ⑤ ⑥

4. Have I used transitions (*but, and, so*) to connect parts of sentences?
Self ① ② ③ ④ ⑤ ⑥
Partner ① ② ③ ④ ⑤ ⑥

Revise With Technology Use the grammar check feature in your word processing program to help you fix any sentences that don't have a sturdy construction.

How Can I Finish a Great Paper?

Grammar: Fragments and Run-ons

A fragment is an incomplete sentence. It must be changed into a complete sentence. Run-on sentences have more than one complete thought, and must be broken up into more than one sentence.

- Fix a fragment by adding words or joining it to another sentence.
- Fix a run-on by breaking it into two or more sentences, adding a semi-colon, or using a comma with a conjunction.

No: When I joined. The debate team it was fun I could argue forever.

Yes: When I joined the debate team, it was fun. I could argue forever.

▶ **Practice** Rewrite this paragraph correctly below.

When my brother got sick. I was upset. It took a while to figure out what was wrong. Because the doctor didn't recognize the symptoms at first. After we learned that it was type 1 diabetes. I knew I needed to learn more about it.

_____

_____

_____

Mechanics: Using End Punctuation Marks

All sentences end with a punctuation mark.

- If it's a statement, use a period.
- If it's a question, use a question mark.
- If you want to show strong emotion, use an exclamation mark.

Example: I aced my science test. Was I happy? Of course I was!

▶ **Practice** Rewrite this paragraph correctly below.

On a boat ride, I saw trash in the water? It was disgusting? Do people realize what happens to their trash. That's how I became interested in the environment!

_____

_____

_____

► **Proofread** Find and correct any errors in your essay. Put a check beside the types of errors you find. Then write three corrected sentences below.

❏ fixing fragments and run-ons

❏ using end punctuation correctly

❏ using commonly confused words correctly

❏ spelling commonly confused words correctly

❏ capitalization

❏ other: _____

1. _____

   _____

2. _____

   _____

3. _____

   _____

PRESENTATION

PUBLISH/PRESENT

► **Write Your Final Draft** Now, using your edited draft, begin creating a final draft for presentation.

Use word processing software to type your final draft. Make sure to format your margins and spacing according to your teacher's request.

Check your final draft against the Traits of Writing Scoring Guide on pages 338–341 and correct any errors before you present it.

► **Beyond the Classroom** Extend your finished personal narrative.

List two ideas for photos that could illustrate your personal narrative:

_____

_____

Look online for a blog, message board, magazine, or newspaper where you could publish your personal narrative.

List two places you could upload or share your personal narrative for publication.

_____   _____

Quick Check

► Check your personal narrative for correct use of conventions. Then have a writing partner rate it, too.

6 = Expert

5 = Well Done

4 = Almost There

3 = Making Strides

2 = On The Way

1 = Getting Started

Conventions

1. Did I fix fragments and run-ons correctly?

Self ① ② ③ ④ ⑤ ⑥
Partner ① ② ③ ④ ⑤ ⑥

2. Did I use end punctuation correctly?

Self ① ② ③ ④ ⑤ ⑥
Partner ① ② ③ ④ ⑤ ⑥

3. Did I follow the rules of capitalization?

Self ① ② ③ ④ ⑤ ⑥
Partner ① ② ③ ④ ⑤ ⑥

4. Is the spelling in the essay correct?

Self ① ② ③ ④ ⑤ ⑥
Partner ① ② ③ ④ ⑤ ⑥

READ ONLINE

expert space
Go to **www.expert21.com/ student** to find photographs and other visuals to illustrate your personal narrative.

Expert Reading

You have learned about various career paths you can take after high school. Now, apply your expert reading strategies to the following article about ground-breaking educational programs. ▶

ON THE CUTTING EDGE

By Jonathan Gromer and Alex Hutchinson

Welcome greenfuzz

Game Culture and Technology

University of California, Irvine

Computer and video gaming these days is a growing industry that thrives on new technology. It is also starving for creative talent. UC Irvine's program looks beyond the basic skills like programming and computer graphics. For example, the World Building course teaches students how to produce complex virtual environments. Projects include a Web-based game that will interact with a $5.5 million dinosaur exhibit at the Discovery Science Center in Santa Ana, California.

Looking ahead: As video games grow ever more popular, UC Irvine will be a breeding ground for the industry's most forward-thinking professionals.

Green Interior Design

Rocky Mountain College of Art + Design

Powering office buildings accounts for 36 percent of the United States' energy usage. Solar panels and extra insulation are useful for conserving energy. But in order for the building to be truly "green," the entire structure has to be carefully thought out. This includes the inside as well as the outside. Designers in the Green Interior Design program think about everything from using natural light to avoiding certain types of paint that release dangerous fumes. In addition to taking classes in green design, students create models using the U.S. Green Building Council's rating system.

Looking ahead: Green design is becoming mainstream. Rocky Mountain students tackle real-world projects, such as revamping a historic office building in nearby Denver.

Robotics
Carnegie Mellon University

This Pittsburgh institute is the world's biggest academic robotics research center. Undergrads take courses in which they build a LEGO robot every week based on what they're learning in class. "If the robot works, they get their A," says instructor Howie Choset. But the real fun happens in the research labs. There, students work on projects such as a slithering snake robot used for search-and-rescue missions. Students also participate in fun competitions. One example is the RoboCup, which pits teams of Sony AIBO robot dogs against each other in a soccer game.

Looking ahead: "Undergrads leave thinking robots are everywhere," Choset says. That may not be true yet. But thanks to these students, it soon could be.

Engineering
Olin College

The mission of this Needham, Massachusetts, college is to provide practical learning opportunities for students pursuing robotics and agricultural engineering. "Instead of spending two years learning [engineering] theory, you start using it in projects right away," says student Katerina Blazek. Last year, 13 companies paid $50,000 each to hire teams of Olin seniors. Projects included a model solar-powered house and a robotic tractor that sprays orchards automatically.

Looking ahead: Olin's project-based program is as real world as it gets. As creativity and problem-solving skills become more important, Olin grads may lead the way in changing how engineering gets taught and practiced.

Underwater Crime Scene Investigation
Florida State University, Panama City

The goal of CSI is to collect evidence to figure out what happened. But you can't dust for fingerprints underwater. This program teaches deep-sea detective skills. "We get called out pretty often to work with law enforcement, and we bring our students with us," says professor Mike Zinszer. That doesn't just mean investigating crimes. They've also studied plane crashes and bridge failures.

Looking ahead: As crime evolves, so must crime fighters. Many graduates of FSU's program go on to work for law enforcement agencies such as the FBI. As certified "science divers," they also take on new challenges, such as tracking down environmental criminals who spill oil or dump garbage on coral reefs.

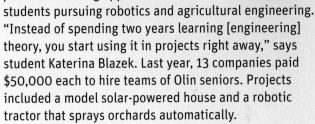

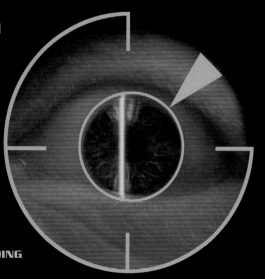

BIOMETRIC SCAN PROGRESS:

CARD: VALID

IRIS: COMPLETE

RETINA: 62%

PATTERN MATCHING:

IN PROGRESS

AUTHENTICATION: PENDING

Transportation Design
Art Center College of Design

The list of cool cars that have come from the minds of Art Center graduates is long and impressive. In fact, it has long been seen as the premier place to learn car design. Now the Pasadena, California, program is evolving to include other forms of transportation. Recent student projects include an automated rapid-transit bus. For another project, students brainstormed car interiors for disabled and elderly drivers. Working with specialists, five teams designed sample cars with swiveling seats, simplified controls, and easy entry.

Looking ahead: The auto industry is due for a major shake-up in the next decade. The role of the designer will definitely change, says program leader Geoff Wardle. "Coming up with cool-looking products isn't enough anymore. You have to balance passion with responsibility." Students at Art Center are learning to think about safety and energy usage as well as design.

Security and Intelligence
The Ohio State University

It's an international studies program for the post-9/11 era. "The name kind of grabs your attention," says Ben Wheat, a 2005 graduate of the Columbus school. The program's biggest selling point, he says, is its teachers. Electives are taught by professors from throughout the university—a plant expert teaches bioterrorism, and a language expert explains how to make and break codes. This year, the Introduction to Intelligence course is being taught by a CIA agent. For hands-on experience, the National Air and Space Intelligence Center is located an hour down the road.

Looking ahead: For better or worse, security is a growth industry these days. While some graduates go on to work for federal agencies such as the FBI, many find private-sector jobs. Wheat, for example, is working for a defense contractor. His company provides Arabic and Pashtun speakers for government contracts in Iraq and Afghanistan.

electives *(n.)* optional courses
bioterrorism *(n.)* the use of living things, such as bacteria or insects, for terroristic purposes

MORE WAYS TO MOVE OFF THE BEATEN PATH

Molecular Gastronomy.
The French Culinary Institute

Culinary studies get a cutting-edge makeover in the classrooms of the French Culinary Institute in New York City. Students can take courses in molecular gastronomy along with the usual classes in gourmet cooking and pastry creation. Molecular gastronomy combines chemistry with cooking to make off-the-wall edible creations.

Special Effects Make-Up.
The Douglas Education Center

Students in the Special Effects Make-Up program at the Douglas Education Center in Monessen, Pennsylvania, are taught by award-winning artist Tom Savini, known for his make-up on such famous films as Dawn of the Dead and Creepshow. Their task is to create fantastical make-up effects that defy the imagination ... and sometimes turn the stomach. Students then move on to work in film, television, theater, or for costume-design companies, amusement parks, museums, or special-effects labs.

Turfgrass Science
Penn State University

Playing well and preventing injuries depend on the quality of the playing field. Luckily, there are students who can turn their love of sports and the outdoors into well-paying, in-demand careers. Students in the Turfgrass Science program at Penn State University learn to build better playing fields. They research issues that affect turfgrass quality, such as pollution, diseases, and insects. At the same time, they gain real-world experience at local golf courses, athletic fields, or lawn care companies. ∎

Reflect

1. Circle the expert strategies you used while reading this article.

   A. Summarize   **B.** Clarify

   C. Other _____

   D. Other _____

   E. Other _____

2. Use the letters above to label where in the article you applied the expert strategies.

3. Select one expert strategy you used. Explain why you applied that strategy where you did.

   _____

   _____

RESEARCH ONLINE

 expert space
Go to **www.expert21.com/student** to learn more about The College Curriculum; Financial Aid; Internships.

PROJECT INNOVATE

FUTURE 101

THE OPPORTUNITY

College or work? A technical job or an office job? A career in the arts or a career in the sciences? Before long, you'll have to make a big choice about your future—what to do with the rest of your life!

YOUR MISSION

In four short years, you'll be graduating from high school. To help you prep for the future you want, explore a variety of paths and create an action plan.

To create your action plan, you will

- Target your skills and interests.

- Interview people who know you well.

- Identify job/career options.

- Decide on a path you'd like to explore.

- Write your plan.

CAREER CONNECTION
Human Services
www.careerclusters.org

Go to **21 ToolKit Expert File 6.25** to learn more about careers in career counseling.

1 Target Your Talents.

Everyone has talents and interests. Spend some time figuring out exactly what you are good at and what interests you—as well as what you just can't stand to do. To get started, complete this survey.

What Makes You TICK?

1. What do you enjoy doing in your free time?

_____

2. Subjects You Like at School:

_____

Subjects You Don't Like at School:

_____

3. What are your talents? Write down three things you can do well.

_____

_____

4. What chores or tasks outside of school do you really hate to do?

_____

5. Circle which kind of activities you prefer:

indoor	**outdoor**	**physical**
mental	**solitary**	**social**

6. Check off the three adjectives that best describe you.

❑ organized	❑ curious	❑ competitive
❑ creative	❑ patient	❑ adventurous
❑ outgoing	❑ tech-savvy	❑ compassionate
❑ shy	❑ determined	❑ persuasive
❑ active/athletic	❑ helpful	

2 Conduct Interviews

Sometimes other people can see a spark in you that you overlook. Use the following questions to conduct an interview with one person who knows you well (a family member, teacher, coach, or good friend).

What would you say are my strongest qualities?

_____

What do you think I'm good at?

_____

_____

What kind of job can you picture me in? Why?

_____

_____

3 Identify Options

Review the selections you've read in this workshop. Then use the information in the **Resource Bank** and resources from **Expert Space** to help you identify some college and career options.

4 Time to Decide

In your **Expert Journal**, write down three careers from your research that caught your interest. Think about which of these careers best suits you. Circle it and write a brief explanation telling why you'd like to explore this path.

Job/Career Choice _____

_____

I'd like to explore _____

because _____

_____

5 Make an Action Plan

Learn the requirements for the career you're interested in by exploring the States' Career Clusters Initiative Web site (www.careerclusters.org) as well as **Expert Space**. Then, create an action plan to achieve your goal!

My ACTION Plan

Job/Career I want to have:

Knowledge and skills needed for this job (e.g., general research skills, expertise with certain tools, etc.):

Education or training needed for this job (e.g., a graduate degree, internship, apprenticeship):

Actions I can take now to prepare myself:

People who can help me:

PROJECT
RESOURCE BANK

CAREER FACTS
Source: www.careerclusters.org
Date Accessed: March 24, 2009

www.adviser.com

Career Clusters

These 16 career clusters represent all the different kinds of jobs you can have. They can help you focus on an area of interest or a possible career path.

	SAMPLE CAREERS
Agriculture, Food & Natural Resources	Veterinarian, park manager, farmer/rancher
Architecture & Construction	Landscape designer, carpenter, electrician
Arts, A/V Technology & Communication	Soundboard operator, artist, reporter, actor, musician
Business Management & Administration	Chief executive officer, public relations manager, administrative assistant
Education & Training	Teacher, coach, day care provider, social worker
Finance	Financial advisor, bank teller, accountant
Government & Public Administration	Mayor, intelligence analyst, infantry officer, county clerk
Health Science	Pharmacist, nurse, doctor, dietary technician, microbiologist
Hospitality & Tourism	Chef, hotel manager, reservationist, tour guide
Human Services	Marriage counselor, barber, cosmetologist, funeral director
Information Technology	Network administrator, computer programmer, Web designer
Law, Public Safety, Corrections & Security	Firefighter, private investigator, police officer, attorney
Manufacturing	Machine operator, industrial engineer, lab technician
Marketing	Sales representative, merchandise buyer, store manager, market research associate
Science, Technology, Engineering & Mathematics	Biologist, statistician, aeronautical engineer
Transportation, Distribution & Logistics	Pilot, truck or bus driver, air traffic controller

Farm workers make up 46% of workers in the agriculture, forestry, and fishing industries. 32% of farm workers are 55 or older.

Nearly 7 out of 10 visual artists are self-employed.

There are about 6.8 million teachers in the U.S. The largest demand for teachers through 2016 will be in the South and West.

Health care is the largest industry in the U. S., with 14 million jobs in 2006. Seven of the 20 fastest-growing occupations are health-care related, and the industry will generate more than 3 million new jobs by 2016.

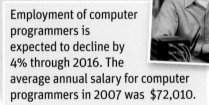

Employment of computer programmers is expected to decline by 4% through 2016. The average annual salary for computer programmers in 2007 was $72,010.

Place a star by the three career clusters that most interest you. Then circle one or two jobs within each of those clusters that catch your eye.

Career Profiles

Sha-Ella Shelton, *Hairstylist*

What she does: "I help clients look their best. I cut hair and create new styles. I also help clients keep their hair healthy."

How she got here: "I studied cosmetology in high school. My first job was at a top New York City salon. I started as a shampoo girl. Within months, I was a stylist. Now, I am the head stylist."

Advice for others interested in this career: "Make sure you love it. Some hairstylists just do their work, and others have a passion for their gift. To succeed in this business, you really have to care."

Gina Riley, *Dolphin Trainer*

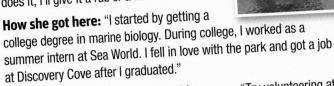

What she does: "My job is to care for 14 dolphins at Discovery Cove, an animal theme park in Orlando, Florida. I also train dolphins to respond to my signals. For example, I'll swing my arm to get them to do a jump. If the dolphin does it, I'll give it a rub or a fish as a reward."

How she got here: "I started by getting a college degree in marine biology. During college, I worked as a summer intern at Sea World. I fell in love with the park and got a job at Discovery Cove after I graduated."

Advice for others interested in this career: "Try volunteering at an animal shelter or an animal hospital. Also, try to swim as much as you can. Trainers must swim well."

> What education or training did Riley need for her job? Circle the answer in the text. Then summarize the advice Shelton gives.
>
> _____
>
> _____

JOB-TRAINING INFORMATION

DIFFERENT PATHS TO YOUR FUTURE

College/University: A four-year college degree is needed for many professional jobs, such as a marketing associate or teacher.

Community/Junior College: One can gain an associate's degree in roughly two years. Jobs in many fields, such as health care, accept this degree.

Job Corps: This no-cost training program administered by the U.S. Department of Labor helps young people ages 16 through 24 get a better job.

Graduate School: Some highly specialized jobs require advanced degrees. If you want to be a doctor, attorney, marine biologist, or professor, plan to spend a lot of time in school.

Technical/Vocational/Trade Schools: They teach job-specific skills for fields such as criminal justice, the culinary arts, information technology, and tourism.

Military School or Boot Camp: The military offers many paths to a fulfilling career. Navy pilot, infantry soldier, graphic designer, and nuclear engineer are just a few of hundreds of career paths available.

> Circle the path that you will take to pursue the career path you want.

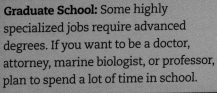

Strategy Check

Use your knowledge and strategies from the workshop to answer these questions.

COMPREHENSION

Main Idea and Details

1. Complete the chart below using information from the selection "How to Survive, Thrive, and Prepare for What's Next."

Main Idea:
Detail:
Detail:
Detail:

Summarize

2. Which detail would not be included in a summary of "My People"? Fill in the circle next to the correct answer.

Ⓐ Lindley was from Appalachia.

Ⓑ No one in Lindley's family had gone to college.

Ⓒ Granny dropped out of school in the fifth grade.

Ⓓ Lindley felt out of place among the other kids at Mercer.

LITERARY ANALYSIS

Character and Motivation

3. Think about Drew and Hugh Gallagher. What is each character's motivation for the action listed below?

Action	Motivation
Drew works hard at basketball.	
Hugh Gallagher writes a satirical essay.	

Narrator's Point of View

4. What is the point of view of the narrator in these selections?

"Playing the Game" _____

"Finding Their Futures" _____

"Essays That Make a Difference" _____

NAVIGATING TEXT

Steps in a Process

5. You have learned a lot about what it takes to go to college. What are the next three steps you could complete to get on the path to a college education? Put them in the order you think you should do them.

1. _____

_____

2. _____

_____

3. _____

_____

VOCABULARY/WORD ANALYSIS

Roots and Affixes

6. Fill in the circle next to the correct answer.

In class, Lakeisha is a <u>fastidious</u> note taker. She writes down every important detail neatly, using different-colored pens for different subjects.

Ⓐ good at writing

Ⓑ very careful and precise

Ⓒ extremely fast

Ⓓ artistic

Base Words and Affixes

7. *Place* is the base word of *displace*. Use affixes to create three other words with the same base word.

1. _____

2. _____

3. _____

8. Think of two career options you are interested in, and add them to the chart below. List skills you have or want to develop (for example, helping others, working with your hands, and so on). Judge your options against your skills list, and then circle the option you think best fits your skills.

Option 1: _____

Option 2: _____

Skills
1.
2.
3.
4.

EXPERT QUESTION

How can I get ready for the future I want?

10. Use what you learned in this workshop to respond to the Expert Question. Jot down some notes. Then use a separate sheet of paper to write your response.

_____

_____

_____

CRITICAL THINKING

Synthesize

9. What is one personal trait or quality that all the selections in this workshop seem to stress as a factor in success? Use examples from the selections to support your answers.

_____

_____

_____

_____

_____

_____

_____

_____

_____

_____

_____

_____

_____

_____

_____

_____

_____

DESIGNING THE FUTURE

Expert Question:
What are the costs and benefits of technology?

Read and Synthesize

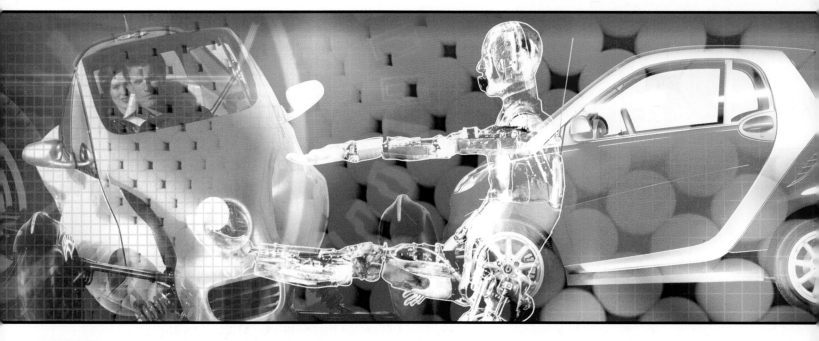

Inquiry 2 Technology to the Rescue

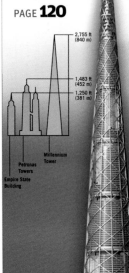

problem started at th
ning of the millenniu
ted posting pictures
files online. Next, the
friends. They posted
sonal information. To
ple are faced with ele
alkers and online bullie
lleges do online searc
th your application. Th
reated a big problem—
ore privacy on the In
o solve this problem,
several new technologie
need to be developed.
program that keeps t
personal information
tracker would allow pe
was searching for in

What are the costs and benefits of technology?

What does the future hold? This workshop offers ideas. Some will excite you; others may disturb you. Imagine the future of technology in this workshop.

▶ Anchor Your Knowledge

Watch the Anchor Media, "Designing the Future," and meet Katie Salen, a video game designer who uses computer technology to create amazing fantasy worlds.

0:00/ 2:30

WORKSHOP GOALS

To gain expert knowledge about technology and the future, you will

- study **informational texts** about how technology can hold people back or help them make the most of their lives.

- read **literature** in which authors imagine what the future will be like.

- learn important **skills** and **strategies** to help you understand what you read.

- develop **21st Century Skills** to **organize information** and **evaluate options**.

- write a **problem-and-solution essay** about a challenge people will face in the future.

- complete an **Expert Project** that helps you invent something.

▶ Anticipation Guide

Before reading this workshop, respond to each statement. In the columns to the left, check **Y (yes)** if you agree with the statement or **N (no)** if you disagree. Then, **after** the workshop, return here to evaluate these statements again in the columns on the right.

BEFORE		TOPIC: **Technology**	AFTER	
Y	N		Y	N
		In 2006, more teens used cell phones than landlines.		
		Less than 3/4 of all U.S. teenagers use the Internet.		
		A car that floats on air and runs on solar power is currently being developed.		
		A robot that can play catch with you has already been invented.		
		The best inventors and scientists must be trained at the most expensive private schools.		
		Artificial arms and legs can be programmed by computers and run on batteries.		

Preview the Expert Project

At the end of this workshop, you'll create your own invention. Preview the **Expert Project** on pages 156–159.

▶ What will you need to know or do to complete the Expert Project?

_____

_____

_____

_____

Explore Expert Space

Go to **www.expert21.com/student** to learn more about the topics in this workshop.

DISCOVER ONLINE

- Careers in Graphic Design
- Animation
- Video Game Development

READ ONLINE

- Katherine Paterson
- Social Networking
- Transportation Innovation
- Robots

RESEARCH ONLINE

- Fashion Design
- Industrial Revolution
- Inventions

Personal Inquiry

Explore the topic of technology and the future by asking your own questions. Return to add questions as you continue reading Workshop 2. Plan to revisit your questions.

Katie Salen: Game Designer

Salen works hard to build the video games that you play.

"You have to convince someone to play, and then convince them to stay. The moment they're not having fun anymore, they'll walk away."

Creating a digital game can take a year or more. The best way to get started is with a 24-hour "game jam." The idea is simple. Throw a team into an office for 24 hours, give them food and energy drinks, deprive them of sleep, and see what happens. Here, **Katie Salen** explains how a game jam kicked off the creation of a new game called *Gamestar Mechanic*.

FACTS AND STATS

NAME: Katie Salen

HOMETOWN: Born in Arvada, Colorado; currently lives in Brooklyn, New York

JOB: Game Designer, Game Lab

EDUCATION: BFA in Graphic Design; MFA in Design

WORKPLACE SKILLS: Leads a team, brainstorms, shares feedback

ADVICE TO KIDS: "Play a lot of games, but think about how and why somebody designed this game."

PAY: Beginning game designers make $45,000 a year; with about 10 years of experience, they make around $65,000 per year.

CAREER CONNECTION

Information Technology
www.careerclusters.org

Go to [21] **ToolKit** Expert File 6.26 to learn more about careers in computer programming.

RELATED JOBS: Programmer, board game designer, help desk staff

12:00 P.M.   Let the Games Begin

At the kickoff for a game jam, we assemble a **team**. For *Gamestar Mechanic*, our challenge was to make a simple tool that allows people to design their own game. We had a visual designer, an audio designer, a programmer, and me, the game designer. As the game designer, I make sure we stick to our goal.

We start out by **brainstorming** with whiteboards, paper, pens, and dice. At the *Gamestar* jam, we threw out ideas such as, what if players could build creatures out of different parts they collected by playing mini-games? Or, what if players were a part of a story about a world that runs on games, but the games are old and broken?

We sketch and model certain parts of the game. We pick the best idea and give it a placeholder title: Game Designer (not very original!).

3:00 P.M.   Research the Parts

Then, the team breaks up, and we all go to our own computers. The visual artists develop concept art. The audio designers scour their library for sounds. I start writing a design specification. A "design spec" is a document that describes the rules for the game. For **inspiration**, I look at anime comics, cool games I like, and books about how people learn.

5:00 P.M. Define the Game

Next, we decide on a format for the game. *Gamestar Mechanic* is a game like *Super Mario Bros.* The characters run, jump, and shoot their way through a two-dimensional environment. We build a space that you can scroll horizontally or vertically.

Once the format is set, I assign behaviors to each character or object. If I want a character to jump when something comes close to it, I assign that behavior and its quality. I decide how high it jumps and the sound it makes when it lands.

9:00 P.M. Build the Program

With the design spec in hand, I sit beside the programmer and we start to work together. We designed *Gamestar Mechanic* in Flash. The programmer types my instructions into Flash using Action Script 3, the programming language attached to Flash.

11:00 P.M. Fill in the Holes

Next, I **share feedback** with the visual and audio designers after looking or listening to what they've done. In *Gamestar Mechanic,* the players built spaces out of different types of blocks. The blocks can be sticky, glass, or asphalt. The visual artists figured out what each block should look like.

9:00 A.M. Practice the Game

We play a test version of the game. Sometimes the characters do things that we didn't know were possible. But if we're frustrated by how the player is limited, we rethink the game.

12:00 P.M. Concept Is Complete

The final product at the end of 24 hours has art and audio. It doesn't work perfectly, but it feels like a functional game. In a short period of time, you produce something that's very rich. And then, home to sleep!

Points: 0/64

ANALYZE EXPERT SKILLS

1. Lead a Team

As the team leader, what are some of Salen's duties?

_____

_____

_____

_____

_____

2. Brainstorm

How does brainstorming help the team get started? Fill out this organizer with the steps in the process.

3. Share Feedback

How does Salen share feedback?

_____

_____

_____

_____

_____

DISCOVER ONLINE

expert space
Go to **www.expert21.com/student** to learn more about Careers in Graphic Design; Animation; Video Game Development.

Short Story

The Last Dog

If pollution destroyed Earth's air and water, where would people live? The author of this story depicts a grim time in the distant future when humans are confined inside a giant dome. Find out what happens when a boy decides to venture out.

QuickWrite

Imagine living your entire life indoors. Write about some things you would never get the chance to experience in the outside world.

Plot and Conflict   LITERARY ANALYSIS

The **plot** is a story's sequence of events.

The **conflict** is the central problem in the plot. The main character must face the conflict and resolve it.

There are two basic types of conflicts.

An **internal conflict** exists when a character struggles with something within, such as fear, shyness, or a moral dilemma.

An **external conflict** exists when a character struggles against something in the outside world, such as a set of rules, a competitor, or an enemy.

▶ Write *internal* or *external* next to each conflict below. Then write who or what the character is struggling against.

> Lars stood up and faced the space alien. He shouted loudly to scare it away.
>
> _____
>
> _____
>
> Devora really wanted this job. "Should I lie on the application even though I know it's wrong?" she wondered.
>
> _____
>
> _____

Problem and Solution   COMPREHENSION

Every story has a **problem** that the characters face.

The **solution** is the way the characters solve the problem.

▶ Read the following passage. Then fill in the graphic organizer to show the problem and solution in the passage.

> Aimeé was getting frustrated. She was trying to teach her puppy, Fredo, to sit, but Fredo just bounded around playfully. He didn't understand. Then Aimeé got an idea. She called to the puppy's mother, Flower.
>
> "Sit, Flower!" Aimeé said firmly. As Fredo watched curiously, Flower obeyed the command instantly. Then Aimeé turned to the puppy.
>
> "Sit, Fredo!" she said. Suddenly Fredo sat, too!

Problem

_____

_____

_____

Solution

_____

_____

_____

Academic Language   VOCABULARY

▶ Rate your knowledge of each word. Then write its meaning and an example sentence.

Word	Meaning	Example
EXPERT WORDS *Use these words to write and talk about the workshop topic.*		
hologram hol•o•gram (noun) ① ② ③ ④	a three-dimensional image created by laser beams	This hologram shows how the rocket ship looks both inside and out.
sensor sen•sor (noun) ① ② ③ ④		A sensor beeped when Tess walked through the security gate.
virtual vir•tu•al (adjective) ① ② ③ ④	generated by a computer; not real	
ACADEMIC WORDS *Use these words in all your subject classes.*		
function func•tion (noun) ① ② ③ ④		
modify mod•i•fy (verb) ① ② ③ ④		
CONTENT AREA WORDS *Use these words to talk and write about science.*		
dome dome (noun) ① ② ③ ④		
interaction in•ter•ac•tion (noun) ① ② ③ ④		
sterile ster•ile (adjective) ① ② ③ ④		

Rating Scale   ① I don't know the word.   ② I've seen it or heard it.   ③ I know its meaning.   ④ I know it and use it.

Word Families   WORD ANALYSIS

A word family is a group of words that share a common base word.

A base word is the part of a word to which prefixes, suffixes, and other endings are added.

▶ Three of the words below are in the same word family. Circle them.

exit	exciting	unexcited
excitement	exterior	excess

Now write the base word that all three words have in common.

The Last Dog

By Katherine Paterson

To find meaning in an empty, futuristic world, a teen boy decides to do the unthinkable.

Brock approached the customs gate. Although he did not reach for the scanner, a feeling it might have labeled "excitement" made him tremble. His fingers shook as he punched in his number on the inquiry board. "This is highly irregular, Brock 095670038," the disembodied voice said. "What is your reason for external travel?"

Brock took a deep breath. "Scientific research," he replied. He didn't need to be told that his behavior was "irregular." He'd never heard of anyone doing research outside the **dome**—actual rather than **virtual** research. "I—I've been cleared by my podmaster and the Research Team...."

"Estimated time of return?" So he wasn't to be questioned further.

"Uh, 1800 hours."

"Are you wearing the prescribed dry suit with helmet and gloves?"

"Affirmative."

"You should be equipped with seven hundred fifty milliliters of liquid and food tablets for one day of travel."

"Affirmative." Brock patted the sides of the dry suit to be sure.

"Remember to drink sparingly. Water supply is limited." Brock nodded. He tried to lick his parched lips, but his whole mouth felt dry.

"Is that understood?"

"Affirmative." Was he hoping customs would stop him? If he was, they didn't seem to be helping him. Well, this was what he wanted, wasn't it? To go outside the dome.

"Turn on the universal locator, Brock 095670038, and proceed to gate."

Why weren't they questioning him further? Were they eager for him to go? Ever since he'd said out loud in group speak that he wanted to go outside the dome, people had treated him strangely—that session with the podmaster and then the interview with the representative from Research. Did they think he was a deviant? Deviants sometimes disappeared. The word was passed around that they had "gone outside," but no one really knew. No deviant had ever returned.

The gate slid open. Before he was quite ready for it, Brock found himself outside the protection of the dome. He blinked. The sun—at least it was what was called "the sun" in virtual lessons—was too bright for his eyes even inside the tinted helmet. He took a deep breath, one last backward look at the dome, which, with the alien sun gleaming on it, was even harder to look at than the distant star, and started across an expanse of brown soil [was it?] to what he recognized from **holograms** as a line of purplish mountains in the distance.

> **disembodied** *(adj.)* not having a physical body
> **parched** *(adj.)* dry

It was, he pulled the scanner from his outside pouch and checked it, "hot." Oh, that was what he was feeling. Hot. He remembered "hot" from a virtual lesson he'd had once on deserts. He wanted to take off the dry suit, but he had been told since he could remember that naked skin would suffer irreparable burning outside the protection of the dome. He adjusted the control as he walked so that the unfamiliar perspiration would evaporate. He fumbled a bit before he found the temperature adjustment **function**. He put it on twenty degrees centigrade and immediately felt more comfortable. No one he really knew had ever left the dome (stories of deviants exiting the dome being hard to verify), but there was all this equipment in case someone decided to venture out. He tried to ask the clerk who outfitted him, but the woman was evasive. The equipment was old, she said. People used to go out, but the outside environment was threatening, so hardly anyone (she looked at him carefully now), hardly anyone ever used it now.

Was Brock, then, the only normal person still curious about the outside? Or had all those who had dared to venture out perished, discouraging further forays? Perhaps he *was* a deviant for wanting to see the mountains for himself. When he'd mentioned it to others, they had laughed, but there was a hollow sound to the laughter.

If he never returned, he'd have no one to blame but himself. He knew that. While his podfellows played virtual games, he'd wandered into a subsection of the historical virtuals called "ancient fictions." Things happened in these fictions more—well, more densely than they did in the virtuals. The people he met there—it was hard to describe—but somehow they were more *actual* than dome dwellers. They had strange names like Huck Finn and M. C. Higgins the Great. They were even a little scary. It was their insides. Their insides were very loud. But even though the people in the ancient fictions frightened him a bit, he couldn't get enough of them. When no one was paying attention, he went back again and again to visit them. They had made him wonder about that other world—that world outside the dome.

> **Question**
> **What questions might Brock ask the people of this other world?**

Perhaps, once he realized the danger the ancient fictions posed, he should have left them alone, but he couldn't help himself. They had made him feel hollow, hungry for something no food pellet or even virtual experience could satisfy. And now he was in that world they spoke of and the mountains of it were in plain view.

Was Brock, then, the only normal person still curious about the outside? Or had all those who had dared to venture out perished, discouraging further forays?

> **irreparable** *(adj.)* not able to be repaired
> **evasive** *(adj.)* avoiding something

He headed for the purple curves. Within a short distance from the dome, the land was clear and barren, but after he had been walking for an hour or so he began to pass rusting hulks and occasional ruins of what might have been the dwellings of ancient peoples that no one in later years had cleared away for recycling or vaporization.

He checked the emotional scanner for an unfamiliar sensation. "Loneliness," it registered. He rather liked having names for these new sensations. It made him feel a bit "proud," was it? The scanner was rather interesting. He wondered when people had stopped using them. He hadn't known they existed until, in that pod meeting, he had voiced his desire to go outside.

The podmaster had looked at him with a raised eyebrow and a sniff. "Next thing you'll be asking for a scanner," he said.

"What's a scanner?" Brock asked.

The podmaster requisitioned one from storage, but at the same time, he must have alerted Research, because it was the representative from Research who had brought him the scanner and questioned him about this expressed desired for an Actual Adventure—a journey outside the dome.

"What has prompted this, uh—unusual ambition?" the representative had asked, his eyes not on Brock but on the scanner in his hand. Brock had hesitated, distracted by the man's fidgeting with the strange instrument. "I—I'm interested in scientific research," Brock said at last.

So here he was out of the pod, alone for the first time in his life. Perhaps, though, he should have asked one of his podfellows to come along. Or even the pod robopet. But the other fellows all laughed when he spoke of going outside, their eyes darting back and forth. Nothing on the outside, they said, could equal the newest Virtual Adventure. He suddenly realized that ever since he started interfacing with the ancient fictions, his fellows had given him that look. They did think he was odd—not quite the same as a regular podfellow. Brock didn't really vibe with the pod robopet. It was one of the more modern ones, and when they'd programmed its artificial intelligence they'd somehow made it too smart. The robopet in the children's pod last year was older, stupider, and more "fun" to have around.

He'd badly underestimated the distance to the mountains. The time was well past noon, and he had at least three kilometers to go. Should he signal late return or turn about now? He didn't have much more than one day's scant supply of water and food tablets. But he was closer to the hills than to the dome. He felt a thrill ["excitement"] and pressed on.

---

requisitioned *(v.)* requested that something be supplied
interfacing *(v.)* connecting with a different thing

LITERARY ANALYSIS

Plot and Conflict
What is Brock's conflict so far?

_____

_____

_____

What kind of conflict is it?

_____

_____

_____

_____

COMPREHENSION

Problem and Solution
Underline the problem you would consider ordinary that Brock encounters when he is outside the dome.

- How does he solve the problem in an unusual way?

_____

_____

_____

_____

VOCABULARY/WORD ANALYSIS

Word Families
Find and circle the word *perished* in the second paragraph on page 92.

- What is the base word in *perished*?

_____

- Draw a box around the word that is in the same family as *perished*.

  died   fished

  shed   perishable

There were actual trees growing on the first hill. Not the great giants of virtual lessons, more scrubby and bent. But they were trees, he was sure of it. The podmaster had said that trees had been extinct for hundreds of years. Brock reached up and pulled off a leaf. It was green and had veins. In some ways it looked like his own hand. He put the leaf in his pack to study later. He didn't want anyone accusing him of losing his scientific objectivity. Only deviants did that. Farther up the hill he heard an unfamiliar burbling sound. No, he knew that sound. It was water running. He'd heard it once when the liquid dispenser had malfunctioned. There'd been a near panic in the dome over it. He checked the scanner. There was no caution signal, so he hurried toward the sound.

It was a—a "brook"—he was sure of it! Virtual lessons had taught that there were such things outside in the past but that they had long ago grown poisonous, then in the warming climate had dried up. But here was a running brook, not even a four-hour journey from his dome. His first impulse was to take off his protective glove and dip a finger in it, but he drew back. He had been well conditioned to avoid danger. He sat down clumsily on the bank. Yes, this must be grass. There were even some tiny flowers mixed in the grass. Would the atmosphere poison him if he unscrewed his helmet to take a sniff? He punched the scanner to read conditions, but the characters on the scanner panel danced about uncertainly until, at length, the disembodied voice said "conditions unreadable." He'd better not risk it.

He pushed the buttons now for liquid and pellets. A tube appeared in his mouth. It dropped a pellet on his tongue. From the tube he sucked liquid enough to swallow his meal. What was it they called outside nourishment in the history virtuals? *Pecnec?* Something like that. He was having a *pecnec* in the *woods* by a *brook*. A hasty consulting of the scanner revealed that what he was feeling was "pleasure." He was very glad he hadn't come with an anxious podfellow or, worse, an advanced robopet that would, no doubt, be yanking at his suit already, urging him back toward the dome.

It was then, in the middle of the post-*pecnec* satisfaction, that he heard the new sound. Like that programmed into a robopet, yet different. He struggled to his feet. The dry suit from storage was certainly awkward when you wanted to stand up or sit down. Nothing on the scanner indicated danger, so he went into the scrubby woods toward the sound. And stopped abruptly.

Something was lying under the shadow of a tree. Something about a meter long. It was furred and quite still. The sound was not coming from

Would the atmosphere poison him if he unscrewed his helmet to take a sniff?

> **malfunctioned** *(v.)* broken down
> **conditioned** *(adj.)* established by learning

it. And then he saw the small dog—the puppy. He was sure it was a puppy, nosing the stiff body of what must once have been its mother, making the little crying sounds that he'd heard from the brook. Later, much later, he realized that he should have been wary. If the older dog had died of some extradomal disease, the puppy might have been a carrier. But at the time, all he could think of was the puppy, a small creature who had lost its mother.

He'd found out about mothers from the Virtuals. Mothers were extinct in the dome. Children were conceived and born in the lab and raised in units of twelve in the pods, presided over by a bank of computers and the podmaster. Nuclear families, as everyone knew, had been wasteful of time, energy, and space. There was an old proverb: The key to survival is efficiency. So though Brock could guess the puppy was "sad" (like that fictions person, Jo, whose podmate expired), he didn't know what missing a mother would feel like. And who would whimper for a test tube?

> **Question**
> **What questions could you ask about families in Brock's world?**

Brock had never seen a dog, of course, but had seen plenty of dog breed descriptions on the science/history virtuals. Dogs had been abundant once. They filled the ancient fictions. They even had names there—Lassie, Toto, Sounder. But now dogs were extinct, gone during the dark ages when the atmosphere had become warm and poisonous. The savages who had not had the intelligence or wealth to join the foresighted dome crafters had killed all animals wild or domesticated for food before they had eventually died out themselves. It was all in one of the very first virtual lessons. He had seen that one many times. He never confessed to anyone how, well, sad it made him feel.

But obviously, dogs were not quite extinct. Cautiously, he moved toward the small one.

"Alert. Alert. Scanning unknown object."

Brock pushed the off button. "Are you sure you want to turn off scanner?"

"Affirmative." He stuck the scanner into his pouch.

The puppy had lifted its head at the sound of his voice. It looked at him, head cocked, as though deciding whether to run or stay.

"It's all right, dog," Brock said soothingly. "I won't hurt you." He stayed still. He didn't want to frighten the little beast. If it ran, he wasn't sure he'd be able to catch it in his clumsy dry suit.

---

presided *(v.)* controlled or guided
foresighted *(adj.)* able to think about the future

Read and Synthesize

COMPREHENSION

Summarize

Write a summary of what Brock has experienced since he left the dome. Use no more than one sentence to summarize each paragraph that describes his experiences.

_____

_____

_____

_____

_____

_____

_____

LITERARY ANALYSIS

Plot and Conflict

Which of these is the most important plot event that occurs on pages 94–95?

- [ ] Brock picks a leaf from a tree.
- [ ] Brock discovers a puppy.
- [ ] Brock has a "pecnec" in the woods

Why is this event significant to the plot?

_____

_____

_____

CRITICAL THINKING

Analyze

 Review the first full paragraph on page 95. (Circle) the proverb.

- What does this paragraph tell you about the qualities that dome dwellers value?

_____

_____

_____

- Box evidence in the paragraph that supports your answer.

> *Slowly he extended his gloved hand. The dog backed away anxiously, but when Brock kept the hand extended, the puppy slowly crept toward him and sniffed, making whimpering sounds.*

Slowly he extended his gloved hand. The dog backed away anxiously, but when Brock kept the hand extended, the puppy slowly crept toward him and sniffed, making whimpering sounds. It wasn't old enough to be truly afraid, it seemed. The pup licked his glove tentatively, then backed away again. It was looking for food, and plasticine gloves weren't going to satisfy.

Brock looked first at the dead mother, whose source of nourishment must have long dried up, then around the landscape. What would a dog eat? A puppy on its own? He took off his glove and reached through his pouch into the inside pocket that held his pellet supply. Making every move slow and deliberate so as not to startle the dog, he held out a pellet. The dog came to his hand, licked it, then the pellet. It wrinkled its nose. Brock laughed. He didn't need the scanner now to tell him that what he felt was "pleasure." He loved the feel of the rough tongue on his palm and the little furred face, questioning him.

"It's all right, fellow. You can eat it."

As though understanding, the pup gulped down the pellet. Then looked around for more, not realizing that it had just bolted down a whole meal. When the dog saw there was no more coming, it ran over to the brook. Brock watched in horror as it put its head right down into the poisonous stream and lapped noisily.

"Don't!" Brock cried.

The puppy turned momentarily at the sound, then went back to drinking, as though it was the most normal thing in the world. Well, it was, for the dog. Where else would a creature in the wild get liquid? If the streams were not all dried up, they must have learned to tolerate the water. But then it was breathing the poisoned atmosphere, wasn't it? Why hadn't it hit Brock before? This was a fully organic creature on the outside *without any life support system*. What could that mean? Some amazing mutation must have occurred, making it possible for at least some creatures to breathe the outside atmosphere and drink its poisoned water. Those who couldn't died, those who could survived and got stronger. Even the ancient scientist Darwin knew that. And Brock had come upon one of these magnificent mutants.

> **Question**
> What other questions might Brock ask about the foreign environment?

The puppy whimpered and looked up at Brock with large, trusting eyes. How could he think of it as a mutant specimen? It was a puppy. One who had lost its mother. What would it eat? There was no sign of food for a carnivore.

---

tentatively *(adv.)* with uncertainty or hesitation
deliberate *(adj.)* thought out carefully

COMPREHENSION

Problem and Solution

What problem does finding the puppy present for Brock?

_____

_____

_____

What is Brock's solution?

_____

_____

LITERARY ANALYSIS

Plot and Conflict

As the plot develops, how does Brock's knowledge of the outside world start to change?

_____

_____

_____

_____

What conflict does this knowledge cause for Brock?

_____

_____

_____

_____

_____

21 SMALL GROUPS/INDEPENDENT

COLLABORATE

Debate In your group, debate whether it was wise for Brock to leave the dome. Develop arguments for and against leaving. Brainstorm reasons to support each argument.

COMMUNICATE

React and Write Is the environment actually poisonous? Jot down details you read about it. Then, write a paragraph expressing your view.

Perhaps way back in the mountains some small mammals had also survived, keeping the food chain going, but the puppy would not live long enough to find its way there, much less know how to hunt with its mother gone. For the first time in his life something deep inside Brock reached out toward another creature. The thought of the puppy languishing here by the side of its dead parent until it, too . . .

"Your name is Brog, all right?" The ancient astronomers had named stars after themselves. He had discovered something just as wonderful. Didn't he have the right to name it sort of after himself while preserving the puppy's uniqueness? "Don't worry, Brog. I won't let you starve."

Which is why Brock appeared at the customs portal after dark, the front of his dry suit stained, carrying a wriggling *Canis familiaris* of uncertain breed.

If there had been any way to smuggle the dog in, Brock would have. But he couldn't for the life of him figure out how. As it was, every alarm in the area went off when he stepped into the transitional cubicle. The disembodied voice of the monitor queried him:

"Welcome back, Brock 095670038. You're late."

"Affirmative."

"And you are carrying contraband."

"I pulled a leaf."

"Deposit same in quarantine bins."

"Affirmative."

"**Sensors** denote warm-blooded presence not on official roster."

"I found a dog," Brock mumbled.

"Repeat."

"A dog."

"*Canis familiaris* is extinct."

"Well, maybe it's just a robopet that got out somehow."

"Correction. Robopets are bloodless. Leave dry suit for sterilization and proceed to quarantine inspection."

The officials in quarantine inspection, who rarely had anything to inspect, were at first nervous and then, as they watched the puppy happily licking Brock's face, interested despite themselves. An actual dog! None of them had ever seen one, of course, and Brock's dog was so much, well, more vital than a robopet. And although, on later reflection, they knew they should

> *An actual dog! None of them had ever seen one, of course, and Brock's dog was so much, well, more vital than a robopet.*

---

transitional *(adj.)* acting as a means of passing between two places
sterilization *(n.)* the process of making something free of microorganisms

have terminated or expelled it, they couldn't quite bring themselves to do so that night.

"It will have to go to Research," the chief inspector finally declared.

"Permission requested to hand carry the dog known as Brog to Research," Brock said. There was a bit of an argument about that. Several inspectors sought the honor, but the chief declared that Brock, having shed his dry suit and being already contaminated, should be placed with the dog in a hermetically sealed air car and transported to Research.

The scientists in Research were predictably amazed to see a live *Canis familiaris*. But being scientists and more objective than the lower-grade quarantine inspectors, they kept a safe distance both physically and psychically from the creature. Only the oldest scientist, dressed in proper protective clothing, came into the laboratory with Brock and the dog. He scanned and poked and prodded the poor little fellow until it began to whimper in protest.

> **QUESTION**
> **What questions do you have about the scientists' reaction to Brock and Brog?**

"Brog needs to rest," said Brock, interrupting the scientist in the midst of his inspection. "She's (for by this time gender had been indisputably established) had a hard day. And if there's some actual food available—she's not used to pellets."

"Of course, of course," said one of the researchers through the speaker in the observation booth. "How thoughtless. Send someone out for a McLike burger without sauce. She may regard it as meat. Anyhow, it will seem more like food to her than a pellet, affirmative, Brock?"

The scientists, Brock soon realized, were looking to him for advice. He was, after all, the discoverer of the last dog. It gave him sudden scientific status. Brock had sense enough to take advantage of this. After Brog had swallowed the McLike burger in three quick gulps, Brock insisted that he be allowed to stay with Brog, so that he might interact with her. "She's not like us," he explained. "She's used to tumbling about and curling up with other warm bodies. In the old myths," he added, "puppies separated from their litters cried all night long. She will need constant **interaction** with another warm-blooded creature or she might, well, die of," he loved using his new vocabulary, "loneliness."

The scientists agreed. After all, Research was rather like quarantine, and since Brock had touched the dog ungloved and unprotected, he might well have picked up some germ from her. It was better to keep them both isolated in the research lab, where proper precautions would be taken.

---

hermetically *(adv.)* being airtight
indisputably *(adv.)* without doubt

COMPREHENSION

Problem and Solution
What problem does Brock solve by bringing the puppy back to the dome?

_____

_____

What potential problems might this action cause?

_____

_____

_____

_____

_____

LITERARY ANALYSIS

Plot and Conflict
How might having Brog inside the dome advance the plot?

_____

_____

_____

_____

_____

_____

_____

CRITICAL THINKING

Analyze
Review pages 98–99. Why do the researchers allow Brock to keep the puppy?

_____

_____

_____

_____

- Circle passages in the text that support your answer.

Cloning—it's the only thing to do. If she's the last, we owe it to posterity to keep the line going.

For nearly a week, Brock lived with Brog in the research center, eating McLike burgers, playing "fetch," teaching Brog to "sit," "heel," "come"—all the commands he could cull from the ancient texts. The dog quickly learned to obey Brock's commands, but it wasn't the automatic response of a robopet. Brog delighted in obedience. She wanted to please Brock, and those few times when she was busy nosing around the lab and failed to obey instantly, those times when Brock's voice took on a sharp tone of reproof, the poor little thing put her tail between her legs, looked up at him with sorrowful eyes, begging to be forgiven. Brock was tempted to speak sharply to her even when there was no need, for the sight of her drooping ears and tail, her mournful eyes, was so dear to him that he did what Travis Coates had to Old Yeller. He hugged her. There was no other way to explain it. He simply put his arms around her and helped her to his chest while she beat at him with her tail and licked his face raw. Out of the corner of his eye he was aware that one of the scientists was watching. Well, let him watch. Nothing was as wonderful as feeling this warmth toward another creature.

For the first week, the researchers seemed quite content to observe dog and boy from their glass-paneled observation booth and speak copious notes into their computers. Only the oldest of them would come into the lab and actually touch the alien creature, and he always wore a **sterile** protective suit with gloves. The others claimed it would interfere with objectivity if they got close to the dog, but they all seemed to behave positively toward Brog. No mention was made to Brock of his own less-than-objective behavior. So Brock was astounded to awake in the middle of the night to the sounds of an argument. Someone had forgotten to turn off the communication system.

"Cloning—it's the only thing to do. If she's the last, we owe it to posterity to keep the line going."

"And how are we going to raise a pack of dogs in a dome? One is nearly eating and drinking us out of test tube and petri dish. We can't go on this way. As drastic as it may seem, we have to be realistic. Besides, no one has had the chance to do actual experiments since the dark ages. Haven't you ever, just once, yearned to compare virtual research with actual?"

"What about the boy? He won't agree. Interfacing daily with the dog, he's become crippled by primal urges."

Question
What questions do you have about the argument Brock overhears?

"Can you think what chaos might ensue if a flood of primordial emotions were to surface in a controlled environment such as ours?" another asked. "Apparently, emotions are easily triggered by interactions with primitive beasts, like dogs."

posterity *(n.)* all future generations
primordial *(adj.)* characteristic of an early state

"Shh. Not now. The speaker is—" The system clicked off.

But Brock had already heard. He knew he had lost anything resembling scientific objectivity. He was no longer sure objectivity was a desirable trait. He rather enjoyed being flooded by "primordial emotions." But he was more worried for Brog than for himself. It wasn't hard to figure out what the scientists meant by "actual experiments." Cloning would be bad enough. Ten dogs who looked just like Brog so no one would know how special, how truly unique Brog was. But experiments! They'd cut her open and examine her internal organs, the way scientists had in the dark ages. They'd prod her with electric impulses and put chips in her brain. They'd try to change her personality or **modify** her behavior. They'd certainly try to make her eat and drink less!

In the dark, he put his arm around Brog and drew her close. He loved the terrible smell of her breath and the way she snored when she slept. They'd probably fix that, too.

The next day he played sick. Brog, faithful dog that she was, hung around him whimpering, licking his face. The scientists showed no particular concern. They were too busy plotting what they might do with Brog.

Brock crept to the nearest terminal in the lab. It was already logged in. The scientists had been doing nothing but research on *Canis familiaris*. COMMON CANINE DISEASES. Brock scrolled down the list with descriptions. No, *distemper* wouldn't do. The first symptom was loss of appetite. He couldn't make Brog fake that. On and on it went—no, *heartworms* wouldn't do. What he needed was a disease that might affect *Homo sapiens* as well as *Canis familiaris*. Here it was! "Rabies: A viral disease occurring in animals and humans, esp. in dogs and wolves. Transmitted by bite or scratch. The early stages of the disease are most dangerous, for an otherwise healthy and friendly appearing animal will suddenly bite without provocation."

Rabies was it! Somehow he would have to make Brog bite him. There was no antirabies serum in the dome, he felt sure. There were no animals in the dome. Why would they use precious space to store an unneeded medication? So they'd have to expel him as well as Brog for fear of spreading the disease. He shivered, then shook himself. No matter what lay on the outside, he could not stand to go back to the life he had lived in the dome before he met Brog.

He crept back to bed, pulling the covers over Brog. When one of the scientists came into the observation booth, Brock pinched Brog's neck as hard as he could. Nothing. He pinched again, harder. Brog just snuggled closer, slobbering on his arm.

---

distemper *(n.)* an infectious disease of canines
provocation *(n.)* the act of annoying or angering

VOCABULARY/WORD ANALYSIS

Word Families

Circle the word in the fourth paragraph on page 100 that is in the same word family as *reality*.

• What base word do both words share?

_____

LITERARY ANALYSIS

Plot and Conflict

How does the conversation Brock overhears add to his internal conflict?

_____
_____
_____
_____

Why does Brock love the "terrible smell" of Brog's breath and her snoring?

_____
_____
_____
_____
_____

COMPREHENSION

Problem and Solution

Describe the problem that develops on pages 100–101.

_____
_____
_____
_____

How does Brock plan to solve it?

_____
_____
_____
_____

• Underline the sentences that helped you figure out Brock's solution.

Disgusted, Brock got out of bed. Brog hopped down as well, rubbing against his leg. Pinching obviously was not going to do it. While the scientist on duty in the booth was bending over a computer terminal, Brock brought his foot down on Brog's paw. A tiny yip was all he got from that cruel effort—not enough sound even to make the man look up.

> **Question**
> What question do you have about what Brock is trying to do?

"Feeling better, Brock 095670038?" The oldest researcher had come into the lab.

"Affirmative," Brock answered.

"And how are you, puppy-wuppy?" The old man tickled Brog under her chin with his gloved hand. If I were a dog, I'd bite someone like that, thought Brock, but Brog, of course, simply licked the researcher's glove and wagged her tail.

That was when he got his great idea. He waited to execute it until the proper moment. For the first time, all the scientists had gathered in the lab, all of them in protective garb, some of them twitching nervously in their chairs. They were sitting in a circle around Brock and Brog, explaining what must be done.

"It has to be done for the sake of science," they began. Then they went on to, "For the sake of the dome community, which is always, as you well know, short on food, and particularly short on water." Brock listened to their arguments, nodding solemnly, pretending to agree. "It won't be as if she'll really be gone, you know. We've made virtuals of her—a special series just for you to keep. You can virtually play with her whenever you like."

That was the cue. Brock turned and bit Brog on the tail so hard that the blood started. Brog, surprised and enraged, spun around and bit Brock on the nose.

There was a shocked silence. Every scientist leaned backward, body pressed hard against his or her chair back. Every eye was on the two of them.

"I—I don't know what got into me," Brock said. "I've been feeling very weird." The scientists continued to stare. "I was checking the historical records...."

All of the scientists fled the room. Someone ran to a computer terminal. When Brock offered to take Brog out of the dome and let her loose in the mountains, no one argued. Neither did they say, "Hurry back," or even, "Take care." No one came close as he loaded his pouch with water and food pellets. The customs gate monitor asked no questions.

Brock turned and bit Brog on the tail so hard that the blood started. Brog, surprised and enraged, spun around and bit Brock on the nose.

> **solemnly** *(adv.)* gravely or seriously
> **enraged** *(adj.)* marked by extreme anger

Out of sight of the dome, Brog was delirious with joy, jumping and running about in circles around Brock's boots. Why wasn't the atmosphere choking Brog if it was as poisonous as the dome dwellers claimed? His heart beating rapidly, Brock unscrewed his helmet just enough to let in a little of the outside atmosphere. Nothing happened. In fact, he seemed to be breathing perfectly normally. He took off the helmet entirely. He was still breathing freely. But his heart was beating so hard, he couldn't be sure. He waited for the choking sensation he had been warned of. It didn't occur. Could they be wrong? Could the outside world have healed itself? Perhaps—perhaps the reason the scanner had so much trouble reading the outside atmosphere was because it wasn't within the range of computerized expectations.

Could it be? Could it be that fear had kept the dome dwellers prisoner many years longer than a poisoned environment would have?

He unfastened the dry suit and slowly stepped out of it into the sunlight.

It was wonderful how much faster he could walk without the clumsy suit. "Who knows?" Brock said to a frisking Brog. "Who knows, maybe out here you aren't the last dog. Your mother had to come from somewhere."

Brog barked happily in reply.

"And maybe, just maybe, where there are dogs, there are humans as well."

They stopped at the brook where they'd met, and both of them had a long drink. Brock no longer carried a scanner, but he knew what he felt was excitement. The water was delicious. ∎

Katherine Paterson

BORN October 31, 1932, Qing Jiang, China

INSPIRATION FOR "THE LAST DOG" While staying at a hotel in Melbourne, Australia, Paterson noticed a little dog trotting behind the groundskeeper. Paterson was impressed by how faithful the dog appeared and decided that someone should write a story about it.

AUTHOR FILE

MOST FAMOUS WORKS *Bridge to Terabithia, The Great Gilly Hopkins, Lyddie*

FAVORITE PART OF WRITING Rewriting. "First drafts are usually painful, but a good rewrite morning is bliss."

AWARDS Hans Christian Andersen Medal for Writing, Scott O'Dell Award for Children's Literature, ALA Best Books for Young Adults

---

delirious *(adj.)* in a state of wild excitement
frisking *(v.)* leaping or jumping

LITERARY ANALYSIS

Plot and Conflict
How does Brock finally resolve his conflict?

_____

_____

_____

CRITICAL THINKING

Evaluate
Review page 103. What does Brock discover about the world outside the dome community? Should he return to explain his discovery to the dome dwellers? Why or why not?

_____

_____

_____

_____

_____

21 SMALL GROUPS/INDEPENDENT

COLLABORATE

Compare Perspectives Compare Brock's perspective at the end of the story with that of the dome dwellers. What has he learned? Why do the dome dwellers believe differently?

COMMUNICATE

React and Write Imagine what happens next to Brock and Brog. Outline your thoughts. Then write a paragraph that describes what they encounter after leaving the dome.

W

READ ONLINE

expert space Go to **www.expert21.com/student** to learn more about Katherine Paterson; Futurism.

Magazine Feature

EXPOSED to the MAX

How safe and private are emails, text messages, and social networking Web sites? Not as safe—and certainly not as private—as you might think. Learn about some Internet privacy pitfalls and how to avoid them.

 QuickWrite

What sort of personal data and information would you consider safe to post on a Web site? What information would you *never post*? Explain your reasoning.

Make Inferences COMPREHENSION

When you make an inference, you make a logical guess based on information in a text and your own knowledge and experience.

Making inferences can help you figure out what an author does not state directly.

▶ **Read the passage. Then complete the step-by-step chart to make an inference about what the character is doing.**

Martin flipped open his cell phone and studied the screen. A smile spread across his face. He pressed some keys on the keypad and hit a button. "Great!" he said to himself. He ran to his room and grabbed some clothes from the closet.

What does the text directly state that Martin is doing?	**What personal experience or knowledge helps you infer what Martin is doing?**	**What can you infer about how Martin is feeling? Underline the words that helped you infer this.**
_____ _____ _____ _____	_____ _____ _____ _____	_____ _____ _____ _____

Analyze Evidence NAVIGATING TEXT

Authors of nonfiction text often include specific facts, or evidence, to support their ideas.

As you read, identify and analyze the evidence the author cites.

▶ **Read the passage. Draw one line under the main point the author makes. Draw two lines under the evidence she gives to support it.**

The Internet has changed the way newspapers report breaking news. In the past, newspapers were printed once a day. A story that occurred after the paper's deadline could not be printed until the next day. But now that newspapers are on the Internet, breaking stories can be published in minutes.

Academic Language VOCABULARY

▶ Rate your knowledge of each word. Then write its meaning and an example sentence.

Word	Meaning	Example
EXPERT WORDS *Use these words to write and talk about the workshop topic.*		
access ac•cess (noun) ① ② ③ ④	the ability to enter a place or use something	I have access to email only on the weekends.
networking net•work•ing (adjective) ① ② ③ ④		
proportion pro•por•tion (noun) ① ② ③ ④		
SELECTION WORDS *These words are key to understanding this selection.*		
digital dig•it•al (adjective) ① ② ③ ④		
impersonate im•per•so•nate (verb) ① ② ③ ④	to pretend to be someone else	
inflict in•flict (verb) ① ② ③ ④		
privacy pri•va•cy (noun) ① ② ③ ④		
vandalize van•dal•ize (verb) ① ② ③ ④		It is against the law to vandalize walls by painting graffiti on them.

Rating Scale ① I don't know the word. ② I've seen it or heard it. ③ I know its meaning. ④ I know it and use it.

Word Families WORD ANALYSIS

Remember that words in the same word family share the same base word.

You can often figure out the meaning of an unfamiliar word by using your knowledge of the base word.

▶ Circle three words that share the same word family as *impersonate*.

personal	personable	permanent
purchase	impersonal	perimeter

Now write the base word that all three words have in common.

_____

EXPOSED
to the
MAX

By Leah Paulos

LAST YEAR, DAVE*, A 13-YEAR-OLD FROM DENVER, COLORADO, MADE A DIGITAL VIDEO FOR A GIRL HE LIKED. In the two-minute recording, he read a poem he wrote and asked her out on a date—in rhyme. When the girl received it, she showed it to her friends. They thought it was so funny they posted it on YouTube and invited the entire school to view it.

Dave, obviously, was totally humiliated, and he continues to be embarrassed because there's no way for him to get the video offline. There are multiple copies floating around cyberspace now—and they will be there forever.

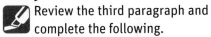

By the Numbers

What happened to Dave is now happening more and more frequently, and it's not because there are more guys with crushes than ever before. It's because the Internet is now playing such a big role in teens' lives. According to a study by the Pew Internet & American Life Project, 93 percent of teens use the Internet; 55 percent of teens have a profile on a social **networking** site like Facebook or MySpace; 47 percent have uploaded photos where others can see them;

and 28 percent have their own blog. That's loads of personal **digital** content that teens are creating.

The truth is there are many amazing things about using the Internet for social purposes: It's a fun and easy way to communicate, and to share pictures and videos. It also helps you keep in touch with people you don't see often and to meet people with whom you have similar interests.

"It's the best way to make plans with my friends," says Brianne Brand, 15, of Kingman, Arizona. "And I feel like I can say anything to them there without worrying that someone will overhear me."

Of course, it's also cool to be able to present yourself to the world any way you want to. Plus, let's be real, it's hard not to use it when everyone else is.

* Name changed to protect privacy.

Well Connected

Today, teens have access to more types of technology than ever before. So, when it comes to chatting, "multi-channel" teens make use of every communication device at their disposal.

Method of Communication	Percentage of Teens
Talk on Cell Phone	70
Send Texts	60
Instant Message	54
Send Messages Over Social Networking	47
Talk to Friends on Landline Telephone	46
Spend Time With Friends in Person	35
Send Email	22

Source: Pew Internet & American Life Project Survey of Parents and Teens, October–November 2006

cyberspace *(n.)* online world of computer networks
content *(n.)* main material offered by a Web site

COMPREHENSION

Make Inferences

Review the first and second paragraphs on pages 106–107. Then, complete the following.

• What can you infer about the author's feelings toward Dave's story?

Ⓐ She is amused by what happened.

Ⓑ She has no strong feelings about it.

Ⓒ She feels bad for Dave.

Ⓓ She thinks the girls were right.

• Circle a detail that supports your response.

NAVIGATING TEXT

Analyze Evidence

Review the third paragraph and complete the following.

• What claim does the author make about the Internet and teens?

_____

_____

_____

_____

Underline at least two facts the author includes to support this claim.

CRITICAL THINKING

Synthesize

Consider the information in "Well Connected" together with your own knowledge of how you and your friends communicate. Do you agree or disagree with the author's description of teens' communication habits? Explain.

_____

_____

_____

_____

_____

_____

_____

_____

How Much Information Is Too Much Information?

Check out this fake social networking profile to learn more. Doing so will help you stay safe online.

www.scholastic.com

KATE

THE BASICS

Female
16 years old
Austin, TX
United States
Last login: 2/11/09

> Don't post any information or photos that you wouldn't want your friends, family, or employers to see.

KATE'S SCHOOL

> Never list specific locations. You don't want to let strangers know where they might find you.

KATE'S SCHOOL

SUPER SURVEY

Name:	Kate Mendez
Birthplace:	San Antonio
Eye color:	Brown
Hair color:	Brown
Height:	5'1"
Right-handed or left-handed:	Right
Weaknesses:	Good music, shopping at the mall, chatting with friends
Ultimate goal:	Become a fashion designer
Favorite saying:	LOL
Chocolate or vanilla:	Chocolate

> Never publish your full name.

> Keep your "Friends" list limited to people you know. Remember, everyone on your friend list can read your bulletins.

> Don't list any hobbies. Online strangers posing as friends or potential friends could strike up a conversation by pretending to have the same interests.

FUN FACTS ABOUT KATE

I love going out, having fun, and sleeping in—even if it means never getting to work or school on time.

KATE'S PHOTOS

> Avoid linking to personal pages on sites where you may have posted photos of your home, family, and friends.

1 2 3 4 5 6 **7** »

For more pix go to http://photobucket/kate

FRIENDS COMMENTS

Kate has 273 friends

 Susanna: Another sick day from school? You're faking it!

Michae What's

 Erin: D cheerle tomorr ville Pa

> Your friends' comments may reveal more than you'd like everyone to know. Be sure to read—and edit—all comments carefully.

Too Much Information

The problem with the Internet is that people often put too much information online. "Teens write about private feelings and post suggestive pictures of themselves, and then assume that only the people they send it to will have **access**," says Katya Gifford of CyberAngels, an Internet safety organization. "The reality is that once you put something out into cyberspace, you lose control of it."

This is true in many ways: Emails can be forwarded with the click of a mouse. Photo-sharing sites that allow you to control who sees your pictures don't prevent those people from downloading the photos and doing whatever they want with them. You or someone else can post something personal about you to a Web site. Even if someone erases it, the search engines often keep a cached, or archived, copy that will keep showing up in search results.

One of the biggest potential downsides to online overexposure is embarrassment. "Everyone has sides of their personality that they don't always show to all people," says Parry Aftab, an Internet **privacy** and security lawyer and the director of WiredSafety. "But offline, people put all sides of themselves out there and don't realize that everyone can see them."

This can cause problems. Teachers can become upset, for example, if they read that people are making fun of their looks; a friend who notices that he or she didn't get invited to your slumber party can get hurt; parents can get angry if they see a photo of their kid doing something he or she shouldn't.

Serious Impact

Putting too much personal information online can also open you up to being cyberbullied. "Sadly, friendships don't always last forever," Aftab says. "Someone who was a friend could become an enemy after a little fight. If that person had access to all of your pictures, emails, IMs, and videos, they could potentially use them against you."

The fact that search engines archive results, making a permanent record of everything online, is the other big problem. "You have to assume that any information you put online will be there forever and that anyone will be able to find it," Gifford says.

Not only can this lead to problems for you now, your future can be adversely affected, too. For example, when you're applying for a job or internship, the company can easily Google your name. You don't want them to see a picture of you on Flickr **vandalizing** school property! Future boyfriends or girlfriends might look for you, too. And then, in the more distant future, how will you tell your own kids not to play with fire if they've seen an online video of you gleefully lighting firecrackers outside the school library?

> **Summarize**
> **Summarize the problems that teens could face on the Internet.**

---

search engines (n.) computer programs used to search for information on the Internet
adversely (adv.) in an unfavorable manner

Read and Synthesize

NAVIGATING TEXT

Analyze Evidence

In the second paragraph on page 109, <u>underline</u> evidence that supports this claim: "[Once] you put something out into cyberspace, you lose control of it."

• Do you find this evidence convincing? Explain.

_____

_____

_____

_____

_____

_____

_____

_____

_____

VOCABULARY/WORD ANALYSIS

Word Families

Circle the words *online* and *offline* in the third paragraph on page 109.

• Write the base word these words share.

_____

What is the difference in their meaning?

_____

_____

_____

_____

COMPREHENSION

Make Inferences

Review pages 108–109 to complete the following.

• The author of this article feels that

☐ the Internet is dangerous for teens.

☐ social networking sites are safe places to post personal details.

☐ the Internet is a great invention, but it has some risks.

• Check ✓ two ideas in the text that support this inference.

Comfort Level

Don't get us wrong: We are not suggesting that you stop using the Internet. We're just saying that everyone needs to pay more attention to security and privacy issues. How do you do that? Gifford offers this guideline: "If you wouldn't be comfortable hanging something on a billboard outside your house so your family, friends, teachers, and neighbors can see it, don't post it online," she says.

Another thing to do is be more discriminating about whom you allow to view your profile. "I never approve anyone as a friend unless I know him or her personally from school," Brianne says.

That's definitely a good idea. It's important to keep your cyberworld based in the real world. But not everyone does this. "A big problem is that the social networking sites encourage people to have as many friends as possible," Aftab says. "Sites like YouTube evaluate success based on the number of page views you get. This is fun, but it is contrary to security issues."

The guy who has 534 MySpace friends, for example, might look very popular, but he's also offering up a lot of personal information and pictures to a good portion of the Internet population, and that could lead to trouble for him.

We haven't even discussed protecting your personal safety. Putting identifying information online (your name, address, age, phone number, and school name) opens you up to more well-known dangers, such as online predators and people who want to steal your identity.

So what's a teen to do? Well, enjoy your online social life, but keep your important information to yourself. And before sending an email or an IM, or posting a blog entry or an online album, always ask yourself how you'd feel if your soccer coach, Sunday school teacher, ex-significant other, future significant other, grandma, the person running against you for class president, and the local sheriff were to see it. If you'd be fine with that, then send it off! ■

[
Summarize
What is the purpose of this article?
]

Cyberbullying

New technology is giving bullies more tools to make their victims miserable.

While bullying is nothing new, advances in communication technology have allowed a new breed of bullies to emerge. Called cyberbullies, these young and technologically savvy villains aren't confined to hassling their victims at school or on the street corner. Armed with cell phones and computers, cyberbullies use technology to **inflict** pain from afar.

According to researchers Sameer Hinduja and Justin Patchin, "Cyberbullying is when someone repeatedly makes fun of another person online or repeatedly picks on another person through email or text message or when someone posts something online about another person that they don't like." As a larger **proportion** of kids go online, cyberbullying is becoming common. Hinduja and Patchin published data in 2008 showing nearly 43 percent of the middle schoolers they polled had experienced cyberbullying in the previous 30 days.

Cyberbullies aren't usually the same kids who torment others in the schoolyard. They are often victims of bullying themselves who seek revenge or want to right perceived wrongs. They use the anonymity of the Internet to launch attacks they'd never make in person.

The techniques used by cyberbullies can be ingenious. They **impersonate** other teens online and send phony messages to friends and classmates. They forward private emails and embarrassing photos to hundreds of people. Through emails, text messages, and IMs, they spread gossip and start arguments. They post hurtful comments to blogs and exclude others from social networks.

So what can you do to stop a cyberbully? An Internet safety group has this advice: First, try to ignore bullies by not responding to their attacks. Block their screen names or telephone numbers. If that doesn't work, save the evidence. Tell an adult what's happening. Surveys show many victims don't tell their parents, for fear of being barred from using the Internet. Nonetheless, keeping quiet is not a good idea. Internet service providers and law enforcement can sometimes stop cyberbullies in their tracks.

If you've never had an online altercation, try to keep it that way. Don't chat with strangers. Change your passwords often. Never give out passwords or personal information. One way to stop cyberbullies is to prevent them from getting started.

---

ingenious *(adj.)* inventive and original
altercation *(n.)* a heated, angry dispute

COMPREHENSION

Make Inferences

Draw a box around the guideline in the first paragraph on page 110. Why does the author include this guideline?

_____

_____

_____

_____

VOCABULARY/WORD ANALYSIS

Word Families

• Circle two words below that are in the same word family.

    identity   ideas

    idolatry   identifying

• In paragraph 5, what is "identifying information"?

_____

_____

21   SMALL GROUPS/INDEPENDENT

COLLABORATE

Create and Innovate Create a 30- to 60-second public service announcement to raise teens' awareness of Internet safety. Suggest several ways to stay safe.

COMMUNICATE

React and Write If you were a parent, what kinds of Web sites would you let your children visit? Make notes. Then write a paragraph explaining your position.

READ ONLINE

expert space
Go to **www.expert21.com/student** to learn more about Social Networking; E-Mail; Privacy Issues.

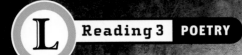

Can a harmless computer game take over your life?

By Neil Gaiman

There was a computer game, I was given it,
one of my friends gave it to me, he was playing it,
he said, brilliant, you should play it,
and I did, and it was.

I copied it off the disk he gave me
for anyone, I wanted everyone to play it.
Everyone should have this much fun.
I sent it upline to bulletin boards
but mainly I got it out to all my friends.

(Personal contact. That's the way it was given to me.)

My friends were like me: some were scared of viruses,
someone gave you a game on a disk, next week or Friday the 13th
it reformatted your hard disk or corrupted your memory.
But this one never did that. This was dead safe.

Even my friends who didn't like computers started to play:
as you get better the game gets harder;
maybe you never win but you can get pretty good.
I'm pretty good.

Of course I have to spend a lot of time playing it.
So do my friends. And their friends.
And just the people you meet, you can see them,
walking down the old motor ways
or standing in queues, away from their computers,
away from the arcades that sprang up overnight,
but they play it in their heads in the meantime,

---

reformatted *(v.)* erased a previous format
queues *(n.)* lines of people

combining shapes,
puzzling over contours, putting colors next to colors,
twisting signals to new screen sections,
listening to the music.

Sure, people think about it, but mainly they play it.
My record's eighteen hours at a stretch.
42,012 points, 3 fanfares.

You play through the tears, the aching wrist, the hunger, after a
while it all goes away.
All of it except the game, I should say.

There's no room in my mind anymore;
no room for other things.
We copied the game, gave it to our friends.
It transcends language, occupies our time,
sometimes I think I'm forgetting things these days.

I wonder what happened to the TV. There used to be TV.
I wonder what will happen when I run out of canned food.
I wonder where all the people went. And I realize how,
if I'm fast enough, I can put a black square next to a red line,
mirror it and rotate them so they both disappear,
clearing the left block
for a white bubble to rise...

(So they both disappear.)

And when the power goes off for good then I
will play it in my head until I die. ■

---

fanfares *(n.)* short tunes played to introduce something
transcends *(v.)* goes beyond the limits of

LITERARY ANALYSIS

Character and Motivation

Review page 112. (Circle) the lines that show the motivation of the **speaker** (narrator in a poem).

- What actions reflect this?

_____

_____

_____

COMPREHENSION

Make Inferences

What is the poet trying to say about playing video games? What can you infer about the poet's perspective on playing video games?

_____

_____

_____

- Underline words and phrases that helped you make this inference.

CRITICAL THINKING

Evaluate

Is the speaker's situation realistic? Why or why not? Why do you think the poet portrays the speaker as someone who has practically stopped eating and interacting with people in order to play a video game?

_____

_____

_____

_____

_____

READ ONLINE

 **expert space**
Go to **www.expert21.com/student**
to learn more about Cybercrime and Computer Vulnerabilities; Computer Security; Computer Virus; Computer Crime.

Think Across Texts

Organize and Synthesize ··

1. What do the three readings say about the pros and cons of technology? Complete this chart using information from "The Last Dog," "Exposed to the Max," and "Virus."

	"The Last Dog"	"Exposed to the Max"	"Virus"
Advantages of Technology			
Disadvantages of Technology			

Compare and Evaluate ··

2. Both "Exposed to the Max" and "Virus" warn about some riskier aspects of technology. In your opinion, which of these selections describes the bigger, more important danger? Explain.

_____

_____

_____

_____

_____

3. Contrast what happens to Brock at the end of "The Last Dog" with the fate of the speaker in "Virus." Who ended up better off? Why?

_____

_____

_____

_____

_____

4. Each of the selections is a different text type. On the line next to each text feature listed below, fill in the text type associated with it. Write **M** for magazine article, **P** for poem, and **S** for science fiction story.

may be set in the future _____

reports factual information _____

fiction _____

can be written in free verse _____

Discuss and Write ····················

5. With a partner, discuss how the three readings in "Human Versus Machine" helped you understand how technology is affecting our civilization. Take notes as you talk. Then use your notes to write a response to the question: *What risks does technology present?*

Apply Word Knowledge

Word Lab

1. **Name them.** List three activities that would be helpful to practice in a **virtual** environment:

- _____
- _____
- _____

2. **Select them.** Look at the list below. Which items are always **digital** devices? Check them.

- ❏ cell phone
- ❏ bicycle
- ❏ piano
- ❏ computer

3. **Describe them.** Give an example of each.

- a place that should be **sterile**

  _____

- a device that contains a **sensor** of some kind

  _____

- a good place to go if you want **privacy**

  _____

4. **Think about it.** Imagine that someone you know is planning to **vandalize** a playground in a public park. What would you say to him or her?

_____

_____

_____

5. **Complete it.** Fill in the dialogue with the following words: **networking**, **access**, **holograms**, and **proportion**.

Zack: A large _____ of the people at this technology conference are video game designers.

Shira: Yes, this is an excellent _____ opportunity. If you want _____ to the smartest people in the video game industry, this is the place to be!

Zack: You said it. I met someone who is creating a game that projects _____ in your living room!

Word Analysis

6. Fill in the missing definition for each word.

Word	Meaning
vandalize (verb)	to purposely destroy or deface property
vandal (noun)	
capitulated (verb)	surrendered
capitulation (noun)	

7. Circle three words below that are in the same word family.

embodiment   body   embarrassed

condiment   embody   harassed

What base word do all three words share?

_____

Solve Problems

CAREER CONNECTION
Business, Management, and Administration
www.careerclusters.org

Go to 21 ToolKit **Expert File 6.19** to learn more about careers in management.

Sometimes a problem can seem overwhelming. However, once you know the steps to effective problem solving, the problem might not seem so challenging.

Music Management Problem

▶ Read these emails to see how one company identified and solved a problem.

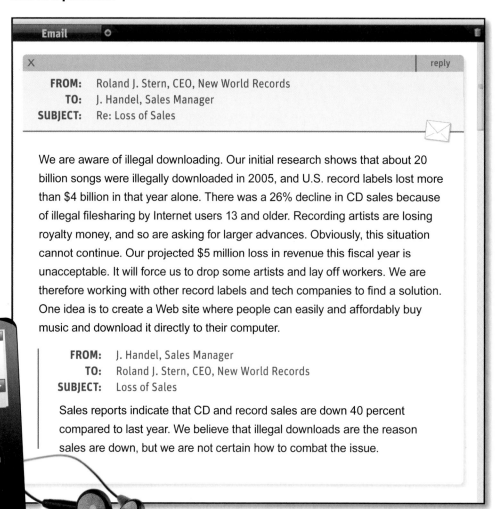

Email

FROM: Roland J. Stern, CEO, New World Records
TO: J. Handel, Sales Manager
SUBJECT: Re: Loss of Sales

We are aware of illegal downloading. Our initial research shows that about 20 billion songs were illegally downloaded in 2005, and U.S. record labels lost more than $4 billion in that year alone. There was a 26% decline in CD sales because of illegal filesharing by Internet users 13 and older. Recording artists are losing royalty money, and so are asking for larger advances. Obviously, this situation cannot continue. Our projected $5 million loss in revenue this fiscal year is unacceptable. It will force us to drop some artists and lay off workers. We are therefore working with other record labels and tech companies to find a solution. One idea is to create a Web site where people can easily and affordably buy music and download it directly to their computer.

FROM: J. Handel, Sales Manager
TO: Roland J. Stern, CEO, New World Records
SUBJECT: Loss of Sales

Sales reports indicate that CD and record sales are down 40 percent compared to last year. We believe that illegal downloads are the reason sales are down, but we are not certain how to combat the issue.

MARK IT

Identify the problem. The sales manager states the problem clearly and directly. Circle the problem.

Identify the effects. One effect, or result of the problem, is that recording artists are asking for larger advances. **Put a star ★** by another effect.

Determine the seriousness of the problem. Draw a line to the number that the CEO finds unacceptable.

Decide what steps to take. Put a **check mark ✔** next to the CEO's solution.

Determine the cause. The sales manager and the CEO state the cause of the problem. **Underline** where the problem is mentioned.

Here's How ▶ Follow these steps to solve problems:

Step 1 Identify the problem. State the problem as clearly and simply as you can.

Step 2 Think about the causes and effects. Look for the reasons this problem exists. Then think about who or what is affected by the problem. List the effects in order of their importance.

Step 3 Determine how serious the problem is. Is the problem widespread? Is it creating strong negative effects? Or are the effects minimal?

Step 4 Decide what actions to take. If the problem is serious, think about what specific things you can do to solve it. You may need more information before taking steps toward a solution, if a solution is needed.

Apply: Solve a Problem in Your Community

▶ Think about a problem in your community that is making life worse, for example, increased traffic.

1. What is the problem?

_____

_____

2. Think about the causes and effects of the problem. In the box on the left, write the cause of the problem. In the box on the right, write the effect of that problem.

Cause	Effect

3. How serious is the problem?

_____

_____

4. What actions can you take to solve the problem?

●Idea	
●Idea	
●Idea	

Will these steps help you work toward solving the problem?

_____

_____

_____

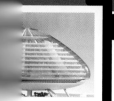
Science Text

Welcome to the Future

Robot insects, egg-shaped office buildings, and cars that float.
Find out about these and other technological advances that
some experts predict the future will bring.

Problem and Solution   COMPREHENSION

The **problem** is a difficult situation
that requires resolution. The **solution**
is the action that leads to resolution.

Sometimes, a text may state several
problems that can be resolved with
one solution. Other times, a text
may propose several solutions to
one problem. In this case, there may
be enough information to help you
evaluate which solution is best.

▶ Read the paragraph below. Draw one line under the problem and two
lines under the solution.

> The car is a useful and convenient form of transportation, but
> that convenience has a price. Cars cause pollution, and pollution
> damages the environment. Hybrid cars offer a clean, fuel-efficient,
> and cost-effective alternative to traditional cars.

Diagrams   NAVIGATING TEXT

A **diagram** is a drawing that
shows what something looks
like, how it is made, or how it
works.

Labels help identify the parts of
the diagram.

Diagrams are often used in
nonfiction articles to provide
information more clearly than
words alone can.

▶ Look carefully at the
diagram at the right.
Then complete these
activities.

• Make a check mark ✓
in front of the title of
the diagram.

• What do the labels
show?

Parts of a Helicopter

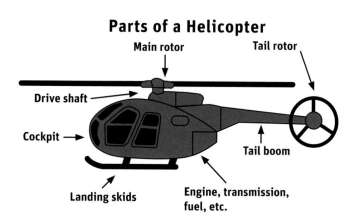

Main rotor
Tail rotor
Drive shaft
Cockpit
Tail boom
Landing skids
Engine, transmission,
fuel, etc.

_____

_____

• Which of the following does this diagram help you to understand?
Circle the answer.

what something   how something   how something
looks like   is made   works

Academic Language VOCABULARY

▶ Rate your knowledge of each word. Then write its meaning and an example sentence.

Word	Meaning	Example
ACADEMIC WORDS *Use these words in all your subject classes.*		
accommodate ac·com·mo·date *(verb)* ① ② ③ ④	to make space for	We squeezed into the van to accommodate everyone on the team.
extract ex·tract *(noun)* ① ② ③ ④	a selection or excerpt	
ACADEMIC WORD *Use this word in all your subject classes.*		
instance in·stance *(noun)* ① ② ③ ④		
SELECTION WORDS *These words are key to understanding this selection.*		
compact com·pact *(adjective)* ① ② ③ ④		
efficient ef·fi·cient *(adjective)* ① ② ③ ④		I don't do efficient work when I am tired.
hazardous haz·ard·ous *(adjective)* ① ② ③ ④		
mobile mo·bile *(adjective)* ① ② ③ ④		
obstacle ob·sta·cle *(noun)* ① ② ③ ④		

Rating Scale ① I don't know the word. ② I've seen it or heard it. ③ I know its meaning. ④ I know it and use it.

Context Clues: Antonyms WORD ANALYSIS

Antonyms are words that have **opposite meanings.** The words *efficient* and *wasteful* are examples of antonyms.

You can use **synonyms** and **antonyms** as **context clues** to figure out the meaning of an unfamiliar word.

▶ Read the sentences below. Circle two words that are antonyms.

Unlike a stationary robot, a mobile robot can move from place to place.

What does *stationary* mean?

_____

Welcome to the Future

Can we predict the future?

To a certain degree, we can. By analyzing current trends, experts can anticipate the scientific and social changes that lie ahead. So what's in store? The future holds plenty of high-tech design. Read about eco-friendly architecture and far-out forms of transportation in this **extract** from a book about future designs.

Environmentally Friendly

Progress has not come without a price. Our cars and factories cause air and water pollution. The carbon and other "greenhouse" gases they give off have damaged the ozone layer and led to potentially catastrophic global warming.

In addition, many of the natural resources we use to power our homes, factories, office buildings, and cars are nonrenewable. Once they are used up, they are gone forever.

Can designers and their designs help save the planet? Check out these designs of the future, meant to conserve energy and give Earth a break.

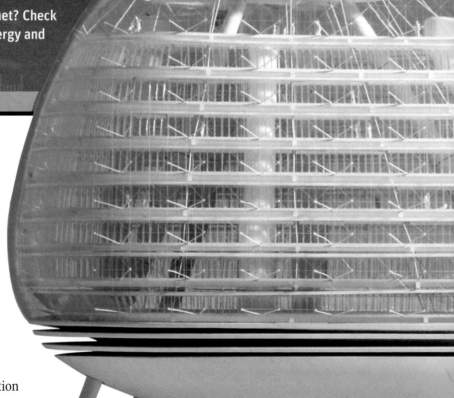

Hot, stale air is vented through louver at the top of the building.

Office of the Future

Most traditional offices are not environmentally friendly. They consume high levels of energy in the winter, and require even more energy to keep cool in the summer. They often lack natural sources of air and light, and so electric lighting and air conditioning are switched on all day. This not only results in high fuel costs, it is unpleasant for the occupants. As the cost and consumption of fuel rises, energy-inefficient offices will need to be redesigned.

This remarkable-looking office building has been designed to maximize the use of both natural ventilation and natural light.

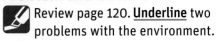

Recycling

Increasingly, people are becoming aware of the value of recycling. Today, we generate an enormous amount of waste, and there are increasing problems with its disposal. In the future we will manufacture products that are built to last and can be repaired. They will be easily dismantled and reused in sometimes surprising ways.

Recycled: a tire becomes a bag.

Streamlined shape allows wind to flow smoothly.

In winter, warm air at the top is used to heat cold air coming in at the bottom.

Air between glass skins is heated by solar radiation.

Air conditioning is replaced by a natural ventilation system.

Mirrors reflect natural light into offices.

Building stands high above ground, away from pollution.

Ideal for the City of the Future

The car is a very popular form of transportation. But people are concerned by the amount of pollution cars now produce and the future scarcity of gas. Manufacturers are designing **compact** cars with clean, fuel-**efficient** engines.

COMPREHENSION

Problem and Solution

Review page 120. **Underline** two problems with the environment.

- What is one possible solution to a problem you underlined?

_____

_____

_____

_____

_____

- Draw a ⬚box⬚ around the text where you found this solution.

NAVIGATING TEXT

Diagrams

How does the office of the future address the use of natural light?

_____

_____

_____

_____

⬭Circle⬭ the part of the diagram that explains the design.

CRITICAL THINKING

Analyze

Review "Ideal for the City of the Future." What are the problems?

_____

_____

_____

_____

What do you think makes the car's design energy efficient?

_____

_____

_____

_____

Futuropolis

People have traditionally been attracted to living in cities because of the cultural and economic opportunities. Cities, or urban areas, usually offer more jobs and social activities than rural areas. It will not be long before most people become urban dwellers. It will be necessary to build new cities and rebuild existing cities to **accommodate** the huge increase in the world's population. High-rise offices and apartment towers, taller than ever before, will become self-contained, with their own shops, restaurants, and leisure facilities. They will operate like small towns, and the occupants will rarely need to leave them.

A Future Underground

Underground transportation is not new—underground trains have been in use for more than a century. To save space in future cities, all vehicles could travel below ground.

self-contained *(adj.)* complete in itself
leisure *(n.)* a time when you are doing things you enjoy

City-Building for the New Millennium

One answer to potential overcrowding is to build upward, constructing huge towers. The Millennium Tower, designed by U.K. architect Norman Foster, was proposed for a site in Tokyo, Japan. It has been planned as a self-contained township 150 stories high, with a population of 50,000. High-speed double-decker elevators will carry a limited number of people at a time to "sky centers," where they can visit restaurants and shops, and enjoy all forms of entertainment, including the movies or discos. From the sky centers, residents will travel by conventional high-speed elevators to their apartments or places of work on the other floors.

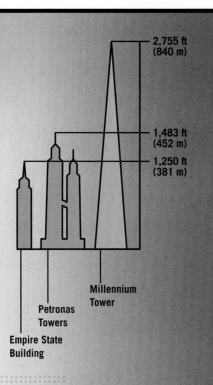

2,755 ft
(840 m)

1,483 ft
(452 m)

1,250 ft
(381 m)

Millennium
Tower

Petronas
Towers

Empire State
Building

Apartments and
offices occupy
other floors

Sky centers for
communal
activities every
30 floors

Cone shape
supported by
steel frame

Large glass
windows to
provide light to
every floor

Question
What questions might the Millennium Tower designers have asked before designing the building?

conventional *(adj.)* ordinary or traditional

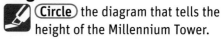
NAVIGATING TEXT

Diagrams

Circle the diagram that tells the height of the Millennium Tower.

- Now find another visual to help you answer this question: Where will "sky centers" be located in the 150-floor Millennium Tower?

_____

- Draw a box around the text where you found this information.

CRITICAL THINKING

Evaluate

Residents of these futuristic self-contained towers will "rarely need to leave them." Do you think this is an added benefit, or a possible problem, or both? Explain why.

_____
_____
_____
_____
_____

COMPREHENSION

Problem and Solution

Review pages 122–123. Where does the author state the main problem on these pages?

_____

- What is the problem?

_____
_____
_____

- What solution does the author think will help?

_____
_____
_____

- Underline another solution the author proposes to solve the problem of overcrowding, especially in cities.

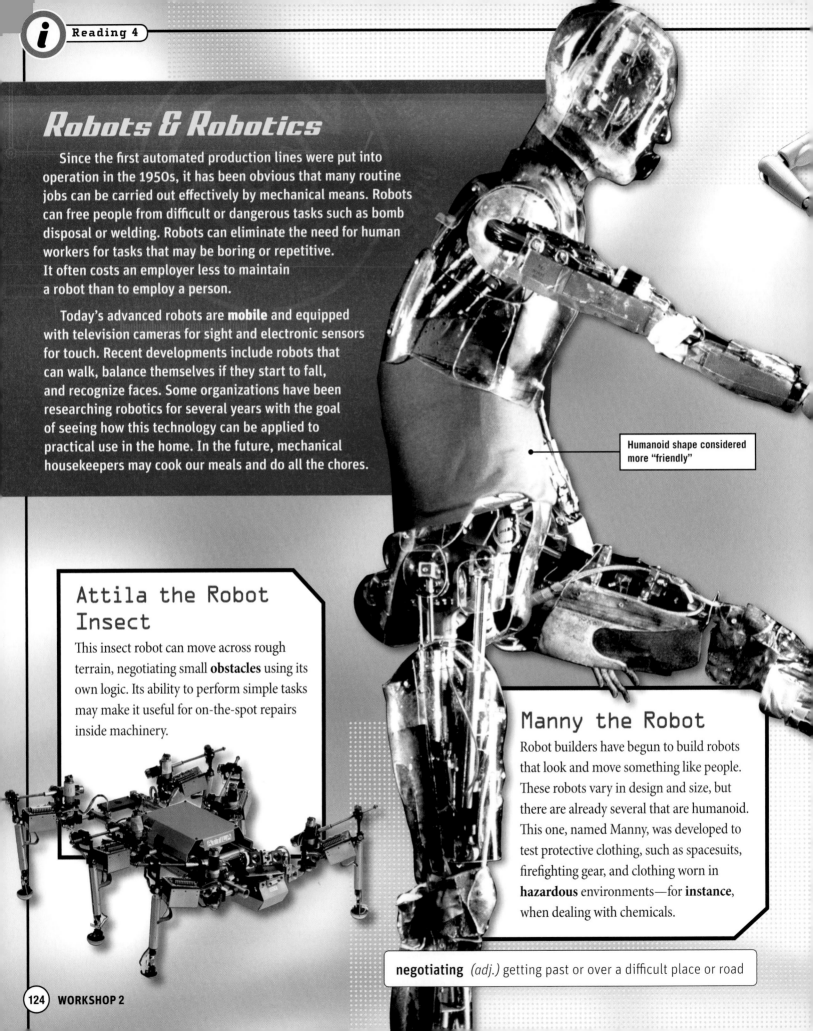

Robots & Robotics

Since the first automated production lines were put into operation in the 1950s, it has been obvious that many routine jobs can be carried out effectively by mechanical means. Robots can free people from difficult or dangerous tasks such as bomb disposal or welding. Robots can eliminate the need for human workers for tasks that may be boring or repetitive. It often costs an employer less to maintain a robot than to employ a person.

Today's advanced robots are **mobile** and equipped with television cameras for sight and electronic sensors for touch. Recent developments include robots that can walk, balance themselves if they start to fall, and recognize faces. Some organizations have been researching robotics for several years with the goal of seeing how this technology can be applied to practical use in the home. In the future, mechanical housekeepers may cook our meals and do all the chores.

Humanoid shape considered more "friendly"

Attila the Robot Insect

This insect robot can move across rough terrain, negotiating small **obstacles** using its own logic. Its ability to perform simple tasks may make it useful for on-the-spot repairs inside machinery.

Manny the Robot

Robot builders have begun to build robots that look and move something like people. These robots vary in design and size, but there are already several that are humanoid. This one, named Manny, was developed to test protective clothing, such as spacesuits, firefighting gear, and clothing worn in **hazardous** environments—for **instance**, when dealing with chemicals.

negotiating *(adj.)* getting past or over a difficult place or road

Ball Partner

A Japanese electronics company has developed a robot that can play catch. It does this by reacting to voice commands, identifying colors, and even recognizing human faces. The makers plan to develop robots that will serve the population in the 21st century. Although this particular robot is programmed only to play catch, it is hoped that later models will be able to work in factories, hospitals, or the home.

Question
What questions do you have about the "ball partner" robot?

COMPREHENSION

Problem and Solution
Review page 124. What does the author state first, the problem or the solution?

_____

- Draw a box around the text that supports your response.
- Circle the text that supports your response.
- According to the "Robots & Robotics" introduction, what are three problems robots could solve?

_____
_____
_____

VOCABULARY/WORD ANALYSIS

Context Clues: Antonyms
Review the section titled "Manny the Robot" and draw a box around *vary*.

- If the robots did not vary in design and size, how would they look?

_____
_____
_____

CRITICAL THINKING

Evaluate
Review pages 124–125. Which robot would most people be more likely to use, Attila, Manny, or the Ball Partner? Why?

_____
_____
_____
_____
_____
_____
_____
_____

Getting Around

Our desire to travel will not diminish in the 21st century—in fact, it will likely increase. Most people will own cars, so roads could become more congested—and polluted. Attention is now focusing on how to ease these potential problems. Smaller, lightweight cars will provide a more environmentally friendly form of ground transportation. In addition, more people will take to the skies. Giant airplanes that travel at supersonic speeds may one day take passengers around the world in a fraction of the time it takes today.

Helicopter-style rotors

Flying Hypersonically

Supersonic travel was possible for transatlantic passengers in the mid-1970s when the British and French built an airliner called the Concorde. But now, NASA is developing the Hyper-X to fly at hypersonic speeds—five times faster than the speed of sound. It will be unpiloted and launched from a B-52 aircraft. Other countries are developing larger and faster versions for the 21st century.

Turboprop engine

NASA 1 X-43A

Passenger entrance

When Is a Car Not a Car?

Many people think it is time we found a replacement for the gas engine. Concept 2096 is truly a vehicle for the future. The vehicle does not have wheels. Instead it floats off the ground on cushions of air and is powered by magnets using an electric current. It is driven by a navigational computer, so there is no need for a driver, brakes, or a steering wheel. With a vehicle like this, pollution will be a thing of the past. It will use rechargeable fuel cells, a clean substitute for gas and diesel fuel.

congested *(adj.)* blocked up; not allowing movement
supersonic *(adj.)* faster than the speed of sound

Flying High

The tilt rotor, used by the military, takes off like a helicopter but flies like a plane. Its wings have helicopter-style rotors, which can be raised into a vertical position for take-off. The tilt rotor would be particularly useful in urban environments because it can take off and land in small spaces, and a passenger version for commercial, short-haul flights will probably become a popular form of transportation in the early 21st century.

Front wheels can tilt body when turning corners

Computers calculate the optimum tilt angle in relation to speed

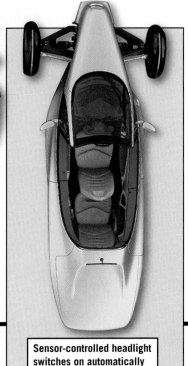

Sensor-controlled headlight switches on automatically

Car of the Future

This lightweight three-wheeler is designed for a driver and one passenger, making it an ideal car for the city. It has an onboard computer that calculates the highest cornering speeds, and the front wheels and body lean when the car is turning corners. This provides the maximum speed with the greatest safety and comfort. To add to the fun, the roof can be removed. ∎

Question
What questions do you still have about 21st century transportation?

CAREER CONNECTION
Architecture and Construction
www.careerclusters.org

Go to **21 ToolKit Expert File 6.17** to learn more about careers in architecture.

COMPREHENSION

Make Inferences

How do you think the author feels about the future of transportation?

_____

_____

• **Underline** the words on pages 126–127 that support your response.

NAVIGATING TEXT

Diagrams

Review the section titled "Car of the Future." Why do you think the author included three images of a car?

_____

_____

_____

21 SMALL GROUPS/INDEPENDENT

COLLABORATE

Make Decisions Review the inventions described in "Welcome to the Future." Imagine that you are a group of investors who want to fund one of the new technologies you just read about. Explain your choice.

COMMUNICATE

Discuss and Write Discuss with a partner why it is important that scientists work to develop technologies that may not be widely available for decades. Take notes as you discuss. Then explain your answer in a paragraph.

W

READ ONLINE

expert space
Go to www.expert21.com/student to learn more about Transportation Innovation; Ships and Shipping; Aviation; Trains and Railroads; Automobiles.

Magazine Feature

LA VIDA ROBOT

In a national science competition, immigrant kids from a public high school in Arizona compete against students from one of America's most elite universities. Find out who wins.

[W] **QuickWrite**

Imagine you are in a competition. Everyone expects the other side to win. You hope to prove them wrong. List three strategies you will use to try to win.

Make Inferences   COMPREHENSION

When you **make inferences** you "read between the lines," or make logical guesses based on evidence and your own knowledge.

When you read a magazine article, you may need to infer the **author's purpose** for writing.

▶ Read the passage below. Then answer the question to make an inference.

> Feeling nervous but still optimistic, the team headed to the competition. They had worked harder than any team the school had ever sent, and their coach was certain they had more drive than any team he had ever seen. The dedicated young athletes were about to discover whether their many months of hard work would finally pay off.

How does the author want readers to feel about the team?

_____

_____

Reading a Magazine Article   NAVIGATING TEXT

As you read a magazine article, pay attention to the different text features.

- The **title** tells what the article is about.

- The **byline** tells who wrote the article.

- The **subheads** tell what each part of the article is about.

- The **captions** give information about illustrations.

▶ Look at the beginning of this magazine article. Label the features with the words *byline, title, subhead,* and *caption*.

Making Science Cool: One School's Campaign

by Manolo Santos

Walking down the school hallway toward Irina Ivanov's 9th-grade science classroom, you can hear the sounds of laughter. It doesn't sound like your typical science lab. But then Ivanov is not your typical teacher.

Science as Adventure

Ivanov has an unusual teaching philosophy—she thinks fun is as important as work. "Kids need to be awake to learn," she says…

Students discover that science can be fun.

Academic Language VOCABULARY

▶ Rate your knowledge of each word. Then write its meaning and an example sentence.

Word	Meaning	Example
EXPERT WORD *Use this word to write and talk about the workshop topic.*		
innovative in·no·va·tive (adjective) ① ② ③ ④	completely new	The scientist has an innovative idea to solve the problem of air pollution.
ACADEMIC WORDS *Use these words in all your subject classes.*		
coordinate co·or·di·nate (verb) ① ② ③ ④		
corporation cor·po·ra·tion (noun) ① ② ③ ④		When I graduate from college, I want to work for a corporation that cares about its employees.
motivate mo·ti·vate (verb) ① ② ③ ④	to encourage to do something; to inspire	
overall o·ver·all (adjective) ① ② ③ ④		
specific spe·ci·fic (adjective) ① ② ③ ④		
CONTENT AREA WORDS *Use these words in all your subject classes.*		
engineer en·gi·neer (noun) ① ② ③ ④		
sponsor spon·sor (verb) ① ② ③ ④		

Rating Scale ① I don't know the word. ② I've seen it or heard it. ③ I know its meaning. ④ I know it and use it.

Context Clues: Synonyms WORD ANALYSIS

Synonyms are words that have almost the same meaning.

You can use synonyms as **context clues** to help you figure out the meanings of unfamiliar words.

▶ **Circle two synonyms in this sentence.**

Our coach's speech inspired us to do our best, but the prize money also motivated us.

What does *inspired* mean?

_____

LEDGE
"THE TEACHER"

ALLAN CAMERON
"THE TEACHER"

LA VIDA ROBOT

▶▶▶ In 2004, a group of students from the mean streets of Phoenix entered a competition to build an underwater robot. These underdogs faced some of the smartest minds in the country. No one could have predicted the outcome.

By **Joshua Davis**
Excerpted from *WIRED* magazine

OSCAR
"The Leader"

CRISTIAN
"The Brains"

LORENZO
"The Mechanic"

LUIS
"The Pick-Up Man"

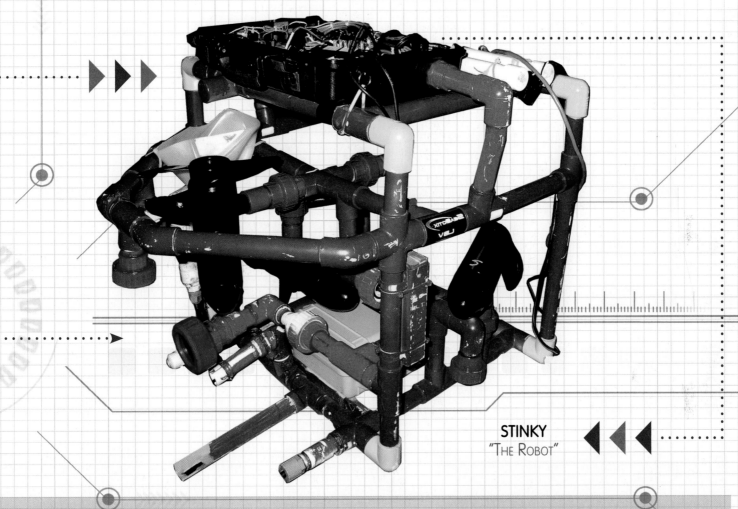

STINKY
"The Robot"

The winter rain makes a mess of West Phoenix. It turns dirt yards into mud and forms reefs of garbage in the streets. Junk food wrappers, diapers, and Spanish-language magazines are swept into the gutters. On West Roosevelt Avenue, security guards, two squad cars, and a handful of cops watch teenagers file into the local high school. A sign reads: *Carl Hayden Community High School: The Pride's Inside.*

Across campus, in a second-floor windowless room, four students huddle around an odd, 3-foot-tall frame constructed of PVC pipe [a plastic pressure pipe]. They have equipped it with propellers, cameras, lights, a laser, depth detectors, pumps, an underwater microphone, and an articulated pincer, a type of claw. It's a cheap but very functional underwater robot capable of recording sounds and retrieving objects 50 feet below the surface.

The four teenagers who built it are all undocumented Mexican immigrants who came to this country through tunnels or hidden in the backseats of cars. They live in sheds and rooms without electricity. But over three days last summer, these kids from the desert proved they are among the smartest young underwater **engineers** in the country.

THE MASTER MECHANIC

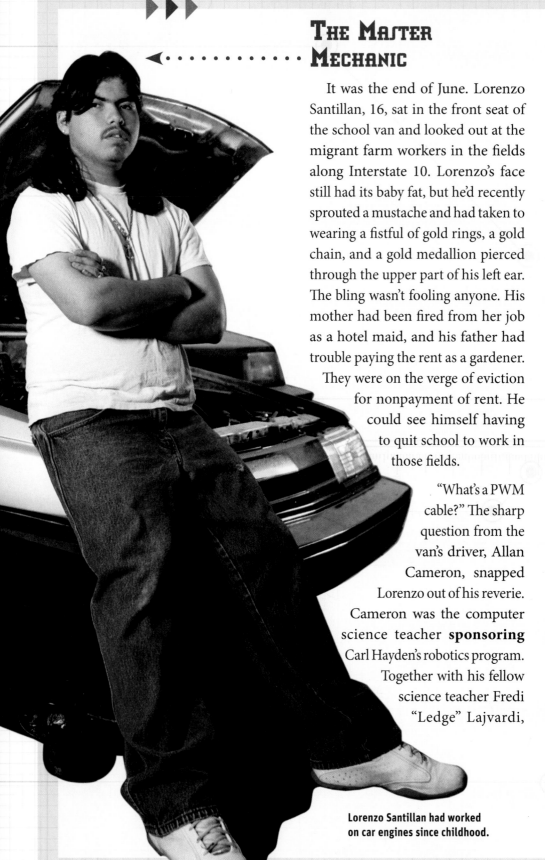

Lorenzo Santillan had worked on car engines since childhood.

It was the end of June. Lorenzo Santillan, 16, sat in the front seat of the school van and looked out at the migrant farm workers in the fields along Interstate 10. Lorenzo's face still had its baby fat, but he'd recently sprouted a mustache and had taken to wearing a fistful of gold rings, a gold chain, and a gold medallion pierced through the upper part of his left ear. The bling wasn't fooling anyone. His mother had been fired from her job as a hotel maid, and his father had trouble paying the rent as a gardener. They were on the verge of eviction for nonpayment of rent. He could see himself having to quit school to work in those fields.

"What's a PWM cable?" The sharp question from the van's driver, Allan Cameron, snapped Lorenzo out of his reverie. Cameron was the computer science teacher **sponsoring** Carl Hayden's robotics program. Together with his fellow science teacher Fredi "Ledge" Lajvardi,

Cameron had put up flyers around the school a few months earlier, offering to sponsor anyone interested in competing in the third annual Marine Advanced Technology Education Center's Remotely Operated Vehicle (ROV) Competition. Lorenzo was one of the first to show up to the after-school meeting last spring.

Cameron hadn't expected many students to be interested, particularly not a kid like Lorenzo, who was failing most of his classes and perpetually looked like he was about to fall asleep. But Lorenzo didn't have much else to do after school. He didn't want to walk around the streets. He had tried that—he'd been a member of a gang. When his friends started to get arrested for theft, he dropped out. He didn't want to go to jail. That's why he decided to come to Cameron's meeting.

"PWM," Lorenzo replied automatically from the van's passenger seat. "Pulse width modulation. *Esto* controls analog circuits with digital output."

Over the past four months, Lorenzo had flourished, learning a new set of acronyms and raising his math grade from an F to an A. He had grown up rebuilding car engines with his brother and cousin. Now he was ready to build something of his own. The team had found its mechanics man.

> **Summarize**
> **Summarize what Lorenzo brought to the team.**

---

reverie *(n.)* condition of being lost in thought
perpetually *(adv.)* constantly

THE "BRAINS"

Ever since his younger sister demanded her own room four years ago, Cristian Arcega had been living in a 30-square-foot plywood shed attached to the side of his parents' trailer. He liked it there. It was his own space. He was free to contemplate the acceleration of a raindrop as it leaves the clouds above him. He could hear it hit the roof and slide toward the puddles on the street outside. He imagined that the puddles were oceans and that the underwater robot he was building at school could explore them.

Cameron and Ledge formed the robotics group for kids like Cristian. He was probably the smartest 16-year-old in West Phoenix—without even trying, he had one of the highest GPAs in the school district. His brains and diminutive stature (5'4", 135 pounds) kept him apart at Carl Hayden. That and the fact that students socialized based on Mexican geography: In the cafeteria, there were Guanajuato tables and Sonora tables [Guanajuato and Sonora are Mexican states]. Cristian was from Mexicali [another state], but he'd left Mexico in the back of a station wagon when he was 6. He thought of himself as part American, part Mexican, and he didn't know where to sit. So he ate lunch in the storage room the teachers had commandeered for the underwater ROV club.

The robot competition (sponsored in part by the Office of Naval Research

Cristian Arcega

and NASA) required students to build a robot that could survey a sunken mock-up of a submarine—not easy stuff. For the competition, the teachers had entered the club in the expert-level Explorer division instead of the beginner Ranger division. They figured their students would lose anyway, and there was more honor in losing to the college kids in the Explorer division than to the high schoolers in Ranger. Their real goal was to show the students that there were opportunities outside West Phoenix. The teachers wanted to give their kids hope.

Just getting them to the Santa Barbara contest in June with a robot would be an accomplishment, Cameron thought. He and Ledge had to gather a group of students who, in four months, could raise money, build a robot, and learn how to pilot it. They had no idea they were about to assemble the perfect team.

"We should use glass syntactic flotation foam [a lightweight foam that can stand the pressure of very deep water]," Cristian said excitedly at that first meeting. "It's got a really high compressive strength."

Cameron and Ledge looked at each other. Now they had their genius.

---

diminutive *(adj.)* tiny or very small
compressive *(adj.)* tending to squeeze together

NAVIGATING TEXT

Reading a Magazine Article

Review pages 132–133. <u>Underline</u> the subheads.

- What do the subheads tell you about Lorenzo and Cristian?

_____
_____
_____
_____

COMPREHENSION

Make Inferences

Review the third and fifth paragraphs on page 132. What impact did joining the team have on Lorenzo?

_____
_____
_____
_____
_____
_____
_____

- (Circle) two details you used to make this inference.

21 SMALL GROUPS/INDEPENDENT

COLLABORATE

Design Draw or describe your own idea for an underwater robot. What functions would your robot serve?

COMMUNICATE

Discuss and Write With a partner, discuss the qualities a team must have to be successful. Make some notes. Then write a few paragraphs describing a successful team.

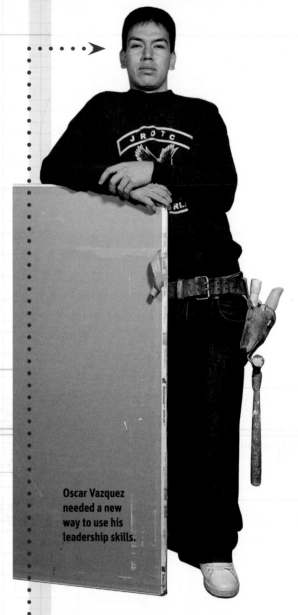

Oscar Vazquez needed a new way to use his leadership skills.

Born Leader

Oscar Vazquez was a born leader. A senior, he'd been in ROTC since ninth grade and was planning on a career in the military. But when he called to schedule a recruitment meeting at the end of his junior year, the officer in charge told him he was ineligible for military service. Because he was undocumented—his parents had brought him to the U.S. from Mexico without proper immigration papers—he couldn't join, wouldn't get any scholarships, and had to start figuring out what else to do with his life. Oscar felt aimless until he heard about the robot club from Ledge, who was teaching his senior biology seminar. Maybe, he thought, engineering could offer him a future.

ROTC had trained Oscar well: he knew how to **motivate** people. He made sure that all of his team members were in the room and focused when he contacted experts to explain tough science concepts. He also helped persuade a handful of local businesses to donate money to the team. Oscar and his team raised a total of about $800.

Teamwork

Now it was up to Cristian and Lorenzo to figure out what to do with the newfound resources. They spoke with Luis Aranda, who was now the fourth member of the team. Luis was the tether man, responsible for the pickup and release of what would be a 100-pound robot. The conversation resulted in Luis going to a hardware store to buy PVC pipe. Despite the donations, they were still on a tight budget. Cristian would have to keep dreaming about glass syntactic flotation foam; PVC pipe was the best they could afford.

But PVC had benefits. The air inside the pipe would create buoyancy as well as provide a waterproof housing for wiring. Cristian calculated the volume of air inside the pipes and realized immediately that they'd need a ballast. He proposed housing the battery system on board, in a heavy waterproof case.

It was a bold idea. If they didn't have to run a power line down to the robot, their tether could be much thinner, making the robot more mobile. Since the competition required that their robot run through a series of seven exploration tasks, mobility was key. Most of the other teams wouldn't even consider putting their power supplies in the water. A leak could take the whole system down. But if they couldn't figure out how to waterproof their case, Cristian argued, then they shouldn't be in an underwater contest.

While other teams machined and welded metal frames, the guys broke out the rubber glue and began assembling the PVC pipe. They did the whole thing in one night, and dubbed their new creation Stinky. Lorenzo painted it garish shades of blue, red, and yellow to designate the functionality of **specific** pipes. Every inch of PVC had a clear purpose. It was the type of machine only an engineer would describe as beautiful.

Test Run

Carl Hayden Community High School doesn't have a swimming pool, so one weekend in May, after about six weeks of work in the classroom, the team took Stinky to a scuba training

---

tether *(n.)* a rope or chain that is used to tie something to something else
ballast *(n.)* a substance that provides stability

pool in downtown Phoenix. Luis lifted the machine up and gently placed it in the water. The team powered it up. Cristian had hacked together off-the-shelf joysticks, a motherboard, motors, and an array of onboard finger-sized video cameras, which now sent flickering images to black-and-white monitors on a folding picnic table. Using five small electric trolling motors, the robot could spin and tilt in any direction. To move smoothly, two drivers had to **coordinate** their commands. The first thing they did was smash the robot into a wall.

"This is good, this is good," Oscar kept repeating, buying himself a few seconds to come up with a positive spin. "Did you see how hard it hit the wall? This thing's got power. Once we figure out how to drive it, we'll be the fastest team there."

By early June, as the contest neared, the team had the hang of it. Stinky now buzzed through the water, dodging all obstacles. The drivers, Cristian and Oscar, could make the robot hover, spin in place, and angle up or down. They could send enough power to Stinky's small engines to pull Luis around the pool. They felt like they had a good shot at not placing last.

> **Summarize**
> Summarize the team's first test run.

As tether man, Luis Aranda was the muscles of the group.

FACING THE COMPETITION

The team arrived at the Olympic-size University of California at Santa Barbara pool on a sunny Thursday afternoon. The pool was concealed under a black tarp—the contest organizers didn't want the students to get a peek at the layout of the mission. Students from cities across the country—Miami, Florida; New Haven, Connecticut; Galveston, Texas; Long Beach, California; and half a dozen others—milled around the water's edge. The Carl Hayden teammates tried to hide their nervousness, but they were intimidated. Lorenzo had never seen so many white people in one place. He was also new to the Pacific Ocean. He had seen it for the first time several months earlier on a school trip to San Diego.

NAVIGATING TEXT

Reading a Magazine Article
What does the photo of Oscar tell you about him that the article doesn't mention?

_____

_____

_____

_____

COMPREHENSION

Make Inferences
Review the sixth paragraph on page 134. What do you think the author thinks about "Stinky"?

Ⓐ Stinky is badly designed.

Ⓑ Stinky is very high tech.

Ⓒ Stinky isn't pretty, but it's well-designed.

• (Circle) two examples that support this inference.

CRITICAL THINKING

Analyze
Review pages 134–135. What obstacles did the Carl Hayden team face and how did they overcome them?

_____

_____

_____

_____

_____

_____

_____

_____

• Draw a **check** ✓ next to the text that supports your response.

The Carl Hayden team poses for a photo with Stinky.

It still unnerved him to see so much water. He said it was incredible and terrifying at the same time.

Even though Lorenzo had never heard of their school—Massachusetts Institute of Technology (MIT)—the students from Cambridge, Massachusetts, scared him. There were 12 of them—six ocean-engineering students, four mechanical engineers, and two computer science majors. Their robot was small, densely packed, and had a large ExxonMobil sticker emblazoned on the side. The largest **corporation** in the U.S. had kicked in $5,000. Other donations brought the MIT team's total budget to $11,000.

As Luis hoisted Stinky to the edge of the practice side of the pool, Cristian heard repressed snickering. It didn't give him a good feeling. He was proud of his robot, but he could see that it looked like a budget car compared to the luxury sports cars around the pool. Luis had thought that Lorenzo's paint job was nice. Now it just looked clownish.

MIT Makes a Move

The first task of the contest was to withdraw 500 milliliters of fluid from a container 12 feet below the surface. Its only opening was a small, half-inch pipe fitted with a one-way valve. Though the

Carl Hayden team didn't know it, MIT had designed an **innovative** system of bladders and pumps to carry out this task. MIT's robot was supposed to land on the container, create a seal, and pump out the fluid. On three test runs in Boston, the system worked fast and flawlessly.

MIT's ROV motored smoothly down and quickly located the 5-gallon drum inside the plastic submarine mock-up at the bottom of the pool. But as the robot approached the container, its protruding mechanical arm hit a piece of the submarine frame, blocking it from going farther. They tried a different angle but still couldn't reach the drum. The robot wasn't small enough to slip past the gap in the frame, making their pump system useless. There was nothing they could do—they had to move on to the next assignment.

Next up was the Carl Hayden team. Luis slowly lowered Stinky into the water for their run. The robot careened wildly as it dived toward the bottom. Luis stood at the pool's edge, paying out the tether cable. Meanwhile, Cristian, Oscar, and Lorenzo monitored Stinky's descent on their video screens in the control tent.

"*Vámonos*, Cristian, this is it!" Oscar said, pushing his control too far forward. They were nervous and overcompensated for each other's joystick movements, causing Stinky to veer off course.

Finally, they settled down and reached the submarine. They saw the

> **repressed** *(adj.)* restrained or held in
> **protruding** *(adj.)* sticking out

drum and tried to steady the robot. Stinky had a bent copper nose, a bilge pump, and a dime-store balloon. First, they had to fit the nose into a half-inch pipe. Then they had to fill the balloon for exactly 20 seconds to get 500 milliliters of water. They had practiced dozens of times at the scuba pool in Phoenix, and it had taken them, on average, 10 minutes to stab the copper structure into the narrow tube. Now they had 30 minutes total to complete all seven tasks on the checklist.

It was up to Oscar and Cristian. They readjusted their grip on the joysticks and leaned into the monitors. Stinky hovered in front of the submarine framing that had frustrated the MIT team. Because Stinky's copper pipe was 18 inches long, it was able to reach the drum. The control tent was silent. Now that they were focused on the mission, both pilots relaxed and made almost imperceptibly small movements with their joysticks. Oscar tapped the control forward while Cristian gave a short backward blast on the vertical propellers. As Stinky floated forward a half inch, its rear raised up and the sampling pipe sank perfectly into the drum.

"*Díos mío,*" Oscar whispered, not fully believing what he saw.

Oscar backed Stinky out of the sub. They spun the robot around, piloted it back to Luis at the edge of the pool, and looked at the judges, who stood in the control tent behind them.

"Can we make a little noise?"

Cristian asked Pat Barrow, a NASA lab operations manager supervising the contest.

"Go on ahead," he replied.

Cristian started yelling, and all three ran out to hug Luis, who held the now-filled blue balloon. Luis stood there with a silly grin on his face while his friends danced around him.

And the Winner Is

The awards ceremony took place over dinner, and the Carl Hayden team was glad for that. They hadn't eaten well over the past two days, and even flavorless iceberg lettuce looked good to them. Their nerves had calmed. After completing all the required tasks, they decided that they had probably placed somewhere in the middle of the pack, maybe fourth or fifth overall. Privately, each of them was hoping for third.

The announcer took to the stage and leaned into the microphone. "The overall winner for the Marine Technology ROV Championship," he said, looking up at the crowd, "goes to Carl Hayden High School of Phoenix, Arizona!"

Lorenzo threw his arms into the air, and looked at Ledge, beaming with pride. Four teenagers from Phoenix did the unthinkable. They beat the team from MIT to win the competition. They beat the brightest minds in the country. ∎

> **Summarize**
> Summarize how the Carl Hayden team won.

COMPREHENSION

Make Inferences

Review the second paragraph on page 136. What inference can you make about the MIT team?

_____

_____

_____

_____

- **Underline** the words that helped you make this inference.

VOCABULARY/WORD ANALYSIS

Context Clues: Synonyms

Circle the word *imperceptibly* in the first paragraph on page 137. What does it mean?

_____

_____

21 **SMALL GROUPS/INDEPENDENT**

COLLABORATE

Negotiate Role-play a conversation between the Carl Hayden team and the corporation that funded the MIT team. Try to convince the funders to support the "underdog" in the upcoming year. List your reasons.

COMMUNICATE

React and Write Imagine you are one of the Carl Hayden team members. How would you feel after winning the competition? What are your hopes for the future? Make some notes. Then write a journal entry describing your thoughts and feelings.

W

READ ONLINE

expert space
Go to www.expert21.com/student to learn more about Robots; Automation.

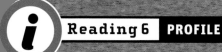
ROBO-LEGS

By Michael Marriott
From *New York Times Upfront*

Won the gold medal in the 100- and 200-meter races

Can run 100 meters in only 18 seconds, swims 20 laps

Competed in the 50-yard freestyle swim

C-Legs can cost more than $40,000 (for one)

Cameron Clapp's high-tech prosthetic legs allow him to compete in the Endeavor Games, a sporting event for disabled athletes.

For many years, amputees have relied on artificial arms and legs, known as prosthetics. Today, new high-tech prosthetic limbs provide increased mobility for many amputees and blur the line between humans and machines.

With his blond hair and megawatt smile, Cameron Clapp is in many ways the typical California teenager. There are, however, a few things that set him apart. For starters, this former skater boy is now making his way through life on a pair of shiny, state-of-the-art robotic legs.

"I make it look easy," he says.

Several years ago, Clapp was hit by a train. As a result, he lost both his legs above the knee and his right arm just short of his shoulder. Years of rehabilitation followed—as did a series of prosthetics, each more technologically advanced than the last. Now, Clapp is part of a new generation of people who are embracing breakthrough technologies as a means of overcoming their own bodies' limitations.

"I do have a lot of motivation and self-esteem," Clapp says. "But I might look at myself differently if technology was not on my side."

The technology he's referring to is a prosthetic device called the C-Leg, which was developed by a German company called Otto Bock HealthCare. The C-Leg contains sensors that monitor how the leg is being placed on terrain, as well as microprocessors that work to simulate a natural step. It literally does the walking for the walker. The technology, however, is not cheap; a single C-Leg can cost more than $40,000. But for many people—especially those who wish to lead a highly active lifestyle—the price is worth it.

66 ...I might look at myself differently if technology was not on my side. 99

The C-Legs have allowed Clapp to remain involved in athletics despite his condition. He has three different sets of specialized prosthetic legs: one for walking, one for running, and one for swimming. In June, he put all of them to use at the Endeavor Games in Edmond, Oklahoma—an annual sporting event for athletes with disabilities. There, Clapp competed in events like the 200-meter dash and the 50-yard freestyle swim.

rehabilitation *(n.)* the act of restoring to a former state
simulate *(v.)* to copy or imitate

NAVIGATING TEXT

Magazine Text Features

Draw a box around the caption on page 138. What do the caption and the photo tell you about Cameron Clapp?

_____
_____
_____
_____
_____
_____
_____
_____

VOCABULARY/WORD ANALYSIS

Context Clues: Synonyms

Circle the word *typical* in the first paragraph. Which word is the best synonym for *typical*?

☐ common   ☐ cheerful
☐ active   ☐ unusual

COMPREHENSION

Make Inferences

Review page 139. How might Cameron's self-image be affected if technology weren't so advanced? Explain.

_____
_____
_____
_____
_____
_____
_____
_____

• **Underline** the text that supports your response.

Man or Machine?

But increased mobility is only part of the story. Something more subtle, and possibly far-reaching, is also occurring: The line that has long separated human beings from the machines that assist them is blurring, as complex technologies become a visible part of the people who depend upon them.

Increasingly, amputees, especially young men like Clapp, are choosing not to hide their prosthetics under clothing as previous generations did. Instead, some of the estimated 1.2 million amputees in the United States proudly polish and decorate their electronic limbs for all to see.

Long an eerie theme in popular science fiction, the blending of humans with machines has often been presented as a sign of a soulless future, populated with flesh and metal cyborgs like the Terminator. But now major universities like Carnegie Mellon and the University of California at Berkeley, as well as private companies and the U.S. military, are all exploring ways in which people can be enhanced by strapping themselves into wearable robotics.

The boundaries between flesh and machine are disappearing, says Sherry Turkle, director of a group at the Massachusetts Institute of Technology that studies technology's impact on humanity. "The notion that your leg is a machine part and that it is exposed is becoming comfortable."

While some users are eager to display their prosthetic marvels, others like them to appear more human. Besides selling prosthetics, Liberating Technologies in Holliston, Massachusetts, for one, offers 19 kinds of silicone sleeves for artificial limbs to make them seem more natural.

> **" The notion that your leg is a machine part ... is becoming comfortable. "**

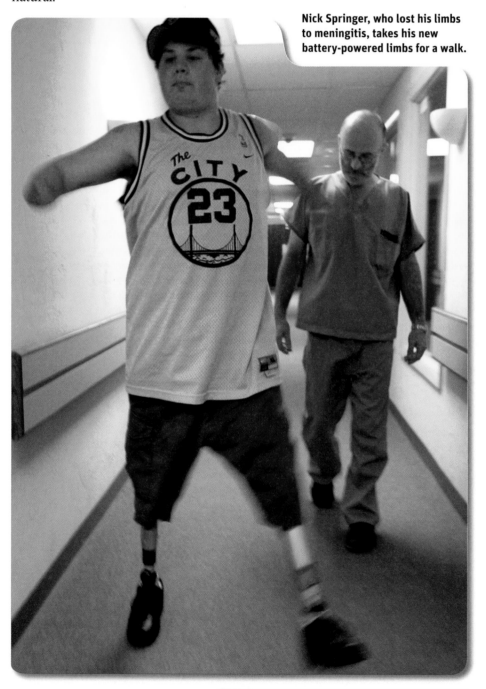

Nick Springer, who lost his limbs to meningitis, takes his new battery-powered limbs for a walk.

---

enhanced *(adj.)* made better or greater
notion *(n.)* an idea

A specialist makes adjustments to Springer's prosthetic leg.

"There are two things that are important: one is functionality and the other is cosmetic," says William Hanson, president of Liberating Technologies. "Various people weigh those differences differently. There are trade-offs."

But many young people—especially those who have been using personal electronics since childhood—are comfortable recharging their limbs' batteries in public and plugging their prosthetics into their computers to adjust the software, Hanson says.

Nick Springer, 20, a student at Eckerd College in St. Petersburg, Florida, who lost his arms and legs to meningitis when he was 14, recalls doing just that at a party when the lithium-ion batteries for his legs went dead.

"I usually get 30 hours out of them before I have to charge them again," he says. "But I didn't charge them up the day before."

Terminator Legs

When his legs ran out of power, he spent most of his time sitting on a couch talking to people while his legs were plugged into an electrical outlet nearby. According to Springer, no one at the party seemed to care, and his faith in his high-tech appendages appears unfazed. "I love my Terminator legs," he says.

Springer also remembers going to see *Star Wars: Episode III—Revenge of the Sith* with his father. While he liked the movie, he found the final scenes in which Anakin Skywalker loses his arms and legs in a lightsaber battle and is rebuilt with fully functional prosthetics to become the infamous Darth Vader a little far-fetched.

"We have a long way to go before we get anything like that," he says. "But look how far humanity has come in the past decade. Who knows? The hardest part is getting the ball rolling. We pretty much got it rolling." ∎

---

cosmetic *(adj.)* relating to beauty
appendages *(n.)* protruding parts of the body

COMPREHENSION

Make Inferences
Review pages 140–141. Why might older and younger people feel differently about using prosthetic limbs that clearly look like electronic devices?

_____
_____
_____
_____
_____
_____
_____
_____
_____
_____

NAVIGATING TEXT

Magazine Text Features
Draw a box around the subhead on page 140 and review the section.

• Why is the subhead written as a question?

_____
_____
_____
_____
_____
_____
_____
_____
_____
_____
_____

READ ONLINE

expert space
Go to **www.expert21.com/student** to learn more about Artificial Body Parts; Prostheses; Artificial Organs.

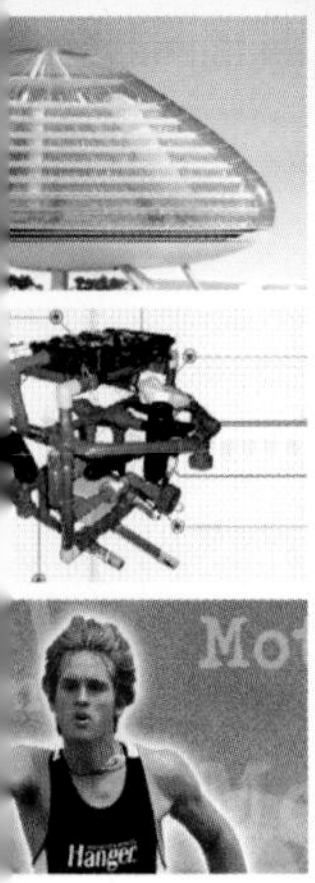

Think Across Texts

Organize and Synthesize ···

1. Complete this chart using information from "Welcome to the Future," "La Vida Robot," and "Robo-Legs."

	Based on what you have read in these selections, predict how technology will change the future.
"Welcome to the Future"	
"La Vida Robot"	
"Robo-Legs"	

Compare and Evaluate ··

2. Think about Lorenzo Santillan from "La Vida Robot" and Cameron Clapp from "Robo-Legs." How are their stories alike? How are they different? Fill in the chart below.

Lorenzo	Both	Cameron

3. In your opinion, which of the three selections does the best job of inspiring future scientists and inventors? Give specific reasons for your choices.

_____

_____

_____

_____

4. All three selections include photos and illustrations. For each selection, choose one piece of art you found particularly interesting and explain why it appeals to you.

"Welcome to the Future": _____

_____

_____

"La Vida Robot": _____

_____

_____

"Robo-Legs": _____

_____

_____

Discuss and Write ····················

5. With a partner, discuss how the three readings in "Technology to the Rescue" show technology's impact on people. Take notes. Then use your notes to write a response to the question: *How is technology paving the way for a better tomorrow?*

Apply Word Knowledge

Word Lab

1. Order these. Put the following items in order from the least to the most **hazardous**, with 1 being the least and 3 being the most hazardous.

___sunbathing without sunblock

___jaywalking across a busy road

___running very fast on the sidewalk

2. Describe them. Give an example of each.

• a device or machine that is **mobile**

_____

• an object that is useful because of its **compact** size

_____

• a **corporation** whose products you use

_____

• an invention you consider **innovative**

_____

3. Check it. What kind of work does an **engineer** do on a typical day?

❏ researches ancient history

❏ designs and builds machines

❏ flies futuristic machines

❏ studies marine mammals

4. Think about it. What would you say to **motivate** your teammates before a competition, knowing that there are many **obstacles** facing you?

_____

_____

5. Select one. If you decide to **accommodate** someone's request, you

Ⓐ deny the request.   Ⓒ agree to the request.

Ⓑ change the request.   Ⓓ ignore the request.

6. Finish them. Complete the sentences below with the words **efficient, coordinate, engineers,** and **sponsor.**

Several corporations have just announced

that they will _____ a competition

to design a more _____ solar panel.

_____ from all over are participating.

If we _____ with some of the top

brains, perhaps we'll have a shot at winning!

Word Analysis

7. Read the passage below and answer the questions.

> The engineers spent years perfecting the rocket's complex technology. Despite the many setbacks they experienced, they appeared completely confident that their efforts would pay off in the end. If they felt uncertain at all about the elaborate machine they were constructing, they did not express it.

Use context clues to locate a synonym for *building*. Write the synonym on the line below.

_____

What is an antonym for *uncertain*?

_____

What is a synonym for *complex*?

_____

Design: Visual Aids

CAREER CONNECTION

Science, Technology, Engineering, and Mathematics
www.careerclusters.org

Go to 21 ToolKit **Expert File 6.30** to learn more about careers in engineering.

When you give a presentation, you can design a visual aid to quickly and easily share complicated information. Visual aids include diagrams, maps, graphs, and illustrations.

Diagram of Text Messaging

▶ See how the design of this visual aid can help readers understand how text messaging works.

How Text Messaging Works

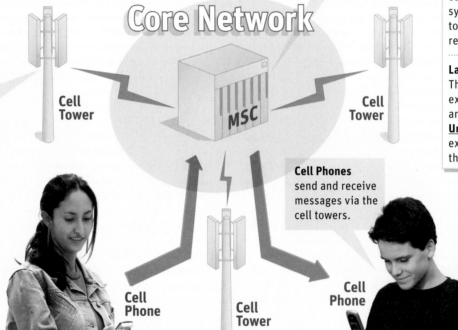

Mobile Switch Centers receive the signals from and send signals to the cell tower.

Cell Towers send signals from cell phones to and from the mobile switch center and other cell phones.

Cell Phones send and receive messages via the cell towers.

Core Network

Cell Tower

MSC

Cell Tower

Cell Phone

Cell Tower

Cell Phone

MARK IT

Content. The visual includes illustrations that show that the Mobile Switch Center can receive messages with many cell towers. Circle the symbols the designer uses to indicate sending or receiving signals.

Labels and explanations. The labels and explanations are short and easy to understand. Underline the words that explain the purpose of this diagram.

[Here's How] ▶ Follow these steps to design a visual aid:

Step 1 **Identify your purpose.** The information you want to show will determine the type of visual aid you use. For example, technical diagrams, like the one above, show how things work and the parts of an object. Step-by-step diagrams show how to do something. Flowcharts show the relationship between things or ideas. Choose a type of visual aid that communicates your purpose. Write a title that explains your purpose.

Step 2 **Break it down and simplify.** Visual aids include only the major details. Before creating a visual aid, ask yourself: What are the most important elements, parts, or steps? Make a list. Then circle the most important information.

Step 3 **Create the visual aid.** Clearly and simply label each element and add any explanations that are necessary to communicate information. Use color, if you feel that would make the information clearer.

Apply: Design a Visual Aid

▶ **Follow the steps to make a diagram that explains something you know or can do. It can be as simple as a family tree or map of your room, or as complex as how to do a skateboarding trick.**

1. **Identify your purpose.** What information will your visual aid show? You may choose simply to show details of what something is, or you may want to show how to do something or how something works. Name the type of visual aid you will create.

   _____

   Write a title that explains your purpose.

   TITLE: _____

2. **Break it down.** List all the parts or steps involved. Circle the most important parts and steps.

   _____

   _____

   _____

   _____

   _____

   _____

3. **Create the visual aid.** In the space below or on a separate sheet of paper, create your visual aid. You can use one of the models to the right as a guide. You can also create your visual aid on a computer.

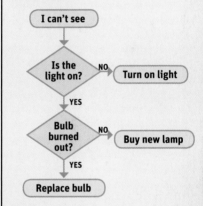
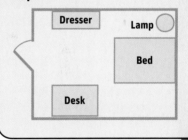

Problem-and-Solution Essay

A problem-and-solution essay explains a problem and offers the best solution. Problem-and-solution writing is used in newspaper editorials, business proposals, government reports, and in many other places.

In this writing workshop, you will write a problem-and-solution essay about a problem people may face in the future and come up with a solution for it.

Example: A do-it-yourself Web site suggests an easy way to solve common problems.

> Laptop computers are getting cheaper and more popular. But have you ever worked with a laptop on your lap? The machine gets too hot. It doesn't feel good to you. And the machine doesn't like it either—the cooling fan has to work harder. So you could buy a $30 laptop stand. Or you could put an empty loose-leaf notebook under the laptop. It lets air circulate under the machine and keeps everything nice and cool.

Traits of Writing

Traits of Writing is a model for assessing and teaching. The traits work within the writing process to support revision and editing.

Each puzzle piece below represents one of the **traits** that define good writing.

Each trait is made up of four **key qualities**. The trait you will focus on in this lesson is Voice.

KEY QUALITIES

Establishing a Tone

▶ Conveying the Purpose

Creating a Connection to the Audience

Taking Risks to Create Voice

▶ **Analyze Features** A strong problem-and-solution essay has the following features:

FEATURE	✏ MARK IT
Look for these features in the Student Model on the next page.	Mark the features as you read the Student Model.
1. An **introduction** that states the problem. (Organization)	Underline the problem that the writer is pointing out.
2. Solutions that the writer believes will help fix the problem. (Ideas)	Circle the solutions that the writer is suggesting.
3. Evidence (experiences, logic, statistics) that supports the solutions. (Ideas)	Check ✓ evidence that supports the solutions.
4. Focus Trait: Voice Language that helps convey the author's purpose.	Star ★ language that conveys purpose.
5. A strong **conclusion** that sums up the problem and how to solve it. (Organization)	Draw a box around the summary in the conclusion.

▶ Read Javier's problem-and-solution essay about solving a problem in the future.

STUDENT MODEL

A New Age for Internet Privacy
By Javier de la Uz

The problem started at the beginning of the millennium. People started posting pictures and profiles online. Next, they connected to friends. They posted all kinds of personal information. Today, some people are faced with electronic stalkers and online bullies. Even colleges do online searches about you with your application. This has created a big problem—people have no more privacy on the Internet.

To solve this problem, there are several new technologies that will need to be developed. One is a program that keeps track of your personal information for you. This tracker would allow people to see who was searching for information about them. People could get lists of people, organizations, and companies that were interested in them. In that way, they could watch the watchers.

However, just knowing who is infringing on your privacy is not really enough. Another solution could be a digital eraser. As a result of this invention, people will no longer have to be embarrassed by a silly video they once uploaded or a thoughtless comment left on someone's page. Your electronic history could be wiped away.

But that's not all. Internet users of today need an online "invisibility cloak." With the cloak turned on, you will leave no trace on any other computers or servers. Not all sites will accept you if you are operating with a cloak, because they rely on marketing information for income. That's part of what keeps the Internet free. But it is a great tool if you do not want things like instant messages to fall into the wrong hands.

After all, no one really wants a complete record of everything they've ever said, done, or bought, do they? Most people want some privacy to learn, and grow, and make mistakes. In the past, that was not an issue. But the digital age creates new problems. We must pursue solutions that will make privacy real again.

▶ Read Javier's notes about how he worked on his problem-and-solution essay.

ORGANIZATION

At first, my paragraphs seemed disjointed. So, I went back and added transitions like "But that's not all" to make sure that my paragraphs made sense from one to the next.

VOICE

At first, I didn't tell the reader what I thought until the second paragraph. When I was revising, I decided to make my point of view clear right away in the first paragraph and I revised it to sound more like me.

▶ Analyze how Javier developed and organized his ideas. Fill in the missing parts of the chart.

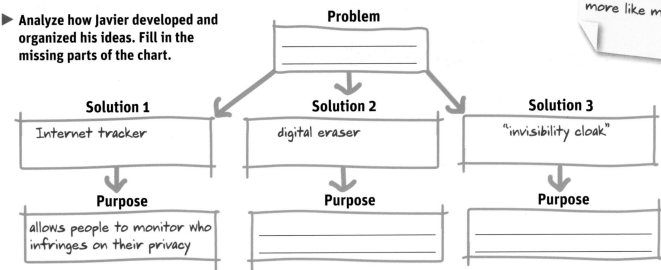

Problem
_____

Solution 1
Internet tracker

Solution 2
digital eraser

Solution 3
"invisibility cloak"

Purpose
allows people to monitor who infringes on their privacy

Purpose
_____

Purpose
_____

How Do I Get Started?

Your Topic:

Assignment: Problem-and-Solution Essay

Purpose: To propose a solution to some future problem

Audience: Readers of your blog

Ideas: Focusing the Topic

Focus your topic to cover only what you need to say. Use these Think-Abouts as you work on your ideas:

• Have I zeroed in on one small part of a bigger idea?

• Can I tell you my idea in a simple sentence?

• Have I chosen the information that captures my idea best?

• Have I thought deeply about what the reader will need to know? *For example, the Student Model explains the limitations of one solution—the "invisibility cloak" will make it difficult to get into most sites.*

○ KEY QUALITIES

Finding a Topic

▶ **Focusing the Topic**

Developing the Topic

Using Details

▶ **Model** Go back to Reading 2, "Exposed to the Max," in this workshop. State the topic of that reading selection in a single sentence.

▶ **Practice** Think about how an aspect of life is changing and what challenges it presents. Now focus your topic by stating this problem in a single sentence.

Future Challenge: _____

Specific Problem: _____

_____

▶ **Plan Your Essay** Use the outline below to plan your essay. Revise as necessary.

Problem

_____

_____

Solution 1

_____

_____

Solution 2

_____

_____

Solution 3

_____

_____

Purpose

_____

_____

Purpose

_____

_____

Purpose

_____

_____

How Do I Get Organized?

ORGANIZATION

Organization: Using Sequence Words and Transition Words

Good writers show sequences and transition in their essays. Ask yourself these Think-Abouts as you work on your organization.

- Have I used sequence words such as *later, then,* and *meanwhile? Look at the first paragraph in the model for examples.*

- Did I use a variety of transition words such as *however, because, also,* and *for instance? Look at the third and fourth paragraphs in the model for examples.*

- Have I shown how ideas connect from sentence to sentence?

- Does my organization make sense from paragraph to paragraph?

KEY QUALITIES

Creating the Lead

▶ **Using Sequence Words and Transition Words**

Structuring the Body

Ending With a Sense of Resolution

▶ **Model** Go back to Reading 1, "The Last Dog," and see if you can find examples of sequence and transition words.

▶ **Practice** Use sequence words and transition words as you rewrite a paragraph from the Student Model.

_____

_____

_____

_____

_____

▶ **Write a Paragraph** Practice using sequence and transition words as you write a first draft of one of your paragraphs here.

_____

_____

_____

_____

_____

▶ **Draft Your Essay** Write a first draft.

Quick Check

▶ Check how well you used sequence words and transition words in your essay. Have a writing partner rate it, too.

6 = Expert   **3** = Making Strides

5 = Well Done   **2** = On the Way

4 = Almost There   **1** = Getting Started

Organization

1. Have I used sequence words such as *later, then,* and *meanwhile?*
  Self ① ② ③ ④ ⑤ ⑥
  Partner ① ② ③ ④ ⑤ ⑥

2. Did I use a variety of transition words such as *however, because, also,* and *for instance?*
  Self ① ② ③ ④ ⑤ ⑥
  Partner ① ② ③ ④ ⑤ ⑥

3. Have I shown how ideas connect from sentence to sentence?
  Self ① ② ③ ④ ⑤ ⑥
  Partner ① ② ③ ④ ⑤ ⑥

4. Does my organization make sense from paragraph to paragraph?
  Self ① ② ③ ④ ⑤ ⑥
  Partner ① ② ③ ④ ⑤ ⑥

How Do I Convey My Purpose to Create a Strong Voice?

FOCUS TRAIT

Voice: Conveying the Purpose

Good writers understand their purpose for writing and make sure that it is clear to the reader in their final drafts. Use these Think-Abouts to convey your purpose in your essay.

- Is the purpose of my writing clear?
- Does my point of view come through?
- Is this the right tone for this kind of writing? *The writer of the Student Model keeps a sincere and serious tone to show that he is talking about a big problem.*
- Have I used strong voice throughout this piece?

VOICE

◊ KEY QUALITIES

Establishing a Tone

▶ Conveying the Purpose

Creating a Connection to the Audience

Taking Risks to Create Voice

▶ **Model** Go back to Reading 6, "Robo-Legs," and decide what the author's tone is and how it relates to his purpose.

▶ Read Ruth Culham's writing blog below to get advice on improving your writing.

Ask the Expert: Ruth Culham

Ruth Culham, an award-winning teacher, is the author of *6+1 Traits of Writing: The Complete Guide for Middle School* and other books on writing.

Q & A: Conveying the Purpose

Pricilla Purpose **Writes:**

> I hate our lunches at school. They taste like gross cardboard. I want a salad bar and soup but I'm told, "No. Forget it." Someone needs to listen to us kids. Do you have any ideas for how to get the attention of the people who make the gross lunches?

Pricilla Purpose, you may find you have more success resolving the problem by dialing down your strident voice. They need to know how you feel, but you don't want to insult them. Try a more thoughtful and sincere voice that includes some practical solutions that show you've done some work to help solve the problem. Your salad bar may be closer to reality than you think!

Posted by: Ruth Culham | December 22 at 04:30 P.M.

▶ **Practice** Read the sample paragraphs and think about which one better conveys the author's purpose.

<u>Underline</u> phrases and words that communicate purpose.

(Circle) the passage in which the author's purpose is expressed more effectively.

Sample 1: Cheating Online

Internet cheating is just out of control and ridiculous. Who thinks they need to cheat to get ahead? People with no morals, that's who. Plus, it's silly to think that teachers won't catch you when you copy and paste stuff from Wikipedia. People who cheat are really, really annoying. It's a serious problem.

Sample 2: Cheating Online

Internet cheating is a problem at our school that must be addressed. Three of my classmates had to rewrite their research papers when the teacher discovered that they had copied from the Web. However, it's unfair to expect students to know about plagiarism if they are not taught about it and shown how not to break the rules.

▶ **Revise** Now use voice to convey the purpose for your writing. Choose a paragraph from your first draft and revise it below. Remember to use words and phrases that make your purpose clear and give your point of view.

_____

_____

_____

_____

_____

_____

_____

_____

_____

Quick Check

▶ Check your essay for how well you conveyed the purpose of your writing. Then have a writing partner rate it, too.

6 = Expert   **3** = Making Strides

5 = Well Done   **2** = On the Way

4 = Almost There   **1** = Getting Started

Voice

1. Is the purpose of my writing clear?
Self ① ② ③ ④ ⑤ ⑥
Partner ① ② ③ ④ ⑤ ⑥

2. Does my point of view come through?
Self ① ② ③ ④ ⑤ ⑥
Partner ① ② ③ ④ ⑤ ⑥

3. Is this the right tone for this kind of writing?
Self ① ② ③ ④ ⑤ ⑥
Partner ① ② ③ ④ ⑤ ⑥

4. Have I used strong voice throughout this piece?
Self ① ② ③ ④ ⑤ ⑥
Partner ① ② ③ ④ ⑤ ⑥

Revise With Technology Use the dictionary feature in your word processing program to be sure your words say exactly what you mean.

How Can I Finish a Great Paper?

Grammar: Using Collective Nouns

Collective nouns are made up of members that can act as a single unit so they usually agree with a verb in the singular.

Example: *class* and *team*

Possessive nouns are nouns that own or have something. Show ownership with **collective nouns** by adding an *'s* to the end of the noun.

Example: the committee's decision

▶ **Practice** Rewrite this paragraph correctly below.

In the future, cars' may be very different. Imagine a fleet's that hover in the air or a model that drives itself. Would a group's of your friends rides with no driver?

_____

_____

_____

Mechanics: Using Capitals for Proper Nouns and Apostrophes for Possessives

Proper nouns are written with capital letters.

Example: Ugo Space Travel's solar system tours are the best.

Possessive nouns have an *'s*. If they end in *s*, they just have an apostrophe at the end.

Example: The engines' roar could be heard from Suzie's front porch.

▶ **Practice** Rewrite this paragraph correctly below.

When the seattle science centers new exhibit was completed, designer dr. evan jones work was on display. Dr. jones was eager for mr. blacks reaction to the exhibit.

_____

_____

_____

► **Proofread** Find and correct any errors in your essay. Put a check beside the types of errors you find. Then write three corrected sentences below.

❏ collective nouns

❏ proper nouns and possessive nouns

❏ fragments and run-ons

❏ end punctuation

❏ misspellings

❏ other: _____

1. _____

_____

2. _____

_____

3. _____

_____

PRESENTATION

PUBLISH/PRESENT

► **Write Your Final Draft** Now, using your edited draft, begin creating a final draft for presentation.

Use word processing software to type your final draft. Make sure to format your margins and spacing according to your teacher's request.

Check your final draft against the Traits of Writing Scoring Guide on page 338–341 and correct any errors before you present it.

► **Beyond the Classroom** Extend your finished problem-and-solution essay.

List two ideas for photos that could illustrate your problem-and-solution essay:

_____

_____

Look online for a blog, message board, magazine, or newspaper where you could publish your problem-and-solution essay.

List two places where you could upload or share your problem-and-solution essay for publication.

_____

_____

Quick Check

► **Check how well you used conventions. Then have a writing partner rate it, too.**

6 = Expert   **3** = Making Strides

5 = Well Done   **2** = On the Way

4 = Almost There **1** = Getting Started

Conventions

1. Did I use collective nouns correctly?
   Self   ① ② ③ ④ ⑤ ⑥
   Partner ① ② ③ ④ ⑤ ⑥

2. Did I capitalize proper nouns and use apostrophes with possessives?
   Self   ① ② ③ ④ ⑤ ⑥
   Partner ① ② ③ ④ ⑤ ⑥

3. Did I follow the rules of punctuation?
   Self   ① ② ③ ④ ⑤ ⑥
   Partner ① ② ③ ④ ⑤ ⑥

4. Is the spelling in the essay correct?
   Self   ① ② ③ ④ ⑤ ⑥
   Partner ① ② ③ ④ ⑤ ⑥

READ ONLINE

expert space
Go to **www.expert21.com/student** to find photographs and other visuals to illustrate your problem-and-solution essay.

You have learned about new developments in technology and how they will affect the future. Now, apply your expert reading strategies to the following article about futuristic fashion. ▶

FUTURISTIC FASHION GETS SMART

By Mark Tutton for CNN

LONDON, England (CNN)—Is that your dress ringing? It could be, if you're wearing an M-Dress—a silk garment that doubles as a mobile phone. Produced by U.K. firm CuteCircuit, the M-Dress works with a standard SIM card. When the dress rings, you raise your hand to your head to answer the call.

This futuristic fusion of fashion and technology is becoming more common as clothes designers are increasingly adding electronics to their garments.

Jane McCann, director of Smart Clothes and Wearable Technology at the University of Wales, says the clothing and electronics industries are collaborating in an unprecedented way—what she describes as "a new industrial revolution."

McCann predicts that in the next 10 years clothes will have all kinds of built-in functionality. "A garment might have devices on it to help you find your way somewhere, or to tell you how fit you are. It could tell you where someone is to help you find them, or tell you what's on at a museum or club," she told CNN.

She says that the sports and fitness industries have led the way in wearable technology; they've produced shoes with built-in pedometers and activewear with iPod controls. However, the fashion industry is currently lagging behind.

"Wearable technology is coming through into useful everyday clothing more than it is on the catwalk. The catwalk still treats

No need to carry a cell phone when you're wearing this dress—just lift your arm to answer calls.

collaborating *(v.)* working together to produce something
catwalk *(n.)* the runway where models show off new fashions

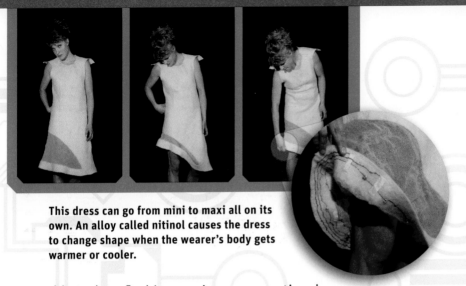

This dress can go from mini to maxi all on its own. An alloy called nitinol causes the dress to change shape when the wearer's body gets warmer or cooler.

Reflect

1. Circle all the expert strategies you used while reading this article.

   A. Summarize

   B. Question

   C. Other: _____

   D. Other: _____

2. Use the letters above to label where in the article you applied the expert strategies.

3. Select one expert strategy you used. Explain why you applied that strategy where you did.

   _____

   _____

   _____

RESEARCH ONLINE

 expert space
Go to **www.expert21.com/student** to learn more about Fashion Design; Industrial Revolution; Inventions.

wearable tech as flashing earrings or sensational things," McCann says.

While high fashion may be slow to adopt practical technology, designers have been quick to embrace technology in order to create dazzling new styles. Hussein Chalayan, twice British Designer of the Year, has used his shows to experiment with dresses that glow or emit spectacular red lasers.

Others, like Angel Chang, have produced beautiful designs using special inks that change color when you touch or breathe on them. Meanwhile Montreal's XS Labs has used a shape-memory alloy called nitinol to produce extraordinary dresses that change shape while you wear them.

As well as functionality, McCann predicts that mass customization will become a major trend in clothing. "You can already go into a sizing booth and get measurements of your size and shape. Perhaps you could store that information on a card and that could be used to customize clothing."

"In theory, if you've got technology that's cutting out garments one at a time, it could produce clothes informed by your own size requirements," she says.

But mass customization could extend beyond getting the perfect fit—you might also be able to customize the technology in your clothes.

McCann explains, "You might want built-in controls for an MP3 player but I might like heart-beat monitoring. I'd like mine to have a digital print on the sleeve but my friend wants a picture of her boyfriend on the back. Some of that could happen in the next 10 years." ■

Become a walking light show when you don this high fashion laser dress.

alloy *(n.)* a metal made by mixing two or more different metals
customization *(n.)* the practice of designing products to suit an individual's needs

PROJECT
RESEARCH

Invention ZONE

THE SITUATION

Every day presents annoying little problems. For example, maybe you've slept through your alarm . . . again. Why doesn't someone invent a clock that just won't give up until you're out of bed? In fact, why can't that someone be you?

The contest: Your school has announced a contest for young inventors called "Invention Zone." It calls for students to identify a problem and solve it by reinventing an everyday item, such as an alarm clock or a spoon.

YOUR CHALLENGE

With a group of classmates, you will figure out an invention to make life a little easier, and enter it in the contest. To devise your invention, you will

- read the contest rules.

- examine a gallery of inventions created by kids and read tips for student inventors.

- brainstorm problems.

- plan your invention.

- complete an entry form.

CAREER CONNECTION **Science, Technology, Engineering, and Mathematics**
www.careerclusters.org

Go to **21** **Tool**Kit **Expert File 6.30** to learn more about careers in engineering.

1 Read the Rules
With your group, read the contest rules shown below and underline the important information. Upon what two qualities will your entry be judged?

_____

_____

2 Examine the Invention Gallery
Review the selections you've read in this workshop to recall the amazing things people have invented. Then use the **Resource Bank** on the following pages and resources from **Expert Space** to learn about other great inventions.

CONTEST RULES Invention ZONE

Welcome to **Invention Zone**, the contest for young inventors in which everyday items are improved or reinvented for new uses. Contestants must agree to the following:

1. Students must be under 16 and live within the boundaries of the school district.

2. Students must work in teams of three to five.

3. Each group is limited to one entry. Entry materials will not be returned. Please retain a copy for your records.

4. Entries that do not include all the required information and/or do not adhere to the rules will be disqualified.

5. Entries are judged on creativity and the usefulness of the invention. The students' age and experience are taken into consideration.

6. Each group will be required to submit an entry form and a sketch or model of the invention. The invention must add to or manipulate an everyday item for the purpose of solving a specific problem.

3 Brainstorm Possibilities

With your group, think of everyday items that could be improved. For example:

- an alarm clock that doesn't wake you
- umbrellas that blow inside out
- movie popcorn that runs out of salt and butter halfway down the container

Use a chart like this one to capture ideas as you brainstorm together. **21 Tool**Kit **Expert File 2.1** has brainstorming tips.

Types of Items	Products Needing Improvement
Household Items	
Sports Equipment	
Makeup	
Tools	

4 Plan Your Invention

As a group, decide which of your ideas you will work on, and place a star by it in your chart. Then use the following questions to help you plan your invention. Remember that you have to reinvent an everyday item, not create something from scratch. And don't worry about how you will manufacture your item—the challenge is to come up with a good idea, not an actual product. Use **21 Tool**Kit **Expert File 2.5** to learn to think like an inventor.

- *What's wrong with the item now?*
- *What do we want it to do better, or to do in addition to what it does now?*
- *How can we add to or manipulate the item to accomplish our goals?*

5 Enter the Contest

Look at the model entry in the **Resource Bank**. Notice how the contestants explained the problem, described how the invention would solve it, and drew a sketch of the proposed invention.

Now work with your group to fill out the entry form below. Remember that you will be judged on your invention's creativity and usefulness.

ENTRY FORM  Invention ZONE

Names of entrants _____

School name/Grade _____

What item are you improving? _____
_____
_____

What problem are you solving? _____

Name of the invention _____
_____

Rationale for the invention (include how it works)
_____
_____
_____
_____
_____
_____
_____

Draw a picture or diagram of your invention.

INVENTOR PROFILES
Source: Magazine Article
Date: November 2008

BRIGHT IDEAS FROM KID INVENTORS

One day, 16-year-old Lisa Marie Wright and her family returned home to find that a candle had been left burning all day. The Columbus, Ohio, teen saw the potential danger. So she devised the Auto-Off Candle, a candle that burns itself out to prevent fires. For her invention, Lisa was inducted into the National Gallery for America's Young Inventors.

AUTO-OFF CANDLE

Lisa Marie Wright's candle allows users to control the time of the burn.

E-Z SHOVE At 13, Jamila Jordan created a prize-winning snow shovel that helps people protect their backs. Thanks to its bent handle and wheels, a shoveler doesn't have to bend over. Jamila got the idea for this device while clearing the walk of her Washington, D.C., home. Jamila says, "I think it's important for other teens not to underestimate themselves. I didn't think I was going anywhere with my invention, but I did."

E-Z SHOVE

Jamila Jordan came up with a "wheely" great idea!

Chris Haas, a native of Murietta, California, was in third grade when inspiration struck. "I stepped onto the basketball courts, and I noticed that a lot of other kids did not know how to shoot correctly," says Chris, now 18. "The solution for this was to paint my hands on an ordinary basketball in the correct position to shoot it, and thus the Hands-On Basketball was born."

HANDS-ON BASKETBALL

Chris Haas's invention is sold in stores.

> **Underline** the features of these inventions that are improvements on older versions.

FACTS ABOUT INVENTING
Source: Invention Contest Web site
Date Accessed: February 23, 2009

Home   Information   **Resources**   Invention News   Contact Us

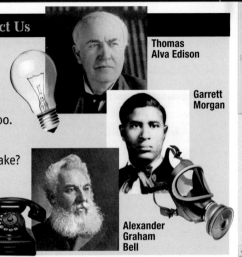

Thomas
Alva Edison

Garrett
Morgan

Alexander
Graham
Bell

5 TIPS FOR STUDENT INVENTORS

1. Survey friends and family for ideas. Ask: What bothers you during your daily routine? What would make your life easier? Answer the questions yourself, too.
2. Read stories about great inventors. How did they get their ideas?
3. Evaluate your idea: Who would use it? Is it practical? Would it cost a lot to make?
4. Make a sketch of your idea.
5. Name your invention by using words that rhyme or have alliteration, your own name, or descriptive words.

▶ **Underline** two ways you can get ideas for this contest.

ENTRY FORM — Invention ZONE

Names of entrants Michael Jones, Jordan Kurczewski, Alicia Herrera

School name/Grade Horace Greeley Middle School, Grade 8

What item are you improving? a trash bin

What problem are you solving? When a trash bin is filled with garbage or cans or bottles for recycling, it can be too heavy for one person to haul outside.

Name of the invention The Garbage-mobile

Rationale for the invention (include how it works)

Not only does the Garbage-mobile make recycling easier, it is made mostly of recycled materials! This garbage transportation device is made of a discarded wooden cabinet door, on which is attached an old skateboard. On the other side of the door is attached a discarded metal chair frame. This is the top of the Garbage-mobile. A large plastic trash bin fits snugly into the chair frame, making the device hold steady. The trash bin's handles become the handles of the Garbage-mobile. Now, with a minimum of lifting, you can transport your trash and/or recycled materials wherever you wish.

Draw a picture or diagram of your invention.

▶ Rate this invention idea below on a scale of 1–10 (1 being bad, 10 being great) based on the two contest criteria, creativity and usefulness. Circle the score you'd give:

Creativity: 1   2   3   4   5   6   7   8   9   10
Usefulness: 1   2   3   4   5   6   7   8   9   10

Now explain your rating. _____

_____

Strategy Check

Use your knowledge and strategies from the workshop to answer these questions.

COMPREHENSION

Problem and Solution

1. Complete the chart to show the problem Cameron Clapp faced and how it was solved.

Problem	Solution

Make Inferences

2. Based on what you read in "The Last Dog," "Exposed to the Max," and "Virus," you can infer that

- (A) technology and science are continually improving.

- (B) technology has many pros and cons.

- (C) young people are smart in their use of technology.

LITERARY ANALYSIS

Plot and Conflict

3. Read the descriptions of the following conflicts. Write *internal* or *external* next to each one.

- A boy is bothered by a bully who will not leave him alone. _____

- A girl feels torn when she can't decide whether or not to try out for a school play. _____

- Two twins get a puppy for their birthday. Each one wants to give the puppy a different name. _____

NAVIGATING TEXT

Analyze Evidence

4. In "La Vida Robot," what evidence does the author give to support the claim that Oscar Vazquez was a good leader?

_____

_____

_____

_____

On a scale of 1–5, how convincing do you find this evidence?

least convincing 1 2 3 4 5 **most convincing**

Explain your answer: _____

_____

_____

Reading a Magazine Article

5. Read the magazine article. Circle the title and byline. Box the subhead.

Scientists Study the Strangest Things!

by Madison Henry

Mold, bugs, jellyfish—sometimes the things scientists study seem bizarre. But some of the greatest scientific discoveries come from unlikely subjects.

Miracle Mold

The discovery of penicillin is a classic example. Less than a century ago, there were no antibiotics. Then in 1928, scientist Alexander Fleming became curious about a mold growing in his lab.

VOCABULARY/WORD ANALYSIS

Word Families

6. Which of the words below are in the same word family?

national   nation   natural

rational   notation   international

Context Clues: Synonyms and Antonyms

7. Read the passage.

> *The sluggish village was transformed into a vital, bustling city, thanks to the advent of the automobile. Indeed, the beginning of the age of mass car travel changed the entire country's way of life.*

Using context clues, identify a synonym for *beginning*.

_____

Now identify an antonym for *bustling*.

_____

Design: Visual Aids

8. Imagine you are doing a presentation about one of the new technologies you have read about in this workshop. In the space below, describe a visual aid you would use in your presentation. Then answer the questions below.

What technology are you presenting?

_____

What is the purpose of your visual aid?

_____

What is the visual aid's title?

_____

Synthesize

9. Will the future be better or worse than today? Think about the selections you have read in "Designing the Future" and make a judgment about this. Explain your judgment, citing at least two selections from the workshop.

_____

_____

_____

_____

_____

_____

_____

_____

_____

_____

_____

_____

_____

_____

_____

_____

_____

_____

? EXPERT QUESTION

What are the costs and benefits of technology?

10. Use what you learned in this workshop to respond to the Expert Question. Jot down some notes here. Then use a separate sheet of paper to write your response.

_____

_____

_____

Life at the Edges

? Expert Question:
How do people survive in extreme environments?

Explore the Expert Question

[21] Expert Knowledge

Watch the Anchor Media!

PAGE **164**

An audiovisual introduction to **Life at the Edges**.

Explore Expert Space

PAGE **165**

expert space

See **Life at the Edges** online at **www.expert21.com/student**.

[21] Meet the Expert

Kendrick Taylor: Polar Scientist

PAGE **166** A scientist explains the challenges of working in the coldest place on Earth.

Read and Synthesize

Inquiry 1 — Lands of Ice and Snow

(L) Reading **1** — SHORT STORY

The Story of Keesh

By Jack London

In the northernmost reaches of the world, a young man takes the ultimate challenge: hunting polar bears.

PAGE **170**

(i) Reading **2** — PERSONAL NARRATIVE

Crisis on Top of the World

By Patty Janes

Earth's arctic regions are getting warmer. Can polar animals survive the heat?

PAGE **180**

(i) Reading **3** — PHOTO ESSAY

Life at the Poles

How does life survive at the frozen top and bottom of the world?

PAGE **192**

[21] 21st Century Skills

Gather Information

PAGE **198**

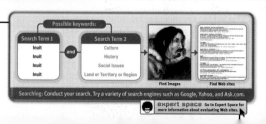

Possible keywords:

Search Term 1		Search Term 2
Inuit		Culture
Inuit	and	History
Inuit		Social Issues
Inuit		Land or Territory or Region

Find Images | Find Web sites

Searching: Conduct your search. Try a variety of search engines such as Google, Yahoo, and Ask.com.

expert space Go to Expert Space for more information about evaluating Web sites.

Inquiry 2 Desert Zones

21 How do people survive in extreme environments?

Scientists and explorers enjoy going to extremes—extreme environments, that is. Find out what it takes to survive in vast searing deserts and the frigid polar regions.

▶ Anchor Your Knowledge

Watch the Anchor Media, Life at the Edges," and meet Kendrick Taylor, a scientist who lives and works in Antarctica.

WORKSHOP GOALS

To gain expert knowledge about life on the edges, you will

- study **informational texts** about life in some of Earth's most extreme environments.

- read **literature** about teens surviving in extreme climates.

- learn **important skills and strategies** to help you understand what you read.

- develop **21st Century Skills** to **synthesize information** and **build an effective team.**

- write a **cause-and-effect essay** about your effects on the environment.

- complete an **Expert Project** about the challenges of life in Antarctica.

▶ Concept Web

Create a concept web of what you know about extreme environments.

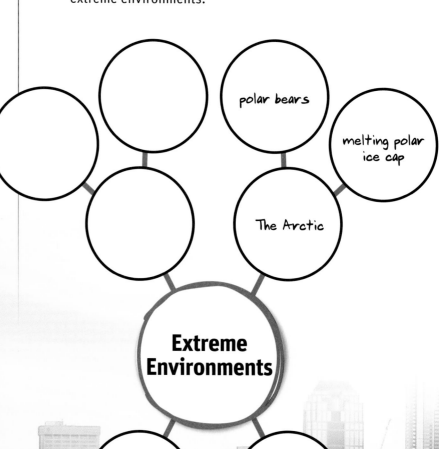

polar bears

melting polar ice cap

The Arctic

Extreme Environments

▶ Preview the Expert Project

At the end of this workshop, you'll create a presentation on life in Antarctica. Preview the **Expert Project** on pages 242–245.

▶ What will you need to know or do to complete the Expert Project?

_____

_____

_____

_____

▶ Explore Expert Space

 Go to **www.expert21.com/student** to learn more about the topics in this workshop.

DISCOVER ONLINE

- Careers in Climatology
- Antarctica
- Arctic Anxiety:
  On the Front Lines

READ ONLINE

- The Arctic
- Polar Bears
- Sandstorms
- Extreme Athletes

RESEARCH ONLINE

- McMurdo Dry Valleys
- South Pole
- Penguins

▶ Personal Inquiry

Explore the topic of surviving in extreme climates by asking your own questions. Return to add questions as you continue reading Workshop 3. Plan to revisit your questions.

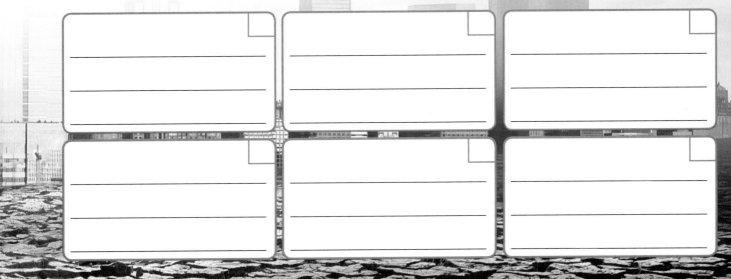

Kendrick Taylor: Polar Scientist

This scientist studies the coolest places on Earth.

"The only way I got to do this job is through having an education. If you have an education, you have a chance to go get your dream job."

At the West Antarctic Ice Sheet (WAIS) field station, Chief Scientist Ken Taylor heads a team of fifty people with a single goal: Drill and recover a deep ice core to research how our climate is changing. Why work in the harshest place on Earth? It's the best place to study and analyze how greenhouse gases affect our planet. Here, the snow never melts. By examining the ice core, Taylor can identify and record what weather was like each year for the past 100,000 years—and how it's changing now.

FACTS AND STATS

NAME: Kendrick Taylor

HOMETOWN: Reno, Nevada

JOB: Polar Scientist

EDUCATION: Ph.D., Hydrogeology/Hydrology; M.S. and B.S., Geophysics

WORKPLACE SKILLS: Social skills; synthesizes information

GOING TO EXTREMES: "I once went from 115 degrees in the desert in Ghana, Africa to 10 degrees at 10,000 feet elevation in Antarctica."

PAY: Beginning research scientists earn about $30,000; those with experience earn about $100,000.

CAREER CONNECTION Science, Technology, Engineering, and Mathematics
www.careerclusters.org

Go to **21** ToolKit **Expert File 6.30** to learn more about careers in environmental science.

RELATED JOBS: meteorologist, geologist, field research assistant, equipment operator

Q: What climate issues have you identified by studying the ice core in Antarctica?

A: That [the climate] is changing all the time. Plus, [the presence of human-caused greenhouse gases indicates that] the current changes are caused by humans.

Q: What skills have you learned that are particular to working in an extreme environment?

A: You have to overcome your environment to get the job done—you're in the cold a lot! You also have to "go with the flow," because plans never unfold the way you expect. And you need good **social skills** because you're dealing with lots of people in small spaces.

Q: What kind of people does an extreme climate attract?

A: A wide mix. But they seem to fall into two categories: scientists and adventurers. The scientists are there to **answer certain questions.** They don't care where they are! The adventurers like to explore and usually work as support staff, like machinists and cooks.

Q: What do you do for fun?

A: Not much! We mostly work, eat, and sleep. And if I'm lucky, I'll get seven hours of sleep a night. We put in lots of time **planning** for these field trips, so we don't want to waste any valuable time.

Q: You're out there two months at a time. Do you ever get lonely?

A: It's not too lonely because there's a **team** environment. There are so few people in Antarctica; the nearest ones may be 600 miles away. But you're **working with fifty people** all the time, enclosed in the modules. So you'd better get along!

Q: What do your friends and family say about your career?

A: They don't think it's abnormal anymore. They say, "Oh, Ken's going to Antarctica again. Oh, well."

Q: What's it like coming back from Antarctica?

A: It takes a while to get used to the media...and all the people. It's hard even to go from the field station to the main research station of 1,000 people. When I get off the plane in Los Angeles, I want to crawl under a rock and hide!

Q: If you were teaching a course on Antarctica, what would you include?

A: It's hard to choose because Antarctica is so big—it's the size of North America. But I might suggest studying the oceans, or glaciers, or how sea levels will change. Or maybe the coastal areas teeming with life, the ice itself, the climate, and the ozone layer.

ANALYZE EXPERT SKILLS

1. Collaborate

How do the two categories of people in Antarctica work as a team?

_____

_____

_____

2. Analyze Data

What climate issues has Taylor learned by studying the West Antarctic ice core?

_____

_____

_____

3. Ask Questions

Part of Taylor's job is to ask questions and analyze information and data to find answers. Use the chart to list questions Taylor might be trying to answer.

What?	
Who?	
Where?	
When?	
Why?	
How?	

DISCOVER ONLINE

expert space
Go to **www.expert21.com/ student** to learn more about Careers in Climatology; Antarctica; Ozone Depletion.

Short Story

THE STORY OF KEESH

In many traditional societies, young men need to prove themselves in order to gain respect. Find out how the poor son of a forgotten hero becomes a legend.

What do young people today do in order to win the respect of their community? Give a specific example.

Setting LITERARY ANALYSIS

Setting **is the time and place in which a story happens.**

Setting can affect the plot of a story by creating challenges or conflicts for the characters.

▶ **Underline sentences and phrases that tell you about the setting of this passage.**

> The shadows lengthened as the sun sank behind the tall pine trees. Emma looked in all directions. There was no sound but the wind. The sky darkened, the temperature dropped, and big, heavy snowflakes began to fall. Emma's heart beat faster as she realized she was lost.

What challenges might Emma have to face in the setting described in the passage?

_____

_____

Compare and Contrast COMPREHENSION

To **compare** two things is to tell how they are alike.

To **contrast** two things is to tell how they are different.

Words such as *also* and *both* often signal a comparison. Words such as *but, however, more,* and *less* often signal a contrast.

▶ **Read each short passage from "The Story of Keesh," and answer the question about each passage.**

It is said that Bok brought home more meat than any of the two best hunters . . .

How was Bok different from the other hunters?

_____

_____

Never did boys of his tender age go forth to hunt, much less to hunt alone.

How is the boy in the passage like the other boys?

_____

How is the boy different from the other boys?

_____

Academic Language VOCABULARY

▶ Rate each word. Then write its meaning and an example sentence.

Invitation

Word	Meaning	Example
ACADEMIC WORDS *Use these words in all your subject classes.*		
decline de•cline (verb) ① ② ③ ④	to turn something down or refuse it	I had to decline Claire's invitation because I had another obligation.
exceed ex•ceed (verb) ① ② ③ ④		
presumption pre•sump•tion (noun) ① ② ③ ④		Chloe's presumption that all petite people wish they were taller is ridiculous.
SELECTION WORDS *These words are key to understanding this selection.*		
affirm af•firm (verb) ① ② ③ ④	to approve something or say it is true	
arrogance ar•ro•gance (noun) ① ② ③ ④		
burden bur•den (noun) ① ② ③ ④		
cunningly cun•ning•ly (adverb) ① ② ③ ④		
prosperous pros•per•ous (adj) ① ② ③ ④		

Rating Scale ① I don't know the word. ② I've seen it or heard it. ③ I know its meaning. ④ I know it and use it.

Multiple-Meaning Words WORD ANALYSIS

Multiple-meaning words are words that have more than one meaning.

Stories that are told in old-fashioned or formal language may contain familiar words that have meanings unfamiliar to modern readers. You can use context clues to figure out these meanings.

▶ **Circle the definition of the word *meanest* as it is used in this sentence.**

*Before Keesh proved he was a great hunter, he was poor and lived in the **meanest** igloo in the village.*

most unkind   poorest and smallest

THE STORY OF KEESH

By Jack London

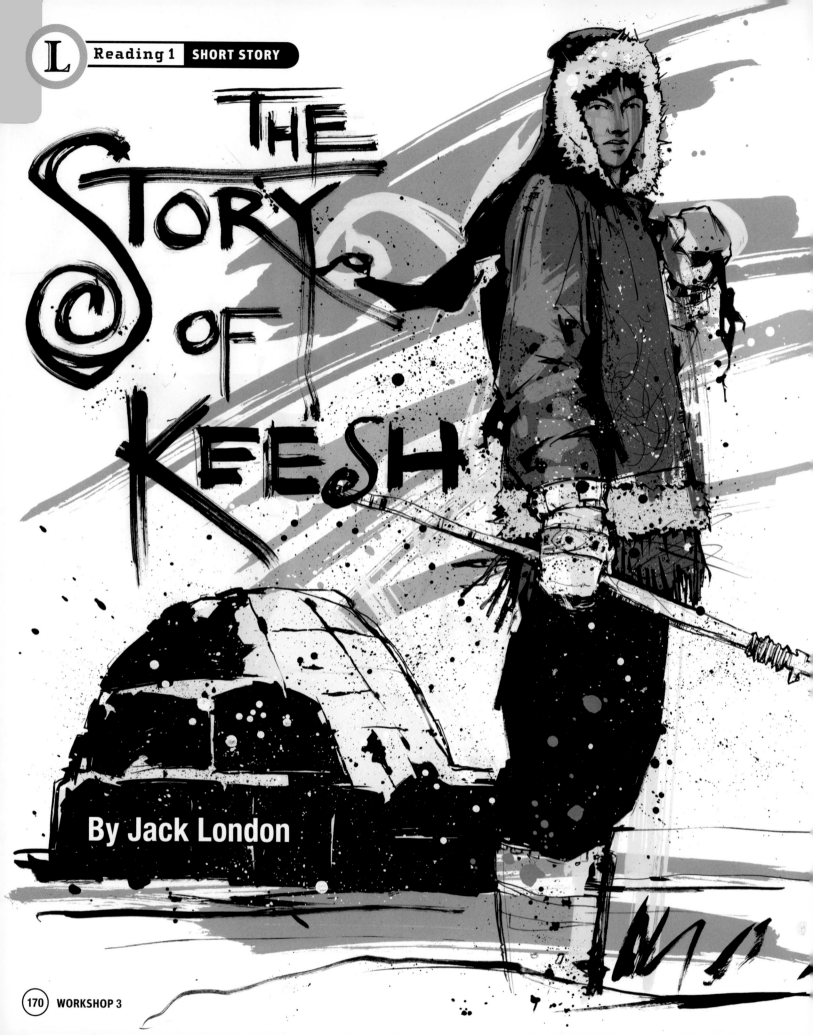

In the icy, northernmost reaches of the world, a young man takes the ultimate challenge: hunting polar bears.

KEESH lived long ago on the rim of the polar sea, was headman of his village through many and **prosperous** years, and died full of honors with his name on the lips of men. So long ago did he live that only the old men remember his name, his name and the tale, which they got from the old men before them, and which the old men to come will tell to their children and their children's children down to the end of time. And the winter darkness, when the north gales make their long sweep across the icepack, and the air is filled with flying white, and no man may venture forth, is the chosen time for the telling of how Keesh, from the poorest *igloo* in the village, rose to power and place over them all.

He was a bright boy, so the tale runs, healthy and strong, and he had seen thirteen suns, in their way of reckoning time. For each winter the sun leaves the land in darkness, and the next year a new sun returns so that they may be warm again and look upon one another's faces. The father of Keesh had been a very brave man, but he had met his death in a time of famine, when he sought to save the lives of his people by taking the life of a great polar bear. In his eagerness he came to close grapples with the bear, and his bones were crushed; but the bear had much meat on him and the people were saved. Keesh was his only son, and after that Keesh lived alone with his mother. But the people are prone to forget, and they forgot the deed of his father; and he being but a boy, and his mother only a woman, they, too, were swiftly forgotten, and ere long came to live in the meanest of all the *igloos*.

It was at a council, one night, in the big *igloo* of Klosh-Kwan, the chief, that Keesh showed the blood that ran in his veins and the manhood that stiffened his back. With the dignity of an elder, he rose to his feet, and waited for silence amid the babble of voices.

"It is true that meat be apportioned me and mine," he said. "But it is oft times old and tough, this meat, and, moreover, it has an unusual quantity of bones."

The hunters, grizzled and gray, and lusty and young, were aghast. The like had never been known before. A child, that talked like a grown man, and said harsh things to their very faces!

---

reckoning *(v.)* counting
apportioned *(v.)* divided and distributed

LITERARY ANALYSIS

Setting

Underline details in the first paragraph on page 171 that help you picture the setting.

- How do you think the setting of this story will influence the plot?

_____

_____

_____

_____

_____

_____

_____

_____

COMPREHENSION

Compare and Contrast

Klosh-Kwan is much older and more powerful than Keesh. How do you think these differences will affect the events in the story?

_____

_____

_____

_____

_____

_____

_____

_____

_____

CRITICAL THINKING

Evaluate

Based on what he says at the council, which statement best describes Keesh?

Ⓐ He is relaxed and easygoing.

Ⓑ He is angry and impatient.

Ⓒ He stands up for his rights.

But steadily and with seriousness, Keesh went on. "For that I know my father, Bok, was a great hunter, I speak these words. It is said that Bok brought home more meat than any of the two best hunters, that with his own hands he attended to the division of it, that with his own eyes he saw to it that the least old woman and the last old man received fair share."

"Na! Na!" the men cried. "Put the child out!" "Send him off to bed!" "He is no man that he should talk to men and graybeards!"

He waited calmly till the uproar died down.

"Thou hast a wife, Ugh-Gluk," he said, "and for her dost thou speak. And thou, too, Massuk, a mother also, and for them dost thou speak. My mother has no one, save me; wherefore I speak. As I say, though Bok be dead because he hunted over-keenly, it is just that I, who am his son, and that Ikeega, who is my mother and was his wife, should have meat in plenty so long as there be meat in plenty in the tribe. I, Keesh, the son of Bok, have spoken."

He sat down, his ears keenly alert to the flood of protest and indignation his words had created.

"That a boy should speak in council!" old Ugh-Gluk was mumbling.

"Shall the babes in arms tell us men the things we shall do?" Massuk demanded in a loud voice. "Am I a man that I should be made a mock by every child that cries for meat?"

The anger boiled a white heat. They ordered him to bed, threatened that he should have no meat at all, and promised him sore beatings for his **presumption**. Keesh's eyes began to flash, and the blood to pound **darkly** under his skin. In the midst of the abuse he sprang to his feet.

"Hear me, ye men!" he cried. "Never shall I speak in the council again, never again till the men come to me and say, 'It is well, Keesh, that thou shouldst speak, it is well and it is our wish.' Take this now, ye men, for my last word. Bok, my father, was a great hunter. I, too, his son, shall go and hunt the meat that I eat. And be it known,

keenly (adv.) in an eager manner
indignation (n.) anger caused by an injustice

now, that the division of that which I kill shall be fair. And no widow nor weak one shall cry in the night because there is no meat, when the strong men are groaning in great pain for that they have eaten overmuch. And in the days to come there shall be shame upon the strong men who have eaten overmuch. I, Keesh, have said it!"

Jeers and scornful laughter followed him out of the *igloo*, but his jaw was set and he went his way, looking neither to right nor left.

Visualize
Describe what Keesh's expression may have been as he left the igloo.

The next day he went forth along the shoreline where the ice and the land met together. Those who saw him go noted that he carried his bow, with a goodly supply of bone-barbed arrows, and that across his shoulder was his father's big hunting-spear. And there was laughter, and much talk, at the event. It was an unprecedented occurrence. Never did boys of his tender age go forth to hunt, much less to hunt alone. Also were there shaking of heads and prophetic mutterings, and the women looked pityingly at Ikeega, and her face was grave and sad.

"He will be back ere long," they said cheeringly.

"Let him go; it will teach him a lesson," the hunters said. "And he will come back shortly, and he will be meek and soft of speech in the days to follow."

But a day passed, and a second, and on the third a wild gale blew, and there was no Keesh. Ikeega tore her hair and put soot of the seal-oil on her face in token of her grief; and the women assailed the men with bitter words in that they had mistreated the boy and sent him to his death; and the men made no answer, preparing to go in search of the body when the storm abated.

Early next morning, however, Keesh strode into the village. But he came not shamefacedly. Across his shoulders he bore a **burden** of fresh-killed meat. And there was importance in his step and **arrogance** in his speech.

"Go, ye men, with the dogs and sledges, and take my trail for the better part of a day's travel," he said. "There is much meat on the ice—a she-bear and two half-grown cubs."

Ikeega was overcome with joy, but he received her demonstrations in manlike fashion, saying: "Come, Ikeega, let us eat. And after that I shall sleep, for I am weary."

assailed *(v.)* attacked
abated *(v.)* became less intense

Read and Synthesize

VOCABULARY/WORD ANALYSIS

Multiple-Meaning Words

Review the next to last paragraph on page 172 and (circle) the word *darkly*. Check the meaning of *darkly* as it is used in this sentence.

Ⓐ without light

Ⓑ angrily

Ⓒ quietly

Ⓓ secretly

LITERARY ANALYSIS

Setting

Place a **check** ✓ in front of the sentence on page 173 that states where Keesh went after leaving the igloo.

• Why do Ikeega and the other women fear for his safety?

_____

_____

_____

_____

_____

_____

_____

CRITICAL THINKING

Analyze

Why do you think the hunters expect Keesh to "come back shortly" and "be meek and soft of speech"?

_____

_____

_____

_____

_____

_____

_____

The Story of Keesh   173

And he passed into their *igloo* and ate profoundly, and after that slept for twenty running hours. There was much doubt at first, much doubt and discussion. The killing of a polar bear is very dangerous, but thrice dangerous is it, and three times thrice, to kill mother bear with her cubs. The men could not bring themselves to believe that the boy Keesh, single-handed, had accomplished so great a marvel. But the women spoke of the fresh-killed meat he had brought on his back, and this was an overwhelming argument against their unbelief. So they finally departed, grumbling greatly that in all probability, if the thing were so, he had neglected to cut up the carcasses. Now in the north it is very necessary that this should be done as soon as a kill is made. If not, the meat freezes so solidly as to turn the edge of the sharpest knife, and a three-hundred-pound bear, frozen stiff, is no easy thing to put upon a sled and haul over the rough ice. But arrived at the spot, they found not only the kill, which they had doubted, but that Keesh had quartered the beasts in true hunter fashion, and removed the entrails.

Thus began the mystery of Keesh, a mystery that deepened and deepened with the passing of the days. His very next trip he killed a young bear, nearly full-grown, and on the trip following, a large male bear and his mate. He was ordinarily gone from three to four days, though it was nothing unusual for him to stay away a week at a time on the icefield. Always he **declined** company on these expeditions, and the people marveled. "How does he do it?" they demanded of one another. "Never does he take a dog with him, and dogs are of such great help, too."

"Why dost thou hunt only bear?" Klosh-Kwan once ventured to ask him.

And Keesh made fitting answer. "It is well known that there is more meat on the bear," he said.

But there was also talk of witchcraft in the village. "He hunts with evil spirits," some of the people contended, "wherefore his hunting is rewarded. How else can it be, save that he hunts with evil spirits?"

"Mayhap they be not evil, but good, these spirits," others said. "It is known that his father was a mighty hunter. May not his father hunt with him so that he may attain excellence and patience and understanding? Who knows?"

Nonetheless, his success continued, and the less skillful hunters were often kept busy hauling in his meat. And in the division of it he was just. As his father had done before him, he saw to it that the least old woman and the last old man received a fair portion, keeping no more for himself than his needs required. And because of this, and of his merit as a hunter, he was looked upon with respect, and even awe; and there was talk of making him chief after old Klosh-Kwan. Because of the things he had done, they looked for him to appear again in the council, but he never came, and they were ashamed to ask.

"I am minded to build me an *igloo*," he said one day to Klosh-Kwan and a number of the hunters. "It shall be a large *igloo*, wherein Ikeega and I can dwell in comfort."

"Ay," they nodded gravely.

"But I have no time. My business is hunting, and it takes all my time. So it is but just that the men and women of the village who eat my meat should build me my *igloo*."

> **Visualize**
> Describe or sketch a picture of what Keesh's igloo may have looked like.

And the *igloo* was built accordingly, on a generous scale which **exceeded** even the dwelling of Klosh-Kwan. Keesh and his mother moved into it, and it was the first prosperity she had enjoyed since the death of Bok. Nor was material prosperity alone hers, for, because of her wonderful son and the position he had given her, she came to be looked upon as the first woman in all the village; and the women were given to visiting her, to asking her advice, and to quoting her wisdom when arguments arose among themselves or with the men.

But it was the mystery of Keesh's marvelous hunting that took chief place in all their minds. And one day Ugh-Gluk taxed him with witchcraft to his face.

> **contended** *(v.)* argued
> **mayhap** *(adv.)* perhaps; possibly

"It is charged," Ugh-Gluk said ominously, "that thou dealest with evil spirits, wherefore thy hunting is rewarded."

"Is not the meat good?" Keesh made answer. "Has one in the village yet to fall sick from the eating of it? How dost thou know that witchcraft be concerned? Or dost thou guess, in the dark, merely because of the envy that consumes thee?"

And Ugh-Gluk withdrew discomfited, the women laughing at him as he walked away. But in the council one night, after long deliberation, it was determined to put spies on his track when he went forth to hunt, so that his methods might be learned. So, on his next trip, Bim and Bawn, two young men, and of hunters the craftiest, followed after him, taking care not to be seen. After five days they returned, their eyes bulging and their tongues a-tremble to tell what they had seen. The council was hastily called in Klosh-Kwan's dwelling, and Bim took up the tale.

"Brothers! As commanded, we journeyed on the trail of Keesh, and **cunningly** we journeyed, so that he might not know. And midway of the first day he picked up with a great he-bear. It was a very great bear."

"None greater," Bawn corroborated, and went on himself. "Yet was the bear not inclined to fight, for he turned away and made off slowly over the ice. This we saw from the rocks of the shore, and the bear came toward us, and after him came Keesh, very much unafraid. And he shouted harsh words after the bear, and waved his arms about, and made much noise. Then did the bear grow angry, and rise up on his hind legs, and growl. But Keesh walked right up to the bear."

discomfited (adj.) frustrated; defeated
corroborated (v.) supported a statement

Read and Synthesize

LITERARY ANALYSIS

Setting

Review the eighth paragraph on page 174. What do Keesh's comments reveal about the igloo that he and his mother currently live in?

_____

_____

_____

_____

Underline words that tell how living in the new igloo changes Ikeega's life.

VOCABULARY/WORD ANALYSIS

Multiple-Meaning Words

Review the seventh paragraph on page 174, and circle the word *fair*.

• What does *received a fair portion* mean in this sentence?

_____

_____

• How do most people feel about the portions Keesh is handing out?

_____

_____

_____

_____

_____

COMPREHENSION

Problem and Solution

Review page 175 and complete the following activities:

• What problem do Ugh-Gluk and others have with Keesh?

_____

_____

_____

_____

• Draw a box around his solution.

"Ay," Bim continued the story. "Right up to the bear Keesh walked. And the bear took after him, and Keesh ran away. But as he ran he dropped a little round ball on the ice. And the bear stopped and smelled of it, then swallowed it up. And Keesh continued to run away and drop little round balls, and the bear continued to swallow them up."

Exclamations and cries of doubt were being made, and Ugh-Gluk expressed open unbelief.

"With our own eyes we saw it," Bim **affirmed**.

And Bawn – "Ay, with our own eyes. And this continued until the bear stood suddenly upright and cried aloud in pain, and thrashed his fore paws madly about. And Keesh continued to make off over the ice to a safe distance. But the bear gave him no notice, being occupied with the misfortune the little round balls had wrought within him."

"Ay, within him," Bim interrupted. "For he did claw at himself, and leap about over the ice like a playful puppy, save from the way he growled and squealed it was plain it was not play but pain. Never did I see such a sight!"

"Nay, never was such a sight seen," Bawn took up the strain. "And furthermore, it was such a large bear."

"Witchcraft," Ugh-Gluk suggested.

"I know not," Bawn replied. "I tell only of what my eyes beheld. And after a while the bear grew weak and tired, for he was very heavy and he had jumped about with exceeding violence, and he went off along the shore-ice, shaking his head slowly from side to side and sitting down ever and again to squeal and cry. And Keesh followed after the bear, and we followed after Keesh, and for that day and three days more we followed. The bear grew weak, and never ceased crying from his pain."

> **Visualize**
> **What details help you visualize the polar bear's condition?**

"It was a charm!" Ugh-Gluk exclaimed. "Surely it was a charm!"

"It may well be."

And Bim relieved Bawn. "The bear wandered, now this way and now that, doubling back and forth and crossing his trail in circles, so that at the end he was near where Keesh had first come upon him. By this time he was quite sick, the bear, and could crawl no farther, so Keesh came up close and speared him to death."

"And then?" Klosh-Kwan demanded.

"Then we left Keesh skinning the bear, and came running that the news of the killing might be told."

And in the afternoon of that day the women hauled in the meat of the bear while the men sat in council assembled. When Keesh arrived a messenger was sent to him, bidding him come to the council. But he sent reply, saying that he was hungry and tired; also that his *igloo* was large and comfortable and could hold many men.

And curiosity was so strong on the men that the whole council, Klosh-Kwan to the fore, rose up and went to the *igloo* of Keesh. He was eating, but he received them with respect and seated them according to their rank. Ikeega was proud and embarrassed by turns, but Keesh was quite composed.

Klosh-Kwan recited the information brought by Bim and Bawn, and at its close said in a stern voice: "So explanation is wanted, O Keesh, of thy manner of hunting. Is there witchcraft in it?"

Keesh looked up and smiled. "Nay, O Klosh-Kwan. It is not for a boy to know aught of witches, and of witches I know nothing. I have but devised a means whereby I may kill the ice-bear with ease, that is all. It be headcraft, not witchcraft."

"And may any man?"

"Any man."

There was a long silence. The men looked in one another's faces, and Keesh went on eating.

"And . . . and . . . and wilt thou tell us, O Keesh?" Klosh-Kwan finally asked in a tremulous voice.

"Yea, I will tell thee." Keesh finished sucking a marrow-bone and rose to his feet. "It is quite simple. Behold!"

> **devised** *(v.)* thought up (something)
> **tremulous** *(adj.)* trembling

He picked up a thin strip of whalebone and showed it to them. The ends were sharp as needlepoints. The strip he coiled carefully, till it disappeared in his hand. Then, suddenly releasing it, it sprang straight again. He picked up a piece of blubber.

"So," he said, "one takes a small chunk of blubber, thus, and thus makes it hollow. Then into the hollow goes the whalebone, so, tightly coiled, and another piece of blubber is fitted over the whalebone. After that it is put outside where it freezes into a little round ball. The bear swallows the little round ball, the blubber melts, the whalebone with its sharp ends stands out straight, the bear gets sick, and when the bear is very sick, why, you kill him with a spear. It is quite simple."

And Ugh-Gluk said "Oh!" and Klosh-Kwan said "Ah!" And each said something after his own manner, and all understood.

And this is the story of Keesh, who lived long ago on the rim of the polar sea. Because he exercised headcraft and not witchcraft, he rose from the meanest *igloo* to be head man of his village, and through all the years that he lived, it is related, his tribe was prosperous, and neither widow nor weak one cried aloud in the night because there was no meat. ∎

Jack London

AUTHOR FILE

BORN January 12, 1876, in San Francisco, California

AWARDS In 1931, Jack London received a Newbery Medal for *The Call of the Wild*. The book, which tells the story of a mistreated dog who becomes the leader of a pack of wolves, is one of his most famous works.

ON INSPIRATION "You can't wait for inspiration. You have to go after it with a club."

NEVER GIVE UP In the first five years of his writing career, London's stories were rejected by publishers 664 times. This included "The Story of Keesh," which was rejected 16 times. The story was ultimately published in *Holiday Magazine for Children* in 1904.

OTHER FAMOUS WORKS *White Fang, The Sea Wolf, The Iron Heel,* and *Martin Eden*

ODD JOBS Oyster pirate, cannery factory worker, deep-sea sailor; London also took part in the Klondike gold rush in 1897.

coiled *(v.)* wound
blubber *(n.)* fat under the skin of a polar animal

LITERARY ANALYSIS

Setting

Review the second column on page 176. Where does the council meet now?

_____

Why do you think the author chose to write about this setting change?

_____

_____

CRITICAL THINKING

Evaluate

Do you think that Keesh's way of killing a bear is clever or cruel? Explain your answer.

_____

_____

_____

_____

21 **SMALL GROUPS/INDEPENDENT**

COLLABORATE

Create Stories Keesh's people handed his story down from one generation to the next. Perform a telling of the story. Have one person in your group start telling Keesh's story, and then take turns continuing the tale.

COMMUNICATE

Discuss and Write With a partner, discuss how the story's message relates to your own life. Then, write a paragraph based on the ideas you come up with.

W

READ ONLINE

expert space
Go to **www.expert21.com/student** to learn more about Jack London; Igloo; Inuit.

Personal Narrative

crisis on top of the world

Minute by minute, little by little, Earth is heating up. Brace yourself to see how this gradual change affects all living things on the planet.

Cause and Effect   COMPREHENSION

A cause is the reason something happens. An effect is the result of a cause.

A series of causes and effects is called a **causal chain**. In a causal chain, an effect becomes the cause of the next effect.

▶ **Read the following passage. Look for a series of causes and effects. Then write them in the boxes below.**

The sound of sirens woke me up. I turned on the radio. There had been an earthquake in Alaska. The quake triggered large waves all down the coast—and one was headed for our town. We had to evacuate—now!

Cause #1	Effect/Cause #2	Effect/Cause #3	Final Effect

Author's Purpose   NAVIGATING TEXT

An author's purpose is his or her reason for writing. The purpose may be to entertain, to inform, to persuade, or to explain.

• An author's purpose affects the kinds of information he or she includes in the text.

• An author might have several different purposes for writing a certain text. For example, he or she might write to both entertain and persuade.

▶ **Fill in each blank with the word that best describes each purpose.**

inform   entertain   persuade   explain

The purpose of a newspaper article is to_____

The purpose of an advertisement is to_____

The purpose of a fictional story is to_____

The purpose of a how-to article is to _____

Academic Language `VOCABULARY`

▶ **Rate each word. Then write its meaning and an example sentence.**

Word	Meaning	Example
EXPERT WORDS *Use these words to write and talk about the workshop topic.*		
conducive con·du·cive *(adj)* ① ② ③ ④	tending to bring about a particular result	Marta's house is not conducive to studying because her brothers are so loud.
emission e·mis·sion *(noun)* ① ② ③ ④	something that is released into the atmosphere	
insulation in·su·la·tion *(noun)* ① ② ③ ④		
ACADEMIC WORDS *Use these words in all your subject classes.*		
convert con·vert *(verb)* ① ② ③ ④		
diminish di·min·ish *(verb)* ① ② ③ ④		
CONTENT AREA WORDS *Use these words to talk and write about social studies.*		
accustomed ac·cus·tomed *(adj)* ① ② ③ ④		Since I dyed my hair blue, I'm accustomed to being stared at.
attendant at·tend·ant *(noun)* ① ② ③ ④		
native na·tive *(adj)* ① ② ③ ④		

Rating Scale   ① I don't know the word.   ② I've seen it or heard it.   ③ I know its meaning.   ④ I know it and use it.

Multiple-Meaning Words `WORD ANALYSIS`

A word can have multiple meanings, or several definitions.

The word *convert* can be a verb that means "to change" or a noun that means "someone who has been changed from one way of thinking to another."

▶ **Read this sentence and underline clues to the meaning of convert.**

This machine can <u>convert</u> corn into fuel.

Which definition of convert is being used in the sentence?

to change   someone who has been changed from one way of thinking to another

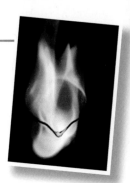

crisis on top of the world

By Patty Janes
From *Science World* Magazine

U.S. COAST GUARD

Earth's arctic regions are getting warmer. Can polar animals survive the heat? *Science World* editor Patty Janes travels to the North to investigate.

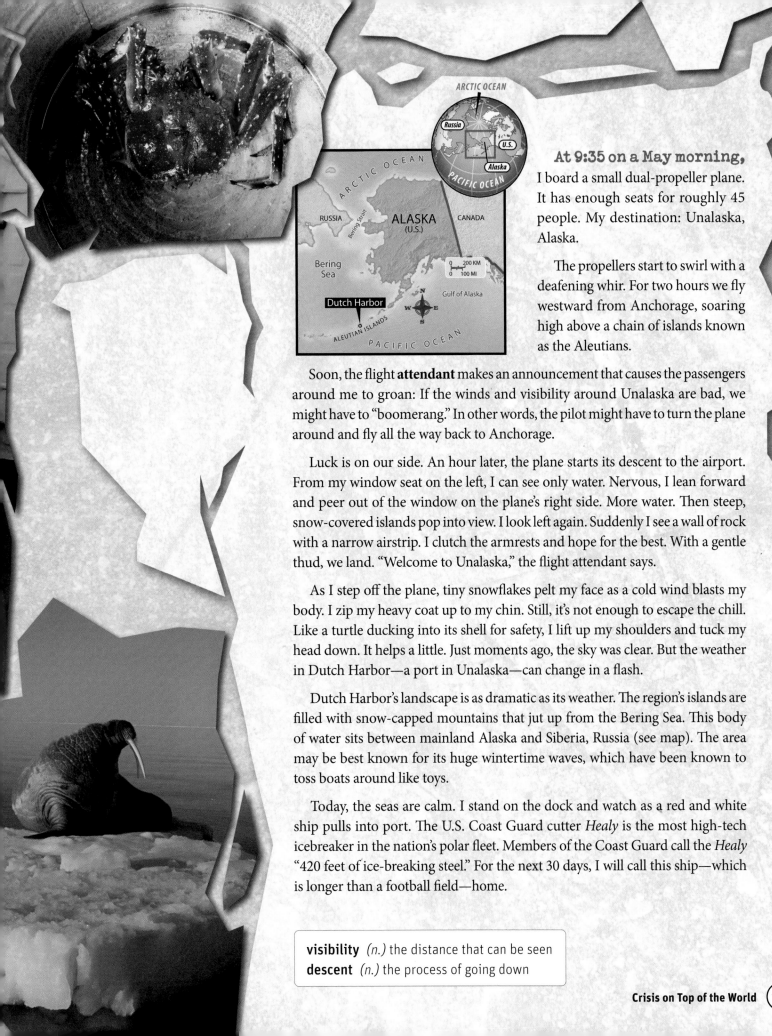

ARCTIC OCEAN

Russia

U.S.

Alaska

PACIFIC OCEAN

ARCTIC OCEAN

RUSSIA

Bering Strait

ALASKA
(U.S.)

CANADA

Bering
Sea

0   200 KM
0   100 MI

Dutch Harbor

Gulf of Alaska

N
W   E
S

ALEUTIAN ISLANDS

PACIFIC OCEAN

At 9:35 on a May morning, I board a small dual-propeller plane. It has enough seats for roughly 45 people. My destination: Unalaska, Alaska.

The propellers start to swirl with a deafening whir. For two hours we fly westward from Anchorage, soaring high above a chain of islands known as the Aleutians.

Soon, the flight **attendant** makes an announcement that causes the passengers around me to groan: If the winds and visibility around Unalaska are bad, we might have to "boomerang." In other words, the pilot might have to turn the plane around and fly all the way back to Anchorage.

Luck is on our side. An hour later, the plane starts its descent to the airport. From my window seat on the left, I can see only water. Nervous, I lean forward and peer out of the window on the plane's right side. More water. Then steep, snow-covered islands pop into view. I look left again. Suddenly I see a wall of rock with a narrow airstrip. I clutch the armrests and hope for the best. With a gentle thud, we land. "Welcome to Unalaska," the flight attendant says.

As I step off the plane, tiny snowflakes pelt my face as a cold wind blasts my body. I zip my heavy coat up to my chin. Still, it's not enough to escape the chill. Like a turtle ducking into its shell for safety, I lift up my shoulders and tuck my head down. It helps a little. Just moments ago, the sky was clear. But the weather in Dutch Harbor—a port in Unalaska—can change in a flash.

Dutch Harbor's landscape is as dramatic as its weather. The region's islands are filled with snow-capped mountains that jut up from the Bering Sea. This body of water sits between mainland Alaska and Siberia, Russia (see map). The area may be best known for its huge wintertime waves, which have been known to toss boats around like toys.

Today, the seas are calm. I stand on the dock and watch as a red and white ship pulls into port. The U.S. Coast Guard cutter *Healy* is the most high-tech icebreaker in the nation's polar fleet. Members of the Coast Guard call the *Healy* "420 feet of ice-breaking steel." For the next 30 days, I will call this ship—which is longer than a football field—home.

visibility (*n.*) the distance that can be seen
descent (*n.*) the process of going down

Oceanographers Jackie Grebmeier and Lee Cooper.

Ice Breaker

The *Healy* can slice through sea ice up to 2.5 meters (8 feet) thick and can operate in temperatures as low as –46° Celsius (–50° Fahrenheit). In addition, the ship has 4,200 square feet of laboratory space and can accommodate up to 50 scientists. That makes it the ideal floating laboratory for researchers investigating Earth's icy arctic regions, or areas within or near the Arctic Circle.

Jackie Grebmeier and Lee Cooper, both oceanographers from the University of Tennessee, are onboard the *Healy* for this trip. They have invited me to join them onboard the cutter. I will be assisting their team of scientists as they study the changes taking place in the Bering Sea.

> **Predict**
> What types of changes do you think might be happening in the Bering Sea?

Sea Change

"The northern Bering Sea is warming," says Cooper over dinner. The *Healy* has just set sail, and I am sitting with the oceanographer at a metal table lined with a long rubber mat. Its sticky grip keeps the cafeteria-style trays in place as the ship rolls with each wave.

For 20 years now, Cooper and Grebmeier have sailed the Bering Sea for weeks at a time to study its environment. Their years of data show that the region's air and water temperatures are rising. These changes are also evident to the naked eye. People **native** to the region, whose ancestors have lived there for thousands of years, have noticed that the amount of seasonal sea ice has been shrinking. The ice also melts earlier than it used to.

Wide-Ranging Effects

I've learned that the Bering Sea isn't alone in its hot spell. In fact, much of the world is experiencing a rise in temperature. What's to blame for the added heat? According to Cooper, it's humans. He explains that people around the world burn oil and other fossil fuels to power appliances, cars, and factories. Fossil fuels are the remains of prehistoric plants and animals. As fossil fuels burn, they release heat-trapping greenhouse gases like carbon dioxide. These gases build up in the atmosphere, causing the entire planet to warm.

This increase in Earth's average temperature—known as global warming—has had a tremendous effect on the environment. Animals and plants that are **accustomed** to thriving in very specific temperatures are now encountering temperatures that are not **conducive** to their survival. As a result, plants and animals all over the planet are moving to cooler climates.

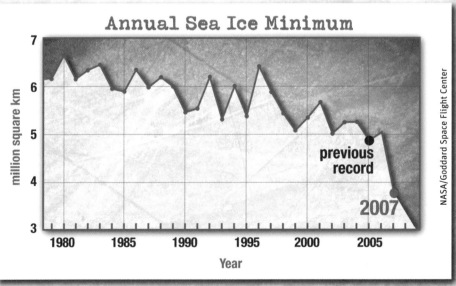

Annual Sea Ice Minimum

previous record

2007

NASA/Goddard Space Flight Center

This graph shows the minimum amount of sea ice in the Arctic each year, from 1979 to 2007. The sea ice has declined dramatically over this time.

> **oceanographer** *(n.)* scientist who studies oceans
> **thriving** *(v.)* becoming strong and healthy

A Warming World

In response to a warming world, animals and plants are relocating to cooler areas. Below are some species in North America that are trekking northward or to higher elevations in search of relief from the heat.

Invertebrate species, such as snails and sea stars, are moving northward, likely because of a rise in water and air temperatures.

Trees from subalpine forests are invading alpine meadows, partly in response to warming temperatures.

The natural habitat of the **Edith's checkerspot butterfly,** which extends from the west coast of southern Canada through northern Mexico, is shrinking.

Robins are migrating from low to high elevations, where temperatures are cooler. The birds now breed two weeks earlier than they did in the late 1970s.

The natural habitat of the **American alligator,** which ranges from the Carolinas south to Florida and west to Texas, seems to be shifting northward in some areas.

invertebrate *(adj.)* lacking a backbone
subalpine *(adj.)* relating to the upland slopes

Read and Synthesize

COMPREHENSION

Cause and Effect

Review the two paragraphs under "Wide-Ranging Effects." Then complete the causal chain below.

> Fossil fuels are burned.

VOCABULARY/WORD ANALYSIS

Multiple-Meaning Words

Check the meaning of the word *spell* as it is used in the first sentence of "Wide-Ranging Effects."

☐ to write the letters of a word
☐ a period of time

NAVIGATING TEXT

Author's Purpose

Review the sidebar "A Warming World."

• Is the author's purpose to inform or to entertain?

• What might the author have included if her purpose was also to persuade?

Ⓐ suggestions for what people should do to stop the world from getting warmer

Ⓑ a humorous description of each animal

Ⓒ more scientific facts about each animal

Earth on Fire

Earth's atmosphere naturally works like a greenhouse. It traps much of the sun's heat, keeping the world from freezing. But trouble arises when a buildup of gases in the atmosphere—caused by humans—traps more heat than normal. This phenomenon, known as the greenhouse effect, causes Earth's temperature to rise.

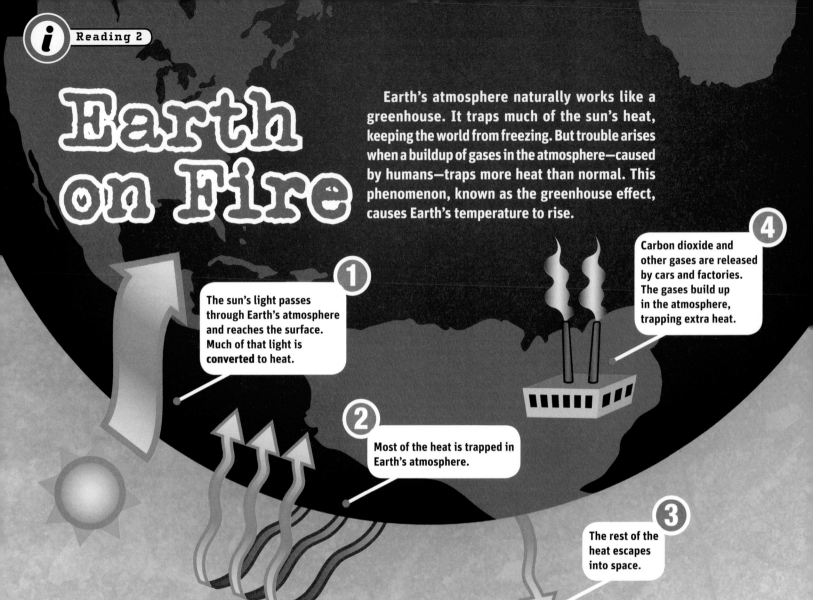

1 The sun's light passes through Earth's atmosphere and reaches the surface. Much of that light is converted to heat.

2 Most of the heat is trapped in Earth's atmosphere.

3 The rest of the heat escapes into space.

4 Carbon dioxide and other gases are released by cars and factories. The gases build up in the atmosphere, trapping extra heat.

Carbon Culprits

Carbon dioxide is the gas that's the leading cause of the greenhouse effect. This map shows the amount of carbon dioxide emissions by each country.

Total CO2 Emissions
(millions metric tons carbon)

- 0-10
- 10-100
- 100-500
- 500-1000
- 1000-1600

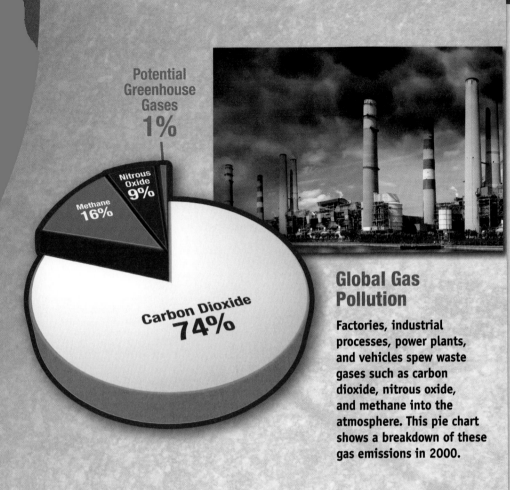

Potential
Greenhouse
Gases
1%

Nitrous
Oxide
9%

Methane
16%

Carbon Dioxide
74%

Global Gas Pollution

Factories, industrial processes, power plants, and vehicles spew waste gases such as carbon dioxide, nitrous oxide, and methane into the atmosphere. This pie chart shows a breakdown of these gas emissions in 2000.

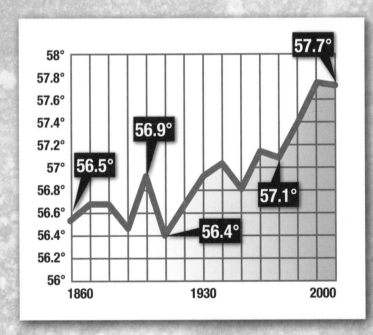

57.7°

56.9°

56.5°

57.1°

56.4°

58°			
57.8°			
57.6°			
57.4°			
57.2°			
57°			
56.8°			
56.6°			
56.4°			
56.2°			
56°			
	1860	1930	2000

Tracking Temperature

This graph shows an increase in Earth's average temperature from 1860 to 2000. To get the average temperature, scientists measure air temperatures at weather stations on continents and sea temperatures along shipping tracks on the oceans. They combine the different measurements to get an average temperature.

Read and Synthesize

COMPREHENSION

Cause and Effect

Review the text and diagram at the top of page 184.

If there were fewer cars and factories, how would that affect the amount of extra gases in the atmosphere?

_____

_____

What would that do to the greenhouse effect?

_____

_____

CRITICAL THINKING

Analyze

Why is it important for scientists to show that humans are contributing to the greenhouse effect?

_____

_____

_____

_____

_____

_____

21 **SMALL GROUPS/INDEPENDENT**

COLLABORATE

Represent Design a button you could wear that symbolizes the dangers of global warming. Include a word or phrase with your design.

COMMUNICATE

React and Write Do you think global warming is a serious problem? Brainstorm a list of facts supporting your position. Then write a paragraph that includes the evidence you collected.

W

Scientists aboard the *Healy* use a metal scooper (above) to collect small creatures from the seafloor (right).

Change in the Arctic

Are warming temperatures also affecting life in the Arctic Circle? For answers, I turn to Jim Lovvorn, an ecologist from the University of Wyoming who is also aboard the *Healy*. According to Lovvorn, "Crabs and fish from the southern Bering Sea are moving northward into the warming waters." Lovvorn tells me that the newcomers are slowly settling into waters that were once too cold for their taste. For the area's native animals that means trouble. After all, these new neighbors will be competing for the same food supply and habitat.

> **Predict**
> What may happen to the native animals if they have to compete for food and habitat?

Digging for Data

Cooper tells me that one of my onboard duties is to help the team study the region's animals. So the next morning I head to the *Healy*'s rear deck. Most of the scientific research takes place there.

Every person working on the deck must wear a survival suit. The suit has built-in flotation and **insulation** that would help me survive if I were to fall overboard. I suit up and get to work.

Twenty-four hours a day, seven days a week, the deck buzzes with experiments. The ship sails to various locations that Cooper and Grebmeier have visited in past years. They come back to these stations to collect data and take note of the plant and animal species that live in each spot.

This long-term data set will help them learn more about the sea's changing conditions over time. At each site we lower a huge metal scooper to the seafloor and grab a chunk of mud. The scientists collect a portion of the mud to take back to their universities for further study. We sift the rest through a screen to catch the small creatures living inside the mud.

During the final activity at each station, the scientists lower a large net to the seafloor. They signal the ship's crew to sail the *Healy* at roughly 2 knots—the speed of a brisk walk—for 20 minutes. As the ship moves, the net glides along the seafloor. As it does so, it gathers bottom-dwelling animals such as clams, crabs, sea stars, and fish.

> **flotation** *(n.)* ability to rest on a fluid's surface
> **sift** *(v.)* to examine something carefully

Trawling for Answers

Once the net is up, everyone helps to sort the catch by species. "We'll look at our catches to learn about the diets, densities, growth rates, and food requirements of the various animals," says Lovvorn. "This will help us understand [how the warming waters have affected] the food web in the northern Bering Sea."

Scientists have noticed that crabs and fish from the southern Bering Sea are moving into this northern region.

These crabs and fish eat things like clams that live on the seafloor. But the bearded seals and other animals that already live in this icy northern region eat similar foods. The scientists want to find out how many relocated crabs and fish are now competing with the ice-dwelling species for food. As competition for food in the Bering Sea increases, the current populations of seals, walruses, and other animals could suffer and decline in numbers, explains Grebmeier.

A scientist aboard the *Healy* sorts the seafloor specimens by species.

Read and Synthesize

NAVIGATING TEXT

Author's Purpose
Review "Digging for Data." Why do you think the author includes so many details about her personal experiences onboard the *Healy*?

_____

_____

_____

_____

VOCABULARY/WORD ANALYSIS

Multiple-Meaning Words
Review the last paragraph in "Digging for Data" and complete the following activities:

• Check the meaning of *knots* in this passage.

☐ a measurement of a boat's speed

☐ fastenings that hold two pieces of rope or string together

• <u>Underline</u> the context clue that helped you figure this out.

COMPREHENSION

Cause and Effect
Review "Trawling for Answers."

How might crabs and fish moving into the northern Bering Sea affect the seal population there?

_____

_____

Why?

_____

_____

_____

_____

_____

_____

_____

Patty Janes sails across the Bering Sea.

Out of Sight

Ring. Ring. I'm awakened by the sound of a phone. Disoriented, I look around to try to figure out where I am. A faint light shines through a nearby porthole. It gently illuminates my surroundings. I can just make out the metal bunk beds crammed inside a small room. At that moment, it all comes back to me: I am on the U.S. Coast Guard icebreaker *Healy*.

Ring. Ring.

The caller is persistent. I look at my watch. It is three o' clock in the morning.

Who would be calling me so early? I pick up the phone to find out.

> **Predict**
> **Why do you think the author is being awoken so early?**

"Come up to the ship's bridge," says Ruth Cooper, a middle school student from St. John Neumann Catholic School in Knoxville, Tennessee. Ruth is onboard the Coast Guard cutter with her parents, Lee Cooper and Jackie Grebmeier. "We've just spotted a polar bear!" she says.

Ursus maritimus, the "bear of the sea," is well adapted to life in this icy environment. Its off-white fur blends with the chunks of ice surrounding the ship. That makes it impossible for me to locate the bear. After a half hour of scanning the horizon, I realize it is hopeless. The carnivore, or meat eater, is probably long gone by now. It is likely prowling the ice in search of ringed seals—its primary prey—to eat.

Polar bears use sea ice as a platform from which to hunt. The bear will search for breathing holes in the ice made by seals and wait patiently by a hole until a seal pops up to breathe. Then, BAM! The polar bear uses its enormous paw to deliver a swift blow to the seal. The bear's dinner is ready.

> **disoriented** *(adj.)* confused
> **illuminates** *(v.)* brightens with light

Polar Problems

Polar bears are massive predators. A male bear can weigh 770 kilograms (1,700 pounds). Only thick ice can support a bear that heavy. From where I stand, the ice where the polar bear was first spotted looks solid. But according to scientists on the *Healy*, sea ice is rapidly melting due to global warming.

In recent history, one of the biggest sea-ice retreats occurred in summer 2004. That year, a pulse of unusually warm Bering Sea water traveled up along the Alaska coast. The warm water caused the seasonal ice north of Alaska to **diminish**. The area's polar bears felt the heat: Scientists came across four polar bears that had drowned. The researchers believe the bears were exhausted from swimming without being able to rest on thick sea ice.

Reduced sea ice threatens more than polar bears. Any animal that depends on sea ice for survival is at risk, says Cooper. He tells me that when he was on the *Healy* in 2004—during the same year and in the general location where the polar bears were found drowned—he and others on the ship spotted baby walruses swimming by themselves in deep waters.

Ringed seals are part of a polar bear's diet. The bears often snag the seals when they surface to breathe.

A polar bear searches for food.

NAVIGATING TEXT

Author's Purpose
Review "Out of Sight." What do you think is the author's purpose for including the humorous story about waking up in the middle of the night to see a polar bear?

_____

_____

_____

COMPREHENSION

Cause and Effect
Review "Polar Problems." Then complete the causal chain below, ending with the cause of death of polar bears in 2004.

First, warm water from the Bering Sea traveled up the Alaska coast.

CRITICAL THINKING

Evaluate
Which would you prefer to read—this personal narrative or an article about global warming in a science book? Why?

_____

_____

_____

_____

A mother walrus huddles with her calf.

Walrus Woes

Normally, for the first one to three months of a walrus calf's life, the baby and its mother are like glue. They usually stick together in waters that are just a couple of hundred meters deep. After that initial period, the walrus mom only separates from her calf to dive to the seafloor. There, she searches for clams and other foods. This nourishment gives her the energy she needs to produce milk and nurse her baby for the first two years of its life. When the mom goes in search of food, she is careful to leave her baby on a chunk of ice, where it can rest.

Cooper says he saw a total of nine baby walruses by themselves in water as deep as 3,000 meters (1.8 miles). Their mothers were nowhere in sight, and the sea ice on which the calves had been resting was gone. The calves were doomed to die, says Cooper.

How do scientists explain the stranded walrus calves? Violent storms could have separated the moms and babies. Or perhaps the mother walruses died, leaving the calves orphaned. But another suspect is global warming.

> **Question**
> **How do you think global warming will affect the walrus calves?**

Some scientists believe that the unusually warm current of Bering Sea water that occurred in the summer of 2004 may have been to blame. This warm water may have caused the ice on which the calves were resting to recede north toward the much-deeper Arctic Ocean. "If sea ice [were to] recede too far north, then the [adult] walruses could not feed," says Carleton Ray. Ray is a walrus expert from the University of Virginia who is also on the *Healy*. "Walruses do not dive in deep water. They can't dive much deeper than approximately 100 m (328 ft)."

Cooper thinks that as the walrus mothers traveled to shallower waters to feed, their calves drifted north with the receding ice. Gradually, the growing distance between moms and calves may have separated them from each other for good.

Uncertain Future

Although Cooper saw nine stranded walrus calves, he believes that there were probably more that he did not spot. Still, the events in 2004 did not threaten the overall walrus population. The population is estimated to be between 150,000 and 250,000.

But global warming is a constant and growing problem. In fact, in the summers of 2002, 2005, and 2006, sea ice retreated at a similar rate as in 2004. So Cooper and other scientists fear that the continued loss of sea ice due to a warming world could make walrus strandings more common.

All of the walruses that I see from the *Healy*'s bridge are safely perched on thick slabs of ice. Mothers and calves are huddled together. But Cooper warns that if global warming doesn't stop, tough times are ahead for the animals of the Bering Sea and other polar regions. "Whether they can adapt or not is uncertain," says Cooper. "I feel optimistic that there's still time to [reverse global warming], but the clock is definitely ticking."

Pulling Into Port

Before I know it, my time aboard the *Healy* has come to an end. Just as the trip began in Dutch Harbor, so it is ending. At 7 o'clock in the morning, the ship pulls into port. I awaken just in time to watch the sun rise over the ocean, its rays revealing the snowy peaks that now surround us.

I pack up my cold weather gear and lug it through the ship's narrow halls, down its steep stairs, and onto solid ground. I turn around to take one last look at the *Healy*. Its bright red hull will forever be etched in my memory, as will all of the events that took place over the last month. It is time to fly home. ■

> **initial** *(adj.)* happening at the beginning
> **recede** *(v.)* to decrease or grow smaller

What Can You Do?

To protect the world from the harmful effects of global warming, people and governments in countries around the globe need to work together to reduce air pollution. But there are also some simple steps that you and your family can take now.

 Change your lightbulbs. Regular incandescent lightbulbs waste a lot of energy. So switch to compact fluorescent bulbs, which use much less energy. If every U.S. family did that, 1 trillion pounds of global-warming air pollution would be kept out of the air.

 Unplug all electric devices when you are not using them. Things like your cell phone charger and DVD player use energy even when they are turned off.

 Convince your family to carpool—or bike ride—whenever possible. Cars are one of the biggest sources of carbon dioxide, so the fewer cars that are on the road, the better!

 In the summer, limit your air conditioner use. Close window shades to keep the sun from heating up your home.

 Wait until you have a full load of dirty clothes before doing your laundry. It takes energy to heat water, so wash your clothes in cold or warm water instead of hot.

 Towel- or air-dry your hair instead of using an electric hair dryer.

Spread the word! Share energy-saving advice with friends and family.

CAREER CONNECTION

Science, Technology, Engineering & Mathematics
www.careerclusters.org

Go to **21 ToolKit Expert File 6.30** to learn more about careers in oceanography.

Walruses rest on a slab of ice.

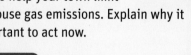

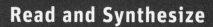
COMPREHENSION

Cause and Effect

Review "Walrus Woes." <u>Underline</u> three reasons that may explain why some walrus calves become stranded.

NAVIGATING TEXT

Author's Purpose

For what purpose do you think the author included the section titled "What Can You Do?"

_____

_____

_____

_____

_____

_____

_____

_____

_____

---

21 SMALL GROUPS/INDEPENDENT

COLLABORATE

Create Stories Invent characters and a plot for a fictional story that has to do with global warming. Present your ideas in a story map or chart.

COMMUNICATE

Discuss and Write With a partner, brainstorm and then write a letter to your mayor suggesting that he or she take action to help your town limit greenhouse gas emissions. Explain why it is important to act now.

W

READ ONLINE

expert space Go to **www.expert21.com/student** to learn more about The Arctic; The Polar Regions; Ozone Layer.

LIFE AT THE P✴LES

The Arctic and Antarctica are the coldest, iciest and windiest places on Earth. How does life survive at the frozen top and bottom of the planet?

THE ARCTIC is the icy, windy region surrounding the North Pole. It consists largely of ice-covered ocean; permanently frozen areas of land lie at the outskirts. Temperatures plummet to -40°C (-40°F). This harsh climate and terrain feeds and houses people and millions of animals. Read on to discover some of their secrets to survival.

People: Outsmarting the Cold

- The Arctic is the only polar region that is home to people. Various groups of indigenous peoples—including the Inuit, the Aleut, and the Nenets—live in different parts of the Arctic. Most live in houses, but the few nomadic groups—mainly reindeer herders—seek refuge from the cold in tents covered with animal skins.

- To keep warm, these groups often dress in clothing and footwear made from animal skins—particularly seal, caribou, polar bear, wolf, and fox. Animal skins are warm and lightweight, making them ideal for living and working in the Arctic.

---

plummet *(v.)* decrease rapidly in value or amount
indigenous *(adj.)* originating in a particular place

Snowy Owl: Extreme Parenting

- Snowy owls nest in shallow depressions in the ground. To keep their eggs warm, these owls favor areas free of snow.

- Snowy owls and their babies have downy feathers, a major cold-weather asset. The thick, fine down under their feathers insulates the birds' bodies from cold, much like a human's down coat.

- The female stays with her babies, while the male guards the nest and hunts for food—usually lemmings. The female then dissects his kill into small portions for the baby owls, called owlets.

Polar Bears: Keeping a Grip, Staying Afloat

- How does a polar bear keep from sliding across the ice? Its fur-covered paws are covered with bumpy pads called papillae, which provide traction. In addition, the bear has strong, sharp claws that work like cleats to keep it from slipping.

- Polar bears spend much time in icy Arctic waters. Each strand of the bears' fur is hollow. Their warm coats are buoyant, so these heavy animals can stay afloat during hours-long swims.

- Believe it or not, the skin under polar bears' gleaming fur is black. The dark color absorbs the sun's rays, keeping the bears warm.

---

depressions *(n.)* sunken or hollow places on a surface
dissects *(v.)* cuts up a dead animal

Author's Purpose

What is the author's purpose for writing the text on these pages?

_____

_____

_____

_____

_____

How might the text have been different if the author's purpose was to persuade people to visit the poles to see the animals described?

_____

_____

_____

_____

_____

_____

_____

COMPREHENSION

Compare and Contrast

What do all these subjects on these pages have in common?

_____

_____

_____

How does the author contrast reindeer herders with most indigenous people who live in the Arctic?

_____

_____

_____

_____

_____

_____

ANTARCTICA is by far the coldest, windiest continent on Earth. During winter months, temperatures can drop below −73°C (−100°F). Wind speeds reach up to 248 kph (154 mph). Much of Antarctica's mainland is covered by a continental ice sheet, while its coastal waters are littered with chunks of ice that range in size from small ice floes to giant ice shelves. Despite these intense challenges, many forms of wildlife live at the South Pole.

Emperor Penguins:
Slip-Sliding Travelers Stand Together

- Emperor penguins spend a great deal of time in icy water. Their scale-like top feathers are water resistant, which prevents ice particles from sticking to the birds as they emerge after swimming. A layer of down underneath traps heat close to their bodies.

- Emperor penguins huddle in large groups—another way to keep warm. They take turns braving the chilly wind along the group's outskirts. Then they move into the center to warm up. As they stand, they rock from toes to heels to minimize contact between their feet and the frigid ground.

- Since these birds have short legs and large, webbed feet, they can only waddle when in an upright position. To pick up speed while moving over land, penguins plop down on their bellies and push forward with their feet and winglike flippers. This tobogganing motion allows them to cover ground at a faster rate.

Elephant Seals:
In Great Shape for the Cold

- The elephant seal is one massive animal. An adult can weigh up to 2,000 kilograms (4,500 pounds). That's heavier than most cars! The seals' hefty size is a necessity in icy Antarctica. Their weight comes largely from blubber, a layer of fat beneath the skin that keeps the animals warm.

- Elephant seals have thick, rounded bodies and short limbs. This compact shape reduces the animals' surface area, so they lose less heat.

---

continental *(adj.)* relating to a large land mass
upright *(adj.)* standing or sitting straight up

Orcas: Natural-Born Killers

- Orcas navigate Antarctica's dangerously ice-filled waters by using echolocation. The whales make a series of clicks and whistles whose sound waves travel through the water until they hit a solid object, then bounce back to the orcas, allowing them to dodge deadly icebergs.

- When you're a sea creature with a taste for Antarctic land animals, finding food can be tricky. Seal-loving orcas use a hunting method called spyhopping. The orcas lift their heads and much of their bodies straight up out of the water and "spy" on their surroundings. When they see a tasty seal on land or on an ice floe, they lunge up to grab their prey. ■

COMPREHENSION

Compare and Contrast
Compare and contrast the adaptations of the Emperor penguin with those of the orca. How are they alike? How are they different?

_____

_____

_____

_____

_____

_____

VOCABULARY/WORD ANALYSIS

Multiple-Meaning Words
Review the text under "Emperor Penguins" and (circle) the word *cover*. Select the meaning of cover as it is used in this sentence.

Ⓐ something put on top of something else to protect it

Ⓑ to travel a particular distance

Ⓒ to investigate or report on

Ⓓ to envelop in a layer of something

CRITICAL THINKING

Synthesize
What did you learn from reading this photo essay?

_____

_____

_____

_____

_____

READ ONLINE

expert space
Go to **www.expert21.com/student** to learn more about Polar Bears; Arctic Wildlife; Antarctic Wildlife.

Think Across Texts

Organize and Synthesize ··

1. Complete this chart using information from "The Story of Keesh," "Crisis on Top of the World," and "Life at the Poles."

	How do animals and people survive in the coldest places on earth?
"The Story of Keesh"	
"Crisis on Top of the World"	
"Life at the Poles"	

Compare and Evaluate ··

2. Polar bears are featured in "The Story of Keesh" and "Crisis on Top of the World." Compare and contrast the part that polar bears play in those two selections.

_____

_____

_____

_____

3. Would you rather visit Antarctica, as described in "Life at the Poles," or the Arctic, as described in "Crisis on Top of the World" and "The Story of Keesh"? Explain your answer using examples from the text.

_____

_____

_____

_____

4. "Crisis on Top of the World" describes the effects of global warming from the first-person perspective of the author, while "Life at the Poles" uses the third-person point of view. Which method do you think is more effective?

_____

_____

_____

_____

_____

_____

Discuss and Write ················

5. With a partner, discuss how the three readings in "Lands of Ice and Snow" helped you understand life in the polar regions. Take notes as you talk. Then use your notes to write a response to the question: *What is life like in permanently frozen places?*

Apply Word Knowledge

Word Lab

1. **Finish it.** Complete the sentence below using the words **convert** and **affirm.**

The body can _____ food into energy. Chapter 3 of my science textbook will _____ this.

2. **Identify it.** Which word or phrase means the same as **decline**?

Ⓐ a climb up

Ⓑ lie down

Ⓒ refuse

Ⓓ decide

3. **Name it.** What foods are you **accustomed** to eating for breakfast?

_____

_____

_____

_____

_____

4. **Think about it.** Do you think a little bit of **arrogance** is a good thing or a bad thing? Explain your answer.

_____

_____

_____

_____

_____

_____

_____

5. **Check them.** Which things are conducive to good health?

❏ getting exercise

❏ eating junk food

❏ eating a healthy diet

❏ being a couch potato

Word Analysis

6. Read each sentence below. Check the meaning of each word in boldface type.

- The **current** in this part of the river is swift.

  ❏ up-to-date

  ❏ the flow of water

- I think that wall is too high to **scale.**

  ❏ an instrument for weighing things

  ❏ to climb up

7. Read the sentence below. Using context clues, figure out the meaning of the word *extremity*.

We walked across the island until we reached its western extremity, where the boats were docked.

In this sentence, *extremity* means

Ⓐ the farthest point

Ⓑ a desperate action

Ⓒ great danger

Ⓓ middle

Gather Information

To gather information about people who live in extreme environments, head to the Internet. But be careful—without good searching skills, you may end up sifting through thousands of Web sites you don't want.

Smart Searches Online

► If you want to learn more about the Inuit people, whom you read about earlier in this workshop, here's how to find information on the Web.

MARK IT 🖊

Put a **checkmark** next to ✔ the question that relates to the territory of the Inuit.

· · · · · · · · · · · · · · · · · · ·

Underline the keywords that you would use to find information about problems in the Inuit community.

⟨Circle⟩ the search engines that you could use to find information.

My research purpose: I want to research the Inuit people. I'm interested in learning more about their culture.

Specific Questions:

• What are the earliest known records of the Inuit?

• Where do they live?

• What is their culture like?

• What problems does their community face?

Possible keywords:		
Search Term 1	**and**	**Search Term 2**
Inuit		Culture
Inuit		History
Inuit		Social Issues
Inuit		Land or Territory or Region

Find Images   Find Web sites

Searching: Conduct your search. Try a variety of search engines such as Google, Yahoo, and Ask.com.

expert space Go to Expert Space for more information about evaluating Web sites.

⌈Here's⌉
⌊How ⌋ ►**Follow these steps to streamline your Web searches:**

Step 1 Determine your purpose. Do you want to find general information or specific facts?

Step 2 Brainstorm your search terms. Your search terms should be as specific as possible.

Step 3 Search. Enter your terms in a search engine, such as Google or Yahoo. If you put words together in quotation marks, the search engine will look for the entire phrase. You can look for two phrases by connecting them with "and."

Step 4 Refine and RE-search. Evaluate the list of sites that comes up and decide if you need to refine your search. You may need to try different search terms.

Apply: Search the Web

▶ **Apply the steps to plan your own Internet search.**

1. **Determine your purpose.** Look again at the questions you wrote under Personal Inquiry on page 165. Choose one of those topics to explore further. Write it again here:

_____

_____

2. **Identify the search terms.** Choose the search terms that you will use. Be as specific as possible.

Search Term No. 1	Search Term No. 2

3. **Conduct your search.** Write down the search engine you are using here:

_____

_____

4. **Evaluate your search results and refine your search.** You may need to rethink your search terms. Write the address for a few Web sites that look useful to you.

_____

_____

_____

_____

Did you find what you needed?   ☐ yes   ☐ no

If not, how can you refine your results? List ideas for search terms here:

_____

_____

_____

Magazine Article

Blue People of the Sahara

The desert is scorching by day. By night, hyenas and jackals prowl. A bowl of rice is considered a luxury. Find out how people survive in this forbidding place.

QuickWrite

Make a list of challenges American middle school students face. Do you think these are harder or easier than the challenges faced by young people living in other parts of the world? Explain.

Compare and Contrast   COMPREHENSION

To **compare** things, an author identifies what they have in common. To **contrast** things, the author identifies how they are different.

In nonfiction, authors often describe people and places that are unfamiliar to most readers. You can get more out of such a description by noticing comparisons and contrasts between what is being described and familiar people and places.

▶ **Read this excerpt from "Blue People of the Sahara." Then complete the sentences below.**

> Fatimata speaks three languages and loves math. But school is only a small part of her work-filled day. She pounds grain and cooks breakfast for her family, draws water from a deep well dug into the ground, and sweeps out the chicken coop.
>
> Her favorite food is rice, "though we can never afford it," she says. There's little time for fun in Fatimata's day, but her favorite game is falango, a version of hide-and-seek. "I imagine American kids have a lot more fun than we do," she says.

One way in which Fatimata is like most American kids is that _____

_____ .

Two ways in which she is different are _____ and _____

_____ .

Analyze Details   NAVIGATING TEXT

In a nonfiction text, authors include details, or ideas that support the main idea.

Details may include facts and examples.

▶ **Read this passage from "Blue People of the Sahara." Circle the main idea of the paragraph. Underline the two details that support the main idea.**

> In the Sahara, modern medicines such as antibiotics are extremely rare. (Sheep urine is the traditional medicine for internal infections.) Clinics and doctors are miles away in distant cities.

Academic Language VOCABULARY

▶ Rate each word. Then write its meaning and an example sentence.

Word	Meaning	Example
EXPERT WORDS *Use these words to write and talk about the workshop topic.*		
arid ar•id *(adj)* ① ② ③ ④	very dry, without much rainfall	Animals in arid places have to live without much water.
drought drought *(noun)* ① ② ③ ④		
ACADEMIC WORDS *Use these words in all your subject classes.*		
adequate ad•e•quate *(adj)* ① ② ③ ④		
internal in•ter•nal *(adj)* ① ② ③ ④	located on the inside	
transition tran•si•tion *(noun)* ① ② ③ ④		
CONTENT AREA WORDS *Use these words to talk and write about social studies.*		
caravan car•a•van *(noun)* ① ② ③ ④		The caravan of trucks drove across the country in four days.
filter fil•ter *(verb)* ① ② ③ ④		
oasis o•a•sis *(noun)* ① ② ③ ④		

Rating Scale ① I don't know the word. ② I've seen it or heard it. ③ I know its meaning. ④ I know it and use it.

Context Clues: Examples and Definitions WORD ANALYSIS

When you come across an unfamiliar word, look for context clues in the same sentence or a nearby sentence that can help you figure out its meaning.

A context clue may be a definition or an example of the unfamiliar word.

▶ In one of the sentences below, the context clue for the word *nomad* is a definition. The other sentence helps you define *nomad* by giving examples. Write *example* or *definition* after each sentence. Then underline the context clues in each sentence.

Nomads are people who roam from place to place in search of food or water for their herds.

_____

The Tuareg nomads of the Sahara rely on camels to sustain their way of life.

_____

Blue People of the Sahara

By Sean McCollum

from *Junior Scholastic* magazine

For centuries, Tuareg nomads have ruled the desert.

To a visitor, the Sahara in dry season looks as if somebody had taken a match to it. The ground is bone-dry and cracked. Stretches of windblown grass are parched a deathly yellow, streaked by fields of black volcanic rock and orangey sand. Skeletons of goats and sheep are a common sight. The only trees, acacias, have thorns so long and sharp that they can pierce the sole of a boot. "Man, this place is so tough," says one visitor, "even the trees have teeth!"

It takes a tough people to live in the Sahara. The Tuareg nomads are certainly that. They have roamed and ruled the Sahara's edges—a desert larger than our lower 48 states—for hundreds of years.

Today, more than a million Tuareg live in the West and North African countries of Mali, Niger, Algeria, Libya, Burkina Faso, Mauritania, and Nigeria. But ask any Tuareg where he or she lives. The answer will always be the same— the Sahara, whatever border it crosses.

"Where others might see a wasteland, we have always seen the beauty of home and freedom," says Nimit Moore, a Tuareg born in the West African country of Mali. To travel in the Sahara is to learn to eat, drink, dress, ride, and sleep like a Tuareg—and to see the beauty of the land through their eyes.

Sahara Desert

parched *(adj.)* extremely dry
nomads *(n.)* tribe members with no fixed home

NAVIGATING TEXT

Analyze Details

Review the first paragraph on page 203. <u>Underline</u> at least three details that support this paragraph's main idea: "the Sahara in dry season looks as if somebody had taken a match to it."

CRITICAL THINKING

Analyze

Why do you think most Tuareg people say they are from the Sahara rather than saying they are from an individual country?

_____

_____

_____

_____

_____

_____

_____

_____

_____

_____

_____

_____

_____

COMPREHENSION

Compare and Contrast

Who would be most likely to make each statement below, a Tuareg or a visitor to the Sahara? Use the information you have read so far to label each statement *visitor* or *Tuareg*.

"This place seems lifeless." _____

"I feel so free here!" _____

"I love wide-open spaces where you can see for miles." _____

"I prefer green forests and high, snowy mountains." _____

The Tuareg use camels to transport cargo across the Sahara.

How Bad Do Camels Smell?

Arabian camels—which have only one hump—have made the Tuareg way of life possible for hundreds of years. Camels have been the trucks that Tuareg traders load with salt slabs from the mines near Timbuktu; the horses that Tuareg warriors ride into battle, swords and daggers flashing; the U-Hauls that Tuareg families pack with household supplies in the move from a water hole to an **oasis.**

These "ships of the desert," as they're called, lug hundreds of pounds, go for days without water, and find the leaves and nasty thorns of the acacia tasty.

> **Visualize**
> **The writer uses several metaphors to describe the camels. How else might you describe them?**

A camel's throaty growls and roars are scary, but not nearly as intimidating as its breath.

Like cows, camels chew their cud. A strong whiff of a mouthful of camel cud—chewed and digested over and over—is enough to sicken a rider new to the Sahara. And if that rider forgets, before mounting, to command his camel to swallow, he may get a splash of stinky green gop in his face.

Watching the Flock

Nomads, by definition and tradition, are herders, or tenders of livestock. The Tuareg are no different. They have lived and died by the health of their herds of camels, sheep and, especially, goats.

Essederg Ag Abuba (ess-eh-DEHRG ak ah-BOO-buh), a 12-year-old herder, lives near the town of Inhinita, a small, dusty settlement in eastern Mali. Each day he cares for his flock of 10 goats and five sheep. He guides them to good grazing grounds, draws water for them from a 50-foot well with a goatskin bucket and rope, milks them morning and evening, and gathers them around him at night to protect them from predators.

"If you only knew how bad things are with the jackals and hyenas," he says, shaking his head. Because of his turban, only Essederg's eyes are visible.

He admits to loneliness in the wide-open desert but amuses himself by daydreaming about the things he

> **settlement** *(n.)* a place where people establish a community
> **turban** *(n.)* a headdress made of wound cloth

wants. A four-wheel drive truck—a rare sight in the Sahara—recently crossed his path and now tops his list. "[It was] so beautiful," he says.

But now, with his animals safe by the well, he can relax beneath the afternoon shade of an acacia tree with the men of Inhinita. He squats with them as they sip small glasses of hot, sweet tea and joins in their joking and laughter.

"The Blue People"

In most places, a 12-year-old boy would be with kids his own age—not in Mali. Essederg's father died when he was 7, forcing him to leave school. He now supports his mother and himself with his small flock.

Essederg Ag Abuba poses with his camel.

Essederg dresses in a blue knee-length robe and pants, flip-flops, and a white turban. The turban is the perfect desert headgear. It blocks powerful sun rays from the head, neck, and face, protects skin from acacia thorns, and **filters** out dust. (It also makes a ready pillow for a quick nap.)

When meeting strangers or important people, Tuareg men pull up part of the turban over their noses and mouths as a sign of respect. The traditional Tuareg turban is made of purple-blue cloth, colored by powdered indigo dye that smells like aspirin. The dye, which gets on the face and hands, gave rise to the Tuareg nickname, "The Blue People."

NAVIGATING TEXT

Analyze Details
Review the section "How Bad Do Camels Smell?"
- **Check** ✓ the sentence that states the main idea.
- <u>Underline</u> details that support this main idea.

VOCABULARY/WORD ANALYSIS

Context Clues: Examples and Definitions
Review the first paragraph in "Watching the Flock." Look for a context clue that is a definition of livestock. Write the definition here.

_____

_____

_____

COMPREHENSION

Compare and Contrast
Review "Watching the Flock" and "The Blue People."

How is Essederg different from typical twelve-year-olds where you live?

_____

_____

_____

_____

_____

How is Essederg like other twelve-year-olds you know of?

_____

_____

_____

_____

_____

_____

Fatimata Wallet Ibrahim is a Tuareg whose family now lives in a city.

Goat's Head for Lunch

In the Sahara, modern medicines such as antibiotics are extremely rare. (Sheep urine is the traditional medicine for **internal** infections.) Clinics and doctors are miles away in distant cities.

If the rainy season—June through September—is below average, **drought** may wipe out livestock by the tens of thousands. Without farming or refrigeration, the food supply is not always **adequate.**

The Tuareg have learned to make the most out of what they have. Essederg's daily diet, for example, consists of goat's milk for breakfast and porridge mixed with wild seeds for supper.

On special occasions, he feasts on meat, bone marrow, and fresh-roasted organs. Since much of the food is spiced with sand, he must be careful not to bite down too hard.

It is not unusual to save the goat's head for lunch the next day. After warming it up by rolling it around in a ground fire, the feaster plucks out and slurps down such delicacies as the eyes, tongue, and brain. A goat's eye tastes pretty good—almost like a piece of fatty pork.

Nomads No More?

For the past 30 years, the Tuareg have experienced a major **transition** in their way of life. Terrible droughts in the 1970s and 1980s destroyed most of their herds.

In 1990, the Tuareg began a five-year violent rebellion against the Mali government to demand better treatment and more assistance. Several factors, including decades of overgrazing and drought, have sped up desertification (see sidebar). Overuse has left fewer grazing areas for goats and sheep.

Such difficulties have forced many Tuareg to abandon nomadic living and settle in villages and cities. Fatimata Wallet Ibrahim (fah-tee-MAH-tah wahl-ETT ee-BRAH-heem), 12, and her family, who used to raise goats, now live in the city of Menaka. They still raise goats, but now they live in a two-room, mud-brick house rather than a tent sewn of rags, hides, and woven mats.

> **Visualize**
> **Sketch a picture of Fatimata's home as you imagine it to look.**

Fatimata is getting an education, unlike her parents before her. (Only about five percent of Tuareg can read or write.) She's a serious fifth-grade student in a class of 40.

Fatimata speaks three languages and loves math. But school is only a small part of her work-filled day. She pounds grain and cooks breakfast for her family, draws water from a deep well dug in the ground, and sweeps out the chicken coop.

Her favorite food is rice, "though we can never afford it," she says. There's little time for fun in Fatimata's day, but her favorite game is falango, a version of hide-and-seek. "I imagine American kids have a lot more fun than we do," she says.

The days of camel **caravans** and desert camps may be numbered for the Tuareg as the modern world of trucks, telephones, and electricity reaches them. But that doesn't mean the smell of camels' breath and the taste of greasy goats' eyes won't always be sweet to these rulers of the Sahara. ∎

---

marrow (n.) soft substance inside some bones
delicacies (n.) foods that are pleasing but rare

The Spread of the Sahara

According to a United Nations (UN) report, one-third of Earth's surface is at risk of becoming a desert. This process—called desertification—has turned large sections of Africa, Spain, and China into dust.

What's causing desertification? Natural changes in the climate are partly responsible, but human activities are largely to blame. The UN report says that much of the land has been deforested to make way for crops—such as peanuts—in areas like Senegal and Niger. Often, the crops aren't suited to the climate of the regions and therefore need large amounts of fertilizers, chemicals, and irrigation to make them grow. These threaten the quality of the land to the point that it becomes a useless desert.

The problem has posed a huge threat to the nomads who call the areas home. Most of these desert-dwellers raise animals including camels, sheep, and goats. These animals must eat vegetation—such as trees and shrubs—to stay alive. However, the **arid** land makes it difficult for plants to grow—consequently threatening the lives of the animals.

Can anything be done to stop the process? The UN report suggests that dryland dwellers need to be provided with alternative livelihoods that don't put pressure on the natural resources.

A giant sand dune threatens to engulf a palm plantation in Libya .

deforested *(adj.)* cleared of forests
irrigation *(n.)* act of supplying water to crops

COMPREHENSION

Compare and Contrast

Review the section "Nomads No More?" Draw a box around the sentences that compare and contrast the Ibrahim family's nomadic life with their way of life in the city.

• What is the same?

_____

• What is different?

_____

_____

VOCABULARY/WORD ANALYSIS

Context Clues: Examples and Definitions

In "The Spread of the Sahara" sidebar find the word *vegetation*.

• <u>Underline</u> two examples that help you figure out what the word means.

• Write the definition here.

_____

21 SMALL GROUPS/INDEPENDENT

COLLABORATE

Examine Perspectives Imagine what it would be like for Essederg or Fatimata to go to your school. Then write a list of things you think would be strange to them.

COMMUNICATE

React and Write List the different challenges the Tuareg face. What do you think is the greatest challenge? Explain your answer.

READ ONLINE

expert space
Go to **www.expert21.com/student** to learn more about Tuareg; Nomads; Caravan.

Novel Excerpt

Shabanu's ailing grandfather disappears . . . just as a huge sandstorm engulfs the part of the desert where they are staying. Will this crisis turn deadly for Shabanu's family?

QuickWrite

Have you ever worried because you didn't know where a family member or friend was? Write an imagined account for someone you care about, who has gone missing for a day.

Mood   LITERARY ANALYSIS

Mood is the feeling or atmosphere that an author creates for readers. An author creates mood by carefully choosing words that can affect how a reader feels, such as:

vivid adjectives:

• glossy, tattered, parched

precise verbs:

• tremble, scrape, bellow

imagery:

• a deep well of terror

• wild laughter

The mood of a piece of writing can be described with words such as *gloomy*, *lighthearted*, or *suspenseful*.

▶ **Read this passage from *Shabanu*, and fill in the web with words and phrases that create a mood of fear and anxiety.**

The storm goes on for hours more, and we are too exhausted to go outside again until the wind dies. The boys whimper. Sher Dil stays under Mama's skirt and never makes a sound. The rest of us are silent, as if our souls have blown outside with Grandfather, tossed with the dust on the wind.

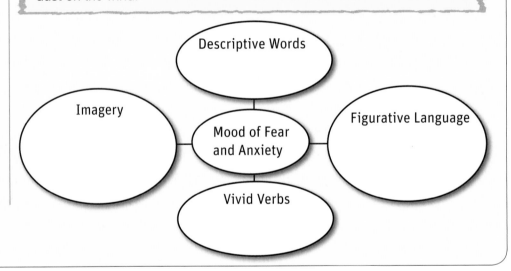

Cause and Effect   COMPREHENSION

A cause is the reason why something happens. An effect is the result of a cause.

Sometimes elements of the setting can be the causes of events in a story or can cause characters to act and feel in certain ways.

▶ **Read the following passage from *Shabanu*, then answer the question below.**

Mama, Phulan, Auntie, and the boys huddle under shawls in the hot, swirling dark. There is no escaping the sand, even indoors, and everything is gritty with the dust that blows with great force through the thatch and around the cracks in the doors and shutters. Mama runs to us and takes the lanterns. She holds me against her for a second. Her eyes are haunted.

List one effect of the sandstorm below.

_____

_____

Academic Language   VOCABULARY

▶ Rate each word. Then write its meaning and an example sentence.

Word	Meaning	Example
ACADEMIC WORDS *Use these words in all your subject classes.*		
colleague col·league *(noun)* ① ② ③ ④	a coworker or fellow member of an organization	My mom is talking on the phone with a colleague from work.
embrace em·brace *(noun)* ① ② ③ ④		
CONTENT AREA WORDS *Use these words to talk and write about social studies.*		
exchange ex·change *(verb)* ① ② ③ ④		
SELECTION WORDS *These words are key to understanding this selection.*		
apprehensive ap·pre·hen·sive *(adj)* ① ② ③ ④	nervous or uneasy about a future event	
envision en·vi·sion *(verb)* ① ② ③ ④		
gaping gap·ing *(adj)* ① ② ③ ④		
haul haul *(verb)* ① ② ③ ④		
wither with·er *(verb)* ① ② ③ ④		Those plants will wither and die if you keep forgetting to water them.

Rating Scale   ① I don't know the word.   ② I've seen it or heard it.   ③ I know its meaning.   ④ I know it and use it.

Context Clues   WORD ANALYSIS

Context clues are the words and phrases in a text that can help you figure out the meaning of an unfamiliar word.

If a word is unfamiliar, look in the same sentence or in a nearby one for context clues that give a general sense of the word's meaning.

▶ Read the following passage from *Shabanu*. Underline clues to the meaning of the word *frustrated*.

The rest of the day drags in a blur of heat and frantic but frustrated effort. First we go to the maker of tombs, but his daughter tells us he has gone to another village. Is there no one else who makes tombs? No, she says, only her father.

What do you think *frustrated* means here?

_____

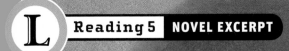
Shabanu

By Suzanne Fisher Staples

Tragedy strikes a young girl and her family living in the Cholistan Desert.

Eleven-year-old Shabanu and her nomadic family live in the Cholistan Desert. The family has several camels, including Mithoo, Sher Dil, and Xhush Dil. To survive the sweltering conditions of the region, the family must drink plenty of freshwater, which they obtain from a toba, or oasis. In this reading, Shabanu's family has situated themselves near a toba, where they had planned to stay for two months. Then, disaster strikes.

Desert Storm

By the time we reach the toba, Grandfather has fallen back into his torpid state, like a beetle in winter. Dadi worries about him, and Mama makes special efforts to make things that he likes to eat.

"He'll come back," she tells Dadi. "He's been this way for years, and he always comes back. Don't worry." But Dadi continues to worry, stopping by Grandfather on his string cot in the shade of the courtyard wall to interest him in a camel that's fallen ill or a batch of new lambs. Grandfather just nods.

The water in the toba is slowly drying up, but Dadi says we have enough for the two months before we leave for Mehrabpur to prepare for [my sister Phulan's] wedding.

One night Phulan shakes me awake in the middle of a deep sleep.

"Shabanu!" she shouts from such a great distance I can barely hear her.

She yanks the quilt away, and suddenly my skin is pierced by thousands of needles. The wind is howling around us. I can't see anything when I open my eyes, but I can tell by the sound and feel that it's a monstrous sandstorm, the kind few living things survive without protection. Phulan pulls me by the hand, but I yank away.

"Mithoo!" I stumble about the courtyard, tripping over huddled chickens, clay pots, and bundles of reeds that have broken away from the entrance. "Mithoo!"

Hands outstretched, I feel my way around the courtyard wall, where Mithoo normally sleeps. When I get to where the reeds were stacked on their stalks, lashed side by side and tied to cover the doorway, there is a **gaping** hole. Quickly I make my way around the courtyard again. Mithoo is gone.

"You can't find him without a light and something to put over your eyes!" Phulan shouts, pulling on my arm. Together we drag the bed through the doorway. Mama struggles to close the window shutters, and Phulan and I manage to push the door shut and wedge the bed against it. Dadi lights a candle and swears softly as the light fills the room. Grandfather and Sher Dil are missing too.

> **sweltering** *(adj.)* oppressively hot
> **torpid** *(adj.)* lacking in energy

"Where can he have gone?" Mama gasps, her eyes bright with fear. Grandfather had been sound asleep, and the storm must have wakened him.

Dadi uses the candle to light the kerosene storm lantern and pulls the bed away from the door. Mama throws a shawl around his shoulders. He pulls it over his head, and I follow him out to the courtyard, where khar shrubs, their shallow roots torn from the dry sand, tumble and hurl themselves against the walls.

With my chadr over my face, I can open my eyes enough to see the haze of the lantern in Dadi's hand, the light reflecting from the dust in a tight circle around him.

Auntie has already closed up her house, and Dadi pounds on the door for several minutes before she opens it again and we slip inside.

"Have you seen Grandfather?" asks Dadi.

"And Mithoo and Sher Dil?" I shout.

She stands in the center of her house, mouth open and speechless, her hands raised helplessly. My cousins stand behind her skirt, their eyes wide. From between her feet Sher Dil's black nose glistens in the lamplight. But no Grandfather and no Mithoo.

"Come to our house," Dadi orders her, handing me the lantern. "I'll close up here. Shabanu, come back for me," he says, bending to light Auntie's storm lantern.

When I return, Dadi holds the light so we can see each other.

"Mithoo will be fine," he says, and I know it is a warning not to ask to look for him. "When the wind has died and it's light, we'll find him standing near a tree by the toba."

Dadi is right. Mithoo has a chance if he can stay with the herd and find shelter in the lee of a dune. But Grandfather can never survive a storm like this.

Dadi holds my hand as we step back into the vicious wind. It slaps us with a terrible force, driving thousands of

"Grandfather! Grandfather!" I shout, but the wind tears the sound from my mouth and hurls it away before I can hear it.

sand grains through our clothes and against our shielded faces.

"Grandfather! Grandfather!" I shout, but the wind tears the sound from my mouth and hurls it away before I can hear it. I catch wisps of Dadi's voice calling out.

In half an hour we know it's no use. We are exhausted and sick, our skin raw from the sand, our voices gone from shouting and gulping in dust. I close my burning eyes and let Dadi lead me home.

Mama, Phulan, Auntie, and the boys huddle under shawls in the hot, swirling dark. There is no escaping

> **Predict**
> Do you think Grandfather and Mithoo will be found alive?

the sand, even indoors, and everything is gritty with the dust that blows with great force through the thatch and around the cracks in the doors and shutters. Mama runs to us and takes the lanterns. She holds me against her for a second.

Her eyes are haunted. I pray Grandfather will die quickly of heart failure and not be skinned alive by the sand and suffocated.

Phulan lifts her hands from over her face, and I can't tell whether she's been crying.

"Your eyes are bright red," she says, looking from Dadi to me and back again.

My vision is blurred, and Phulan leads me to her quilt. Dadi and I both lie down, and Mama dips the corner of her chadr into freshwater in which healing desert mint has soaked, and squeezes drops into our eyes. It burns like fire, and I cry out. Even Dadi grunts as Mama gently squeezes the water into the corners of his eyes.

The storm goes on for hours more, and we are too exhausted to go outside again until the wind dies. The boys whimper. Sher Dil stays under Mama's skirt and never makes a sound. The rest of us are silent, as if our souls have blown outside with Grandfather, tossed with the dust on the wind.

---

lee *(n.)* side that is sheltered from the wind

And then, as suddenly as it began, the storm is over. The wind has torn holes in the thatch, and pale, watery sunlight filters through, even before the wind is quiet.

Still none of us speaks. Our noses and mouths and throats are parched and caked with dust.

Mama lifts the lid from a pot and pours some water into cups, and I pass them around.

It is late afternoon. I shake the dust from my clothes and hair. Mama wets the end of my chadr so I can wipe some of the dust from my eyes, nose, mouth, and ears.

"Quickly," she says, following me to the door. She insists we take a water pot in case we should find Grandfather alive.

The air is calm and cool. The storm has buried all signs of civilization. Even our courtyard looks like a piece of desert, the neat mud walls and storage mounds beaten down and draped with sand.

Outside, the desert has been rearranged. Unfamiliar dunes roll where the land used to lie flat. Stands of shrub and thorn trees are no more. Nothing looks the same. Dadi looks back over his shoulder at the house and fixes a course for the toba, where we hope Grandfather will be, somehow safe with the camels.

As we reach the top of each dune, I expect to see water. When we've gone farther than it should be, we split up, Dadi walking into the sun, quivery and pale on the horizon, and I with my back to it. The sand is powdery underfoot, its fresh whiteness an obscenity to me, covering up the devastation it has wrought.

"Grandfather!" I shout, with little hope. "Grandfather, where are you?" If Mithoo is anywhere within hearing, he'll come to the sound of my voice.

According to the legend of the thirsty dead, men lost in the desert tie a turban into the branches of the highest shrubs, then take shelter underneath and wait for help. My eyes scan the few thorn trees, spiky kharin, and hardy pogh for the pale blue turban Grandfather wore yesterday.

At the foot of a hillock I see a sand-covered lump too small to be a dune, and my heart lurches into my mouth. I turn and shout, "Dadi! Here, Dadi, here!"

I put down the water jar I've been carrying on my head and run toward the thing in the sand.

VOCABULARY/WORD ANALYSIS

Context Clues

Review page 212. Find the word *chadr*. (Circle) words and phrases that provide clues to the meaning of the word.

- What does *chadr* mean?

_____

_____

- Why might a chadr be useful in a desert environment?

_____

_____

_____

_____

LITERARY ANALYSIS

Mood

Underline three examples of descriptive language and imagery that contribute to the mood of the story.

- What words would you use to describe the part of the story that tells about the storm?

_____

_____

COMPREHENSION

Cause and Effect

Review page 213. What effects did the storm have on each of the following?

Grandfather: _____

_____

_____

the house: _____

_____

_____

I fall to my knees and scrape the sand blanket away to find the body of a black baby camel, knees tucked under him, chin on the ground, as if asleep.

"Poor baby," I say softly, stroking the curly dark fur. Where is his mother, and the other camels? And where is the toba?

Dadi runs over the hillock. He stops when he sees the dead baby and clucks his tongue. Hands on hips, he looks around with a strange expression on his face.

Suddenly he falls to the ground and begins digging with his hands. The sand flies out behind him in a powdery shower.

"Here!" he says, holding up a handful of damp sand.

> **Predict**
> What do you think Dadi has discovered?

"This is our toba!"

There on the far edge is the thorn tree where I tied Mithoo's goatskin milk bag, where he and I sat after his birth.

I turn back to Dadi, who continues to dig, the sand flying out behind him now in heavy gray clumps.

Finally he sits back on his heels, hands resting on his thighs, breathing heavily. He throws his head back and looks at the sky.

I go to his side and squat down to peer into the hole he's dug. A small puddle has formed in the wet sand at the bottom.

"Dadi, there's water enough for a day or two, until we find Grandfather. We'll survive."

The sun has slipped below the horizon, and there's little color in the sky; the day has stolen quietly away. Dadi stands and I fetch the water pot. Together we walk home, realizing we must leave the desert as soon as possible.

Mama, Auntie, and Phulan have cleaned the houses and shaken the sand from our bedding. They have put the mats back on the floor, and are busy now carrying debris from the courtyard. The little boys are making piles of khip to repair the thatch in the morning. Sher Dil watches, his chin on his paws.

Dadi sleeps early, waking for a supper of stew made of leftover meat. The new moon is waxing, and Dadi prepares to go out again in search of Grandfather and the camels, using the stars as guides.

"I'm going with you," I say. Dadi shakes his head.

"You help Mama pack. I'll be back by morning."

Phulan, Mama, and I gather our possessions together again, our cooking pots and plates and cups, our ax and ropes and harnesses, our half-empty water pots, our spindles for making cord, wooden spoons, and whisks.

After several hours Phulan and I drag Grandfather's string cot outside to sleep in the courtyard again, in case he should return during the night.

The moon and stars are brighter than before, the storm having cleared the dust from the air. The shadowless blue-white light is eerie. Mama cries quietly inside. Phulan goes to her, Sher Dil trotting at her heels, and I am asleep before she reaches the door.

Sometime later, in the hours before dawn, the magic symphony of the animals' bells wakes us, ta-dong-a-roorna-long-chink-a-dong. I run, **apprehensive** and groggy with fitful sleep, to the courtyard gate. Dadi's turban glows the same blue-white as the stars in a makeshift harness around the neck of Xhush Dil. The others, fifty or so big camels and dozens of babies, follow in a close knot. They look as if they've just been out grazing. Among them is Mithoo, one of the herd now.

Dadi leads Xhush Dil slowly, gently, for slumped against his hump is Grandfather.

"He's alive!" I shout over my shoulder through the doorway. I can tell by the way his limbs jog. A small moan escapes from Mama's throat, and she is up and running to Grandfather's side. I am close behind, Sher Dil and Phulan tripping over my heels.

Grandfather's fingers are twined tightly in the long, curly hair on Xhush Dil's ample hump. The stocky young

"He's alive!" I shout over my shoulder through the doorway.

> **khip** (n.) a brushy desert plant
> **waxing** (v.) increasing in size or intensity

camel sinks gently to his knees without command. We pry Grandfather's fingers loose. Phulan and I fetch the string cot, and we carry him on it into the courtyard, where Auntie is building a fire. Mama covers him with a shawl and brings a pot of water.

Grandfather's eyes are open. His cracked lips are parted and he talks soundlessly, rolling his head from side to side. His fingers move restlessly like the claws of a wounded bird. Mama dips the edge of her chadr into the water and presses it against his lips. He turns his head away.

I bend my ear closer to his mouth. At first I hear only the faint hiss of softly articulated air.

Grandfather pulls me closer with hands that are powerful for a dying man.

"Kalu," he says. "Make Kalu ready. We must get to Derawar quickly."

I stand and repeat his words. Mama puts her hand on his arm and bends over him.

"I want to die at Derawar," Grandfather says, his voice stronger now. "The nawab will bury me in a martyr's grave, with turquoise tiles and lapis carvings."

Mama looks at Dadi.

"We'll leave by first light, Father," says Dadi. "Phulan, help your mother. Shabanu, come with me to get water."

Grandfather closes his eyes. His hands stop moving and lie limp on the shawl that covers him. Mama kneels by his side for a moment, stroking his head and watching him closely.

"Dalil Abassi," says Mama, addressing Dadi formally for the first time that I can remember. Dadi turns wearily toward her.

"I found him huddled among the camels at Mujarawala Toba, where the dunes are high," Dadi says. "It's a miracle he survived."

"He'll be lucky to live through the night," Mama says. "We'll take him to Derawar," Dadi says. "We can't stay here without water. Let him die in peace."

The Thirsty Dead

Dadi and I squeeze enough water from the sand to fill one goatskin. Our half-full water pots are round and fat, sweating and red, tempting our thirsty eyes.

---

articulated *(adj.)* uttered clearly

The light glints orange on Mama's nose disk as she ties the pots with goat hair twine very carefully, as if they hold gems. She hands them up to Dadi, who stands in front of the hump of a gentle old female camel. He handles the pots gingerly, tying them securely to the wooden frame of the saddle and packing clothing and quilts around them so they won't shatter.

We load Xhush Dil last with the most important cargo: Phulan's dowry chest and Grandfather.

Grandfather lies on his string cot, eyes wide and sightless; his once-strong hands, now curled and covered with waxy skin, search restlessly over the pale green quilt that lies across his chest. On his head is the khaki fez of the nawab's army, its tassel crumpled, the felt faded and torn.

In its center is the bronze star for bravery, brass rays surrounding it like a holy emblem. He earned it for leading the charge at Kutch.

Grandfather's lips move wordlessly, and Mama and I stop our rushed packing every few minutes to soothe him.

When it is time to leave, Dadi and Mama carry Grandfather on his cot, beyond the courtyard, and I follow, leading Xhush Dil. It is our custom never to get onto the camels in front of our house for fear we'll never return. In normal times it is sad to leave home. Now it is unbearable.

"Uuusshhhshh," I say softly, and the young camel sinks to his knees with barely a whisper in the sand. Dadi loops cords around the head and foot of the cot, and we hoist Grandfather to where his weight balances the dowry chest on the other side of the wooden pack frame.

Xhush Dil gets to his feet again in a movement so

fluid I think he must know the value of his cargo. Dadi lifts the glass of the lantern and blows out the flame. The eerie blue of near dawn enfolds us, and we move off without looking back.

We pass the place where our raised mud prayer platform stood until yesterday, its delicately molded mehrab facing toward Mecca. Dadi looks at the mound of sand that covers it as if he thinks he should stop to pray, but we keep walking.

Mithoo's head is several inches higher than my own. The bell on the new cord around his neck clangs solemnly as he trots beside me, his feet making no sound in the wind-fluffed sand. The other camels move in syncopation, their loads swaying side to side and back and forth.

We reach the old fort just as the sun slips behind the dunes, and the last pink fingers of light burnish its forty graceful turrets.

The nawab's green and red flag flutters beside the green banner of Pakistan, and we stand on the hill looking over the lake built by the nawab of a hundred years ago for his ladies to paddle little boats across. The wind has died, and the last daylight leaves a silvery skin on the water. Mama lifts Grandfather's head to see the marble dome and vaulted minarets of the nawab's mosque beyond the fort's massive brick walls.

"We won't disturb Nawab-sahib until morning," Grandfather says, then falls back on his pillow, his hands and face relaxed for the first time since we left.

> **Predict**
> How do you think Shabanu's family will be greeted in the morning?

The camels move on, their only sound the kachinnik, kachinnik of their bracelets, the gentle thong of their bells, and the creaking of goat hair cords against their wooden saddles. We stop beside a collection of torn lean-tos built by other nomads. Our reed mats will make walls and a small courtyard. The camp is within walking distance of the well. Phulan and I have been collecting firewood over the last several miles, and Auntie makes a fire while Mama unrolls the mats.

Xhush Dil sinks quietly to his knees. Dadi and I lower the dowry trunk and the cot on which Grandfather sleeps. We have enough water in the goatskin until tomorrow. At first light Dadi, Xhush Dil, and I will go to the well. Only then will we know whether the water is sweet. The well out here on the edge of the settlement is least likely to have good water. But our goatskins will be empty, and we are so thirsty we will drink even salty water. God willing, the monsoon will not fail this year.

---

minarets (n.) tall thin towers on mosques
lean-tos (n.) extensions of a type of building

VOCABULARY/WORD ANALYSIS

Context Clues

On page 216, find the word *gingerly*. Circle details that tell how Mama and Dadi handle the pots.

• What is the meaning of *gingerly*?

_____

Why does Dadi handle the pots gingerly?

_____
_____
_____
_____

LITERARY ANALYSIS

Mood

Check any words below that describe the mood of story on page 216.

☐ quiet
☐ joyous
☐ angry
☐ serious

Underline words that help create this mood.

COMPREHENSION

Problem and Solution

Think back to the sandstorm at the beginning of the story. How might the bells and bracelets of the camels help in a similar situation?

_____
_____
_____
_____

Derawar

"Grandfather is dead, Shabanu," Mama says, leaning over me, shaking me awake in the dark. Dadi leaps up from his quilt and turns Grandfather's head toward Mecca so his soul can pray.

Everyone is calm, and in the morning it seems we all had known Grandfather's soul would take flight once it reached Derawar.

Dadi washes Grandfather's thin and wasted body with the last of our water, chanting prayers for the dead. There's no time to spare. It's shortly after dawn, and the heat of the day will be fierce. As he and Mama wrap the shroud around the body, Dadi chants softly in his wood-smoke voice.

Grandfather's worn foot with the split toenail lies inert and topples sideways like a sack of lentils as Dadi lifts the body to slip the white seamless cloth under him. I bandaged that toe for Grandfather. This lifeless foot will never again feel such a thing as a split toenail, and I grieve for it, as if it embodies all of Grandfather.

Auntie, Mama, and Phulan stay to fetch water at the well and to pray. Grandfather is laid out on his string cot, such a small and insignificant little form for the tall and strong warrior of his stories.

The devil sun creeps into the doorway, chasing the chill from the dark reed enclosure. We must hurry, Dadi and I, to find a burial place before the heat … how we would hate to think of his body stinking, swelling up. Oh, we must hurry!

The camels walk slowly up the long, cobbled ramp that leads to the huge wooden doors, just as Grandfather had described them, the tips of sword blades at the top to keep out the elephants of the Raja of Bikaner.

A door of inch-thick bars stands between us and the wooden gates. Dadi calls out, and a thin old man, brown as mud, with a white beard, stoops through the three-foot doorway of the guardroom behind the bars. He slips a fez like Grandfather's—but red—over his shaved brown head.

"Yes sir, can I help you?" he asks, squinting up at Dadi through the bars. Dadi jumps down and they **exchange** greetings. Through the ancient guard's pure white mustache, three long teeth protrude. Grandfather has told me about those who wear the red fez. They are the nawab's personal guard.

He is Shahzada (his name is a mother's wish that her son had been born a king). The estate and the son of the nawab, as well as several of his cousins, all claim not only the fort at Derawar but the nawab's palace in Bahawalpur and the graveyard and all of the nawab's lands that remained after Pakistan and India were separated.

"Cholistan was once home to a great civilization," he tells us. "Now it is just a patch of sand with weeds. But the nawab **envisioned** pumping the great Hakra River up from under the desert and making this into a fertile valley once again."

Dadi and I are interested, but we explain that we must hurry to find a burial place for Grandfather. He seems truly sorry not to be able to help. He directs us to the village of the tomb maker. We thank Shahzada and ask him to our camp to share our dinner.

The rest of the day drags in a blur of heat and frantic but frustrated effort. First we go to the maker of tombs, but his daughter tells us he has gone to another village. Is there no one else who makes tombs? No, she says, only her father.

> **Predict**
> Do you think Grandfather will be buried inside a tomb?

So Dadi and I go to the dried up toba and dig through the sand down to the clay. The old bed of the Hakra River is hard as rock, with shells still embedded in it, preserved by the desert air. We break up chunks of the clay and pound it into powder, then carry it in wheat sacks to the camels to be **hauled** back to camp.

Mama and Auntie have collected fresh cow dung, and fortunately there is water in the well. Our goatskins and jars are full.

We load Grandfather, rigid now under his shroud, still on the string cot, onto Xhush Dil with the mud and the

---

shroud (n.) cloth placed on a body before burial
inert (adj.) not moving

cow dung and the water, and set out into the desert to find a burial spot where the jackals, foxes, and wolves won't find his body.

In the heat of the afternoon, we dig six feet into the ground, Dadi and I taking turns. Mama and Phulan mix the powdered clay, cow dung, water, and sand into desert cement, and we pave the hole as we work to keep it from filling up again.

Within sight of his beloved Derawar, we lay Grandfather under a bush in a solitary grave. Dadi turns him on his right side so that he faces Mecca, and each of us throws a handful of Cholistan sand over him, whispering a prayer and saying good-bye.

When it's over, we are relieved that his suffering has ended and that his body is safe in the ground. But my heart still carries the promise we made to bury him beside those with whom he fought.

Conversation turns to what we should do next.

"It's too soon to go to Mehrabpur," says Mama, taking charge of our plans. "Hamir and his family don't expect us until Ramadan."

It is two weeks before the fasting month of Ramadan, still a month before the monsoon rains refill the tobas.

"I'll not stay here!" Dadi says. "I'm happy Grandfather's grave does not lie in the village."

Mama nods.

"But there is little choice," she says, and that is that. We will stay here until we move to Mehrabpur just before Ramadan to prepare for the wedding.

The water at the Derawar well is salty. The camels drink little, and my throat is beginning to ache again with thirst.

When we are back in camp, we resume the normal rhythm of our lives and it soothes us. The boys play with Sher Dil. Mama becomes cross with them and sends them outside. We make tea, and with milk and sugar the salt water is not so difficult to drink.

Mama and Phulan talk about final preparations for the wedding. I listen to their chatter about dresses and bangles and furniture and plates while I mix the gray salty water into flour for our evening chapatis. They never once mention Hamir or how Phulan should behave toward Hamir's mother when the wedding is over and they all are living together—everything I want to know about marriage.

LITERARY ANALYSIS

Mood

What is the mood of the story as the family sets out after Grandfather's death?

_____

_____

_____

_____

- (Circle) words or phrases in the story that support your responses.

VOCABULARY/WORD ANALYSIS

Context Clues

Review page 218. Use context clues to help you explain who the nawab is.

_____

_____

What did Shabanu's family hope the nawab would do for them?

_____

_____

_____

_____

CRITICAL THINKING

Analyze

Compare Shabanu with her mother and sister by reviewing the last paragraph on page 219. <u>Underline</u> the sentence that tells what Shabanu is doing.

- How is Shabanu different from her mother and sister? Support your response with details from the story.

_____

_____

_____

_____

_____

_____

Outside the circle of our campfire we hear someone approach, singing. Dadi stands and greets Shahzada with a warm **embrace.** The old guard is wearing a faded tunic over a lungi, and there is no sign of his red fez. His bald head is glossy with the orange glow of the campfire.

"Where have you buried Abassi-bhai?" Dadi is pleased Shahzada uses the affectionate term meaning "brother" for his old **colleague.**

Dadi tells him, and the old man nods.

"I will watch over the grave," he says.

Dadi and Shahzada talk about the drought. We keep few sheep and no cows or goats. But Shahzada says people are beginning to

> **Predict**
> **Do you think Shabanu feels that her grandfather's wishes have been honored?**

leave the desert with their animals because the grasses have **withered** and there is little left for them to eat. Camels can eat almost anything, and our animals haven't had trouble with sickness and hunger yet.

"The old nawab," Shahzada says, "believed we could pump water from under the ground onto the land. He used to say, 'You see how flowers bloom in the sand when there is water? This is not desert. This is land without water.'"

A shepherd plays a sweet melody on his flute far out in the desert, calling his flock to graze. They respond with the muted ringing of their bells, ghostly as they pass among the dunes.

> **lungi** *(n.)* long cloth wrapped around the waist

Grandfather's body lies out under the stars, alone for the first time since the sandstorm. I wonder whether his soul is near enough to hear the flute or, now that it is free, whether he can see inside my heart and know I am thinking of him.

"Shahzada-sahib," I say, "could you help us keep a promise to my grandfather?'

"Shabanu," Dadi says, a warning in his voice.

"I know it was impossible to bury him in the nawab's graveyard," I rush on. "Would you put his fez and sword somewhere in an honored place?"

"Oh, could you?" asks Mama.

Shahzada tells us of a tomb built for a general who died in battle and whose body was never found.

"There are other relics in the empty tomb," he says. "It is a beautiful one with blue and white tiles, lapis with gold script. That would be an appropriate place for the fez and sword of a man who won the medal for bravery."

Grandfather's relics will rest with those of his brothers and finally his soul will rest in peace. ■

AUTHOR FILE

Suzanne Fisher Staples

BORN August 27, 1945, in Philadelphia, Pennsylvania

INSPIRATION FOR *SHABANU* While working on a literacy project for women in Pakistan's Punjab province, she met many women who were eager to share stories about their lives.

ON PAKISTAN "I was constantly surprised by the rural people of Pakistan, most of whom were extraordinarily poor. They were living on the edge of survival yet they were extremely generous. ... They always offered me a meal or tea, whatever they had."

FAVORITE AUTHORS Gabriel García Márquez, Virginia Wolff, Naomi Shihab Nye

CURRENT PASSION "Archeoastronomy—legends and myths about the stars, sciences, and mathematics, in Persia in particular."

AWARDS Newbery Honor for *Shabanu: Daughter of the Wind*

OTHER FAMOUS WORKS *Haveli, Dangerous Skies,* and *Shiva's Fire*

---

lapis *(n.)* a semiprecious stone, usually blue in color

COMPREHENSION

Cause and Effect

 Review page 220. Why are people leaving the nawab's lands?

_____

_____

_____

_____

- (Circle) the part of the story that tells you what the nawab did to try to keep people on his land.

LITERARY ANALYSIS

Mood

Review page 221. How would you describe the mood at the end of the story? Support your answer with details from the story.

_____

_____

_____

_____

_____

[21] SMALL GROUPS/INDEPENDENT

COLLABORATE

 Designing Design a sign for the tomb where Grandfather's belongings will be placed.

COMMUNICATE

 React and Write Write a letter that Shabanu might send to Shahzada, thanking him for helping her family.

READ ONLINE

 expert space Go to **www.expert21.com/student** to learn more about Sandstorms; Oasis; Arid Climate.

Extreme Athletes Run Length of Sahara

Runners log equivalent of two marathons a day across deserts for nearly four months

By The Associated Press

(The Associated Press) A North Carolina man and two other ultra-endurance athletes have just done something most would consider insane: They ran the equivalent of two marathons a day for 111 days to become the first modern runners to cross the Sahara desert's grueling 4,000 miles.

"It will take time to sink in ... but this is an absolutely once-in-a-lifetime thing. They say ignorance is bliss, and now that I know how hard this is, I would never consider crossing the Sahara on foot again," said Charlie Engle, 44, of Greensboro, N.C., hours after he and the others completed the run at Egypt's Red Sea.

Engle said he, Canadian Ray Zahab, 38, and Kevin Lin, 30, of Taiwan, ran the final stretch of their

Runners (from left to right) Kevin Lin, Ray Zahab, and Charlie Engle endured scorching temperatures and strong winds to cross the Sahara Desert.

journey that took them through the Giza pyramids and Cairo to the mouth of the Suez Canal on four hours of sleep. Once they hit the Red Sea, they put their hands in the water to signify crossing the finish line.

"We touched the water in Senegal at the beginning, and we touched the water in the Red Sea at the end. They were the bookends of our journey," Engle said on the telephone from a hotel room in Cairo.

In less than four months, they have run across the world's largest desert, through six countries—Senegal, Mauritania, Mali, Niger,

Libya and finally Egypt.

The trek is one of extremes. The relentless sun can push temperatures above 100 degrees Fahrenheit during the day, but at night it sometimes dips below freezing. Strong winds can abruptly send sand swooping in every direction, making it difficult to see and breathe.

Running through turbulent conditions is nothing new for these athletes who have traveled the world, competing in adventure races. But they say nothing has tested their physical and mental limitations like the Sahara.

Throughout the run, the runners were stricken with tendonitis, severe diarrhea, cramping and knee injuries, all while running through the intense heat and wind—often without a paved road in sight.

"This has been a life changing event," Engle said.

The runners say they undertook the challenge to see if they could accomplish something that many have called impossible. They used GPS devices to track their route and teamed up with local experts and a host of sports professionals who also followed them, in four-wheel drive vehicles.

Typically, the three began each day with a 4 a.m. wake-up call. About an hour later, they started running. Around noon, they took a lunch break at a makeshift camp, devouring pasta, tuna and vegetables. A short nap on thin mattresses in a yellow-domed tent usually followed before they headed out on the second leg of their day's run.

Finally, around 9:30 p.m., they called it quits each day, returning to camp for a protein- and carbohydrate-packed dinner before passing out for the night.

Despite the preparation and drive to finish, the runners said they often questioned—mostly to themselves—what they were doing. Zahab described stopping one recent day for a bathroom break only to discover the wind was blowing so harshly that he couldn't keep the sand out of his clothes. "And I thought to myself, 'What am I doing?'" he said.

But Zahab kept going, as did the other two, never skipping a day.

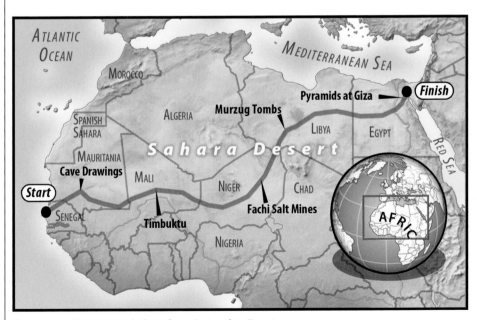

The runners' journey took them from Senegal to Egypt.

> **makeshift** *(adj.)* serving as a temporary substitute
> **devouring** *(v.)* eating hungrily or quickly

COMPREHENSION

Cause and Effect
Review the sixth paragraph on page 222. List three conditions that cause the trek across the Sahara to be an extreme one.

1. _____

2. _____

3. _____

NAVIGATING TEXT

Maps
Maps are often found in news articles. Look at the map on page 223. What city in Mali did the runners pass through?

_____

Why was it a good choice to include a map with this article?

_____

The Science of the Run

from *RunningtheSahara.com*

There's more to running 6,920 kilometers (4,300 miles) across a desert than simply … well, running. You want to know things like how much to drink to keep from dehydrating under temperatures comparable to Phoenix, Arizona, on a hot summer day; and what to eat to keep your body from wasting away as the miles, days, and weeks mount.

To figure out the optimal game plan, runner Charlie Engle approached scientists at a sports laboratory for help.

"His biggest fear was dehydration," said Beth Stover, one of the lab's scientists, who noted that on previous desert runs, Charlie had problems with hallucinations and dizziness.

Stover and her colleagues put the runners on treadmills in a room heated to 47°C (117°F), mimicking the temperatures in which they were expecting to run. There were even heat lamps to simulate sunlight.

There, the three ran at their expected effort level while the scientists measured the rate at which they sweated.

"We also measured their sweat's electrolyte concentration," Stover said, "because depletion of sodium, the primary electrolyte in sweat, can lead to muscle cramping."

The scientists then gave the team a mountain of powdered sports drink, which each runner was to consume according to an individual plan, ranging from 0.9 liters (1 quart) to 1.4 liters (1.5 quarts) per hour.

The scientists also measured the runners' oxygen usage, an indicator of how many calories they would be burning per mile. The tests indicated they would need between 6,000 and 9,000 calories per day—three to four times the intake of the average American.

Scientist Beth Stover applies a sweat patch test to Charlie Engle. The test will determine if Engle is dehydrated.

Once the run started, Stover and another colleague went with the team to Africa to monitor the runners for the first few days. "Our goal was to see if we'd accurately measured their sweat rates in the lab," she said.

Another scientist had the runners swallow a vitamin-sized capsule containing a radio-transponder that monitored their body temperature. The runners' temperatures stayed within a degree or two of normal, which meant the hydration plan was working, since runners who get dehydrated will quickly begin to overheat.

Most people can't imagine running a 40-mile (64-kilometer) day in perfect conditions, let alone in a desert. But to cross the Sahara, these runners had to accomplish this feat daily for nearly four months.

During that time, a lot of things can happen to your body.

There are inevitable aches and pains. "I like to say that this type of running is 90 percent mental, and the other part is all in your head," runner Ray Zahab jokes. "They told us that after a certain amount of time your body's going to adapt or fall apart."

optimal *(adj.)* most desirable or satisfactory

mimicking *(v.)* imitating

TOP: Small children run alongside the three runners as they pass through a village in Mauritania.

LEFT: Lin, Zahab, and Engle meet with expedition experts to assess their route.

Most days, the three ran a total of 44 to 50 miles—sometimes a little more, sometimes a little less.

They were interviewed by *The Associated Press* on Saturday—day 108—on the side of a road about 112 miles from Cairo in Egypt's harsh Western Desert, part of the greater Sahara.

At several points in their trek, the athletes stopped near sparsely populated wells to talk with villagers and nomads about the difficulties they face finding water. That marked another goal of the run—raising awareness for the clean water nonprofit group H_2O Africa.

"We have seen firsthand the need for clean water, which we take for granted in North America. It's such a foundation for any community," Zahab said during day 108's lunch break. The three plan to fundraise for the group after they return home and finish recuperating.

"It started off as a huge motivator, especially as we passed through countries where the water wasn't clean," Engle said.

But as the trio's bodies became more depleted, the focus was "the day-to-day battle to stay alive and keep moving," he said. ▪

recuperating *(v.)* recovering slowly

COMPREHENSION

Cause and Effect

Review page 225. What difficulty did the runners face, and speak about with local people in the Sahara each day?

_____

_____

_____

_____

What were two effects of facing this difficulty?

1. _____

_____

_____

_____

2. _____

_____

_____

_____

CRITICAL THINKING

Evaluate

Do you think the three athletes were foolish to complete their run across the Sahara, or do you admire them for doing it? Explain your response.

_____

_____

_____

_____

_____

_____

_____

READ ONLINE

expert space
Go to **www.expert21.com/student** to learn more about Extreme Athletes; Extreme Deserts; Sahara.

Think Across Texts

Organize and Synthesize

1. Complete this chart using information from "Blue People of the Sahara," *Shabanu*, and "Extreme Athletes Run Length of Sahara."

	"Blue People of the Sahara"	**Shabanu**	**"Extreme Athletes Run Length of Sahara"**
How have people adapted to life in the desert?			
What is the greatest challenge facing the people in each selection?			

Compare and Evaluate

2. The two informational texts are set in the Sahara desert. What do the runners in "Extreme Athletes Run Length of Sahara" have in common with the Tuareg from "Blue People of the Sahara"? How are they different?

_____

_____

_____

_____

_____

_____

3. Which of the three selections did you find the most surprising? Explain your answer.

_____

_____

_____

_____

4. Think about how the visual features in each text added to your understanding of each of the selections below. Give specific examples.

"Blue People of the Sahara":_____

_____

_____

_____

"Extreme Athletes Run Length of Sahara":_____

_____

_____

_____

Discuss and Write

5. With a partner, discuss how the three readings in "Desert Zones" helped you understand desert life. Take notes as you talk. Then use your notes to write a response to the question *How do people survive in the hottest places on earth?*

Apply Word Knowledge

Word Lab ....

1. **Explain it.** Which two conditions would make garden plants **wither**?

❏ extreme heat

❏ extreme cold

❏ enough space and light

❏ enough water

2. **Choose.** Who would be a **colleague** to a teacher at your school?

❏ you

❏ your entire class

❏ another teacher at the school

3. **Decide.** Would you enjoy living in an **arid** place? Give a reason for your answer.

_____

_____

_____

_____

_____

_____

_____

4. **Finish it.** Complete the sentence below with the words **apprehensive** and **adequate.**

Belen was _____ during

our hike because she felt we did not pack

an _____ water supply.

5. **Think about it.** What career do you **envision** having when you grow up? Why?

_____

_____

_____

_____

_____

_____

_____

_____

_____

_____

Word Analysis ....

6. Use context clues to figure out the meaning of *syncopation* in the sentence below. Then circle the letter next to the meaning.

The other camels move in syncopation, their loads swaying side to side and back and forth.

Ⓐ a rhythm

Ⓑ a confused manner

7. As you read the sentences below, use context clues to figure out the meaning of the word *torpid*. Then circle the letter next to the correct meaning.

The insect was nearly dead. It went into a torpid state, and didn't move at all.

Torpid means

Ⓐ numb and still.   Ⓑ very sad.

Ⓒ frantically afraid.   Ⓓ no longer alive.

Build an Effective Team

In a successful team, all the members talk to each other, listen respectfully, and make decisions together. The person who heads the team helps make sure the process runs smoothly.

Work Together to Survive

▶ Read the conversation below to see how one team, with the guidance of a team leader, worked together to make a plan.

Transcript
Season 10: The Survivors Episode 1

RITA (Team Leader): We have to live in the forest for three days to win the survival contest. First, we need to find drinking water and wood for a fire.

CARLOS: I think we should try to find more food first. I can't work without food.

RITA: What do you think, Olivia?

OLIVIA: We can get by without extra food, but we can't live without water. And we need a fire to keep us warm and cook the food we brought with us.

CARLOS: OK, that makes sense.

ETHAN: We also need to find a place to set up camp.

RITA: Let's make a list of tasks and assign people to do them. Use the walkie-talkies to keep me posted on how things are going.

MARK IT

Set a goal. <u>Underline</u> the team leader's statement of the team's goals.

Hand out tasks and check progress. (Circle) the text that shows how Rita will monitor the team's progress.

Resolve differences. Draw a line to the text where Carlos declares the problem solved.

Lead the team. Rita guides the team to discuss what they should do first. Put a **star ★** by the text that shows how Rita does this.

[**Here's How**] ▶ Follow these steps to build an effective team:

Step 1 Identify your goal. Do you have to solve a problem? Accomplish a task? Create something? Make sure everyone has a clear understanding of the goal.

Step 2 Discuss what needs to be done. What steps need to be taken to achieve your goal? Listen to everyone's ideas, and respond positively. Resolve any disagreements or conflicts and be willing to compromise.

Step 3 Assign tasks. Assign roles such as leader and divide the work among team members. Set priorities and deadlines.

Step 4 Monitor progress and evaluate. Meet regularly and report what tasks have been completed. If necessary, adjust tasks or roles to make sure the goal is fully met and completed on time.

Apply: Build a Successful Team

▶ **Follow the steps below to lead a team. You find a Web site that advertises a contest for funding to create an original animation short. You and a group decide to enter the contest. How will you build an effective team to get the job done?**

Ripax Studios

ABOUT US | MAKING MOVES | ART OF ANIMATION | CONTACT US | **CONTEST**

ANIMATION CONTEST

Calling all young animators! Ripax Studio is sponsoring the world's greatest animation contest. We want you to create a short video that uses any form of animation—from computer to hand-drawn to stop-motion. The only restrictions are that it can't be longer than five minutes and must be set either in a desert or a polar region. Your film will be judged on originality and execution. The contest is open to anyone under 17. The creator or creators of the winning entry will receive **$10,000** and an internship at our studio in Los Angeles. Best of all, some of your ideas might be used in a future Ripax film! **Get all the _details_.**

Terms of use. Privacy. © 2009

1. **Identify your goal.** What are you trying to accomplish?

_____

2. **Talk about what needs to be done.** What steps do you need to take to achieve this goal?

_____

_____

3. **Assign the tasks.** Who will do what?

_____

_____

4. **Monitor progress and evaluate.** Have a teammate use the following rubric to determine how well you participated in the collaborative process.

	Always	Usually	Seldom or Never
Contributed ideas			
Listened to the ideas of others			
Responded positively			
Willing to compromise			

Cause-and-Effect Essay

Traits of Writing

Traits of Writing is a model for assessing and teaching. The traits work within the writing process to support revision and editing.

Each puzzle piece below represents one of the **traits** that define good writing.

Each trait is made up of four **key qualities.** The trait you will focus on in this lesson is **Word Choice.**

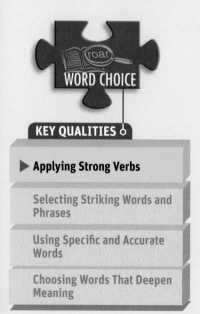

A cause-and-effect essay explains what happened (the effect) and why (the cause). Cause-and-effect writing is used in news stories, science lab reports, history reports, safety alerts, and in many other places.

In this writing workshop, you will write an essay about a cause-and-effect relationship that impacts the way you live in your environment.

Example: Posted notices let people know about possible dangers. In this notice, people are being alerted to the danger of avalanches.

> The snowfall this winter has increased the danger of avalanches in the backcountry. Be sure your party is carrying safety equipment, such as a first-aid kit, shovel, and beacon. This will help you survive the first fifteen minutes, which is critical. Also, pay attention to the weather. A sudden warming can loosen the snow pack.

▶ **Analyze Features** A strong cause-and-effect essay has the following features:

FEATURE	🖊 MARK IT
Look for these features in the Student Model on the next page.	Mark the features as you read the Student Model.
1. The **introduction** states the essay's topic and gets the reader interested. (Organization)	<u>Underline</u> the problem that the writer is pointing out.
2. Paragraphs explain the **effects** (what happened) and the **causes** (why). (Organization)	(Circle) three effects that resulted from the same cause.
3. Evidence gives more information about cause-and-effect relationships. (Organization)	Check ✓ evidence.
4. **Focus Trait: Word Choice** Strong verbs help make the causes and effects clear.	Star ★ strong verbs.
5. A strong **conclusion** summarizes the information in the essay and ends the essay in an interesting way. (Organization)	Draw a box around the summary of the essay in the conclusion.

▶ **Read Sarah Wong's cause-and-effect essay about surviving a power outage.**

STUDENT MODEL

Powerless in the Heat

by Sarah Wong

Summer in the South can be really hot, so most people try to stay inside to avoid the heat. Most places crank up the air conditioning. It feels good when you first step inside, but after a while, you wish you had a sweater. People can take air conditioning too far, but when it's been over 100 degrees every day for over a month, air conditioning is definitely your friend.

A power outage can give you a taste of what the South was like before air conditioning or even fans existed. There can be strong summer storms, and it's not unusual for the wind to take down trees and power lines. When everything zaps off, an eerie quiet fills the house. The background hum of the AC and the ceiling fan vanish. Then things really heat up.

When the power goes out, my mom grabs the biggest cooler she can find and fills it with ice. Without power, all the food in the refrigerator and the freezer can go bad quickly. We open all the windows and doors. It can get boring without any TV or computers.

Even with the windows open, the house traps the heat. So we slither outside, and most of our neighbors do the same. The kids start squirting each other with hoses to keep cool. Sometimes people have barbeques to use up meat before it goes bad. A big barbecue makes the neighborhood smell delicious. Some people play guitars and sing. It's fun to have a big feast with everyone, but since there's no ice, it all gets washed down with lukewarm drinks.

After dark, everyone shuffles inside for the night. If the power is still out, we might play board games by candlelight until it's time for bed. Before bed, we take ice-cold showers and try to fall asleep before the cool feeling wears off. I wouldn't want to give up modern conveniences like air conditioning, refrigerators, television, and computers

▶ **Read Sarah's notes about how she worked on her cause-and-effect essay.**

When I went back to my essay, I added the detail about how it can be over 100 degrees for a month or more here. That fact is interesting to people who don't live in this climate.

When I revised my essay, I made some verbs stronger, for example: "cranked" and "slithered" to make it more interesting and give it energy.

▶ **Analyze how Sarah developed and organized her ideas. Fill in the missing parts of the outline.**

Cause

No Power

1st Effect	2nd Effect	3rd Effect
	Without AC, it was cooler outside, so everyone went outside.	People make their own fun. You can have a barbeque or play games.

How Do I Get Started?

Your Topic:

Assignment: Cause-and-Effect Essay

Purpose: to explain a cause-and-effect relationship that impacts the way you live in your environment

Audience: classmates

Ideas: Developing the Topic

Developing your topic deepens what you have to say. Use these Think-Abouts as you work on your ideas.

- Am I sure my information is right?
- Are my details chock-full of interesting information?
- Have I used details that show new thinking about this idea? *For example, in the Student Model, the author suggests that the power outage allows people to experience what life was like in the past.*
- Will my reader believe what I say about this topic?

◇ KEY QUALITIES

Finding a Topic

Focusing the Topic

▶ Developing the Topic

Using Details

▶ **Model** Go back to Reading 1, "The Story of Keesh," in this workshop. List some interesting information that Jack London sprinkles throughout the story.

▶ **Practice** Think of an interesting detail about a cause and about an effect of that cause.

Cause: _____

Effect: _____

_____

▶ **Plan Your Essay** Use the organizer to jot down ideas for your essay. Revise as needed.

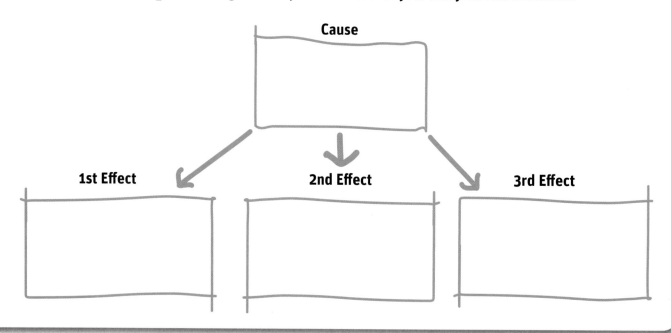

Cause

1st Effect

2nd Effect

3rd Effect

How Do I Get Organized?

Organization: Structuring the Body

Good writers think about how to order and chunk their ideas. Ask yourself these Think-Abouts as you work on your organization.

ORGANIZATION

- Have I shown the reader where to slow down and where to speed up?
- Do all the details fit where they are placed? *For example, in the Student Model, the information is given in chronological order.*
- Will the reader find it easy to follow my ideas?
- Does the organization help the main idea stand out?

○ KEY QUALITIES

Creating the Lead

Using Sequence Words and Transition Words

▶ **Structuring the Body**

Ending With a Sense of Resolution

▶ **Model** Go back to Reading 3, "Life at the Poles," and see if you can find details that fit into the main idea of each section. Hint: use a text feature to find the main ideas.

▶ **Practice** Add new details as you rewrite a paragraph from the Student Model on page 231. Remember to be sure these details make sense with the main idea of the paragraph.

_____

_____

_____

_____

_____

▶ **Write a Paragraph** Practice structuring your ideas as you write a first draft of one of your paragraphs here.

_____

_____

_____

_____

_____

▶ **Draft Your Essay** Write a first draft.

Quick Check

▶ Check how well you developed the topic of your essay. Have a writing partner rate it, too.

6 = Expert   **3** = Making Strides

5 = Well Done   **2** = On the Way

4 = Almost There **1** = Getting Started

Organization

1. Am I sure my information is correct?
   Self   ① ② ③ ④ ⑤ ⑥
   Partner ① ② ③ ④ ⑤ ⑥

2. Are my details chock-full of interesting information?
   Self   ① ② ③ ④ ⑤ ⑥
   Partner ① ② ③ ④ ⑤ ⑥

3. Have I used details that show new thinking about this idea?
   Self   ① ② ③ ④ ⑤ ⑥
   Partner ① ② ③ ④ ⑤ ⑥

4. Will my reader believe what I say about this topic?
   Self   ① ② ③ ④ ⑤ ⑥
   Partner ① ② ③ ④ ⑤ ⑥

How Do I Apply Strong Verbs to Make My Writing Exciting?

FOCUS TRAIT

Word Choice: Applying Strong Verbs

Good writers choose their words carefully and get the most bang for their buck from each one. Use these Think-Abouts to make sure you apply strong verbs in your essay.

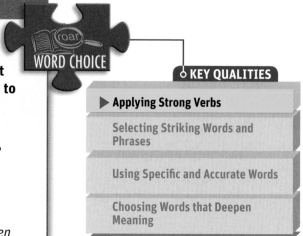

- Have I used action words?
- Did I stretch to get a better word—*scurry* rather than *run*? *For example, the Student Model uses the phrase "zaps off" instead of "turns off."*
- Do my verbs give my writing punch and pizzazz?
- Did I avoid using *is, am, are, was, were, be, being,* and *been* whenever I could?

○ KEY QUALITIES

▶ **Applying Strong Verbs**

Selecting Striking Words and Phrases

Using Specific and Accurate Words

Choosing Words that Deepen Meaning

▶ **Model** Go back to Reading 5, *Shabanu*, and find examples of strong verbs the author used.

▶ Read Ruth Culham's writing blog below to get advice on improving your writing.

Ask the Expert: Ruth Culham

Ruth Culham, an award-winning teacher, is the author of *6+1 Traits of Writing: The Complete Guide for Middle School* and other books on writing.

Q & A: Word Choice: Using Strong Verbs

Vernon Verb Writes:

> Going through all these revisions is not much fun. I'm going nuts trying to use all these traits. Going through draft after draft? I'm going to need a vacation after going through all this.

Dear Vernon Verb: Revision is the hardest part of writing. And you are right, it's not a lot of fun, though when it all comes together, revision is very rewarding. Why don't you take on one issue at a time, such as verbs? You've used "going" four times in your question to me. Try rewriting it without using that word at all; challenge yourself. Going, going, gone!

Posted by: Ruth Culham | April 15 at 02:54 P.M.

► **Practice** Read the sample paragraphs and think about which one applies strong verbs to make the writing more interesting to read.

(Circle) the strong verbs.

Star ★ the sample that shows the best example of applying strong verbs.

Sample 1: Snow Days

It snows a lot here in the winter. You might think that we would get more snow days. But it has to snow an amazing amount before our school closes. If it snows a couple of inches or even a foot, we go. The bulldozers are out early. They get most of the snow, and the salt melts the rest.

Sample 2: Snow Days

Snow blankets this part of the country. You might think that our schools would shut their doors for most of the winter. But the snow must be dumped on us like an avalanche before we get a snow day. Bulldozers quickly scrape away a foot or two of snow. The salt they sprinkle on the road melts the rest.

► **Revise** Now apply strong verbs to spice up your writing. Choose a paragraph from your first draft and revise it below. Remember to use active verbs and to avoid forms of the verb *be* whenever possible.

_____

_____

_____

_____

_____

_____

_____

_____

_____

_____

_____

_____

Quick Check

► **Check your essay for how well you applied strong verbs to your writing. Then have a writing partner rate it, too.**

6 = Expert   **3** = Making Strides

5 = Well Done   **2** = On The Way

4 = Almost There   **1** = Getting Started

Word Choice

1. Have I used action words?
   Self   ① ② ③ ④ ⑤ ⑥
   Partner ① ② ③ ④ ⑤ ⑥

2. Did I stretch to get a better word—*scurry* rather than *run*?
   Self   ① ② ③ ④ ⑤ ⑥
   Partner ① ② ③ ④ ⑤ ⑥

3. Do my verbs give my writing punch and pizzazz?
   Self   ① ② ③ ④ ⑤ ⑥
   Partner ① ② ③ ④ ⑤ ⑥

4. Did I avoid using *is, am, are, was, were, be, being,* and *been* whenever I could?
   Self   ① ② ③ ④ ⑤ ⑥
   Partner ① ② ③ ④ ⑤ ⑥

Revise with Technology Use the thesaurus feature in your word processing program to help you stretch for stronger verbs.

How Can I Finish a Great Paper?

Grammar: Using Correct Verb Tense

Verb tenses show when an action happens.

- Regular past-tense verbs end in *–ed*.
- Regular present-tense verbs add *–s* to the root in 3rd person singular.
- Regular future-tense verbs have *will* or *going to* before the verb.

Other verb tenses use a helping verb (*be* or *have*) with a participle.

- Participles are verbs that end in *–ing*, *–ed*, or *–en*.
- Don't mix up past-tense verbs with past participles of irregular verbs.

► **Practice** **Rewrite this paragraph correctly below.**

Last year, the newspapers say that there was a drought. The city will make laws about how often people were allowed to water their lawns. Even after the drought was over, we still will take shorter showers.

Mechanics: Comma in a Series

Items in a series, or list, are separated by commas.

- Put a comma after each item.
- Also put a comma after the last item before the word *and*.

Example: Dust, pollen, and ozone can make it difficult for some people to breathe.

► **Practice** **Rewrite the paragraph below correctly.**

The Coast Guard scientists gathered clams crabs and sea stars from the seafloor. They found species that normally live further south. This puts seals walruses and other animals in danger of running out of food.

▶ **Proofread** Find and correct any errors in your essay. Put a check beside the types of errors you find. Then write three corrected sentences below.

❏ verb tenses

❏ capitalizing proper nouns, using apostrophes with possessive nouns

❏ commas in a series

❏ misspellings

❏ using nouns correctly

❏ other: _____

1. _____

   _____

2. _____

   _____

3. _____

   _____

PRESENTATION

PUBLISH/PRESENT

▶ **Write Your Final Draft** Now, using your edited draft, begin creating a final draft for presentation.

Use word processing software to type your final draft. Make sure to format your margins and spacing according to your teacher's request.

Check your final draft against the Traits of Writing Scoring Guide on pages 338–341 and correct any errors before you present it.

▶ **Beyond the Classroom** Extend your finished cause-and-effect essay.

List two ideas for photos that could illustrate your cause-and-effect essay:

_____

_____

Look online for a blog, message board, magazine, or newspaper where you could publish your cause-and-effect essay.

List two places you could upload or share your cause-and-effect essay for publication.

_____

Quick Check

▶ **Check your essay for how well you used conventions. Then have a writing partner rate it, too.**

6 = Expert   **3** = Making Strides

5 = Well Done   **2** = On The Way

4 = Almost There   **1** = Getting Started

Conventions

1. Did I use verb tenses correctly?

Self   ① ② ③ ④ ⑤ ⑥
Partner ① ② ③ ④ ⑤ ⑥

2. Did I correctly use commas in a series?

Self   ① ② ③ ④ ⑤ ⑥
Partner ① ② ③ ④ ⑤ ⑥

3. Did I use nouns correctly?

Self   ① ② ③ ④ ⑤ ⑥
Partner ① ② ③ ④ ⑤ ⑥

4. Did I capitalize proper nouns and use apostrophes with possessive nouns?

Self   ① ② ③ ④ ⑤ ⑥
Partner ① ② ③ ④ ⑤ ⑥

READ ONLINE

expert space
Go to **www.expert21.com/ student** to find photographs and other visuals to illustrate your essay.

21
Expert Reading

You have learned about the conditions in extreme regions. Now, apply your expert reading strategies to the following article about surviving in Antarctica. ▶

HOW TO SURVIVE IN ANTARCTICA

By Lucy Jane Bledsoe

Traveling to the coldest and windiest place on the planet takes a lot of courage—and preparation. Here's what you'll need to know before making the journey.

➔ What to Pack

Surviving a trip to Antarctica starts with packing. Lots of warm clothes are a must! It's necessary to bring good sunglasses that have 100 percent ultraviolet protection. Why? Not only does the sun shine all day and night in the summertime in Antarctica, it also reflects off the snow, making for a very bright world. Glasses frames should be plastic, rather than metal, so they won't freeze to your skin! Snow goggles are a good idea, as is lots of sunscreen, with an SPF of 15 or greater.

Keeping warm in Antarctica requires dressing in layers. For most people, the first layer is long underwear. This can be made of either polypropylene or, for even greater warmth, fleece. Over the long underwear, some people wear a fleece suit, a lot like the snowsuits that children wear. Wind pants and a fleece jacket cover this layer. Finally, a huge down parka tops off the ensemble.

polypropylene *(n.)* a plastic that softens when heated
ensemble *(n.)* an outfit of complementary clothing

How to Build a Snow Shelter

Most likely, you'll have a room on a ship or in a dorm, or a heavy-duty tent to house you in Antarctica. But in case of an emergency, knowing how to make a quick shelter is an essential survival skill.

The beauty of snow caves is that they are very warm. No matter how cold the air gets, snow is always 0°C (32°F), so a snow cave is always at least that warm. In a good, tightly constructed snow cave, a person's body heat can warm it up even more.

There are many kinds of snow shelters. Some are more elaborate than others. Below are instructions for building a very easy kind. You'll need a shovel.

Step 1: Throw all your gear, including duffels, sleep kits, buckets—whatever you have—into a big pile. Be sure to keep your shovel out!

Step 2: Shovel lots of snow onto your pile of gear.

Step 3: When your gear is completely buried, climb up on the mound and stamp the snow solid. Then, pile more snow on and stamp it again.

Step 4: Dig a tunnel to your gear. Beginning a few feet away from the mound, dig down and forward, so that the tunnel will come out under your mound of gear.

Step 5: Pull your gear, piece by piece, out of the tunnel.

Step 6: Scoot into the tunnel yourself. There is your snow shelter!

Layers are important for a couple of reasons. For one, air gets trapped between each of the layers. That air is warmed by your body and helps keep you insulated against the cold. Also, sweating is dangerous in very cold places. If you sweat, the sweat will freeze. Then you'll end up much, much colder. If you dress in layers, you can always take a layer off when you feel yourself overheating. Or you can add one if you feel yourself getting too cold.

It's very important to pay attention to your extremities—feet, hands, nose, and ears. These are the first to get frostbite. You'll definitely want a wool or fleece hat that covers your ears. To help keep the nose warm, most people wear a neck gaiter, which is a tube of material worn around the neck and pulled up over the mouth and nose. You'll want to wear liners under your mittens. People who work in Antarctica are issued a full set of clothing called extreme cold weather gear, including all the clothes mentioned above and more.

In Antarctica, it's important to take the time to make body temperature adjustments, no matter how inconvenient. Getting too cold, or too warm, can be life threatening.

adjustments *(n.)* changes
inconvenient *(adj.)* causing difficulties

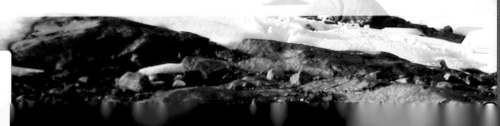

Visiting McMurdo Station

How To Tell Penguins Apart

To be an Antarctic expert, it is essential to know how to tell the different kinds of penguins apart. There are 18 species of penguins, four of which live on the continent of Antarctica, while several other species live on the islands around the continent.

The names of many species will help you remember them. The chinstrap penguin has a thin black line that extends from either side of its black "cap," all the way under its white chin. The Adélie penguin, small with a white ring around its eyes, is named after the wife of a nineteenth-century French explorer. The biggest, most regal penguins are the emperors, distinguished by their three-and-a-half-foot height, an orange tinge to their neck feathers, and an orange streak along their beak. Also regal, the slightly smaller king penguins can dive to depths of 800 feet. The gentoo penguins can be identified by their white forehead patches. Gentoo penguins are very fast swimmers, having been clocked at over 22 miles an hour.

Chinstrap

Adélie

Emperor

Gentoo

regal *(adj.)* of notable excellence
distinguished *(v.)* marked as different

If you're like some explorers, you might think you haven't really been to Antarctica until you've been on the mainland. Maybe you crave endless ice fields, volcanoes, and mind-numbing temperatures. Or maybe you'd like to arrive by air, avoiding that long, multiday crossing of the southern sea. In that case, you'll want to visit McMurdo Station—the biggest American research base.

McMurdo Station is more than a research site—it's a small town, with about 80 buildings and, in the summertime, 1,200 residents. Besides science laboratories, there is a firehouse, a church, a library, a hospital, a bowling alley, and even a greenhouse where fresh vegetables are grown. People who are going nuts from never seeing any plant life can lie in the greenhouse hammock, enjoy the moist warmth, and gaze at the deep red chilies and bright green lettuces.

Getting Supplies To McMurdo

The people at McMurdo Station are isolated from the rest of the world. Supplying the station with food and equipment is challenging. During the short summer, Air Force LC-130s bring in mail and food, but they can't carry large loads. Each year, a Coast Guard icebreaker called the Polar Star carves a path through the sea ice so that a resupply ship, the Green Wave, can make it into McMurdo Station. The Green Wave carries machinery, trucks, and large loads of food for the winter. It also takes the year's waste back to the United States to be recycled or disposed of properly.

To make docking and loading such large ships easier, the Coast Guard has built a pier of ice. During the winter, workers set up a large rectangular enclosure on top of the sea ice. They pump a layer of water from under the sea ice into this big tray. After the layer of water freezes, they pump in another layer. They keep adding layers of water and letting them freeze until there is one large ice cube. Then, during the summer when the sea ice melts, the big ice cube remains floating. That's the pier!

isolated *(adj.)* kept separate from others
disposed of *(v.)* gotten rid of

Trip's End

Traveling to Antarctica is a life-changing adventure. No one comes back the same person. You've looked into the eyes of penguins. You've walked on snow and ice only a handful of people have walked on before you. You've learned how to survive in the most extreme climate on Earth. Congratulations! You're now a true Antarctic explorer. ■

Reflect

1. Circle all the expert strategies you used while reading this article.

   A. Visualize

   B. Predict

   C. Other _____

2. Use the letters above to label where in the article you applied the expert strategies.

3. Select one expert strategy you used. Explain why you applied that strategy where you did.

   _____
   _____
   _____

RESEARCH ONLINE

expert space
Go to **www.expert21.com/student**
to learn more about McMurdo Dry Valleys; South Pole; Penguins.

PROJECT
RESEARCH

Extreme Habitat

THE SITUATION

The Amundsen–Scott South Pole Station is a research facility in Antarctica, the coldest, highest, driest, windiest, and emptiest place on Earth. About 200 people live at South Pole Station during the summer; a few dozen keep it operational in winter.

YOUR CHALLENGE

You are a scientist at South Pole Station. You must create a presentation to give workers realistic expectations for living conditions there. Your group will present the top five challenges of living in Antarctica.

In order to create your presentation, you will

- ask questions.
- analyze resources that describe life at the South Pole.
- describe the Antarctic habitat.
- categorize the challenges of living in Antarctica.
- create a brief computer presentation.

CAREER CONNECTION Human Services

www.careerclusters.org

Go to **21** ToolKit **Expert File 6.25** to learn more about recruiting workers.

1 Discuss What's "Normal"

Newcomers to Antarctica can experience culture shock. With your group, discuss the things people in the United States take for granted. Jot down your thoughts here.

THINGS TAKEN FOR GRANTED IN THE U.S.

2 List Questions

It's good to think about questions applicants are likely to ask so you can be ready with the answers. With your group, brainstorm a list of questions about life in Antarctica. Write them here.

_____

_____

_____

_____

3 Analyze Resources

Review the selections you've read in this Workshop for information about living and working in Antarctica. Then use the **Fact File** on the following pages and **Expert Space** to gather more information.

4 Describe the Habitat

Look at this photo of the Antarctic. Go to the [21] **Tool**Kit and use **Expert File 2.2** to brainstorm adjectives that describe the habitat in Antarctica as shown in the photo. Write a short descriptive paragraph about the environment.

_____

_____

_____

_____

5 Synthesize Data to Create Categories

With your group, use the information from the Workshop selections, the **Fact File**, and **Expert Space** to come up with five categories of challenges facing those working at South Pole Station. Write them here.

_____

_____

_____

_____

_____

6 Assemble Your Presentation

Go to the [21] **Tool**Kit and use **Expert File 2.9** to make a storyboard of your presentation. Then, use **Expert File 4.4** to create a multimedia presentation.

PROJECT
FACT FILE

ANTARCTIC FACT SHEET
Source: Polar Adventures Magazine
Date: December 24, 2008

FASCINATING FACTS ABOUT ANTARCTICA

- The average temperature in Antarctica is –30°F in inland areas. The lowest recorded temperature was –128.6°F. It is so cold inland that if a steel bar is dropped, it will shatter like glass.

- Antarctica is the world's windiest continent. Wind speeds of more than 185 mph have been recorded. Inland research stations can be quickly buried by snow.

- There is very little precipitation in Antarctica, but what snow does fall never melts. The average depth of the ice in Antarctica is about 1.5 miles. Only about 2.4% of Antarctica is not covered by ice—it's exposed rock.

- The interior of Antarctica has almost continuous daylight during the summer and almost continuous darkness during the winter.

- About 4,000 people work in Antarctica during the summer and 1,000 in the winter. From April to October or November, it is impossible to leave—ice conditions prevent ships and planes from getting through.

Place a **star** ★ next to three statements that you think describe the most difficult challenges of living in Antarctica.

POLAR INFORMATION CARD
Source: Australian Antarctic Division Brochure
Date Accessed: February 23, 2009

ADD Transport Survival Gear

Ship • Aircraft • Vehicle

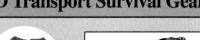

Carry-On Survival Bag

Woolen Thermals

Polar Fleece

Freezer Suit

AERIAL PHOTOS

Source: South Pole Station Web site
Date Accessed: February 5, 2009

The New South Pole Station

Introductions | Science Goals | Video Tour | Contact

ICE CREEP

The new station faces into the wind and is airfoil-shaped.

The shape forces the lower air stream to accelerate through the gap.

Years later, if snow still builds up, the building can be lifted two more stories on its support columns.

A new station was recently built at the South Pole to replace a dome built in the 1970s that is gradually being buried by snow. In what two ways does the design of the new station building address the challenges created by blowing wind?

1. _____

2. _____

INTERIOR PHOTO

Source: Polar Scientist's Photostream
Date Accessed: February 6, 2009

South Pole Accommodations

Image Gallery

How might you feel living here—especially knowing you can't leave for months?

_____

_____

_____

_____

_____

_____

A dorm room inside the Pole Station. The station can house 154 people in single rooms.

uploaded January 4, 2009
(0) comments

Strategy Check

Use your knowledge and strategies from the workshop to answer these questions.

Compare and Contrast

1. Write a comparison of Keesh, from "The Story of Keesh," and Shabanu, from *Shabanu*. Compare and contrast their survival skills and their personalities.

Keesh: _____

_____

_____

Shabanu: _____

_____

_____

Cause and Effect

2. In "Crisis on Top of the World" and "Blue People of the Sahara," you learned about the effects of human actions on the environment. Complete the two causal chains below.

"Crisis on Top of the World"
Human actions release greenhouse gases.

↓

↓

"Blue People of the Sahara"

↓

Land in the Sahara turns into desert.

↓

Setting

3. In what ways does the setting affect plot in *Shabanu*?

_____

_____

_____

Mood

4. How is the mood of "The Story of Keesh" similar to the mood of *Shabanu* at the beginning and at the end of each selection?

_____

_____

_____

Author's Purpose

5. What is the author's purpose for writing the selections below: to inform, to entertain, to persuade, or to explain? Choose one or more author's purposes for each selection.

"Life at the Poles"

_____

Shabanu

_____

"Extreme Athletes Run Length of Sahara"

_____

Multiple-Meaning Words

6. Use context clues to figure out the meaning of the word *material* in the sentence below. Then fill in the circle next to the correct answer.

My goal is to be happy and to win the respect of my family; <u>material</u> things, such as fancy clothes, mean nothing to me.

Ⓐ a piece of cloth

Ⓑ important to all

Ⓒ unimportant to all

Ⓓ having to do with the physical world

Context Clues

7. Using context clues, figure out the meaning of the word *thatch* in this sentence. Then fill in the circle next to the correct answer.

The boys collected branches to repair the torn <u>thatch</u> on the roof.

Thatch is _____

Ⓐ bricks used for a roof

Ⓑ a chimney

Ⓒ plant material woven into a roof

Ⓓ stones on the ground

Gather Information

8. You have learned about desert life from "Blue People of the Sahara" and *Shabanu*. Complete the chart below by incorporating facts from both selections.

climate	
transportation	
food	
challenges	

Evaluate

9. Based on the selections in this workshop, do you think it is more difficult to live in extremely cold environments, such as the Arctic region and Antarctica, or very hot environments, such as the Sahara and Cholistan deserts? Support your answer with evidence from the selections.

_____

_____

_____

_____

_____

_____

How do people survive in extreme environments?

10. Use what you learned in this workshop to respond to the Expert Question. Jot down some notes here. Then use a separate sheet of paper to write your response.

_____

_____

1960s: STAND UP. BE HEARD

Expert Question:
How can we be heard?

WELCOME HOME, VETS!

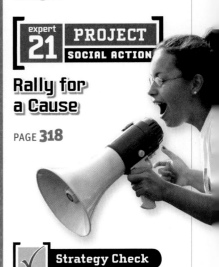

en are the largest
p in the world, maki
st exactly half of t
ulation. The size of
uld make it easy fo
ieve equal rights. Ri
ing a woman can be b
alth. Around the worl
ocking number of wo
xperience some form
uring their lifetimes
nother source of da
In countries that pr
to good health care, t
low. But in developing
the number is much
have not yet achieved
equality either. They

How can we be heard?

The 1960s were a time of social and political change in the United States. Young people were speaking out on a number of issues, such as the Vietnam War and civil rights. What are some of the issues that you care about today? Explore the ways that people spoke out in the past and think about how you can speak out today.

▶ Anchor Your Knowledge

Watch the Anchor Media, "The 1960s: Stand Up, Be Heard," to see how Erica Fernandez, an activist, fought to protect her community from environmental dangers.

0:00/ 2:30

WORKSHOP GOALS

To gain expert knowledge about social change, you will

- study **informational texts** about the events that shaped the 1960s.

- read **literary texts** about this era of political and social change.

- learn important **skills** and **strategies** to help you understand what you read.

- develop **21ˢᵗ Century Skills** to **understand persuasive techniques** and **analyze media messages**.

- write a **persuasive essay** about a social issue you care about.

- complete an **Expert Project** about organizing a rally.

▶ Opinionaire

Before starting this workshop, put a check mark to the left of each statement you agree with. Then, come back **after** you complete the workshop to see if you changed your mind.

BEFORE Workshop	TOPIC: **Social Change**	AFTER Workshop
	Individual people can't make a difference in society.	
	Most people don't really care about the rights of other people.	
	In wartime, soldiers always believe in the cause that they are fighting for.	
	It's difficult for young people to change society.	
	Youths today are just as outspoken as previous generations.	
	It takes bravery to stand up for what is right.	
	Groups are more effective than individuals at making a difference.	

We the People

▶ Preview the Expert Project

At the end of this workshop, you'll organize a rally for an issue you care about. Preview the Expert Project on pages 318–321.

Chicago, Illinois—About 300,000 demonstrators in Chicago did not report to work today, but instead took to the streets to protest restrictions on immigration. Among them were thousands of young people from predominantly Latino schools. The protests were part of a nationwide event called "A Day Without Immigrants."

▶ What will you need to know or do to complete the Expert Project?

_____

_____

_____

_____

▶ Explore Expert Space

 Go to **www.expert21.com/student** to learn more about the topics in this workshop.

DISCOVER ONLINE

- The Environmental Movement
- The Vietnam War Era
- Public Speaking

READ ONLINE

- Dr. Martin Luther King, Jr.
- The 1960s
- American Indian Movement
- Bob Dylan

RESEARCH ONLINE

- Student Movements
- First Amendment Freedoms
- Hispanic Americans

▶ Personal Inquiry

Explore the topic of standing up for equal rights by asking your own questions. Return to add questions as you continue reading Workshop 4. Plan to revisit your questions.

Erica Fernandez: Activist
This young woman rallied her community for a cause.

"I love to see people empower themselves, to find their voice, and to realize how much power they have when they get together."

FACTS AND STATS

NAME: Erica Fernandez

HOMETOWN: Originally Michoacán, Mexico; now Oxnard, California

JOB: Activist and student

EDUCATION: High school diploma; currently pursuing a bachelor's degree at Stanford University

PLANS FOR THE FUTURE: To become an attorney and continue helping people and communities.

WORKPLACE LITERACIES: Leading people, understanding persuasive techniques, determining priorities, understanding multiple perspectives, building teams, creating effective presentations

PAY: Many activists volunteer. Others can earn $20,000 to $45,000 a year.

CAREER CONNECTION Human Services
www.careerclusters.org

Go to **21** **Tool**Kit **Expert File 6.25** to learn more about careers in activism.

RELATED JOBS: Social worker, local, state, or national political representative

At age 12, Erica Fernandez learned of a corporation's plan to run a liquefied natural gas (LNG) pipeline through her mostly Latino neighborhood in Oxnard, California. She joined a small group, Latino No on LNG, to fight the project. Four years later, Erica found herself speaking in front of 3,000 people and persuading the government to cancel the plan. Below, she explains how she did it.

STEP 1 Recruiting a Team

To build the pipeline, the company needed permission from two state commissions. We decided the best **strategy** was to **persuade** the commissions to say "No" by **organizing** rallies on the day of their votes. We needed a lot of support from the community. I **recruited** hundreds of student volunteers.

STEP 2 Knocking on Doors

We went door to door to encourage our neighbors to join our cause. At each house, volunteers explained why we were against the pipeline and we **connected** to people's concerns. If a person worked in agriculture, we explained how the pipeline would ruin the fields and that people would lose their jobs. On the day a commission voted, we called people and reminded them to come protest.

STEP 3 Finding My Voice

Latino No on LNG chose me to speak at our rallies. I wrote my speech, but speech trainers helped. They told me how to **deliver** an effective speech by focusing on the most important points. They also helped me with my grammar. My English was bad, so I held a pencil in my teeth while practicing to help improve my pronunciation.

STEP 4 — Gathering the Masses

We held a rally on the day the first commission voted in Oxnard. We thought we had **convinced** 500 people to attend, but we did much better than we expected. The crowd grew to 3,000 people! I **trained** volunteers to direct people to parking. We **coordinated** with other organizations who wanted to help us. We ordered T-shirts, made posters, and brought hula hoops that represented the diameter of the pipeline.

STEP 5 — Moment of Truth

At first, I didn't worry about my speech, because I didn't think anyone would listen. But I became nervous standing in front of so many people. I gave the speech, explaining how the LNG pipeline would hurt us. No one was supposed to clap for the speakers. But when I was done, the whole crowd stood up and cheered. We won the vote, 2 to 1.

STEP 6 — Inspiring Others

The second commission voted two days later in Santa Barbara—40 miles away. So I gave the speech again. After I spoke, a 90-year-old woman was crying. She told me, "I have lived so long, and I have seen so many things. I thought I couldn't make a difference, but you **inspired** me." She stood at the podium and said, "Because of Erica, I'm standing up here, and I'm speaking for future generations." We won the vote, unanimously. A month later, the governor vetoed the project. We had won—a group of everyday people had beaten a big corporation.

ANALYZE WORKPLACE SKILLS

1. Understand Multiple Perspectives

How did the volunteers persuade people to fight the pipeline?

_____

_____

_____

_____

2. Build an Effective Team

What steps did Erica take to build an effective team to help her group fight the LNG pipeline?

3. Present Effectively

Why was it important for Erica to speak clearly while giving her speech?

_____

_____

_____

DISCOVER ONLINE

expert space
Go to **www.expert21.com/student** to learn more about The Environmental Movement; The Vietnam War Era; Public Speaking.

Speech

I Have a Dream

Civil rights leader Dr. Martin Luther King, Jr. had a dream that inspired millions of people to help change the nation. Read about it in King's own famous words.

QuickWrite

Describe a cause you believe in. How could you convince others to support your cause? Describe one method you think would be effective.

Figurative Language   **LITERARY ANALYSIS**

Figurative language uses words and expressions that mean something other than their literal meaning. Figurative language helps readers form vivid mental pictures.

- A **simile** compares two unlike things using the word *like* or *as*.
- A **metaphor** compares two unlike things directly.
- **Imagery** uses descriptive words and phrases that appeal to one or more of the five senses—sight, hearing, smell, taste, and touch.

▶ Write an *M* next to the sentence that contains a metaphor, an *S* next to the sentence that contains a simile, and an *I* next to the sentence that contains examples of imagery. Underline the examples of figurative language in the sentences.

_____ This momentous decree came as a great beacon light of hope ...

_____ With this faith we will be able to hew out of the mountain of despair a stone of hope.

_____ With this faith we will be able to transform the jangling discords of our nation into a beautiful symphony of brotherhood.

Draw Conclusions   **COMPREHENSION**

When you **draw a conclusion**, you use details from the text, your own knowledge, and reasoning to form a judgment about a subject.

To draw a conclusion, combine details from the text with what you already know.

▶ Read the following excerpt from Dr. King's speech. Then complete the graphic organizer to draw a conclusion about what King means.

Fivescore years ago, a great American, in whose symbolic shadow we stand today, signed the Emancipation Proclamation. This momentous decree came as a great beacon light of hope to millions of ... slaves who had been seared in the flames of withering injustice.

What the text says		What I already know		My Conclusion
A great American signed the Emancipation Proclamation and brought hope to millions of slaves.	**+**		**=**	

Academic Language `VOCABULARY`

▶ Rate each word. Then write its meaning and an example sentence.

Word	Meaning	Example
EXPERT WORDS *Use these words to write and talk about the workshop topic.*		
momentous mo•men•tous *(adjective)* ① ② ③ ④	of great importance	My graduation from college is going to be a momentous event for my entire family.
oppression op•pres•sion *(noun)* ① ② ③ ④		
rally ral•ly *(verb)* ① ② ③ ④		
revolt re•volt *(noun)* ① ② ③ ④		
CONTENT AREA WORDS *Use these words to talk and write about social studies or science.*		
decade dec•ade *(noun)* ① ② ③ ④		
echo ech•o *(verb)* ① ② ③ ④		
SELECTION WORDS *These words are key to understanding this selection.*		
invigorating in•vig•o•ra•ting *(adjective)* ① ② ③ ④	energizing	
legitimate le•git•i•mate *(adjective)* ① ② ③ ④		Hank's illness was a legitimate excuse for missing the test.

Rating Scale ① I don't know the word. ② I've seen it or heard it. ③ I know its meaning. ④ I know it and use it.

Suffixes `WORD ANALYSIS`

A suffix is a word part that has been added to the end of a base word to change its meaning.

A suffix often changes the word's part of speech. For example, the suffix *-ion,* which means "the state of being," changes a verb to a noun.

▶ **Write the base word and the suffix of *confusion.***

_____ + _____

Confuse means "to mix up or bewilder." What does *confusion* mean?

_____

I Have a Dream

By Dr. Martin Luther King, Jr.

"Martin the Dreamer"
Elizabeth Shapiro, age 17

One of the greatest speeches of all time inspires us to dream of a free and fair America.

The 1960s was a defining **decade** in America, and Dr. Martin Luther King, Jr. was one of its most significant leaders. King led the Montgomery Bus Boycott, which ended racial segregation[1] on public transportation in Montgomery, Alabama. Later, he founded the Southern Christian Leadership Conference (SCLC), a civil rights organization that helped to organize the March on Washington for Jobs and Freedom. Held on August 28, 1963, in Washington, D.C., the march drew an estimated 200,000 to 300,000 participants, who **rallied** against racial inequality. It became one of the most successful peaceful demonstrations in American history.

Several speakers made their voices heard at the March on Washington. Yet, only one speaker's powerful message continues to **echo** in American hearts and minds today. King's "I Have a Dream" speech, excerpted below, has become a symbol of the fight to achieve justice for all.

"I am happy to join with you today in what will go down in history as the greatest demonstration for freedom in the history of our nation.

Fivescore years ago, a great American, in whose symbolic shadow we stand today, signed the Emancipation Proclamation. This **momentous** decree came as a great beacon light of hope to millions of Negro[2] slaves who had been seared in the flames of withering injustice. It came as a joyous daybreak to end the long night of their captivity.

But one hundred years later, the Negro still is not free. One hundred years later, the life of the Negro is still sadly crippled by the manacles of segregation and the chains of discrimination. One hundred years later, the Negro lives on a lonely island of poverty in the midst of a vast ocean of material prosperity. One hundred years later, the Negro is still languished in the corners of American society and finds himself an exile in his own land.

---

[1] Racial segregation, or the forced separation of people based on race, was legal in many states.

[2] The term "Negro" was considered an acceptable term in the 1960s. Today, it is viewed as an ethnic slur, but still appears in historical texts.

founded (v.) established
fivescore (adj.) one hundred

COMPREHENSION

Draw Conclusions

Using what you know plus information in the text, why do you think the organizers chose Washington, D.C., as the location of the march?

_____

_____

_____

_____

_____

LITERARY ANALYSIS

Figurative Language

<u>Underline</u> the metaphor that discusses African Americans and poverty.

- To what does King compare African American poverty?

_____

_____

_____

CRITICAL THINKING

Analyze

How does the metaphor help communicate how African Americans felt in the 1960s?

_____

_____

_____

_____

_____

_____

_____

_____

_____

_____

And so we've come here today to dramatize the shameful condition.

... It would be fatal for the nation to overlook the urgency of the moment. This sweltering summer of the Negro's **legitimate** discontent will not pass until there is an **invigorating** autumn of freedom and equality.

Nineteen sixty-three is not an end, but a beginning. Those who hope that the Negro needed to blow off steam and will now be content will have a rude awakening if the nation returns to business as usual. There will be neither rest nor tranquility in America until the Negro is granted his citizenship rights. The whirlwinds of **revolt** will continue to shake the foundations of our nation until the bright day of justice emerges. . . .

I say to you today, my friends, that even though we face the difficulties of today and tomorrow, I still have a dream. It is a dream deeply rooted in the American dream. I have a dream that one day this nation will rise up, live out the true meaning of its creed: "We hold these truths to be self-evident, that all men are created equal."

I have a dream that one day on the red hills of Georgia, the sons of former slaves and the sons of former slave owners will be able to sit down together at the table of brotherhood.

I have a dream that one day even the state of Mississippi[1], a state sweltering with the heat of injustice, sweltering with the heat of **oppression**, will be transformed into an oasis of freedom and justice.

I have a dream that my four little children will one day live in a nation where they will not be judged by the color of their skin but by the content of their character. I have a dream today.

I have a dream that one day down in Alabama, with its vicious racists[2], with its governor having his lips dripping with the words of interposition and nullification[3], one day, right there in Alabama, little black boys and little black girls will be able to join hands with little white boys and white girls as sisters and brothers. I have a dream today.

... This is our hope. This is the faith that I go back to the South with. With this faith we will be able to hew out of the mountain of despair a stone of hope. With this faith we will be able to transform the jangling discords of our nation into a beautiful symphony of brotherhood. With this faith we will be able to work together, to pray together, to struggle together, to go to jail together, **to stand up for freedom together, knowing that we will be free one day.**

This will be the day when all of God's children will be able to sing with new meaning, 'My country, 'tis of thee, sweet land of liberty, of thee I sing. Land where my fathers died, land of the Pilgrim's pride, from every mountainside, let freedom ring.' And if America is to be a great nation this must become true.

> **Make Inferences**
> Why do you think King quotes the song, "My Country 'Tis of Thee"?

So let freedom ring from the prodigious hilltops of New Hampshire.

---

[1] Mississippi had a particularly poor record of violating voting rights. Black and white civil rights workers from other states often traveled there and risked their lives to register voters.

[2] Alabama was known as a state that was unfriendly to civil rights activists. Activists were often bombed.

[3] Governor George Wallace refused to desegregate Alabama's public schools, even when required by federal law. He was famous for saying, "Segregation now, segregation tomorrow, segregation forever."

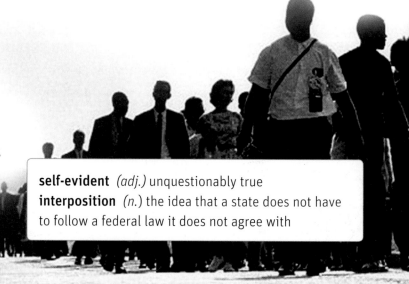

self-evident (adj.) unquestionably true
interposition (n.) the idea that a state does not have to follow a federal law it does not agree with

Let freedom ring from the mighty mountains of New York.

Let freedom ring from the snowcapped Rockies of Colorado.

Let freedom ring from the curvaceous slopes of California.

But not only that. Let freedom ring from Stone Mountain of Georgia.

Let freedom ring from Lookout Mountain of Tennessee.

Let freedom ring from every hill and molehill of Mississippi. From every mountainside, let freedom ring.

And when this happens, when we allow freedom to ring, when we let it ring from every village and every hamlet, from every state and every city, we will be able to speed up that day when all of God's children—black men and white men, Jews and Gentiles, Protestants and Catholics—**will be able to join hands and sing in the words of the old Negro spiritual, 'Free at last! Free at last! Thank God Almighty, we are free at last!'"**

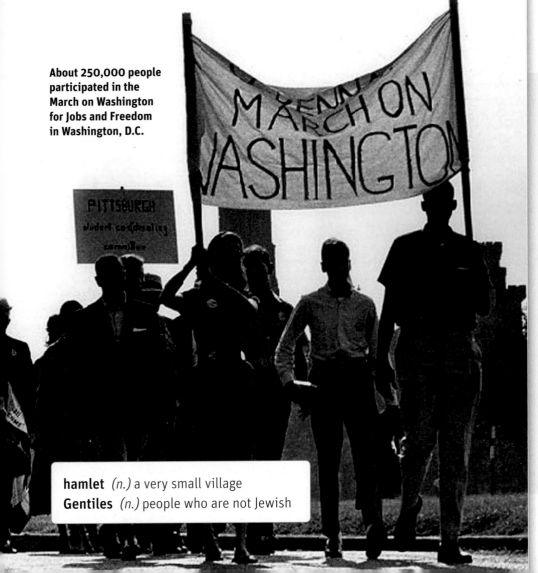

About 250,000 people participated in the March on Washington for Jobs and Freedom in Washington, D.C.

hamlet *(n.)* a very small village
Gentiles *(n.)* people who are not Jewish

VOCABULARY/WORD ANALYSIS

Suffixes

 (Circle) the word *nullification* in the eighth paragraph on page 258. The word *nullify* means "to erase from existence."

• What does the governor want to *nullify*?

_____

_____

_____

LITERARY ANALYSIS

Figurative Language

Review the sixth paragraph on page 258. <u>Underline</u> three images King uses.

• What does the paragraph mean?

_____

_____

_____

21 **SMALL GROUPS/INDEPENDENT**

COLLABORATE

Design You have been asked to create a poster to carry at the March on Washington. Come up with a slogan and create one or more images to express your ideas.

COMMUNICATE

 Reflect and Write Write a paragraph about what King means when he uses the terms "brother," "sister," and "brotherhood."

W

READ ONLINE

 expert space
Go to **www.expert21.com/student**
to learn more about Dr. Martin Luther King, Jr.; March on Washington; Pacifism and Nonviolence.

Correspondence

ON THE FRONT LINE IN VIETNAM

The Vietnam War cost the United States more than 58,000 lives and divided the American people. Find out what it was like to be a soldier on the front line—from the soldiers themselves.

W QuickWrite

Imagine you are a soldier writing a letter to your family. What news would you share with them? What news would you want to hear from them in return?

Fact and Opinion   **COMPREHENSION**

A **fact** is a statement that can be proved.

An **opinion** is a statement that cannot be proved. An opinion expresses a belief or a feeling.

▶ Complete the chart. The first example has been done for you.

Statement	Fact?	Opinion?	How do you know?
59,939 U.S. soldiers died or disappeared during the Vietnam War.	✗		The statement can be proved.
Vietnam veterans should be treated with great respect.			
The Vietnam War was not worth the huge loss of life.			

Primary Sources   **NAVIGATING TEXT**

A **primary source** is a document, recording, or other resource that gives firsthand information about a subject.

Primary sources include letters, speeches, original literary works, diaries, journals, and historical documents.

▶ Check the box next to the primary sources in the list below.

❑ Dr. Martin Luther King, Jr.'s "I Have a Dream" speech

❑ a book that discusses the impact of the Vietnam War

❑ Mark Twain's novel, *The Adventures of Tom Sawyer*

❑ a term paper that analyzes *The Adventures of Tom Sawyer*

❑ a letter from a soldier in Vietnam to his parents

Academic Language VOCABULARY

▶ Rate each word. Then write its meaning and an example sentence.

Word	Meaning	Example
ACADEMIC WORDS *Use these words in all your subject classes.*		
hostile *hos•tile (adjective)* ① ② ③ ④	threatening or aggressive	My enemy glared at me and raised her fists in a hostile way.
inevitable *in•ev•i•ta•ble (adjective)* ① ② ③ ④		It was inevitable that my sister would notice the hole I'd made in her sweater.
CONTENT AREA WORDS *Use these words to talk and write about social studies.*		
ambush *am•bush (verb)* ① ② ③ ④		
captor *cap•tor (noun)* ① ② ③ ④		
SELECTION WORDS *These words are key to understanding this selection.*		
angst *angst (noun)* ① ② ③ ④		
bittersweet *bit•ter•sweet (adjective)* ① ② ③ ④		
brace *brace (verb)* ① ② ③ ④	to prepare for something unpleasant, usually by tightening your muscles	
profound *pro•found (adjective)* ① ② ③ ④		

Rating Scale   ① I don't know the word.   ② I've seen it or heard it.   ③ I know its meaning.   ④ I know it and use it.

Suffixes WORD ANALYSIS

A suffix is a word part that is added to the end of a word to change its meaning.

You can figure out the meanings of many words that look unfamiliar by identifying the base word and suffix and thinking about their combined meaning.

▶ The suffix *–ity* means "the state of being" and can change a word from an adjective to a noun.

      EXAMPLE: *inevitable* ("impossible to prevent") + *-ity* ("the state of being")
           base word   **suffix**

         inevitability ("the state of being impossible to prevent")
         new term

Using what you know about suffixes, what does *hostility* mean?

_____

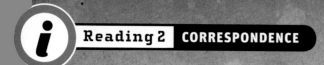

ON THE FRONT LINE IN VIETNAM

MAR 22 P.M. 1967

FROM Memories of Vietnam:
War in the First Person

The Vietnam War, half a world away, nearly tore the United States apart.

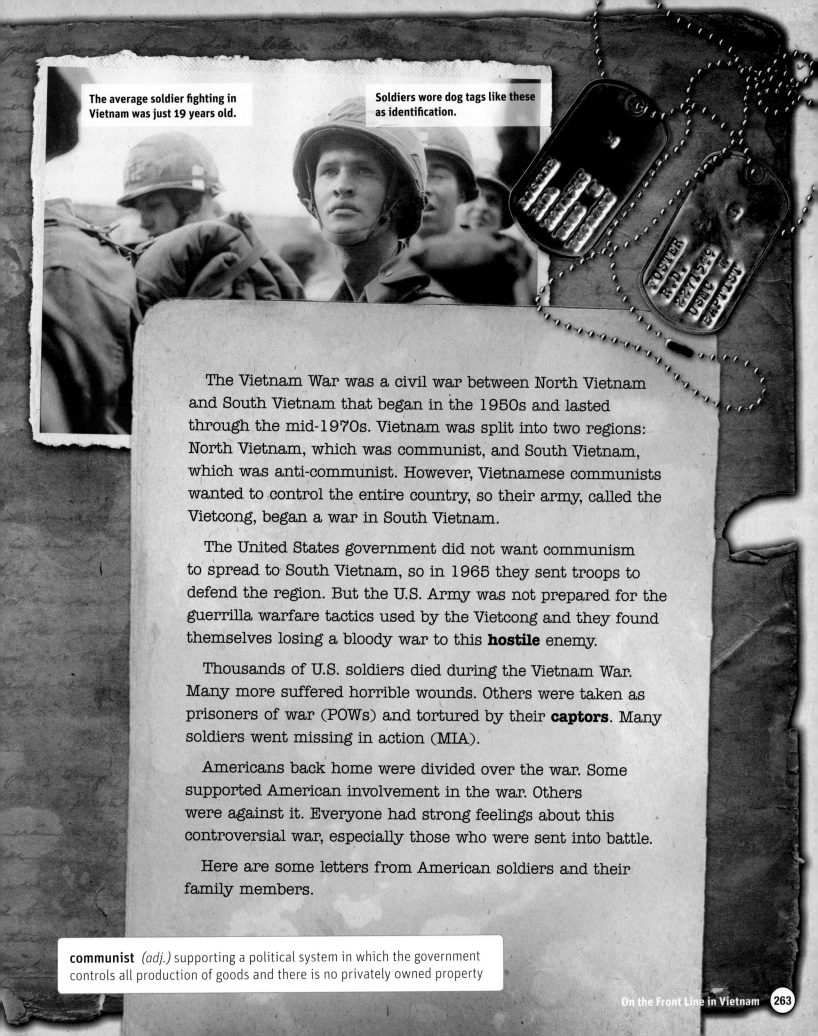

The average soldier fighting in Vietnam was just 19 years old.

Soldiers wore dog tags like these as identification.

The Vietnam War was a civil war between North Vietnam and South Vietnam that began in the 1950s and lasted through the mid-1970s. Vietnam was split into two regions: North Vietnam, which was communist, and South Vietnam, which was anti-communist. However, Vietnamese communists wanted to control the entire country, so their army, called the Vietcong, began a war in South Vietnam.

The United States government did not want communism to spread to South Vietnam, so in 1965 they sent troops to defend the region. But the U.S. Army was not prepared for the guerrilla warfare tactics used by the Vietcong and they found themselves losing a bloody war to this **hostile** enemy.

Thousands of U.S. soldiers died during the Vietnam War. Many more suffered horrible wounds. Others were taken as prisoners of war (POWs) and tortured by their **captors**. Many soldiers went missing in action (MIA).

Americans back home were divided over the war. Some supported American involvement in the war. Others were against it. Everyone had strong feelings about this controversial war, especially those who were sent into battle.

Here are some letters from American soldiers and their family members.

communist *(adj.)* supporting a political system in which the government controls all production of goods and there is no privately owned property

THE REALITY OF WAR

The reality of war came as a shock to most soldiers, especially if it was their first experience on the battlefield. They were forced to confront what they were witnessing outside as well as the **angst** they were feeling inside.

Somebody's Boots

We got to the airstrip at Pleiku. Someone said to me, "Oh, man, go over to the [other side of the] airstrip. Get yourself a couple of extra pairs of boots." I was the only one who went across the airstrip. I started noting men's names in the boots, and I said, "These are somebody's boots. I don't want these boots." Then I noticed piles of uniforms with lots of blood. It hit me like a ton of bricks. All of a sudden I realized what was going on and where those guys were coming from. They were coming from [a battle at] Ia Drang [where I was going].

—Thomas Bird

Private Anguish

April 1967

How are things back in the World? I hope all is well! Things are pretty much the same. Vietnam has my feelings on a seesaw.

This country is so beautiful when the sun is shining on the mountains. I see farmers in their rice paddies, with their water buffalo. I love the palm trees, monkeys, birds and even the strange insects. For a moment I wasn't in a war zone at all, just on vacation.

There are a few kids who hang around, some with no parents. I feel so sorry for them. I do things to make them laugh. And they call me dinky dow. That means "crazy." But it makes me feel good. I hope that's one reason why we're here, to win a future for them. It seems to be the only excuse I can think of for the things that I have done!

Love to all. Your son, George

—George Williams

After a Month in Battle

The Marines looked nothing like any Marines I had ever seen. The spit and polish was long gone. Every one of them was weighted down with enormous packs on their backs. They could hardly lift their feet when they walked, and most of them needed a shave. Their trousers were rolled up to just below their knees. The bare skin on their legs was caked with a red-tinted mud.

—Paul O'Connell

MESSAGES HOME

Most soldiers who wrote home carefully chose what kind of news to tell loved ones.

No Sympathy Please

January 14, 1969

This is to let you know that I'm OK. I want to tell you about that 12-day mission so that you can keep Mom from worrying. Don't show her this letter because the following is what I'll be doing for the next 11 months.

First it rained for six days solid. I got muddy and wet. My hands are covered with cuts. The jungles have thousands of leeches and mosquitoes. I think I have gotten bitten almost all over my body. I personally had to dig up two dead bodies. The smell was terrible. I just about got sick. About three or four guys got hurt through accidents.

The fighting is not heavy yet. But the rumor is we're moving south. I walk up and down mountains with a heavy pack on my back. But if everyone else does it, so can I. It's not so hard, actually. But one thing is for certain: you surely learn to appreciate some of the finer things you once had. Don't get me wrong. I'm not complaining or expecting sympathy. All I want to do is lay the line on what I'm doing. In return you must tell Mom that I'm probably out in the field doing hardly anything at all.

Love, Sal

—Salvador Gonzalez

airstrip (n.) a long, narrow piece of land that airplanes can fly from and land on
leeches (n.) small, soft worms that attach themselves to an animal in order to drink its blood

Soldiers carry
injured man.

The Worst Battle

July 3, 1966

I don't know how I can say this without alarming you. But I know I'll have to tell you about it. NBC News was there. I'm afraid you might have seen me on film or read about the dreadful fighting. When I think about what I've been through the last few days, I can't help but cry. I wonder how I am still alive. My company suffered the worst losses. I believe it was something close to 50 dead and wounded. Friends I took training with have been killed. Some are seriously wounded. In my squad of nine men, only four of us survived.

This was the worst battle that this company has experienced.

How I made it, I don't know. Perhaps you didn't read about it, but in case you did I just wanted to tell you I'm OK.

I can't help crying now because I think about the horror of those three days. I was carrying the bodies of wounded and dead onto helicopters when I saw NBC. They were taking pictures.

Yesterday we were rescued from that area by helicopter. I thought they'd never come for us. The area is less than two miles from Cambodia, where VCs [Vietcong soldiers] have regiments. They **ambushed** us.

Try to hold up. By the time you receive this, I hope to be **somewhat** recovered and at ease.

Love, Kenny

—Kenneth Peeples, Jr.

> **Make Inferences**
> How do you think Kenneth felt about NBC News's presence at the battle he describes?

---

regiments (*n.*) large groups of soldiers
somewhat (*adv.*) slightly, but not very much

NAVIGATING TEXT
Primary Sources
Explain why letters are useful for learning about the Vietnam War.

_____

_____

_____

_____

_____

COMPREHENSION
Compare and Contrast
Review the letters in "Private Anguish" and "The Worst Battle." How are the experiences and attitudes of the writers different? How are they similar?

_____

_____

_____

_____

_____

_____

_____

_____

_____

21 **SMALL GROUPS/INDEPENDENT**

COLLABORATE

Design Plan a monument to honor Vietnam veterans in your town or city. Decide what it would be and sketch the monument. Write a caption to explain its design.

COMMUNICATE

React and Write Write a letter to one of the soldiers. Review the soldier's letter and note the hardships he mentions. Try to address these issues in your letter.

ANTIWAR PROTEST

Back in America, the war had become very unpopular. Demonstrators crowded the streets, pressuring the government to bring the soldiers home. American troops began to leave Vietnam, and some soldiers questioned what they were doing there. Meanwhile the battle for equal rights was still raging, even as African American and Latino soldiers risked their lives in the war. Unrest seemed inevitable.

Tired of Suffering

August 1969

Things are picking up around here. We're starting to train the Vietnamese to do our jobs. That way they can take over when the time comes for the Air Force to pull out. The local people are not very happy about our leaving. They don't want to lose all the money they are making off the American GIs.

We cannot blame them for wanting a way of life that they have never had, and the war is not going to bring any solution. They do not want to fight. They're tired of suffering. They realize this is a war with no gains for the common people.

I've learned only one lesson from this. The United States, as powerful as it may be, cannot play the role of God. It cannot solve all the problems of the world. . . .

Love, Chicky

—Hector Ramos

Healing Words From Home

February 21, 1967

Hello Kenny,

How are you feeling today, Son? Hope this letter will find you recovering. Today we received your Purple Heart medal. I looked at it with mixed emotions. Happy, because you are out of Vietnam. Sad, because of the price you had to pay to get away from there. I also realize the thousands of boys who will never return home. Those parents have received the Purple Heart because of their son's death. When I think of these things, I know that I shouldn't feel too bad about your condition.

Let me say here and now that I'm extremely proud of you, Son. Not because you were awarded the Heart, but because you did an honorable thing. I know that you were bitterly against going into the service and rejected our reasons for being in Vietnam. I also knew of your feelings about the U.S. and its treatment of Negroes. Yet, in spite of these conditions, you did everything that was asked of you.

But I do know that you made an honorable decision, Kenny. It may not matter at all to you, but you are coming home a hero to us. Not a war hero, because you had to fight and get shot, but more so because you made a man's decision and stuck it out. You should feel proud of yourself! You can hold your head high everywhere you go, and you can go anywhere you wish.

You know, I was thinking that for a person who never traveled much, you are really seeing the world. Who would have thought that you would be writing from Japan, and your letters would arrive here in just two days. Hope ours reach you just as fast.

Rest good, and eat hearty. Relax, and don't worry about anything. Will write again soon. Until then, may God continue to bless you.

Love, Mom & Pop

> **GIs** *(n.)* Government Issue; American soldiers
> **honorable** *(adj.)* morally correct and deserving respect and admiration

THE BRAVE SON

Kenneth Peeples, Jr. wrote this letter to his parents (the writers of the letter in "Healing Words From Home") two weeks after he was wounded and moved to a hospital in Japan. Kenny was one of many African Americans who fought in Vietnam.

Just Bearing It

February 23, 1967

Dear Mom & Dad,

I was just about giving up on mail when I received your letter. It sure did a lot to cheer me up.

To be honest, I'm getting sick and tired of being in a hospital. I'm constantly on my back. I'm not able to walk as yet. It will probably be a few months before I'm even able to try.

This morning they took the cast off, and the doctor changed my dressing. I felt brave enough to peek at my wound for the first time. What I saw didn't make me feel too good. The wound doesn't give me any more pain. But I get a tremendous shock of pain at the sole of my foot and toes. The doctor said it is caused by the damaged nerves. There is nothing they can give me to relieve it. So all I do is just scream day and night. Everyone in the ward knows about it. I yell at the top of my lungs to relieve the pressure. Don't worry, I'll just "scream and bear it" (smile).

I guess I'll try to read a few pages or listen to the radio. My foot is acting up again.

So long for now.
Love, Kenny

An injured soldier rests.

COMPREHENSION

Fact and Opinion

Review "Tired of Suffering." Identify one piece of evidence Ramos could provide to support the opinion that the Vietnamese people "do not want to fight."

_____
_____
_____
_____

VOCABULARY/WORD ANALYSIS

Suffixes

Find the word *honorable* in the second paragraph of "Healing Words from Home." Write its base word and suffix below.

_____ + _____
(base word)   (suffix)

• Why did Mom and Pop say their son's actions were honorable?

_____
_____
_____

NAVIGATING TEXT

Primary Sources

(Circle) the text that explains the connection between "Healing Words From Home" and "Just Bearing It."

• What information can you infer from Mom and Pop's mention of Peeples's race and how he felt about fighting?

_____
_____
_____
_____
_____
_____

A soldier returning from battle greets his family.

HOMECOMING

Toward the end of the war, U.S. soldiers returned home in waves. They were met with a **bittersweet** homecoming. The war had changed Americans in **profound** ways, and those who had fought in it found themselves still on the front lines—even at home.

Bittersweet

I have been in the navy for two years and this is the end of my second tour to Vietnam. My wife Jeanne will be in San Francisco to greet me upon my arrival. My mother, father, aunt, and uncle will be there as well. They saw me off before the first tour so it is nice that they will be here when I come home.

I stay on the flight deck until we dock. It's a time to think and reflect on the times that have passed during the past two years. Times containing laughter and fun, but not overshadowing the episodes of death and pain.

I can see the [San Francisco Golden Gate Bridge] clearer now, as well as the surrounding land. You just don't know how good it feels to see America.

The USS *Coral Sea* had been adopted by the city of San Francisco two years before. Last year the city put on a nice homecoming for us. I hope they do the same this time; it really means a lot to us.

The bridge is getting closer now. I can see people waving to us. Last year they had a sign that said "Welcome Home," and they dropped flowers from the bridge.

We are passing under the bridge now. The people are shouting [dirty words] and are dumping garbage on us. A sign unfolds. It says "MURDERERS." A terrible [emptiness] fills my heart as if someone just kicked me in the chest. My country asked me to go. I went. I did what was expected of me as an American. I did not run away from my duty. I fought for what I believed in, freedom. Was I wrong?

—Michael Murphy

overshadowing *(v.)* being more important than

> ## "They were tears coming not from the joy of being home, but from the memory of the cabbie's simple offering of welcome and thanks."

A Simple Offering

When I was released from [the hospital], there seemed to be more enemies here than there had been in Vietnam. [. . .] Much later that night the bus delivered me and my duffle bag to downtown Sacramento, California, but still some ten miles short of home. It was much too early in the morning to wake up the family. I stood alone on that deserted street pondering the next step when a cab drove by. I waved him down.

He looked me over carefully before saying a word. "You just back from the war?" he asked. I told him that, in a way, yes, that was true.

I **braced** for what might follow, that he might deliver a lecture and boot me out. But all he said was, "Where you headed?" and I told him the address.

"Okay, this ride's on me."

Not another word was spoken until he pulled to a stop in front of my folks' house and offered me his hand. "Thanks," he said. "Good luck, kid." And he was gone.

It took me a while before I found the [self-control] to quietly let myself in and start again the life I'd left behind. I sat there in the living room, all alone except for the family's beloved and equally delighted Irish setter. I hugged and stroked him while he licked my face clean of the tears that had found their way down my cheek. They were tears coming not from the joy of being home, but from the memory of the cabbie's simple offering of welcome and thanks. I would never forget that morning or the kindness of that wonderful man.

—Mike Kelly

> **Make Inferences**
> Why do you think this soldier was so moved by this homecoming?

deserted (adv.) empty of inhabitants
boot (v.) to force to leave

CRITICAL THINKING

Synthesize

Review "Bittersweet" and "A Simple Offering" and complete the following activities:

- Circle the paragraph in both letters that shows how Murphy and Kelly felt about coming home.
- How do you think Murphy's and Kelly's experiences affected how they felt about fighting in the Vietnam War?

_____

_____

_____

_____

_____

_____

_____

21 SMALL GROUPS/INDEPENDENT

COLLABORATE

Examine Perspectives Identify at least three different perspectives on the war presented in these letters. Which view do most of the people in your group agree with? Why?

COMMUNICATE

Discuss and Write Discuss the pros and cons of fighting in the Vietnam War. Then write a paragraph about whether you would have fought in the war and why.

READ ONLINE

expert space
Go to **www.expert21.com/student** to learn more about The Vietnam War; Vietnam Veterans Memorial; G.I. Bill of Rights.

A DECADE TO REMEMBER

THE 1960s WERE FILLED WITH MEMORABLE MOMENTS.

By Lydia Okutoro

1960

On November 8, **John F. Kennedy (age 43)** becomes the youngest person in U.S. history to be **elected president.**

1962

In August, **Spider Man** makes his **first appearance** when Marvel Comics publishes *Amazing Fantasy (#15).*

In September, **Rachel Carson** publishes *Silent Spring,* which becomes a best seller and sparks the **environmental movement**. Chemical companies threaten to sue her to keep her quiet.

1961

On May 5, **Alan B. Shepard,** Jr. becomes **the first American in space**. On May 25, President **Kennedy** outlines a **plan** to **land an American on the moon.**

Throughout the spring and summer, interracial groups of students called **Freedom Riders** ride through the South to **protest segregation** on public transportation.

1963

The March on Washington

▼ On February 19, **Betty Friedan** publishes *The Feminine Mystique*, helping to fuel the **Women's Liberation Movement**, which sought to **gain more social, political, and financial opportunities for women.**

▼ On June 12, **Medgar Evers**, a well-known civil rights activist, is **assassinated** in front of his home in Mississippi.

▼ On August 28, **The March on Washington for Jobs and Freedom** draws about 250,000 participants. At the march, **Dr. Martin Luther King, Jr.** gives his **"I Have a Dream"** speech.

▼ On November 22, **President John F. Kennedy** is **assassinated** in Dallas, Texas, while riding in a motorcade. Lyndon B. Johnson is sworn in as the thirty-sixth president.

1964

On January 13, Bob Dylan's famous protest album **"The Times They Are A-Changin'"** is released.

On July 2, 1964, President Lyndon B. Johnson signs the **Civil Rights Act, outlawing discrimination** on the basis of race, color, religion, sex, or national origin.

1965

On February 21, **Malcolm X**, controversial Nation of Islam leader and major civil rights activist, **is assassinated** while giving a speech in New York City.

fuel *(v.)* to give something more energy
motorcade *(n.)* a group of vehicles that travel together

COMPREHENSION

Cause and Effect

Review the events that occurred before 1964. (Circle) events that might have led to the passage of the Civil Rights Act of 1964.

• Which event do you think was the most important in leading to the passage of the Civil Rights Act?

_____

_____

_____

_____

_____

_____

_____

_____

CRITICAL THINKING

Evaluate

When do you think time lines are more helpful than magazine articles or books? When are they less helpful?

_____

_____

_____

_____

_____

_____

_____

_____

_____

_____

_____

_____

_____

_____

_____

_____

_____

1966

In July, tennis player Billie Jean King **wins her first Wimbledon singles championship** (seven years later, she beats male player Bobby Riggs in the highly publicized "Battle of the Sexes" tennis match). King uses her fame to fight for **equal treatment and pay for female athletes**.

National Organization for Women, 1966

In June, **The National Organization for Women (NOW)** is founded to help **women speak up for equal rights** and fair treatment in all areas of life, such as employment and health.

1967

In April, Muhammad Ali, heavyweight boxing champion, is arrested for refusing to join the U.S. Army on the basis of his religion, Islam. He is known for his provocative anti-war statement: **"I ain't got no quarrel with them Vietcong!"**

1968

On April 4, **Dr. Martin Luther King, Jr. is assassinated** on the balcony of the Lorraine Motel in Memphis, Tennessee. Riots break out in more than 100 cities.

On June 4, Presidential candidate **Robert ("Bobby") Kennedy**, brother of John F. Kennedy, **is assassinated** in Los Angeles, California.

fame *(n.)* the state of being well known
provocative *(adj.)* intending to cause a lot of discussion

1969

On July 20, the National Aeronautics and Space Administration (NASA) launches **Apollo 11,** making Neil Armstrong and Buzz Aldrin the **first people to walk on the moon**.

Man on the moon, 1969

Woodstock, 1969

On August 15–17, more than 250,000 young people gather on a farm in Bethel, New York for **Woodstock**—a three-day **festival of music and peace.**

On October 15, a nationwide **protest against the Vietnam War** called **the Peace Moratorium** draws 250,000 demonstrators to Washington, D.C. More than a million others participate in street rallies, marches, school seminars, religious services, and public meetings around the country.

On Novermber 9, **Native American protestors occupy Alcatraz** Island in California to claim the land for "Indians of all tribes."

On November 10, *Sesame Street* makes its **first appearance** on television.

1970

Singer Edwin Starr releases the wildly popular protest song **"War"** with unforgettable lyrics:
"War! / Hunh! Yeah / What is it good for / Absolutely nothing . . ."

moratorium *(n.)* an official announcement stopping an activity

COMPREHENSION

Draw Conclusions

Review the time line events of 1966 and 1967. (Circle) the things sports figures did to bring about social change.

• Why do you think these people were able to make an impact?

_____

_____

_____

_____

_____

_____

_____

CRITICAL THINKING

Synthesize

Compare Muhammad Ali's statement with what you have read in "On the Front Line in Vietnam." Why was his statement provocative? Do you agree or disagree with it?

_____

_____

_____

_____

_____

_____

_____

_____

_____

_____

_____

_____

_____

READ ONLINE

expert space
Go to **www.expert21.com/student** to learn more about The 1960s; John Fitzgerald Kennedy; Betty Friedan.

Think Across Texts

Organize and Synthesize

1. Complete this chart using information from "I Have a Dream," "On the Front Line in Vietnam," and "A Decade to Remember." Identify one important conflict from each reading and describe the effort or efforts to resolve the conflict.

"I Have a Dream"	"On the Front Line in Vietnam"	"A Decade to Remember"

Compare and Evaluate

2. Which of the readings gave you the best sense of what life was like in America during the 1960s? Explain your answer with details from the passages.

_____

_____

_____

_____

_____

3. What did the soldiers fighting in Vietnam have in common with civilians fighting for civil rights? How are the battles different?

_____

_____

_____

_____

_____

4. How have race relations improved since before the civil rights movement? Support your opinion with facts from the texts and your own knowledge.

_____

_____

_____

_____

_____

_____

_____

_____

Discuss and Write

5. With a partner, discuss how the three readings in "The Power of Free Speech" relate to the idea of free speech. Take notes as you talk. Then use your notes to write a response to the question: *What does freedom sound like*?

Apply Word Knowledge

Word Lab

1. **Think about it.** Think about the injustices in our world today.

What form of **oppression** would you fight against?

_____

_____

What do you think is the biggest problem of the current **decade?**

_____

_____

2. **Check it.** Which two of the following could be called **momentous?**

❑ electing a president

❑ buying lunch at school

❑ passing the Civil Rights Act

3. **Describe them.** Write an example of each.

a **profound** event in your life

_____

a possible cause of **angst**

_____

something you should **brace** yourself for

_____

4. **Finish it.** Complete the sentence with the words below.

inevitable   **ambush**

Once it was clear that battle

was _____,

the general decided on a plan to

_____ the enemy.

5. **Name them.** Name two **legitimate** reasons to stay home from school.

● _____

● _____

Word Analysis

6. Write the base word and suffix of each word below.

WORD	BASE WORD	SUFFIX
captivity		
joyous		
containable		

7. Draw a line to match each base word with a suffix. Then write the three new words you made.

bear   _-ity_

able   _-ous_

poison   _-able_

New Words:

_____ _____ _____

21

Understand Persuasive Techniques

We see thousands of powerful media messages every day. Understanding how these messages persuade and influence us helps us make decisions as citizens and consumers.

Persuading the Public to Support Veterans

▶ Study this poster. See how it uses words and images to influence how you think and act.

WELCOME HOME, VETS!

Nearly 1 in 5 veterans suffers from problems such as depression and stress. With less than one percent of the U.S. population serving in these conflicts, vets returning home often feel alone. You can help by reaching out. Let them know they are not alone. Let them know you care.

Sponsored by the **WELCOME HOME CAMPAIGN**

MARK IT

Study the image. The image shows one soldier walking down a deserted street. Put a **check mark** ✔ next to the slogan in the poster that is an ironic comment on the scene.

Analyze the words. The text uses powerful words such as *depression* and *stress* to talk about the veterans. ⟨Circle⟩ another word the text uses to describe how veterans feel.

Recognize facts. The poster presents some facts and statistics to support the message. <u>Underline</u> the statistics.

[Here's How] Follow these steps to understand persuasive techniques in a media message:

Step 1 Study the image. Look at the environment, the people, and the objects in the image. How do you react to them? The people who create media messages choose a particular image to make you feel a certain way.

Step 2 Analyze the words. Look for loaded language. Are words with positive or negative connotations used? Is there irony (a statement or image that means the opposite of what it actually says)? Does the message include a catchy slogan designed to influence you?

Step 3 Recognize facts and emotional appeals. Does the media message present facts that appeal to your sense of logic? Or does it appeal to your emotions, such as loyalty or fear? Are there techniques like testimonials by famous people or the bandwagon appeal that urges people to not be left out?

Step 4 Identify and evaluate the message. Use the image, facts, and your analysis of persuasive techniques to identify the message. What does the poster or ad want you to think or do? Is the message convincing?

Apply: Analyze Persuasive Techniques in a Poster

▶ Follow the steps below to help you analyze the message in the poster.

1. **Look carefully at the image.** How do you react to it?

_____

_____

2. **Analyze the words.** Do you think the message uses negative or positive language? Explain.

_____

_____

3. **Check for facts and emotional appeals.** Write one fact and one emotional appeal here.

_____

_____

4. **Identify and evaluate the message.** What is the message? Is it effective? Why or why not?

_____

_____

Social Studies Text

AMERICA DREAMING: How Youth Changed America in the '60s

If you had been a teenager in the 1960s, you might have protested against the Vietnam War or fought for civil rights. The article you are about to read will show you how various young Americans banded together to change the nation.

 QuickWrite

If you lived in the 1960s and could only protest against one issue, which issue would you choose? Why is this issue the most important to you?

Fact and Opinion `COMPREHENSION`

A **fact** is a statement that can be proven true. It is supported by evidence.

To check a fact, you can look in a reference source, such as an encyclopedia, almanac, or government Web site.

An **opinion** cannot be proven because it expresses a belief or feeling.

A **valid opinion** is supported by facts. When evaluating an opinion, evaluate whether it is supported by facts.

▶ **In each sentence, circle any opinions and underline any facts. Then write the source you would use to check the fact.**

1. John F. Kennedy was the youngest person elected to be president.

   Source: _____

2. Because America produced over 10 million bushels of corn in 2006, it was the most important crop that year.

   Source: _____

3. The Civil Rights Act passed in 1964.

   Source: _____

4. War is wrong.

   Source: _____

Text Features `NAVIGATING TEXT`

Text features highlight the organization of a text or show what is important.

They include

- **headings and subheadings—** the title of a section of text that expresses its main idea.

- **photos and captions.**

- **maps, graphs, charts, and tables.**

- **pull quotes**—quotations set in large type that highlight important ideas.

▶ **Read the passage below. Then write an appropriate heading that expresses the main idea of the passage.**

Heading: _____

It is estimated that nearly 20 million Americans participated in the first Earth Day in 1970. By 1990, more than 141 countries participated in Earth Day celebrations. Now, every year on April 22, more than a billion people around the world celebrate Earth Day. They renew their commitment to preserving and improving the environment.

Academic Language VOCABULARY

▶ **Rate each word. Then write its meaning and an example sentence.**

Word	Meaning	Example
EXPERT WORDS *Use these words to write and talk about the workshop topic.*		
collectively col·lec·tive·ly (adverb) ① ② ③ ④	together as a whole	Collectively, the team scored 102 points and won the game.
resistance re·sist·ance (noun) ① ② ③ ④		
ACADEMIC WORDS *Use this word in all your subject classes.*		
expansive ex·pan·sive (adjective) ① ② ③ ④		The view from the top of the mountain was expansive.
SELECTION WORDS *These words are key to understanding this selection.*		
chaos cha·os (noun) ① ② ③ ④		
charismatic char·is·mat·ic (adjective) ① ② ③ ④	having a powerful ability to charm and influence people	
disperse dis·perse (verb) ① ② ③ ④		
etch etch (verb) ① ② ③ ④		
unprecedented un·prec·e·dent·ed (adjective) ① ② ③ ④		

Rating Scale   ① I don't know the word.   ② I've seen it or heard it.   ③ I know its meaning.   ④ I know it and use it.

Prefixes WORD ANALYSIS

A prefix is a word part that can be added to the beginning of a word to change its meaning.

This chart shows some common prefixes and their meanings.

Prefixes	Meaning	Examples
un-, il-, in-	not	unwanted, illegitimate, inorganic
mis-	incorrect	misunderstand
inter-	between	interaction

▶ **Write the meaning of each word below.**

illegal: _____

misprint: _____

AMERiCA
DREAMiNG

How Youth Changed America in the '60s

A group of young American women protest in the rain for women's rights.

By Laban Carrick Hill

An unforgettable decade brought about a world of change to American society— and young people led the way.

★ ★ ★ ★ ★ ★ ★ ★ ★ ★

Students protest educational segregation.

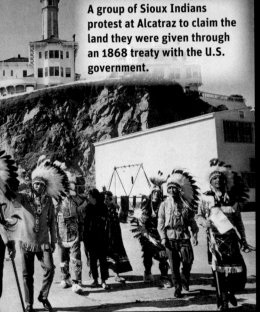

A group of Sioux Indians protest at Alcatraz to claim the land they were given through an 1868 treaty with the U.S. government.

Those who came of age in the 1960s make up the most influential generation ever in American history. These youths changed their world like no other generation has before or since. Their music, their language, and their style still define our culture today.

The full impact of the '60s on American culture has been obscured by the media. When we think of this era, we imagine a period of extremes. The real story of the '60s depicts the largest generation in American history. They came of age in an **unprecedented** period of economic growth. They questioned the very basis of our government, culture, and economy.

This is the story of young African Americans, young Latinos, young women, young Native Americans, and simply young Americans who woke up one day and decided they wanted something more. These were teens who dared to dream of an America that was fair and just.

obscured *(v.)* prevented from being understood
basis *(n.)* the ideas on which something develops

A NEW PRESIDENT, A NEW AGE

> ❝ **Ask not what your country can do for you; ask what you can do for your country.** ❞
>
> **President John F. Kennedy,**
> Inaugural Address, January 20, 1961

When a hatless, coatless John F. Kennedy stepped up to the podium in wintry Washington, D.C., to deliver his inaugural presidential address, he did nothing less than recast the national image. At forty-three, Kennedy was the youngest elected president in this country's history. He was also the first president to be born in the twentieth century.

Kennedy took the presidential oath just when the country needed him. America was experiencing an identity crisis. For the previous fifteen years, the country had lived through the greatest economic expansion in the world's history. The United States had become the most powerful nation in the world's history. The only country that challenged its supremacy was the Communist Soviet Union. What this unprecedented transformation meant to the nation's citizens was still not clear. So much seemed possible.

Kennedy was able to harness the incredibly **expansive** idea of national possibility. He offered an answer to the seeming contradiction between the values that led to prosperity and the values that were essential to its survival. In his acceptance speech at the Democratic convention in the summer of 1960, Kennedy called this new era the "New Frontier."

---

harness *(v.)* use the natural power of something
contradiction *(n.)* a difference between two facts that shows they cannot both be true

Kennedy took the presidential oath just when the country needed him.

He said:

"We stand today at the edge of a New Frontier ... a frontier of unfulfilled hopes and threats. ... The New Frontier of which I speak is not a set of promises—it is a set of challenges. It sums up not what I intend to offer the American people but what I intend to ask of them."

With these words Kennedy was able to marry American prosperity to a mission: Unfettered consumption was not only good for America but also for the world. Kennedy was saying that now that we have achieved this incredible prosperity, we must use it for the good of everyone. It was our duty to take our good fortune and use it to better the world.

NATIONAL TRAGEDY

Kennedy served as president less than three years. On the afternoon of November 22, 1963, whatever hope America held that everything would be okay was destroyed by gunshots. President Kennedy was assassinated in a Dallas motorcade. It was as if everyone in the country stopped and **collectively** held their breath. Almost every person who was old enough to remember still has that moment **etched** in his or her memory.

For the first time, an entire nation gathered in front of their television sets to witness the events unfold live. More than 100 million Americans watched John Kennedy's funeral.

John F. Kennedy, Jr. ("John-John"), Kennedy's three-year-old son, stood bravely at the grave site and saluted, breaking hearts across the country. Dressed in black, Jacqueline Kennedy, the president's wife, wore a mask of grief. Hour after hour, the three television networks presented the same pictures to a mourning nation.

> **Make Inferences**
> How do you think President Kennedy's death affected Americans?

The country also witnessed Kennedy's assassin, Lee Harvey Oswald, gunned down in front of the police by Jack Ruby on November 24. This vigilante execution came to underscore the powerlessness of the government to protect us from evil. The too-short years of unlimited possibility seemed to come to an end.

The Kennedy family mourns the president's death.

---

unfettered *(adj.)* not restricted in any way
vigilante *(adj.)* without any legal authority

Read and Synthesize

COMPREHENSION

Fact and Opinion

Review the fifth paragraph of "A New President, a New Age." <u>Underline</u> the sentence that states Kennedy's opinion on how America must use its prosperity.

• Do you agree with Kennedy's opinion?

_____

_____

_____

_____

_____

_____

NAVIGATING TEXT

Text Features

A heading summarizes the main idea of a reading or a section of a reading. How does the heading "A New President, A New Age" express the main idea of pages 282–283?

_____

_____

_____

_____

_____

_____

_____

CRITICAL THINKING

Evaluate

Review the quotation from Kennedy's acceptance speech. How would Americans respond to Kennedy's message today? Is it demanding or empowering? Discuss your opinion with a partner. Support your opinion with evidence from your own experiences.

STUDENTS SIT-IN TO STAND UP FOR EQUALITY

Around 4:30 P.M. on February 1, 1960, long after the lunch rush, college students Frank McCain, Junior Blair, Joe McNeil, and David Richmond sat down at the Woolworth's lunch counter in Greensboro, North Carolina. Nearly everyone gasped. One of the black waitresses motioned for the young men to leave, warning them not to sit there. The counter where they had seated themselves was reserved exclusively for whites. McCain, Blair, McNeil, and Richmond were black. No African American had ever sat at the whites-only counter before.

Years later, Joe McNeil recalled that quiet winter afternoon at Woolworth's:

"I don't think there's any specific reason why that particular day was chosen … but we did walk in that day … and we sat at a lunch counter where blacks never sat before. … We asked for service, and we were denied, and we expected to be denied. We asked why couldn't we be served … and it was our intent to sit there until they decided to serve us. We had planned to come back the following day and to repeat that scenario. Others found out what we had done, because the press became aware of what was happening. So the next day when we decided to go down again, I think we went with fifteen, and the third day it was probably a hundred and fifty, and then it probably mushroomed to a thousand or so, and then it spread to another city."

Within days, protests had spread across the South to fifteen cities in five states. Over the next two years, lunch counter sit-ins occurred across the South. Whites, however, reacted strongly to the protests.

In 1960, segregation was legal, and some states had laws banning African Americans from using public lunch counters.

motioned *(v.)* gave instructions by moving the head or hand
exclusively *(adv.)* only

We Shall Overcome

This anthem, originally published in 1947, became the "unofficial anthem" of the civil rights movement.

We shall overcome,
We shall overcome,
We shall overcome some day.
Oh, deep in my heart, I do believe
We shall overcome some day.

We shall all be free,
We shall all be free,
We shall all be free some day.
Oh, deep in my heart, I do believe
We shall all be free some day.

VOCABULARY/WORD ANALYSIS

Prefixes

The prefix *de-* means "reverse" or "make the opposite of." What does it mean to "desegregate public facilities"?

_____

_____

_____

_____

NAVIGATING TEXT

Text Features

Think about the photo and caption on page 284. How do these text features contribute to your understanding of the section "Students Sit-In to Stand Up for Equality?" Use specific details from the photo to support your answer.

_____

_____

_____

_____

_____

_____

In Greensboro, it took seven months of sit-ins to desegregate public facilities there. In Marshall, Texas, the local authorities used fire hoses to **disperse** sit-in protesters.

Most of the sit-ins were met with heavy **resistance**, with whites pouring ketchup and mustard over the heads of the protesters and committing other physical assaults. In a wade-in at a public beach in Biloxi, Mississippi, as many as ten African Americans were wounded by gunfire. In Jacksonville, Florida, a race riot erupted and at least fifty people were injured. In Atlanta, Georgia, acid was thrown in a protester's face.

Question
What questions do you have about whites' reactions to the protests?

In the end, more than seventeen school districts and countless stores, beaches, libraries, and movie theaters were integrated. The success of the sit-ins taught young African Americans that they did not have to wait for their elders in more established civil rights organizations such as the NAACP (National Association for the Advancement of Colored People) to take action. They did not have to wait for arduous court cases to wind their way to the Supreme Court, only to be ignored by local authorities. They didn't have to wait for big companies to see how discrimination hurt their business. They could lead the fight to end racism and discrimination with direct and immediate action.

The lunch counter sit-ins marked the first civil rights events of the '60s. What set them apart from previous protests against segregation was that these actions occurred on a national, not just a local, level. This would make them the model for the mass protests on college campuses and around the country that would follow in the coming years.

wade-in *(n.)* a demonstration in which people enter a segregated pool or beach as a protest

arduous *(adj.)* hard to endure

---

21 SMALL GROUPS/INDEPENDENT

COLLABORATE

Examine Perspectives Work in pairs to plan an interview with the four college students who sat-in at Woolworth's lunch counter. Make a list of questions you would ask your subjects.

COMMUNICATE

React and Write Choose your favorite photograph from the selection so far. Write a journal entry explaining why it appeals to you.

In the '60s, young Native Americans came together to protest the U.S. government's takeover of Indian land. Above, protest graffiti adorns a wall at Alcatraz.

TAKEOVER OF THE
ROCK

"We hold the rock!" came the cry across San Francisco Bay on the afternoon of November 20, 1969. This roar was extraordinary not simply because approximately 100 Native Americans had occupied Alcatraz Island, the notorious federal penitentiary closed five years earlier. Perhaps more incredible was that the call came from a group of young urban Native American college students who hailed from different tribes. They called themselves "Indians of All Tribes." They were the first to unite Native Americans from

different tribes to work together against the injustices committed by the U.S. government. Prior to Alcatraz, Native American activism had been generally tribal in nature. It centered in small geographic areas and focused on specific issues, such as illegal trespass or fishing rights.

Occupying Alcatraz was the brainchild of Richard Oakes, a young **charismatic** Mohawk Indian and college student from the [San Francisco] Bay area. He was inspired by an earlier occupation on March 9, 1964, led by Richard McKenzie and four other Sioux. McKenzie and his group stayed only four hours, but their demands for the use of the island for a cultural center and an Indian university resonated with Oakes.

On November 9, 1969, Oakes, along with Native American students he had met at the American Indian Studies Center at UCLA and Bay area Native Americans symbolically occupied the island. They claimed the island in the name of the Indians of All Tribes and departed that evening. Afterward, Oakes and the others realized that they actually could take hold of the island. Over the following week, they organized a long-term occupation of Alcatraz Island. On November 20, these students climbed into a chartered boat, the *Monte Cristo*, and made their way across San Francisco Bay to Alcatraz.

> **notorious** *(adj.)* famous for something bad
>
> **trespass** *(v.)* to go onto someone's land without permission

"We hold the rock!" came the cry across the San Francisco Bay on the afternoon of November 20, 1969.

These idealistic men and women quickly began to organize, electing a council and giving everyone on the island a job: security, sanitation, cooking, and laundry. All decisions were made by unanimous consent. For the first few days, this remarkable utopian community worked well, but as the resistance from the federal government to their demands continued and the weeks passed, the organization could not hold. Many of the students began returning to school in January 1970. They were replaced by less disciplined participants from urban areas and reservations.

A TURNING POINT

When tragedy occurred on January 5, the organizers were shattered. Richard Oakes's thirteen-year-old stepdaughter, Yvonne, fell three floors to her death within the prison. Oakes immediately departed, and competing groups began to battle for leadership.

Perhaps wisely, the government decided to wait the insurgents out. The FBI and Coast Guard surrounded the island but did not remove anyone or prevent anyone from landing on Alcatraz. As no progress was made in meeting their demands, the remaining protesters on Alcatraz Island became more entrenched.

Summarize

What were these students hoping to accomplish by taking over Alcatraz?

By June, nothing less than full title to the island and the establishment of a university and cultural center would end the siege. In response to this hardening of their position, the government cut off electricity and clean water to the island. At this point, a fire broke out and several historic buildings were destroyed. Whatever organization there had been now devolved into **chaos**. There was no visible leadership with which the government would negotiate.

As the situation became more desperate on the island, people began looting, stripping copper wiring and copper tubing from the buildings and selling it as scrap metal. Finally, on June 10, 1971, one and a half years after the initial occupation, armed federal marshals, FBI agents, and special-forces police launched an attack on the island. They removed five women, four children, and six unarmed Native American men. With this action, the occupation ended.

It is ironic and sad in some ways how extreme measures almost always fail but often empower more moderate groups to take up the broader cause and change society. While the island was occupied, President Nixon made a dramatic shift in policy. He returned Blue Lake and 48,000 acres of land to the Taos Indians. Eventually, a Native American university was created near Davis, California. In the bigger picture, Native Americans might have lost the battle on Alcatraz, but they clearly won the war, giving birth to a political movement.

utopian *(adj.)* relating to an imaginary, perfect world where everyone is happy

insurgents *(n.)* people fighting against the government of their own country

NAVIGATING TEXT

Text Features

 (Circle) the subheading on page 287.

- How does it relate to the heading on page 286?

_____

_____

_____

_____

- Why do you think the author chose the pull quote on page 287?

_____

_____

_____

_____

COMPREHENSION

Draw Conclusions

Review the first paragraph on page 287. Why do you think the organization began to break down as time passed?

_____

_____

_____

_____

_____

CRITICAL THINKING

Evaluate

What is something the protesters could have done to make their occupation of Alcatraz more successful? Use details from the text to support your answer.

_____

_____

_____

_____

_____

_____

Marine biologist Rachel Carson

UNITED TO SAVE
THE PLANET

We are poisoning ourselves, and everything we touch. That was the frightening message Rachel Carson voiced in her ground-breaking article in *The New Yorker* magazine and then in her best-selling book *Silent Spring* in 1962. Writing the book while she was dying of cancer, perhaps poisoned by the very world she was writing about, Carson redefined the way Americans thought about their environment. She explained how humankind's relationship with nature was an "intricate web of life whose interwoven strands lead from microbes to man."

For the first time, someone was offering a devastating critique of the chemical industry. She revealed the effects that indiscriminate use of inorganic chemicals, such as the now banned DDT [a synthetic pesticide], had on the world's ecological system. After World War II, the new and amazing pesticides, herbicides, and fungicides that industry produced seemed like miracles. According to their producers, they "controlled" all kinds of pesky insects, fungi, and weeds. What no one really understood until Carson put all the pieces together was that these new wonder chemicals were also poisoning us and our environment. Her research exposed cancer-inducing chemicals that remained as residues in virtually everything we ate or drank.

Because Carson's *Silent Spring* was a national best-seller, her message reached some surprising places. Some of the first people to realize that Carson's message contained hard truths were hunters and fishermen. Over the years, they'd watched as their lakes and rivers became polluted with improperly treated sewage and industrial waste. They were catching fish with odd growths and mutations. They were experiencing a wildlife population crash. What was unusual about them, however, was that most of them were not traditional activists. Instead they were professionals and business owners. They had political and community clout. They weren't radical youths. They were part of the establishment and were used to being listened to.

A DAY TO
CELEBRATE
EARTH

The biggest symbol of the rise in awareness and power of the environmental movement was the establishment of Earth Day on April 22, 1970. *American Heritage* magazine called the event "one of the most remarkable happenings in the history of democracy . . . 20 million people demonstrated their support. . . . American politics and public policy would never be the same again."

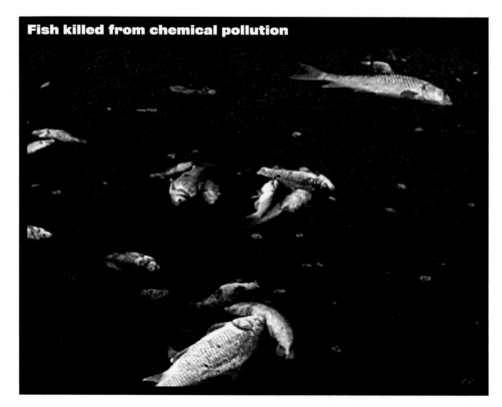

Fish killed from chemical pollution

intricate *(adj.)* containing a lot of parts or details
inorganic *(adj.)* not consisting of anything that is living

The idea for Earth Day began more than seven years earlier when Senator Gaylord Nelson of Wisconsin came to the decision to find a way to put environmental issues into the forefront of everyone's mind. On Earth Day, ten million children participated and planted thousands of trees in commemoration of the event. Schools organized special Earth Day fairs and assemblies. More than 10,000 people demonstrated at the Washington Monument in Washington, D.C. All across the country, at various landmarks, speakers described the destruction of the environment by reckless industries. They expressed hope that we as members of the human race could work together to preserve the earth's continued health.

Earth Day created an overwhelming momentum in Washington, D.C. Republicans and Democrats were united on this issue. The result was the creation of the Environmental Protection Agency and the Occupational Safety and Health Act. A host of new regulations, cleanup programs, and technological solutions were suddenly proposed. Clearly, ecology was an issue on which all of America could unite. It contained none of the divisive issues such as poverty, race, and war. It transcended race riots, assassinations, and generational conflicts.

Make Inferences
Why do you think this issue united all Americans?

In 1969, the polluted Cuyahoga river in Cleveland, Ohio, caught fire.

reckless *(adj.)* not caring about the danger of your behavior
preserve *(v.)* to keep from being destroyed

VOCABULARY/WORD ANALYSIS

Prefixes

Review the third paragraph in "United to Save the Planet." Circle two words that have a prefix that means "not."

• Complete the chart with the words you underlined.

PREFIX	BASE WORD	DEFINITION

COMPREHENSION

Fact and Opinion

Review page 288. Underline the first two pieces of evidence in the text that support the claim "We are poisoning ourselves and everything we touch."

NAVIGATING TEXT

Text Features

How do the photographs and captions in this section support Rachel Carson's ideas? Use details from the photos to support your answer.

_____
_____
_____
_____
_____
_____
_____
_____
_____
_____
_____
_____
_____
_____

MOVEMENTS OF THE '60s

	Women's Liberation Movement	Civil Rights Movement	Free Speech Movement
Movement Goal	**To challenge** the traditional ideas that restricted women to the roles of mother, wife, and homemaker	**To secure** the personal freedoms of African Americans and other minority groups who were targets of discrimination	**To protect** students' rights to free speech and academic freedom
Defining Moment	**1963.** The publication of *The Feminine Mystique* encouraged women to begin questioning traditional gender roles.	**1964.** Congress passed the Civil Rights Act, which made it unlawful to discriminate based on race, religion, sex, or national origin.	**1964.** After school officials banned civil rights groups from recruiting on campus, students at the University of California–Berkeley organized sit-ins, rallies, and strikes. This inspired students around the nation to make their views on a variety of issues heard.
Leading Figures	**Betty Friedan,** author of *The Feminine Mystique* and cofounder of NOW (National Organization for Women)	**Dr. Martin Luther King, Jr.; Rosa Parks,** seamstress who refused to give up her seat on the bus to a white man	Berkeley students **Mario Savio** and **Bettina Apthecker**
Lasting Slogans	"Sisterhood is powerful!"	"We shall overcome."	"I am a student. Please do not fold, spindle, or mutilate me."

mystique *(n.)* the quality that makes something mysterious, special, or interesting

mutilate *(v.)* to damage severely by removing part of something

These defining movements helped change America.

Antiwar Movement	American Indian Movement
To stop further U.S. involvement in the Vietnam War	**To organize and support** Native American groups to challenge the U.S. government's historically racist policies toward American Indians
1969. Over one quarter of a million people gathered in Washington, D.C., for what was, at the time, the largest antiwar demonstration in U.S. history.	**1969.** Native Americans took over Alcatraz Island for 19 months demanding that the U.S. government change its racist policies.
John Lennon, Joan Baez, and **Bob Dylan**, famous musicians whose popular songs were often protests against the Vietnam War	**Dennis Banks**, founder of the American Indian Movement organization; **Richard Oakes**
"Give peace a chance."	"Remember Wounded Knee"

CRITICAL THINKING

Evaluate

When is it useful to see information organized in a table? When would it be more useful to see information organized in a time line?

_____

_____

_____

_____

_____

_____

_____

_____

_____

_____

21 SMALL GROUPS/INDEPENDENT

COLLABORATE

Invent Think of an issue that affects you and your fellow students. Write three or four slogans that express your views on the issue. Share your best slogan with the class.

COMMUNICATE

Discuss and Write With a partner, consider Hill's statement: "Those who came of age in the '60s make up the most influential generation ever in American history." Jot down ideas that support or refute this statement. Then write a paragraph telling whether you agree or not and why.

W

READ ONLINE

expert space
Go to **www.expert21.com/student** to learn more about American Indian Movement; Environmental Movements; Earth Day; Rachel Carson.

Images and Design

ICONS OF THE TIMES

A peace sign, the first man on the moon—these images instantly bring to mind the memory of the 1960s. This article will give you the inside scoop on some of the most famous visuals of that exciting time.

QuickWrite

What do you think of when you imagine the 1960s? List images, clothing, music, and anything else you associate with that time.

Draw Conclusions COMPREHENSION

When you **draw conclusions**, you make a judgment based on text evidence, your own experience, and reasoning.

To draw a conclusion

- think about details in the text.
- think about what you know.
- make a judgment.

▶ Complete the chart to draw a conclusion about the characters and setting of the passage below.

> Marsha stared in awe as the new president of the United States stepped up to the podium to deliver his inaugural address. She had never seen a president this young elected to office before. He spoke clearly and confidently and the audience cheered wildly. Then he said something that inspired in her a feeling of patriotism: "Ask not what your country can do for you; ask what you can do for your country."

What the text says:	
What I know:	
My conclusion:	

Symbols NAVIGATING TEXT

A **symbol** is a picture, person, place, object, or activity that stands for a general idea.

For example, a heart is a symbol of love. The American flag is a symbol of the United States. Shaking hands with someone is a symbol of friendship.

▶ Write the meaning of each of the symbols below.

 _____

 _____

 _____

Academic Language VOCABULARY

▶ Rate each word. Then write its meaning and an example sentence.

Word	Meaning	Example
ACADEMIC WORDS *Use this word in all your subject classes.*		
externally *ex•ter•nal•ly (adverb)* ① ② ③ ④	having to do with the outside of something	Externally, my house is painted white, but internally, the walls are very colorful.
CONTENT AREA WORDS *Use this word to talk and write about social studies.*		
universal *u•ni•ver•sal (adjective)* ① ② ③ ④	common to everyone or everything	
SELECTION WORDS *These words are key to understanding this selection.*		
catapult *cat•a•pult (verb)* ① ② ③ ④		
discarded *dis•card•ed (adjective)* ① ② ③ ④		
encircle *en•cir•cle (verb)* ① ② ③ ④		The soldiers began to quietly encircle the enemy's camp.
fiery *fi•er•y (adjective)* ① ② ③ ④		
popularize *pop•u•lar•ize (verb)* ① ② ③ ④		
prominent *prom•i•nent (adjective)* ① ② ③ ④		

Rating Scale ① I don't know the word. ② I've seen it or heard it. ③ I know its meaning. ④ I know it and use it.

Prefixes WORD ANALYSIS

You have learned that a prefix is a word part that can be added to the beginning of a word to change its meaning.

Some words with a prefix, such as *enrobe*, can stand by themselves when their prefix is removed. Other words, such as *predict*, cannot stand alone without their prefix.

▶ Complete the chart with two examples of each prefix.

Prefixes	Meaning	Examples
en-	to put into or on	encircle, _____, _____
pre-	before	preview, _____, _____
ex-	outside of	external, _____, _____

SAY IT LOUD I'M BLACK AND I'M PROUD

ICONS OF THE TIMES

The 1960s in Images

The 1960s was the decade of "peace and love"—and a time of change and conflict. The civil rights movement. A man on the moon. Power to the people. Assassinations. War. **Externally,** the country was at war in Vietnam. Internally, the nation seemed to be at war with itself. Here are key images from an incredible decade of change.

Clockwise from top left:

GUITARIST JIMI HENDRIX: Hendrix was an iconic 1960s rocker. His far-out, **fiery** style on the electric guitar — complete with loud feedback from amps — made him one of the most influential guitarists of all time.

UNITED STATES ARMY SOLDIER: U.S. involvement in the Vietnam War created conflict between Americans at home. Many young Americans who fought in this war were drafted.

UNITED FARM WORKERS BOYCOTT POSTER: Mexican-Americans César Chavez and Dolores Huerta led United Farm Workers protests and boycotts to gain rights for farm workers who toiled for low pay in poor conditions.

AMERICAN INDIAN MOVEMENT (AIM) LOGO: AIM spoke out for the rights of Native Americans, and supported the reclamation of tribal land.

WOMEN'S LIBERATION LEADER GLORIA STEINEM: Steinem was a **prominent** leader of "Women's Lib." The women's movement stood up for equal pay for equal work, and wanted to **discard** traditional gender roles in favor of equality for women and men.

DR. MARTIN LUTHER KING, JR.: King gave his famous "I Have a Dream" speech in 1963. He led a huge, years-long campaign of peaceful but insistent protests against discrimination. The assassination of this civil rights leader in April 1968 was a national trauma.

BLACK PRIDE BUTTON: James Brown's 1968 anthem, "Say It Loud—I'm Black and I'm Proud," gave the black pride movement a new catchphrase.

DETAIL FROM A CONCERT POSTER: The Fillmore in San Francisco, CA, and the Fillmore East in New York City were concert halls famed for their counterculture music lineups and groovy posters.

U.S. SOLDIER HOLDING A DOVE: This uniformed soldier holds a white dove, a symbol of peace.

MAN ON THE MOON: As U.S. astronauts became the first people on the moon, hundreds of millions of people around the world watched via live television broadcast.

PEACE RALLY: A large peace sign encircles a common sight in the 1960s: a peace rally. Antiwar and antidraft rallies and vigils were common across the nation during the height of U.S. involvement in the war.

Center:

JOHN F. KENNEDY: The youngest president ever elected, "JFK" symbolized youth and change. He asked people to join together against war, poverty, and tyranny. This film still shows Kennedy riding in an open car with his wife, Jacqueline. The same day, November 22, 1963, Kennedy was shot to death by an assassin. The nation was stunned.

iconic *(adj.)* representing an idea or an era

vigils *(n.)* silent political protests in which people gather outside

Read and Synthesize

COMPREHENSION

Draw Conclusions

Review pages 294 and 295. What conclusions can you draw from the images and the text?

_____

_____

_____

_____

_____

_____

_____

_____

NAVIGATING TEXT

Symbols

One soldier shown has a tear in his eye. Another holds a white dove. What do these visual symbols communicate? Use what you know about the Vietnam War in your response.

_____

_____

_____

_____

_____

_____

VOCABULARY/WORD ANALYSIS

Prefixes

On this page, review the paragraph with the subheading Peace Rally. Use your knowledge of the prefix *en-* to write the definition of the word *encircle*.

_____

_____

_____

_____

Gerald Holtom: Symbols of Peace

Certain images are recognized in America as **universal** symbols of peace: a white dove, an olive branch, two fingers held up in the shape of a V, a circle around an upside-down broken cross.

Many Americans associate the latter peace symbol with the 1960s antiwar protest. However, it originated in England in 1958 when antiwar protesters marched to a factory where atomic bombs were being built. The protesters were calling for nuclear disarmament, which means a ban on nuclear bombs around the world.

Gerald Holtom, the artist and designer of this particular peace symbol, used the naval flag signs for two letters: "N" (for "nuclear") and "D" (for "disarmament"). He combined the two signs into one image, and then **encircled** them. The resulting image became the peace sign.

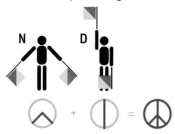

Holtom's peace sign was adopted by protesters in the U.S. calling for an end to the Vietnam War. Eventually, the sign became a symbol of protest against war in general. Youth protesters and famous musicians such as John Lennon of the Beatles **popularized** the sign.

> **CLARIFY**
> Explain in your own words how the "peace" sign evolved.

Robert Indiana: Spreading Love

In 1964, Robert Indiana first created the *LOVE* design as a Christmas card for the Museum of Modern Art. Then in 1966, he exhibited the 3-D version of the image at an art show in New York.

The image was simple. Arranged in a square, the capital letters were stacked and the "O" was tilted slightly.

The 1960s youth movement adopted the *LOVE* image and **catapulted** it into broad use. Soon, *LOVE* was everywhere: on greeting cards, in jewelry designs, on T-shirts, mugs, and rugs. In 1973, the *LOVE* icon premiered as one of the biggest-selling U.S. postage stamps. The *LOVE* series is still in use today.

The *LOVE* design is one of the most recognizable art icons of all time, not only in the U.S. but around the world. Versions of it still appear on clothes, mugs, book covers, posters, and paintings. Several cities across the U.S. display *LOVE* sculptures in public spaces, such as parks. Among these cities is Philadelphia, which is known as "the city of brotherly love." ■

> **latter** *(n.)* the last of things that are mentioned
> **disarmament** *(n.)* a reduction in numbers of weapons

More Icons From the 1960s

FASHION'S HOTTEST FOOTWEAR: GO-GO BOOTS

ULTIMATE HIPPIE COOL: LONG HAIR, HEADBANDS, AND FRINGE VESTS

"BLACK IS BEAUTIFUL": THE AFRO HAIRSTYLE

"FLOWER POWER": SYMBOLS OF HARMONY AND PEACE

COSMIC EXPRESSION: PETER MAX MAKES ART THAT TOUCHES THE SOUL

DOMINATING THE POP CHARTS: THE BEATLES

hippie *(n.)* someone who usually had long hair and opposed the standards of society

cosmic *(adj.)* having to do with the universe

Read and Synthesize

CRITICAL THINKING

Analyze

Think about the *LOVE* symbol. Why do you think this symbol became so popular? Why is it still popular today?

_____
_____
_____
_____
_____

NAVIGATING TEXT

Symbols

How can a musical group, like the Beatles, become a symbol of an era?

_____
_____
_____
_____

21 SMALL GROUPS/INDEPENDENT

COLLABORATE

Represent Create a list of three images that might serve as symbols of today's youth culture. Select your best image, and present it to the class.

COMMUNICATE

Discuss and Write Given what you know about the 1960s, do you think the symbols discussed in this article accurately represent the era? Write a journal entry explaining why you believe they do or do not.

W

READ ONLINE

expert space
Go to **www.expert21.com/student** to learn more about Jimi Hendrix; Pop Art; Robert Indiana; Museum of Modern Art; The Beatles.

THE TIMES THEY ARE A-CHANGIN'

BY BOB DYLAN

This popular song by one of America's most famous folksingers captured the struggles and the voice of a generation living through enormous change.

Painting by Milton Glaser

Come gather 'round people wherever you roam
And admit that the waters around you have grown
And accept it that soon you'll be drenched to the bone.
If your time to you is worth savin'
Then you better start swimmin' or you'll sink like a stone
For the times they are a-changin'.

Come writers and critics who prophesize with your pen
And keep your eyes wide the chance won't come again
And don't speak too soon for the wheel's still in spin
And there's no tellin' who that it's namin'.
For the loser now will be later to win
For the times they are a-changin'.

Come senators, congressmen please heed the call
Don't stand in the doorway don't block up the hall
For he that gets hurt will be he who has stalled
There's a battle outside and it is ragin'.
It'll soon shake your windows and rattle your walls
For the times they are a-changin'.

Come mothers and fathers throughout the land
And don't criticize what you can't understand
Your sons and your daughters are beyond your command
Your old road is rapidly agin'.
Please get out of the new one if you can't lend your hand
For the times they are a-changin'.

The line it is drawn the curse it is cast
The slow one now will later be fast
As the present now will later be past
The order is rapidly fadin'.
And the first one now will later be last
For the times they are a-changin'. ∎

> **drenched** *(adj.)* completely wet
> **prophesize** *(v.)* to make predictions

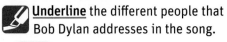

COMPREHENSION

Draw Conclusions

Underline the different people that Bob Dylan addresses in the song.

- Circle the lyrics in which he tells people what to do.

- Given the lyrics of the song and what you know about the 1960s, what do you think the song is protesting against?

_____

_____

_____

_____

_____

_____

_____

_____

LITERARY ANALYSIS

Figurative Language

Review the first verse of the song. Dylan uses a metaphor to compare change to the tide coming in. What does this verse mean?

_____

_____

_____

_____

_____

_____

- List another metaphor he uses for change in the song.

_____

_____

_____

_____

READ ONLINE

expert space
Go to **www.expert21.com/student** to learn more about Bob Dylan; Woodstock Festival; Folk Music.

Think Across Texts

Organize and Synthesize ·······························

1. Complete this chart using information from "America Dreaming," "Icons of the Times," and "The Times They Are A-Changin'."

Issue	Who Fought for It	Outcomes
Civil rights for all		
Peace		
Environmental awareness		

Compare and Evaluate ·····································

2. Each of the readings discuss one or more messages that the people of the 1960s wanted to pass on to future generations. Choose one message and explain why it is important today.

_____

_____

_____

_____

3. How does the *Signs* collage discussed in "Icons of the Times," relate to the events that happened in the Social Studies Text, "America Dreaming"?

_____

_____

_____

_____

4. "The Times They Are A-Changin'" states that change will always happen, even if people fight it. Give two examples from "America Dreaming" that support that idea.

_____

_____

_____

_____

Discuss and Write ··················

5. With a partner, discuss how the three readings in "Changing Times" helped you understand what happened to America in the 1960s. Take notes as you talk. Then use your notes to write a response to the question: *What is it like to live in a time of great change?*

Apply Word Knowledge

Word Lab

1. **Describe them.** Write an example of each.

- a **universal** human emotion:

  _____

- a **universal** human need:

  _____

2. **Finish it.** Complete the sentences below.

- A **fiery** speaker speaks with

  _____

- A **charismatic** person is

  _____

- **Chaos** can occur when

  _____

3. **Name them.** Name three events in your life that were **unprecedented** for you.

  _____

  _____

  _____

4. **Think about it.** How is a new music group **popularized**? Use your own experience to answer.

  _____

  _____

  _____

  _____

5. **Sort them.** Which of the activities listed below are usually done **collectively**? Which are not usually done **collectively**? Write each activity in the chart.

playing baseball   **reading a book**

writing a story   **marching in a band**

Collectively	Not Collectively

Word Analysis

6. Use your knowledge of the words below to infer the meaning of each word's prefix. Complete the chart by writing each word next to the meaning of its prefix. Then write the word's definition.

antiwar   **unhappy**   **transform**

Prefix Meaning	Word	Definition
"not"		
"change" or "across"		
"against"		

7. Underline the prefix in each word below. Then write its meaning on the line next to it.

inorganic means: _____

transplant means: _____

unarmed means: _____

21 Analyze Media Messages

The Vietnam War was the first war to be televised. The images shown on TV and in the news greatly influenced how people felt about the war. Media continues to influence how we feel about events and issues today.

Recognize the Influence of the Media

▶ Analyze how the images and captions below could influence how you feel about Vietnam War protesters.

Nonviolent protesters hold up a peace sign.

An angry student screams at a police officer during an antiwar demonstration

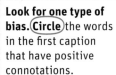

MARK IT

Look for one type of bias. Circle the words in the first caption that have positive connotations.

Identify techniques. In the second image, the viewer first notices the look of anger on the student's face. In the first image, **draw a line** to what the viewer's eyes are immediately drawn to.

Look for another kind of bias. The second caption has words with negative connotations. <u>Underline</u> the negative words in this caption.

[Here's How] ▶ **Analyze the message of media:**

Step 1 Study the information in the message. The people who create media messages choose what to include or leave out. Be sure more than one side is presented.

Step 2 Identify the techniques. Look carefully at the image and read any captions or titles. What persuasive techniques or emotional appeals are being used?

Step 3 Identify bias. Media messages often reflect the values and opinions of the people who create them. Ask yourself what values or opinions are being communicated.

Step 4 Think about your reaction. Ask yourself how the message makes you feel. Do you feel angry, upset, or inspired? Then ask yourself whether your reaction is a fair one, or caused by the carefully chosen words and images.

Apply: Analyze a Media Image

▶ An editor selected this image for a story about injured soldiers receiving war medals. Follow the steps to analyze its intended message.

A U.S. Army sergeant holds his 9-month-old daughter, after receiving the Purple Heart during a ceremony in Washington, D.C. He lost both of his legs during an enemy attack while on tour in Iraq.

1. **Study the information in the message.** What information does the image include? What emotions do you think it's designed to create?

_____

_____

_____

2. **Identify the techniques.** Review the caption and look again at the image. What persuasive techniques or emotional appeals are used?

_____

_____

_____

How do the camera angle and composition affect the way you feel?

_____

_____

_____

3. **Identify bias.** Does the editor's decision to use this image show bias about the war? Explain.

_____

_____

_____

4. **Think about your reaction.** How does this image make you feel?

_____

_____

_____

Traits of Writing

Traits of Writing is a model for assessing and teaching. The traits work within the writing process to support revision and editing.

Each puzzle piece below represents one of the **traits** that define good writing.

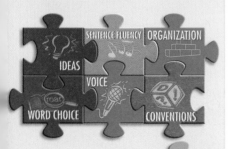

Each trait is made up of four **key qualities**. The trait that you will focus on in this lesson is **Sentence Fluency**.

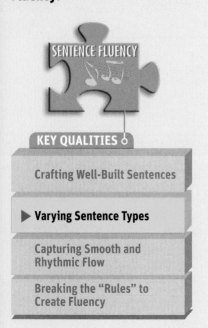

KEY QUALITIES

Crafting Well-Built Sentences

▶ **Varying Sentence Types**

Capturing Smooth and Rhythmic Flow

Breaking the "Rules" to Create Fluency

Persuasive Opinion Essay

A persuasive opinion essay states an opinion and then supports it with facts, logic, or personal stories. Persuasive writing is used in political speeches, ad copy, newspaper editorials, consumer blogs, and in many other places.

In this writing workshop, you will write a persuasive opinion essay on a social issue about which you feel deeply.

Example: Policy papers argue for new laws. In this example, a policy paper uses research information to suggest that the voting age be lowered.

> Right now, there are different standards that decide when a person becomes an adult. Each year about 200,000 defendants are tried as adults in criminal court. Yet young adults in this same age group are not allowed to vote.

▶ **Analyze Features** A persuasive opinion essay has the following features:

Look for these features in the Student Model on the next page.	Mark these features as you read the Student Model.
1. An **introduction** that explains the issue and states the opinion. (Organization)	Underline the opinion that the writer has.
2. One or more reasons backed by evidence that support this opinion. (Ideas)	Circle the reasons that support this opinion.
3. Focus Trait: Sentence Fluency Varied sentence types that make writing fluent.	Check ✓ examples of varied sentence types.
4. A good **counterargument** for a different opinion and a reason that discredits the counterargument. (Ideas)	Star ★ the counterargument for a different opinion.

► Read Henry's persuasive opinion essay about achieving equality for women.

STUDENT MODEL

The Unequal Half
by Henry Johnson

Women are the largest minority group in the world, making up almost exactly half of the population. The size of that group should make it easy for women to achieve equal rights. Right? Wrong.

Being a woman can be bad for your health. Around the world, a shocking number of women experience some form of violence during their lifetimes. Another source of danger comes from pregnancy and childbirth. Women can die from complications. In countries that provide access to good health care, the number is low. But in developing countries, the number is much higher.

Women have not yet achieved economic equality either. They are still making, on average, 78 cents to the dollar earned by men in the United States. They also bear most of the burden of poverty. More women than men in the United States have income below the poverty line. Most researchers agree that women make up the majority of people living in poverty throughout the world, although there have been no conclusive studies to prove this.

Women are not equally represented in society. Certain professions still attract only a small number of women, such as medicine, architecture, and engineering. Women are not equally represented in government. Out of 435 members of the U.S. House of Representatives, only 74 are women. Of the senators, only 16 of 100 are.

Today, half the population struggles to obtain the same rights as its male counterpart. Half still cannot feel equally safe. Half does not earn equal pay for equal work, and half has not been equally represented in many areas of life. So will our generation be the one to lead the way toward true equality? If we want to make it happen, there will be no stopping us. We must join together in the fight for equality.

► Read Henry's notes about how he worked on his persuasive opinion essay.

ORGANIZATION

I wanted to add to the conclusion to give the reader something to think about, so I asked the reader to join the fight for equality.

SENTENCE FLUENCY

The third sentence of my last paragraph used to be two sentences. I combined them to vary the sentence types and sound smoother.

► Analyze how Henry developed and organized his ideas. Fill in the missing parts of the mind map.

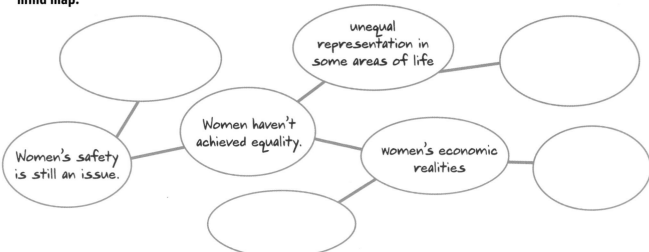

How Do I Get Started?

Your Topic:

Assignment: Persuasive Opinion Essay

Purpose: To write a persuasive essay on a social issue about which you feel deeply

Audience: Political rally attendees

Ideas: Using Details

Developing your topic deepens what you have to say. Use these Think-Abouts as you work on your ideas.

- Did I create a picture in the reader's mind?
- Did I use details that draw upon the five senses (sight, touch, taste, smell, hearing)?
- Do my details support the main topic? *For example, the paragraph about women's safety has details about violence and the risks of pregnancy and childbirth.*
- Did I stretch for details beyond the obvious?

IDEAS

KEY QUALITIES

Finding a Topic

Focusing the Topic

Developing the Topic

▶ **Using Details**

▶ **Model** Go back to Reading 2, "On the Frontline in Vietnam," in this workshop. List some details that create a picture in the reader's mind.

▶ **Practice** Think about details that will help persuade your audience.

What issue do you care the most about? _____

What details will help you create a convincing argument? ____

_____

▶ **Plan Your Essay** Use the mind map below to plan your persuasive opinion essay. Add circles as needed. Revise as necessary.

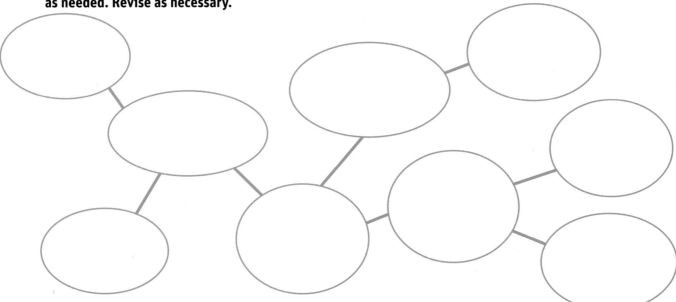

How Do I Get Organized?

ORGANIZATION

Organization: Ending With a Sense of Resolution

Good writers end their essays with a sense of resolution. Ask yourself these Think-Abouts as you work on your organization.

- Have I wrapped up all the loose ends? *Notice how the author summarizes the arguments in the conclusion, addressing safety, money, and representation.*

- Have I ended at the best place?

- Do I have an ending that makes my writing feel finished?

- Did I leave the reader with something to think about?

○ **KEY QUALITIES**

Creating the Lead

Using Sequence Words and Transition Words

Structuring the Body

▶ **Ending With a Sense of Resolution**

▶ **Model** Go back to Reading 4, *America Dreaming: How Youth Changed America in the '60s,* and explain what makes the essay end with a sense of resolution.

▶ **Practice** Rewrite the last paragraph of the Student Model on page 305. Remember, you can wrap up the loose ends in different ways. You can also leave the reader with something different to think about.

_____

_____

_____

_____

_____

_____

▶ **Write a Paragraph** Practice ending your essay with a sense of resolution as you write a first draft of your conclusion here.

_____

_____

_____

_____

_____

▶ **Draft Your Essay** Write a first draft.

Quick Check

▶ Check how well you ended your essay with a sense of resolution. Have a writing partner rate it, too.

6 = Expert   **3** = Making Strides

5 = Well Done   **2** = On the Way

4 = Almost There **1** = Getting Started

Organization

1. Have I wrapped up all the loose ends?
Self   ① ② ③ ④ ⑤ ⑥
Partner   ① ② ③ ④ ⑤ ⑥

2. Have I ended at the best place?
Self   ① ② ③ ④ ⑤ ⑥
Partner   ① ② ③ ④ ⑤ ⑥

3. Do I have an ending that makes my writing feel finished?
Self   ① ② ③ ④ ⑤ ⑥
Partner   ① ② ③ ④ ⑤ ⑥

4. Did I leave the reader with something to think about?
Self   ① ② ③ ④ ⑤ ⑥
Partner   ① ② ③ ④ ⑤ ⑥

How Do I Vary My Sentences to Make My Writing Fluent?

FOCUS TRAIT

Sentence Fluency: Varying Sentence Types

SENTENCE FLUENCY

Good writers choose their words carefully to get the most from each one. Use these Think-Abouts to make sure you vary your sentence types in your essay.

- Did I use different kinds of sentences?
- Did I make some of my sentences complex?
- Did I make some of my sentences simple? *The Student Model uses some very simple, one-word sentences, like "Right? Wrong."*
- Did I vary my sentence types from one to the next?

KEY QUALITIES

Crafting Well-Built Sentences

▶ Varying Sentence Types

Capturing Smooth and Rhythmic Flow

Breaking the "Rules" to Create Fluency

▶ **Model** Go back to Reading 1, "I Have a Dream," and find examples of ways the speaker varied sentence types.

▶ Read Ruth Culham's writing blog below to get advice on improving your writing.

Ask the Expert: Ruth Culham

Ruth Culham, an award-winning teacher, is the author of *6+1 Traits of Writing: The Complete Guide for Middle School* and other books on writing.

Q & A: Sentence Fluency: Varying Sentence Types

Seth Sentence Writes:

Is there a formula for sentences? Shazam: It's short. Pow: It's a longer one with more information. I'm never sure if I have the right combination of short and long sentences, so I keep writing new ones, hoping they will be right. Am I on the right track?

Dear Seth Sentence: Your sentences don't need magic; they already work. You used simple, compound, and complex sentences in your question to me, so you obviously know what you are doing! When you write, do you read your sentences aloud? That will give you a sense of which kind of sentences should come next. Nice variety, nice flow. You are a sorcerer of sentences!

Posted by: Ruth Culham | January 9 at 10:14 A.M.

▶ **Practice** Read the sample paragraphs, and think about which one varies sentence types to make the writing more fluent.

Underline the complex sentences.

Circle the simple sentences.

Star ★ the sample that shows the best example of varying sentence types.

Sample 1: Peace Out

Some people think it's time to stop fighting wars to solve disagreements. They say that war costs a lot of money. Wars also cost many lives. People want to stop fighting wars. They do not want to make problems between groups of people worse. But they feel it's time to find a better way to resolve differences.

Sample 2: Peace Out

People who are opposed to violence feel that nations should stop fighting wars. The violence has gone on for too long. While people have been fighting each other for thousands of years, the conflicts remain. Ultimately, everyone wants the nations of the world to learn to get along. Some people say that time is now.

▶ **Revise** Now choose a paragraph from your first draft and revise it below. Remember to use complex and simple sentences.

_____

_____

_____

_____

_____

_____

_____

_____

_____

_____

Quick Check

▶ **Check your essay for how well you varied sentence types in your writing. Then have a writing partner rate it, too.**

6 = Expert   **3** = Making Strides

5 = Well Done   **2** = On the Way

4 = Almost There **1** = Getting Started

Sentence Fluency

1. Did I use different kinds of sentences?
Self   ① ② ③ ④ ⑤ ⑥
Partner ① ② ③ ④ ⑤ ⑥

2. Did I make some of my sentences complex?
Self   ① ② ③ ④ ⑤ ⑥
Partner ① ② ③ ④ ⑤ ⑥

3. Did I make some of my sentences simple?
Self   ① ② ③ ④ ⑤ ⑥
Partner ① ② ③ ④ ⑤ ⑥

4. Did I vary my sentence types from one to the next?
Self   ① ② ③ ④ ⑤ ⑥
Partner ① ② ③ ④ ⑤ ⑥

Revise With Technology Use the grammar feature of the word processing program to be sure your complex sentences are constructed properly.

How Can I Finish a Great Paper?

Grammar: Subject/Verb Agreement

When nouns and verbs in a sentence match, they agree in number.

- The <u>sign</u> <u>has</u> a peace symbol as its design.
- The <u>signs</u> <u>have</u> integrated the school.

Words Between Subject and Verb

Don't be fooled by phrases that come between the subject and verb. You may have to look back in longer sentences to find the subject in order to make sure the verb agrees.

- <u>One</u> of the songs <u>was</u> a protest song.

▶ **Practice** **Rewrite this paragraph correctly.**

Marches, sit-ins, and boycotts is nonviolent ways people can show the world that something are unfair. Fighting back make both sides seem equally wrong. One of the risks of violence are creating new victims.

_____

_____

_____

Mechanics: Using Contractions

Contractions are two words that are combined into one. The missing letters are replaced with an apostrophe. Contractions make writing less formal or rigid and are usually not used in formal writing.

Example: have not = haven't

▶ **Practice** **Rewrite this paragraph without contractions.**

During the 1960s, many people decided that they should've been treated better. They hadn't received the same opportunities. Before the 1960s, racism wasn't considered abnormal. Today, everyone's expected to reject prejudice.

_____

_____

_____

_____

▶ **Proofread** Find and correct any errors in your essay. Put a check beside the types of errors you find. Then write three corrected sentences below.

❏ ensuring subject/verb agreement
❏ using contractions correctly
❏ using verb tenses correctly

❏ using commas in a series correctly
❏ misspellings
❏ other: _____

1. _____
   _____

2. _____
   _____

3. _____
   _____

PRESENTATION

PUBLISH/PRESENT

▶ **Write Your Final Draft** Now, using your edited draft, begin creating a final draft for presentation.

🖥 Use word processing software to type your final draft. Make sure to format your margins and spacing according to your teacher's request.

Check your final draft against the Traits of Writing Scoring Guide on pages 338–341 and correct any errors before you present it.

▶ **Beyond the Classroom** Extend your finished persuasive opinion essay.

List two ideas for photos that could illustrate your persuasive opinion essay:

_____

_____

Look online for a blog, message board, magazine, or newspaper where you could publish your persuasive opinion essay.

List two places where you could upload or share your persuasive opinion essay for publication.

_____

Quick Check

▶ Check your persuasive opinion essay for how well you used conventions. Then have a writing partner rate it, too.

6 = Expert   **3** = Making Strides
5 = Well Done   **2** = On the Way
4 = Almost There   **1** = Getting Started

Conventions

1. Were my verbs in agreement with my subjects?
   Self ① ② ③ ④ ⑤ ⑥
   Partner ① ② ③ ④ ⑤ ⑥

2. Did I use contractions correctly?
   Self ① ② ③ ④ ⑤ ⑥
   Partner ① ② ③ ④ ⑤ ⑥

3. Did I follow the rules of capitalization?
   Self ① ② ③ ④ ⑤ ⑥
   Partner ① ② ③ ④ ⑤ ⑥

4. Is my spelling in the essay correct?
   Self ① ② ③ ④ ⑤ ⑥
   Partner ① ② ③ ④ ⑤ ⑥

READ ONLINE
expert space
Go to **www.expert21.com/student** to find photographs and other visuals to illustrate your persuasive opinion essay.

You have learned about young people taking a stand. Now apply your expert reading strategies to the following profile about two student leaders. ▶

BOO!

HE'S NO GOOD!

THE FOOTBALL PLAYER
and the *Student Council President*

By Phillip Hoose

FOOTBALL MEANT EVERYTHING TO 16-YEAR-OLD NETO, HIS TEAM'S STAR RUNNING BACK. AND YET WHEN HE HEARD FANS SCREAMING RACIAL INSULTS AT HIM AND HIS LATINO TEAMMATES, HE WONDERED HOW HE COULD KEEP PLAYING FOR PEOPLE WHO FELT THAT WAY. WHAT HAPPENED WHEN NETO TEAMED UP WITH THE STUDENT COUNCIL PRESIDENT AND ENLISTED THE SUPPORT OF THE ENTIRE STUDENT BODY?

FROM THE BEET FIELDS TO THE FOOTBALL FIELD

When the whistle blew, ending football practice, Jesse Paz and Ernesto "Neto" Villareal unsnapped their helmets and jogged off the field together in silence. Just before they reached the locker room, Jesse stopped. "Aren't you getting tired of white fans yelling at us Latino players?" he asked Neto. "They yell we're 'no good' whenever we mess up. Haven't you heard that at the games?"

"I never really paid attention to it," Neto replied. Something about this made him uncomfortable.

Jesse kept on, his voice rising in anger. "We shouldn't stand for it. We should quit the team. We have twenty-one players on the team, and ten of us are Latino. Most of the best players are Latino. Without us, there wouldn't even be a team. If we quit, we could wake up this whole community."

This was the last thing in the world Neto wanted to hear. For him, football wasn't the problem. Football was the one thing that had made life with whites possible.

Until football, Neto hadn't had a chance to get to know white people around Marsing, Idaho. Most of the Latino families had come to Idaho from Texas or Mexico to pick beets, and they lived together in one part of town. White families lived in another area. Many Latinos spoke only Spanish, and most whites spoke only English. They went to different churches, too.

Every summer since he was seven, Neto had worked from dawn till dusk with his family in the beet fields, chopping up clusters of beets with a metal hoe. Every now and then white workers would join the Latinos in the beet fields, but they would usually give up after two or three days. Neto grew up thinking that if more whites knew what it was like to work that hard, they couldn't possibly think they were better than he was.

Now, as a 220-pound tenth-grader, Neto was the starting fullback and middle linebacker on the Marsing High School football team. He loved to lower his shoulder and blast through a thicket of arms and bodies. He was a charismatic player on an exciting team. On Friday nights, hundreds of people from all around the valley piled into trucks, cars, and vans and headed to Marsing Field to watch the Huskies.

THE STRUGGLE FOR RESPECT

Now Jesse Paz was proposing to take away the thing Neto loved most, to turn him into just another big kid at school, and maybe even ruin his chances for a college scholarship, all because a few jerks had said things that turned Jesse off. Neto didn't answer for a while. Finally he said, "I've never heard anyone say those things, Jesse," and walked away.

But Jesse's words stayed with Neto. What if it were true? Could he really perform in front of people who felt that way about him? Could he represent a school that would let that happen?

"The next game, I decided to see if I could hear what Jesse was hearing," Neto recalls. "In one play, we were running a pass pattern that ended up very near the Marsing cheering section. Our receiver, who was Latino, dove for the ball and missed it. Suddenly I could hear voices in our crowd saying, 'Get that stupid Mexican off of there! Put in a white player!'

thicket *(n.)* a group of bushes and small trees

"I looked up. Most of the voices belonged to parents. One was a guy on the school board.

"All game long I kept listening. When a white player would drop a pass, they'd go, 'Nice try.' But they were always negative toward us. Our whole race. I guess I had been blocking it out. Jesse was right. We couldn't just ignore it anymore."

After the game, Neto found Jesse at his locker and said he was ready to act. They called a team meeting. All the players—white and Latino—were invited, but not coaches.

The players sat down together on the benches in the locker room. Jesse and Neto repeated the words they had heard and said it hurt too badly for them to play in the next game.

"Yeah, I've heard those things, too," said one player. "Sure it's terrible, but you can't quit! If you guys leave, it will destroy our team."

"Look," Neto said, "if we don't take a stand now, those fans will say those things forever. Even after we graduate, they'll keep putting Latino players down. We have a chance to stop it now."

Finally there was no more to say. The question came: "Who votes not to play the next game?" Every player raised his hand.

That night, Neto, Jesse, and another teammate walked into the coach's office and handed him their uniforms and pads. They explained why they were leaving and expected him to understand, but they were disappointed. "The coach said, 'Quitting will just make it worse,'" Neto remembers. "He said the fans would call us losers and quitters instead of respecting us. Nothing could convince him. After a while we just walked out."

Now there was no turning back.

UNLIKELY ALLIES

There was no one to talk to when Neto went home that night. His father was no longer living at home, and his mother was away on a trip. Neto made a sandwich, sat down, and looked through the kitchen window at the autumn sky. It wasn't enough just to quit the team, he decided. They had to tell the community why they were quitting, so the fans would at least have a chance to change. But how?

Neto decided to ask Andy Percifield for help. Percifield was the student council president—a tall, red-haired senior who always read the morning announcements over the loudspeaker. Neto didn't know him, but people who did said Percifield was smart and fair. Maybe he would know what to do and become an ally.

Neto was waiting by Andy's locker the next morning. "He had tears in his eyes," Andy remembers. "He said that adult fans were swearing at the Mexican players and that it wasn't fair. He was really hurting. He said 'Is there any way you can help?' I told him I'd try."

When Neto left, Andy walked to the principal's office and repeated Neto's story. He asked for the school's support in dealing with the crowd. "The principal told me he hadn't heard adults say those things," Andy recalls. "He said some of the parents

> "Look," Neto said, "If we don't take a stand now, those fans will keep putting Latino players down. We have a chance to stop it now."

> **ally** (n.) a person who helps another

would have to call him and complain before the school administration could get involved. He said Neto had probably heard it out of context anyway." Andy stormed out angrily.

Soon there was even worse news for Neto and Jesse. Most of the players who had voted not to play had suddenly changed their minds—even the Latino players. They could barely look at Neto and Jesse as they explained that they loved football too much to give it up. In the end, only four players—Jesse, Neto, Rigo Delgudillo, and Johnny Garcia—were committed to staying off the field.

TAKING A STAND

The more Neto thought about it, the more determined he became. "I knew we were right," he recalls. "I didn't care what anybody else thought. And I also knew the team couldn't afford to lose me. If the school really wanted me, the fans had to stop saying those things. Only then would I play—not before."

That afternoon, a Latino teacher named Baldimar Elizondo, whom everyone called Baldy, suggested that Neto tell the school board about the racist remarks. It was important to say in public why they were quitting, Baldy said, so that the school couldn't ignore it or pretend the protest was about something else.

The board was meeting that night. Baldy offered to pick Neto up and take him. Neto hesitated. He knew he had the courage to blast through tacklers and the toughness to work all day in the beet fields, but this seemed harder. When Jesse Paz said he'd go, Neto finally agreed.

Baldy picked up Neto first, but when they got to Jesse's, Jesse was nowhere to be found. Now Neto had to choose: did he testify alone or forget it? "All right," Neto finally said, letting out a long breath. "We've gone this far. Let's finish it."

When they entered the board's meeting room, Neto was terrified. They were alone with the ten white men who were members of the Marsing school board. "I couldn't believe I was really doing this," Neto recalls. "Then I heard Baldy say, 'Neto wants to talk with you about the football team.'

"So I just started. I told them I was quitting and why. I told them word-for-word what I had heard. Only one of them looked like he was really listening. When I was finished, they thanked me for coming, but they didn't say they would do anything about it. I went home thinking, Well, at least I tried. Now they can't say nobody told them."

THE LETTER

Andy Percifield had been busy, too. There were only two days before the next game. He was determined that his school would do the right thing, no matter what the principal said. He had an idea: rally the student body around this cause. Maybe the students themselves could write a letter against racism that could be read over the microphone in the press box to everyone at the game. It would have to be powerful enough to satisfy the protesting players and shame the racist fans.

Andy was inspired by Neto, who was willing to risk his football career—his main source of power and popularity at Marsing High—for something that was right. Andy considered his own power: as council president, he could get out of class more easily than any other student. He could use the office photocopy machine whenever he wanted, and nobody ever asked him what he was reproducing. He read the morning announcements every day, so he could speak to the whole student body. If Neto was willing to risk it all, so was he.

---

context (n.) the situation, events, or information related to something
testify (v.) to make a formal statement about what is true

The next morning during study hall, Andy drafted a letter from the students, ran off a hundred copies, and then went to the office microphone to read the morning announcements. "There will be a student council meeting in the chemistry lab at ten," he said. "Attendance is required. Then there will be a meeting of all the students in the same room at 10:30. Attendance is encouraged."

At 10:30, students from all grades packed themselves into the lab. Andy stood up and reported what was happening, then read his letter aloud and asked for suggestions to improve it. There were a few. Then he asked for, and got, the students' unanimous approval to have it read at halftime. Next, Andy took the letter to the striking players and asked if it was good enough for them. They studied it carefully. It read:

> We, the student body of Marsing High School, are appalled by the racist behavior of certain people in the audience. Not only does this set a bad example for some younger students, it also reflects very badly on our entire school and community.
>
> Although we appreciate the support of our fans for our team, which is composed of students from many ethnic backgrounds, we do not need bigots here.
>
> We are asking the authorities to eject from the premises anyone making such rude and racist remarks.

—**Marsing High School Student Body**

The four players looked up and grinned. You get this letter read to the crowd, they said, and we'll play. Since the letter wouldn't get read till halftime, Andy said they would have to start the game and trust him. They looked at each other. "You got it," said Neto.

POWERFUL ALLIANCES, POWERFUL RESULTS

Andy had the students and the strikers behind him, but he still needed permission to read the letter. He took it to the principal, hoping for a change of heart. The principal read it, handed it back, and refused permission. They looked at each other. "I kept asking him, 'Well, how are we going to solve this problem?'" Andy recalls. "He didn't have an answer."

Andy was down to his last card: the school superintendent, the most powerful official in the Marsing school district. If he said no, the students would have to act outside school channels. That would be tougher, but not impossible. Baldy went with Andy to see the superintendent. The superintendent listened carefully to Andy's story and read the letter. "Then he looked up and said he was proud of us," Andy recalls. "He said he would be willing to read the letter himself if we wanted him to. I said no, we wanted to do it ourselves."

On the morning of the homecoming game, while other students were constructing floats and preparing for the parade, Andy Percifield was in the office photocopying one thousand copies of the students' letter. After school, he passed them out to the students who would be working as parking lot attendants at the game and told them to make sure two copies of the students' letter were handed into every car that entered the lot.

At halftime, as the homecoming floats circled the field, Allison Gibbons, a member of the student

---

superintendent *(n.)* the person responsible for all the schools in an area
floats *(n.)* large vehicles that are decorated to be part of a parade

council, entered the press box, stood before the microphone, and asked for everyone's attention. The crowd grew silent as she began to read the letter.

"I was watching the crowd while Allison read it," Andy said. "When she finished, there was a silence, and then almost everyone stood up and cheered. All the students stood up. And the football players were all clapping. It was a wonderful feeling to know that we had people behind us."

Since the letter was read, there have been no more racial slurs from the Marsing Husky fans, at least none loud enough for the players to hear. Neto and Andy know that they and Jesse and Rigo and Johnny didn't do away with racial prejudice in their town. Many white parents still won't let their sons and daughters date Latinos, and the two groups still don't mix much outside school. But they also know that they did what no one before them had done. "At least," says Neto, "we made it known that we wouldn't accept racism in our school or from our fans. We made a difference in the part of our lives that we really could control." ■

High school football was one of the Marsing community's favorite pastimes.

slurs *(n.)* offensive remarks

Reflect

1. Circle the expert strategies you used while reading this profile.

A. Question

B. Clarify

C. Other: _____

D. Other: _____

E. Other: _____

2. Use the letters above to label where in the profile you applied the expert strategies.

3. Select one expert strategy you used. Explain why you applied that strategy where you did.

_____

_____

_____

_____

READ ONLINE

expert space
Go to **www.expert21.com/ student** to learn more about Student Movements; First Amendment Freedoms; Hispanic Americans.

PROJECT
SOCIAL ACTION

ONE UNION ONE FIGHT

Rally for a Cause

THE SITUATION

The problem: Pick up any newspaper or flip on the TV and you'll be overwhelmed by all the things that are wrong with the world.

The question: Can kids make a difference?

The answer: Absolutely!

YOUR CHALLENGE

With a group of classmates, you will take a look at your own school and community to identify one problem or cause that you care about. You'll then plan a rally and show how a group of kids can really make a difference.

To hold a rally, you will

- Choose an issue to focus on.
- Set a goal for your rally.
- Check out information about planning and staging a rally.
- Create a slogan and artwork.
- Make a plan for your rally.

CAREER CONNECTION

Human Services

www.careerclusters.org

Go to **21 ToolKit Expert File 6.25** to learn more about careers in community services.

1 Choose Your Cause

With your group, talk about the problems in your school or community that really bother you. Take a look at the local newspaper for ideas, and talk to students, teachers, or other adults. Then, use the categories here to help you brainstorm more ideas. Write specific issues under each category, and then circle the issue you decide to focus on.

Student Issues:

Community Issues:

Kid Issues:

Volunteering Issues:

2 Be Creative

Every rally needs some creative visuals. Posters, banners, and signs with memorable slogans and eye-catching artwork will help unify your group and attract attention—especially of the media, which can really spread your message. Read the tips and look at the symbol collection in the **Resource Bank** on the following pages. Then sketch your poster (slogan and artwork) below.

3 Make a Plan

Now it's time to figure out exactly what you need to do to get ready for your rally. With your group, use the following template to make a plan. Brainstorm a list of tasks for each step. Go to [21] **ToolKit Expert File 2.1** to learn about brainstorming. Some ideas have been included for you.

Rally Plan

STEP 1: Choose the date and place to hold the rally.

Tasks:

STEP 2: Find and train volunteers.

Tasks:

STEP 3: Figure out a budget and raise money.

Tasks: Hold a car wash.

STEP 4: Get the word out.

Tasks: Post on social networking sites.

STEP 5: Find speakers and entertainers. Choose music.

Tasks:

STEP 6: Make posters, signs, and banners.

Tasks:

STEP 7: Create a schedule.

Tasks:

PROJECT
RESOURCE BANK

FACTS ABOUT RALLIES
Source: Activist's Blog
Date Accessed: September 23, 2008

YOUTH VOICES

Email This Article | Printer-Friendly

LESSONS FROM AN ACTIVIST

Posted at 3:50 P.M. on March 1, 2007 By Tim O'Leary

Here is what I've learned about holding protest rallies in my years as an activist.

- **Connect the place to the message.** Hold a rally about dumping chemicals in front of a lake—not in front of a bake shop. No cupcakes but better media coverage.

- **Be a marketer.** Unless you talk up your rally, you could end up with a "crowd" of seven people. Post flyers, give out handbills, post on social networking sites, email Listservs, and most of all, talk to people and get them to spread the word.

- **Money matters.** You'd be surprised how expensive rallies can be. Raise money by holding a bake sale, collecting change, or doing whatever works.

- **Don't be late! Big duh?** Hey, it once happened to me! Give yourself plenty of time to get to your event—especially if you're the one carrying the signs, leaflets, and bullhorns. Because if you're not on time, everyone may head home.

- **Make sure everything works.** There's nothing dorkier than talking into a megaphone that doesn't work. Be sure it's loaded with batteries. And check that the signs are clean and readable. Do this a few days before your event to avoid seriously unpleasant surprises.

- **Details, details! Be organized.** If you've planned a demonstration in front of your school, be sure that the street isn't being closed off for a parade on that day. Plan for enough space for the crowd. Don't forget speakers and entertainers who will donate their time, and double-check that they know where to go and when.

Name three things that can go wrong with your event if you don't plan properly.

_____

_____

_____

SYMBOLS OF PROTEST
Source: Visual Dictionary
Date: August 12, 2009

SIGNS OF PROTEST

Peace
peace sign started as anti-nuclear movement symbol

Raised fist
stands for resistance, protest, equality

Dove
a symbol of peace

V
is for victory over war and inequality

Rainbow
stands for diversity

Heart
stands for caring

Which symbols would most likely be used at an antiwar rally?

_____

_____

ARTICLE
Source: News Magazine Article
Date Accessed: December 18, 2008

Kids Who Care

Peaceful Rally to Save the Seals
by Karen Reilly

Armed with homemade posters and original songs, about 25 children from Kids for Peace joined a "Save Our San Diego Seals" coalition at Casa Beach. They were protesting the city's attempts to remove the seals from the beach. The children signed a petition to the San Diego City Council stating their wish to allow seal colonies access to the beach. The children hope to present the petition to the council. They also handed out flyers asking people to contact their councilperson about the situation.

> This article describes a successful rally planned by kids. Name one thing you learned from the entry that you can use in planning your rally.
>
> _____
>
> _____

PHOTOS
Source: Daily Newspaper
Date Accessed: May 3, 2006

Chicago, Illinois—About 300,000 demonstrators in Chicago did not report to work today, but instead took to the streets to protest restrictions on immigration. Among them were thousands of young people from predominantly Latino schools. The protests were part of a nationwide event called "A Day Without Immigrants."

> Do you think the title of this protest was effective?
>
> _____
>
> _____

Strategy Check

Use your knowledge and strategies from the workshop to answer these questions.

Draw Conclusions

1. What conclusion can you draw about why young people played a large role in the social changes of the 1960s? Support your answer with reasoning.

_____

_____

_____

_____

_____

_____

_____

_____

_____

_____

_____

Fact and Opinion

2. Based on the selections in this workshop, write two statements about the events of the 1960s. Make one a fact and the other an opinion. Provide evidence to support your opinion.

Fact: _____

_____

_____

Opinion: _____

_____

_____

Figurative Language

3. Write an example of these three things: a metaphor, a simile, and an image.

metaphor: _____

_____

simile: _____

_____

image: _____

_____

Primary Sources

4. Check the box next to the primary sources in the list below.

❏ A speech on global warming.

❏ A journal kept by a Peace Corps volunteer.

❏ A book analyzing global warming trends.

❏ A magazine article about the Peace Corps.

Text Features

5. Which text feature is a repetition, in larger type, of an important part of the text? Fill in the circle next to the correct answer.

Ⓐ a caption   Ⓑ a heading

Ⓒ a table   Ⓓ a pull quote

Suffixes

6. Complete the chart below with three words that have suffixes.

Word	Base word	Suffix

Prefixes

7. Read the sentence below, and circle each word that contains a prefix. Then rewrite the sentence in your own words. Use other words in place of the words you circled.

In an unprecedented move to halt water pollution, state legislators made it illegal to dump inorganic substances into rivers and lakes.

_____

_____

_____

_____

Understand Persuasive Techniques

8. What are the four steps you should use when analyzing a persuasive image, like a poster?

Step 1: _____

_____

Step 2: _____

_____

Step 3: _____

_____

Step 4: _____

_____

Evaluate

9. The U.S. Constitution says that all Americans have certain rights. If our civil rights are not protected, what is the best way to fight for your rights? Answer this question using examples from the selections in this workshop.

_____

_____

_____

_____

_____

_____

_____

_____

_____

_____

_____

_____

_____

_____

_____

_____

_____

_____

? EXPERT QUESTION

How can we be heard?

10. Use what you have learned in the workshop to respond to the Expert Question. Jot down some notes here. Then use a separate piece of paper to write your response.

_____

_____

Glossary

A glossary is a useful tool found at the back of many books. It contains information about key words in the text. Look at the sample glossary entry below.

This is an **entry word** — the word you look up. It is divided into syllables.

This tells you the **part of speech** of the entry word.

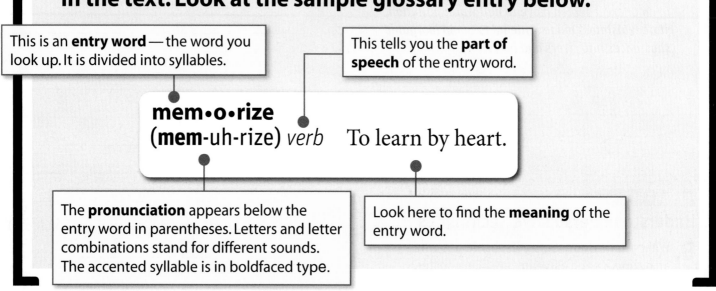

mem•o•rize
(**mem**-uh-rize) *verb*   To learn by heart.

The **pronunciation** appears below the entry word in parentheses. Letters and letter combinations stand for different sounds. The accented syllable is in boldfaced type.

Look here to find the **meaning** of the entry word.

ab•stract
(**ab**-strakt *or* ab-**strakt**) *adjective*
Showing imagined things rather than what people or objects actually look like.

ac•cess
(**ak**-sess) *noun*   The ability to enter a place or use something.

ac•com•mo•date
(uh-**kom**-uh-date) *verb*   To make space for.

ac•cus•tomed
(uh-**kuss**-tuhmd) *adjective*   To be familiar with something and accept it as normal.

Prefixes

Unaccustomed begins with the prefix *un-*, meaning "not" or "the opposite of." A **prefix** is a letter or letter group added to the beginning of a word to change its meaning. **Unaccustomed** means "not used to" or "the opposite of accustomed."

ac•quire
(uh-**kwire**) *verb*   To obtain or get something.

ad•e•quate
(**ad**-uh-kwit) *adjective*   Enough, or just what is needed.

ad•min•is•tra•tion
(ad-min-uh-**stray**-shuhn) *noun*   The people in the executive branch of government during a certain president's term.

a•dore
(uh-**dor**) *verb*   To worship or love a lot.

ad•van•tage
(ad-**van**-tij) *noun*   A benefit; something that helps you get ahead.

ad•vise
(ad-**vize**) *verb*   To guide; to suggest something.

af•firm
(uh-**furm**) *verb*   To approve something or say it is true.

ag•o•ny
(**ag**-uh-nee) *noun*   Great pain or suffering.

al·le·giance
(uh-**lee**-junss) *noun* Loyalty; obedience.

al·ter·nate
(**awl**-tur-nit) *adjective* Every second time.

am·bush
(**am**-bush) *verb* To attack by surprise from a hidden place.

angst
(**angst**) *noun* A feeling of anxiety.

ap·point
(uh-**point**) *verb* To choose someone for a position or job.

ap·pre·hen·sive
(ap-ri-**hen**-siv) *adjective* Nervous or uneasy about a future event.

ap·ti·tude
(**ap**-ti-tood) *adjective* Having to do with the natural ability to do well.

ar·du·ous
(**ar**-joo-uhss) *adjective* Very difficult; demanding great effort.

ar·id
(**ar**-id) *adjective* Very dry, without much rainfall.

ar·ro·gance
(**a**-ruh-guhnss) *noun* Behavior that is conceited or too proud.

as·sess
(uh-**sess**) *verb* To evaluate.

as·ter·oid
(**ass**-tuh-roid) *noun* A piece of rock that orbits the sun.

a·troc·i·ty
(uh-**tross**-uh-tee) *noun* A terrible cruelty done to a person or group.

at·tend·ant
(uh-**ten**-duhnt) *noun* Someone who serves or waits on people.

au·di·tion
(aw-**dish**-uhn) *verb* To try out for a role or part by giving a performance.

a·wry
(uh-**rye**) *adverb* Wrong; amiss.

bit·ter·sweet
(**bit**-ur-sweet) *adjective* Producing both pain and happiness.

brace
(**brayss**) *verb* To prepare for something unpleasant, usually by tightening your muscles.

bur·den
(**bur**-duhn) *noun* Something that is heavy and hard to carry.

cap·i·tal·ist
(**kap**-uh-tuh-list) *noun* A person who favors a society in which most goods and property are owned by individuals, not the government.

cap·tor
(**kap**-tuhr) *noun* A person who takes someone as a prisoner.

car·a·van
(**kar**-uh-van) *noun* A group of people, animals, or vehicles carrying cargo and traveling as a group.

Noun Endings

To make most nouns plural, add an *s*, as in ***caravans***. But nouns that already end in *s* need *–es*, as in ***losses***. Nouns that end in *y* need *–ies*, as in ***casualties***.

---

cas·u·al·ty
(**kazh**-oo-uhl-tee) *noun* Death or injury that occurs as a result of war.

cat·a·pult
(**kat**-uh-puhlt) *verb* To cause something to rise forcefully and suddenly.

cen·tu·ry
(**sen**-chuh-ree) *noun* A period of 100 years.

cha·os
(**kay**-oss) *noun* A state of total disorder and confusion.

char·is·mat·ic
(ka-riz-**mat**-ik) *adjective* Having a powerful ability to charm and influence people.

clut·tered
(**kluht**-urd) *adjective* Crowded, messy, and disorderly.

col·league
(**kol**-eeg) *noun* A coworker or fellow member of an organization.

col·lec·tive·ly
(kuh-**lek**-tiv-lee) *adverb* Together as a whole.

com·et
(**kom**-it) *noun* Chunks of rocks, frozen gas, and ice that orbit the sun.

com·pact
(**kom**-pakt) *adjective* Designed to take up very little space.

com·pas·sion
(kuhm-**pass**-shuhn) *noun* A feeling of sympathy for and a desire to help someone who is suffering.

com·po·si·tion
(kom-puh-**zish**-uhn) *noun* Something whole formed in a certain way from parts.

com·prise
(kuhm-**prize**) *verb* To consist of; to be made up of.

con·cen·tra·tion
(kon-suhn-**tray**-shuhn) *noun* Focusing your thoughts and attention on something.

con·du·cive
(kuhn-**doo**-siv) *adjective*   Tending to bring about a particular result.

con·sole
(kuhn-**sole**) *verb*   To comfort; to try to make someone feel better.

con·struc·tive
(kuhn-**struhk**-tiv) *adjective*   Useful; helping with improvement.

con·tour
(**kon**-toor) *noun*   The outline or edge of an object, or a line that represents it.

con·vert
(kuhn-**vert**) *verb*   To change into another form.

co·or·di·nate
(koh-**or**-duh-nate) *verb*   To move or work together smoothly and easily.

co·or·di·na·tion
(koh-or-duh-**nay**-shuhn) *noun*   The act of working together smoothly.

cor·po·ra·tion
(kor-puh-**ray**-shuhn) *noun*   A company or other business group.

course
(**korss**) *noun*   A class or series of classes in a subject.

Idioms

When something is **"par for the course"** it is typical or expected. This expression is an **idiom**, a phrase that means something different from the meanings of its separate words.

cun·ning·ly
(**kuhn**-ing-lee) *adverb*   In a clever, sneaky way.

cus·tom·ize
(**kuhss**-tuh-mize) *verb*   To prepare something to meet a particular need or requirement.

cyl·in·der
(**sil**-uhn-dur) *noun*   A shape like a tube or can.

dec·ade
(**dek**-ayd) *noun*   A period of ten years.

de·cep·tive·ly
(di-**sep**-tiv-lee) *adverb*   In a way that is misleading or false.

de·cline
(di-**kline**) *verb*   To turn something down or refuse it.

de·flect
(di-**flekt**) *verb*   To make something go in a different direction.

de·ject·ed
(di-**jekt**-id) *adjective*   Unhappy, disappointed, or sad.

de·mise
(di-**mize**) *noun*   Death or disappearance.

de·pict
(di-**pikt**) *verb*   To show something in a picture or with words.

de·port
(di-**port**) *verb*   To send people back to the country of their birth.

de·prive
(di-**prive**) *verb*   To prevent someone from having something, especially something necessary.

des·o·late
(**dess**-uh-luht) *adjective*   Empty; deserted.

de·spise
(di-**spize**) *verb*   To greatly dislike someone or something.

de·tect
(di-**tekt**) *verb*   To discover or notice something.

de·vice
(di-**visse**) *noun*   An object or mechanism used for a particular purpose.

de·vi·ous
(**dee**-vee-uhss) *adjective*   Winding or roundabout; deceitful or tricky.

de·void
(di-**void**) *adjective*   Without something or empty of something.

dig·it·al
(**dij**-uht-uhl) *adjective*   Relating to electronic or computer-based technology.

di·lem·ma
(duh-**lem**-muh) *noun*   A hard choice between two difficult alternatives.

di·men·sion
(duh-**men**-shuhn) *noun*   A measurement of space; in science fiction, a universe.

di·min·ish
(duh-**min**-ish) *verb*   To decrease or to become decreased.

dis·card·ed
(diss-**kard**-ed) *adjective*   Thrown away or abandoned.

dis·creet
(diss-**kreet**) *adjective*   Showing good judgment in the way information is shared.

dis·dain
(diss-**dayn**) *verb*   To treat with lack of respect; to look down on something.

dis·perse
(diss-**purss**) *verb*   To break up or scatter in various directions.

dome
(**dohm**) *noun*   A round structure shaped like half of a sphere.

drought
(**drout**) *noun*   An unusually long period of time without rain.

ech·o
(**ek**-oh) *verb* To be repeated or heard over and over.

ef·fi·cient
(uh-**fish**-uhnt) *adjective* Wasting as little time, energy, and effort as possible.

ef·fi·cient·ly
(uh-**fish**-uhnt-lee) *adverb* In a way that gets the best results with the least waste of time or effort.

el·i·gi·ble
(**el**-uh-juh-buhl) *adjective* Having the right qualifications for something.

e·lu·sive
(i-**loo**-siv) *adjective* Difficult to find or catch.

em·brace
(em-**brayss**) *noun* A hug.

em·i·nent
(**em**-uh-nuhnt) *adjective* Well-known and respected.

Suffixes

Eminently ends with the suffix *-ly,* meaning "like or in a way that is." A suffix is a letter or letter group added to the end of a word. The suffix *-ly* changes **eminent** from an adjective to an adverb meaning "in a way that is eminent, or widely respected."

---

e·mis·sion
(i-**mish**-uhn) *noun* Something that is released into the atmosphere.

en·cir·cle
(en-**sur**-kuhl) *verb* To form a circle around.

en·crust·ed
(en-**kruhst**-ed) *verb* Covered with a hard coating.

en·gi·neer
(en-juh-**nihr**) *noun* A professional trained to use math and science to design machines and buildings.

en·grossed
(en-**grohst**) *adjective* Wholly absorbed.

e·nor·mi·ty
(i-**nor**-muh-tee) *noun* The quality of being very wicked or evil.

en·vi·sion
(en-**vi**-zhuhn) *verb* To imagine something.

e·ro·sion
(i-**roh**-zhuhn) *noun* The gradual wearing away of something.

etch
(**ech**) *verb* To impress strongly.

e·val·u·ate
(i-**val**-yoo-ate) *verb* To look at and judge the worth or quality of something.

e·voke
(i-**voke**) *verb* To call to mind a certain feeling or idea.

ex·ceed
(ek-**seed**) *verb* To be greater or better than something else.

ex·cel
(ek-**sel**) *verb* To do something very well.

ex·change
(eks-**chaynj**) *verb* To give something to someone and receive something in return.

ex·clu·sive
(eks-**kloo**-siv) *adjective* Limited; private; restricted.

ex·hi·bi·tion
(eks-uh-**bish**-uhn) *noun* A public display of works of art or objects of special interest.

ex·pan·sive
(eks-**pan**-siv) *adjective* Grand or large in scale.

ex·ter·nal·ly
(ek-**stur**-nuhl-lee) *adverb* Having to do with the outside of something.

ex·tract
(**ek**-strakt) *noun* A selection or excerpt.

ex·tra·cur·ric·u·lar
(ek-struh-kuh-**rik**-yuh-lar) *adjective* Connected with a school but not an academic class.

fate·ful
(**fayt**-fuhl) *adjective* Having an important and usually unpleasant effect on future events.

fi·er·y
(**fye**-ree *or* **fye**-uh-ree) *adjective* Full of emotion; enthusiastic and energetic.

fil·ter
(**fil**-tur) *verb* To pass liquid or gas through an object to strain out larger particles.

fore·front
(**for**-fruhnt) *noun* The most important or noticeable position.

foun·da·tion
(foun-**day**-shuhn) *noun* The base or basis of something.

fric·tion
(**frik**-shuhn) *noun* The rubbing of two objects against each other.

fu·gi·tive
(**fyoo**-juh-tiv) *noun* A person who is running from the law.

func·tion
(**fuhngk**-shuhn) *noun* The assigned job or duty of something.

fun·da·men·tal
(fuhn-duh-**men**-tuhl) *adjective* Basic and necessary.

fu·tur·is·tic
(fyoo-chur-**iss**-tik) *adjective*   Relating to the future.

gap·ing
(**gape**-ing) *adjective*   Wide open.

ge·nial·ly
(**jeen**-yuhl-ee) *adverb*   In a friendly and welcoming manner.

gru·el·ing
(**groo**-uh-ling) *adjective*   Tiring and difficult.

haul
(**hawl**) *verb*   To drag or pull something heavy.

haz·ard·ous
(**haz**-urd-uhss) *adjective*   Dangerous.

hol·o·gram
(**hol**-uh-grahm) *noun*   A three-dimensional image created by laser beams.

Root Words

The word **hologram** comes from the Greek root *holo* which means "whole" or "complete." A **root** is a word or word part from another language that is the basis of an English word.

hos·tile
(**hoss**-tuhl) *adjective*   Threatening or aggressive.

im·pact
(**im**-pakt) *noun*   The effect that something has.

im·pend·ing
(im-**pend**-ing) *adjective*   Upcoming; going to happen very soon.

im·per·so·nate
(im-**pur**-suh-nayt) *verb*   To pretend to be someone else.

im·ple·ment
(**im**-pluh-ment) *verb*   To put a plan or an idea into action.

im·press
(im-**press**) *verb*   To make people think highly of you.

in·come
(**in**-kuhm) *noun*   The amount of money a person earns.

in·crim·i·nat·ing
(in-**krim**-uh-nate-ing) *adjective*   Evidence that makes someone look guilty.

in·ev·i·ta·ble
(in-**ev**-uh-tuh-buhl) *adjective*   Impossible to prevent.

in·flict
(in-**flikt**) *verb*   To make someone else experience something unpleasant.

in·her·ent·ly
(in-**her**-ent-lee) *adjective*   Basically; by nature.

in·no·va·tive
(**in**-uh-vay-tiv) *adjective*   Completely new.

in·stance
(**in**-stuhnss) *noun*   One case or example of something.

in·su·la·tion
(in-suh-**lay**-shuhn) *noun*   Material used to prevent the passage of heat into or out of something.

in·teg·ri·ty
(in-**teg**-ruh-tee) *noun*   Honesty.

in·tel·lec·tu·al
(in-tuh-**lek**-choo-uhl) *adjective*   Involving thought or reason.

in·ter·ac·tion
(in-tur-**ak**-shuhn) *noun*   The activity of talking with other people and working together with them.

in·ter·fere
(in-tur-**fihr**) *verb*   To prevent something from happening; to get in the way of something.

Synonyms

To **interfere** is "to prevent something from happening" or "to get in the way." To **hinder** is "to make something difficult for someone to do." These words are **synonyms**, words that have the same or similar meanings.

in·ter·mit·tent
(in-tur-**mit**-uhnt) *adjective*   Starting and stopping, over and over.

in·ter·nal
(in-**tur**-nuhl) *adjective*   Located on the inside.

in·tern·ship
(**in**-turn-ship) *noun*   A job a student works at in order to gain work skills and experience.

in·ter·val
(**in**-tur-vuhl) *noun*   A period of time between two events or activities.

in·tol·er·a·ble
(in-**tol**-ur-uh-buhl) *adjective*   Impossible to endure or experience.

in·tri·cate
(**in**-truh-kit) *adjective*   Having a lot of fine detail; complex.

in·vig·o·ra·ting
(in-**vig**-uh-ray-ting) *adjective*   Energizing.

ir·rev·o·ca·ble
(ihr-**rev**-oh-kuh-buhl) *adjective*   Unable to be taken back, changed, or stopped.

jus·ti·fy
(**juhss**-tuh-fye) *verb* To show that something is fair or reasonable.

jux·ta·pose
(juhk-stuh-**poze** or **juhk**-stuh-poze) *verb* To place side by side for the purpose of comparing and contrasting.

lad·en
(**layd**-uhn) *adjective* Loaded or weighed down.

le·git·i·mate
(luh-**jit**-uh-mit) *adjective* Lawful and reasonable.

lei·sure·ly
(**lee**-zhur-lee) *adverb* In an unhurried or relaxed manner.

ma·neu·ver
(muh-**noo**-ver) *verb* To carefully direct or steer.

mech·a·nism
(**mek**-uh-nizm) *noun* A system of moving parts inside a machine.

mem·o·rize
(**mem**-uh-rize) *verb* To learn by heart.

me·te·or
(**mee**-tee-ur) *noun* A bright streak caused by a space rock entering Earth's atmosphere.

mo·bile
(**moh**-buhl) *adjective* Capable of moving.

mod·i·fy
(**mod**-uh-fye) *verb* To change or alter in some way.

mo·men·tous
(moh-**men**-tuhss) *adjective* Of great importance.

mo·ti·vate
(**moh**-tuh-vate) *verb* To encourage to do something; inspire.

na·tive
(**nay**-tiv) *adjective* Originally from a certain place.

net·work·ing
(**net**-wurk-ing) *adjective* Related to sharing interests and making connections.

nom·i·nate
(**nom**-uh-nate) *verb* To recommend someone for an award, honor, or job.

nur·ture
(**nur**-chur) *verb* To bring up; to take care of someone's needs, especially a child.

o·a·sis
(oh-**ay**-siss) *noun* A small area in a desert where water rises to ground level.

ob·jec·tive
(uhb-**jek**-tiv) *noun* A goal one plans to achieve; the job at hand.

ob·sta·cle
(**ob**-stuh-kuhl) *noun* Something that blocks a path or gets in the way.

op·pres·sion
(uh-**press**-shuhn) *noun* The placement of unfair burdens and restrictions on a person or group.

o·ri·en·ta·tion
(or-ee-uhn-**tay**-shuhn) *noun* A course introducing a new situation or environment.

o·ver·all
(oh-vur-**awl**) *adjective* In all; including everything.

par·a·noid
(**pa**-ruh-noid) *adjective* Believing unreasonably that you cannot trust people or that they are trying to harm you.

pe·cu·liar
(pi-**kyoo**-lyur) *adjective* Strange, unfamiliar, or slightly surprising.

per·cep·tion
(pur-**sep**-shuhn) *noun* Understanding; awareness.

per·va·sive·ness
(pur-**vay**-siv-niss) *noun* The state of being extremely common or widespread.

pla·gia·rize
(**play**-juh-rize) *verb* To steal another person's words or ideas and pass them off as your own.

pop·u·lar·ize
(**pop**-yuh-lur-ize) *verb* To make popular and well-known.

por·trait
(**por**-trit) *noun* A drawing, painting, or photograph of a person.

pre·fer
(pri-**fur**) *verb* To like better than something else.

pre·sump·tion
(pri-**zuhmp**-shuhn) *noun* Something you think must be true.

pri·or
(**prye**-ur) *adjective* Done or planned earlier than something else.

pri·va·cy
(**prye**-vuh-see) *noun* Freedom from unwanted exposure.

pro·found
(pruh-**found**) *adjective* Far-reaching and very significant.

pro·hib·it·ed
(proh-**hib**-it-ed) *adjective* Forbidden by law or authority.

prom·i·nent
(**prom**-uh-nuhnt) *adjective* Obvious and easily visible.

Glossary

prop·a·gan·da
(prop-uh-**gan**-duh) *noun*   Incomplete or biased information designed to influence the way people think.

pro·pel
(**pruh**-pel) *verb*   To cause something to move.

pro·por·tion
(pruh-**por**-shuhn) *noun*   A certain part or fraction of a whole.

pros·per·ous
(**pross**-pur-uhss) *adjective*   To be successful; to have wealth.

pur·sue
(pur-**soo**) *verb*   To try to accomplish or obtain.

quan·da·ry
(**kwahn**-duh-ree) *noun*   A state of confusion or uncertainty.

ral·ly
(**ral**-lee) *verb*   To gather together with others to support a common purpose.

ra·tion
(**rash**-uhn) *verb*   To distribute sparingly.

re·cit·al
(ri-**sye**-tuhl) *noun*   A music or dance performance.

re·cruit
(ri-**kroot**) *noun*   Someone who has recently joined a group or team.

reg·u·la·tion
(reg-yuh-**lay**-shuhn) *noun*   A rule or law.

re·ject
(ri-**jekt**) *verb*   To refuse to accept something.

re·lo·ca·tion
(ri-loh-**kay**-shuhn) *noun*   A move to a new place.

rep·re·sent
(rep-ri-**zent**) *verb*   To serve as an excellent example.

re·pulse
(ri-**puhlss**) *verb*   To make someone feel sick or disgusted.

re·quire·ment
(ri-**kwire**-ment) *noun*   Something you need to do or have.

re·sist·ance
(ri-**ziss**-tuhnss) *noun*   The act of resisting or fighting against something.

re·stric·tion
(re-**strikt**-shuhn) *noun*   Something that limits or takes away rights.

ret·ri·bu·tion
(ret-trib-**yoo**-shuhn) *noun* Punishment that is deserved.

re·volt
(ri-**vohlt**) *noun*   A rebellion.

rev·o·lu·tion
(rev-uh-**loo**-shuhn) *noun*   A sudden, sometimes violent change in government.

Multiple-Meaning Words

Revolution means "a sudden, sometimes violent change in government." It also means "the orbiting of one body in space around another." **Multiple-meaning words** are words that have more than one meaning.

---

re·vul·sion
(ri-**vuhl**-shuhn) *noun*   A strong feeling of disgust.

rig·or
(**rig**-ur) *noun*   Strict devotion to something.

rue·ful·ly
(**roo**-fuhl-lee) *adverb*   In a way that shows shame or regret.

rum·mage
(**ruhm**-ij) *verb*   To search through, especially by moving, turning, or looking through the contents of a container.

sal·vage
(**sal**-vij) *noun*   Something that has been saved from destruction or loss.

sat·el·lite
(**sat**-uh-lite) *noun*   A machine sent into space to orbit Earth, used for radio, television, and other electronic communication.

saun·ter
(**sawn**-tur) *verb*   To walk in a slow or casual way.

schol·ar·ship
(**skol**-ur-ship) *noun*   Money given to a student to pay for school.

scope
(**skohp**) *verb*   To look at, often for the purpose of evaluation.

sculp·ture
(**skuhlp**-chur) *noun*   A three-dimensional work of art made by carving, modeling, or constructing.

seep
(**seep**) *verb*   To flow or trickle slowly.

se·mes·ter
(suh-**mess**-tur) *noun*   Half of the school year, usually about four months long.

sen·sa·tion
(sen-**say**-shuhn) *noun*   A feeling that comes from heightened interest or emotions.

sen·sor
(**sen**-sur) *noun*   A device that scans an object and senses its characteristics.

shun
(**shun**) *verb*   To deliberately avoid something or someone.

Antonyms

Shun means "to deliberately avoid something or someone." *Welcome* means "to greet in a friendly way." These words are **antonyms**, words that have opposite meanings.

---

sol·i·ta·ry
(**sol**-uh-teh-ree) *adjective*   Completely alone; without human contact.

spe·ci·fic
(spi-**sif**-ik) *adjective*   Particular.

spon·sor
(**spon**-sur) *verb*   To help and support, often in an official and/or financial way.

sta·tion·a·ry
(**stay**-shuhn-eh-ree) *adjective*   Not moving or not able to be moved.

ster·ile
(**ster**-uhl) *adjective*   Free from bacteria or other germs.

strat·e·gy
(**strat**-uh-jee) *noun*   Plan of action.

sub·se·quent
(**suhb**-suh-kwuhnt) *adjective*   Coming after; next.

suc·ces·sion
(suhk-**sesh**-shuhn) *noun*   A series of events that happen one after the other.

sup·port·ive
(suhp-**port**-iv) *adjective*   Ready to help out; understanding.

sus·pend
(suhs-**pend**) *verb*   To stop something for a short time.

sus·pense·ful
(suhs-**penss**-ful) *adjective*   Filled with excitement over an uncertain outcome.

swift·ly
(**swift**-lee) *adverb*   In a very fast manner; quickly.

tran·sit
(**tran**-zit) *noun*   Related to a system of buses or trains that moves people or goods.

tran·si·tion
(tran-**zi**-shuhn) *noun*   Movement from one place to another or from one lifestyle to another.

trau·ma
(**traw**-muh) *noun*   Serious physical, mental, or emotional damage.

tra·verse
(tra-**verss**) *verb*   To travel across.

un·der·foot
(uhn-der-**fut**) *adverb*   In the way.

Compound Words

Underfoot is a compound word. A **compound word** is made up of two smaller words, like *under* + *foot*.

---

un·der·tak·ing
(**uhn**-dur-tayk-ing) *verb*   To commit oneself to and begin.

u·ni·ver·sal
(yoo-nuh-**vur**-suhl) *adjective*   Common to everyone or everything.

un·prec·e·dent·ed
(un-**press**-uh-dent-id) *adjective*   Never seen or done before.

up·roar
(**uhp**-ror) *noun*   State of disturbance.

van·dal·ize
(**van**-duhl-ize) *verb*   To harm or destroy property that belongs to someone else.

var·si·ty
(**var**-si-tee) *noun*   The main team that represents a school in a sport.

vi·o·la·tion
(**vye**-uh-lay-shuhn) *noun*   An action that breaks a rule.

vir·tu·al
(**vur**-choo-uhl) *adjective*   Generated by a computer; not real.

vul·ner·a·ble
(**vuhl**-nur-uh-buhl) *adjective*   Able to be harmed or damaged.

wince
(**winss**) *verb*   To flinch; to draw back from as if in pain.

with·er
(**with**-ur) *verb*   To dry up and shrivel from lack of water.

wretch·ed
(**rech**-id) *adjective*   Extremely unpleasant or miserable.

Glossary of Literary Terms

alliteration
The repetition of initial (beginning) consonant sounds in a string of words. Notice the alliteration in this line: *a sweet, sad song.*

assonance
The repetition of vowel sounds within non-rhyming words. The repetition of the "aw" sound in the following line is an example: *the soft wings of the moth.*

author's perspective
A writer's way of looking at a topic. Perspective is usually influenced by the author's background and experiences.

author's purpose
A writer usually writes for one or more of these purposes: to express thoughts or feelings, to inform or explain, to persuade, or to entertain.

autobiography
A writer's account of his or her own life. It is usually told from the first-person point of view.

biography
The true account of a person's life, written by another person. Biographies are usually told from a third-person point of view. The writer of a biography researches his or her subject through interviews, primary sources, and/or reference materials.

cast of characters
A list of all the characters in a play, usually in order of appearance. It appears at the beginning of a script, and may contain a brief description of each character.

character
The people, animals, or imaginary creatures in a work of literature.

main character Main characters are the most important characters in literary works.

minor characters The less important characters in a literary work are known as minor characters.

dynamic character A dynamic character is one who changes over the course of a story.

static character A static character is one who stays the same throughout a story, no matter what experiences he or she has.

characterization
The way a writer creates and develops characters. There are five basic methods of characterization:
- The story's narrator makes direct comments about a character.
- The writer describes the character's physical appearance.
- The writer presents the character's own thoughts, speech, and actions.
- The writer shows how other characters think about or interact with the character.
- The writer reveals a character's motivation, or the reason why the character acts a certain way.

See also **character; character traits.**

character traits
The character's qualities. These qualities may include physical traits (strength) as well as personality traits (stubbornness).

climax
The point of greatest interest in a story. At the climax, the outcome of the plot usually becomes clear.

See also **plot.**

conflict

A struggle between opposing forces. Almost every story has a main conflict that is the focus of the story.

external conflict A struggle between a character and a force outside him or herself: nature, a physical obstacle, another character, or society.

internal conflict A struggle that occurs within a character; for example, deciding whether to betray a friend.

consonance

The repetition of consonant sounds within and at the ends of words: *o̱n a lo̱nely aftern̲oon.*

See also **alliteration.**

dialect

A variation on a language spoken in a particular place or by a particular group of people. Dialects may feature unique pronunciations, vocabulary, and grammar.

dialogue

Written conversation between two or more characters. Writers use dialogue to bring characters to life and move the story's action along.

diary

A daily record of a person's experiences and feelings, written by that person. The terms *diary* and *journal* are often used to mean the same thing.

drama

A form of literature meant to be performed by actors in front of an audience. In a drama, the characters' dialogue and actions tell the story. The written form of a play is known as a script. A script usually includes a cast of characters, dialogue, and stage directions. Dramas are usually divided into acts and scenes.

epic

A long narrative poem on a serious subject. It is usually written in formal style and tells the adventures of a great hero whose actions reflect the ideals of his or her society. *Beowulf* and *The Odyssey* are examples.

essay

A short work of nonfiction that deals with a single subject. An *expository essay* presents or explains information and ideas. A *personal essay* usually tells about the writer's experiences, feelings, and beliefs. A *persuasive essay* attempts to convince the reader to take action or accept a certain opinion.

exposition

The first stage of a typical story plot. The exposition introduces the setting and the important characters. The exposition may also introduce the story's conflict.

fable

A brief tale told to illustrate a moral or teach a lesson. Often the moral of a fable is directly stated near the tale's beginning or end.

falling action

The stage of the plot in which the story begins to come to a close. The falling action comes between the climax and the resolution. Events in the falling action begin to show the results of an important decision or action that happened at the climax.

See also **climax; plot.**

fiction

Writing that tells an imaginary story. It includes both short stories and novels. The writer of a fictional work might invent all the events and characters or might base parts of the story on real people and events. The basic elements of fiction are *plot, character, setting,* and *theme.*

See also **novel; short story.**

figurative language

Words or phrases that go beyond the literal meanings of words. Writers use figurative language to create a picture in readers' minds, to emphasize ideas, and to create strong emotion.

See also **metaphor; onomatopoeia; personification; simile.**

first-person point of view

See **point of view**.

flashback

Interrupts the sequence of events to tell about something that took place at an earlier time. A flashback provides information that can help a reader better understand a character's current situation.

folk tale

A story that has been passed from generation to generation originally by word of mouth. Folk tales often take place in the distant past and involve supernatural events. Characters may be animals, people, or superhuman beings.

foreshadowing

Provides hints about what will happen in a story. Foreshadowing creates suspense and makes readers eager to find out what will happen.

form

The structure or organization of a piece of writing. The form of a poem, for example, includes the arrangement of its words and lines on the page.

genre

A category, or group, in which a work of literature is classified. The major genres in literature are fiction, nonfiction, poetry, and drama.

graphic story

A story that combines text and visuals and tells the plot through a series of panels. Graphic stories often include speech bubbles to convey dialogue and captions to present information to the reader.

hero

A main character in a story. In older literary works, the heroes are often courageous, strong, honorable, and intelligent. In today's stories, a hero may be an ordinary person with ordinary problems.

historical fiction

A short story or a novel set in the past which includes real places and real events.

hyperbole

Figurative language in which the truth is exaggerated for emphasis or humorous effect: *I tried a million times, but I could not do that puzzle.*

idiom

An expression with a meaning different from the meaning of its individual words. For example, if a job is said to be "a piece of cake," it can be done easily.

imagery

Descriptive words and phrases that appeal to one or more of the five senses—sight, hearing, smell, taste, and touch. Writers use imagery to help readers picture what the writers describe.

interview

A conversation between a writer or reporter and another person in which the writer asks questions to gather facts and information. Interviews may be recorded, broadcast, or published.

journal

See **diary**.

legend

A story handed down from the past about a hero or someone who has achieved something great. Legends usually have some basis in historical fact.

line

The core unit of a poem. In a poem, lines may end, or break, at the end of a phrase or in the middle of one.

memoir

A form of autobiographical writing in which a writer shares his or her personal experiences and observations.

See also **autobiography**.

metaphor

A comparison of two things that are different but have some qualities in common. Unlike a simile, a metaphor does not include the words *like* or *as*. If a person is described as "a beast," he probably is big and mean.

See also **figurative language; simile**.

meter

In poetry, the repeated pattern of rhythm in a poem.

See also **rhythm**.

mood

The feeling or atmosphere that a writer creates in a piece of writing. For example, *gloomy, lighthearted,* or *suspenseful* could be the mood of a piece.

See also **tone**.

moral

A lesson that a story teaches. A moral is often stated at the end of a fable. A reader must often infer a story's moral from what happens to the characters.

See also **fable**.

motivation

See **characterization**.

myth

Stories that explain the creation of the world or something in nature, such as the changing seasons. They often focus on both gods and mortals, and in ancient times were used to comment on personality traits and human behavior.

narrative poetry

Poetry that tells a story. Like fiction, a narrative poem contains characters, a setting, and a plot.

narrator

The voice that tells a story. Sometimes the narrator is a character in the story. At other times, the narrator is an outside voice created by the writer. The narrator is not the same as the writer. In drama, the narrator is a character who explains the action in the play to the audience.

See also **point of view**.

nonfiction

Writing that tells about real people, places, and events. Nonfiction is mainly written to communicate facts and information. Nonfiction includes a wide range of writing: newspaper articles, Web sites, biographies, essays, movie reviews, speeches, blogs, and more.

See also **fiction**.

novel

A long, complex work of narrative fiction, usually divided into chapters. Novels most often feature invented characters and events, but sometimes include characters based on real people and events drawn from history or the news. Novels include the basic elements of fiction: *plot, character, setting,* and *theme.*

See also **fiction**.

omniscient point of view

See **point of view**.

onomatopoeia

A word that sounds like the action it describes. An example is the word *buzz.*

See also **sound devices**.

oral literature

Stories that have been passed down by word of mouth from generation to generation. Oral literature includes folk tales, legends, and myths.

personification

The giving of human qualities to an animal, object, or idea. For example, the wind is personified in this poem by James Stephens: *The wind stood up and gave a shout./He whistled on his fingers and/kicked the withered leaves about.*

See also **figurative language**.

play

See **drama**.

plot

The series of events in a story. The plot usually centers on a conflict, or struggle, faced by the main character. The main stages of a plot include exposition, rising action, climax, falling action, and resolution.

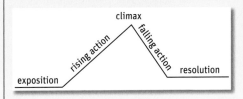

See also **climax; conflict; exposition; falling action; resolution; rising action.**

poetry

Literary works in which words are chosen and arranged in rhythmic verses that express emotions and ideas in imaginative ways.

point of view

The method of narration used in a short story, novel, narrative poem, or work of nonfiction.

first-person point of view

The narrator is a character in the story and refers to himself or herself as "I."

second-person point of view

The main character is presented using "you" as the main pronoun.

third-person point of view

The narrator is outside of the action, and is not one of the characters.

third-person omniscient

or all-knowing point of view: The narrator sees into the minds of all characters.

third-person limited point of view

The narrator tells what only one character thinks, feels, and observes.

protagonist

The main character in a story, play, or novel. The protagonist is involved in the main conflict of the story.

repetition

A technique in which a sound, word, phrase, or line is repeated. Repetition helps to emphasize meaning and create an appealing rhythm in a speech or poem. For example, the phrase "I have a dream" is repeated throughout Dr. Martin Luther King, Jr.'s most famous speech.

See also **alliteration; sound devices.**

resolution

See **falling action.**

rhyme

Similar or identical sounds at the end of two or more words, such as *beat, heat,* and *complete.* Lines in a poem often end with rhyming words.

rhyme scheme

A pattern of end rhymes in a poem. A letter of the alphabet is assigned to each line. Lines that rhyme are given the same letter. Notice the rhyme scheme in this poem by Christina Rosetti:

Is the moon tired? she looks so pale *a*
Within her misty veil; *a*
She scales the sky from east to west *b*
And takes no rest, *b*

rhythm

A pattern of stressed and unstressed syllables in a line of poetry. Poets use rhythm to bring out the musical quality of language and to create moods. Outside of poetry, rhythm refers to the repetition of specific phrases, images, or ideas.

See also **meter.**

rising action

The stage of the plot that develops the conflict, or struggle. The events in the rising action build toward the climax, or turning point.

See also **plot.**

script

The text of a play, film, or broadcast.

second-person point of view
See **point of view.**

sensory details

Words and phrases that appeal to the reader's senses of sight, hearing, touch, smell, and taste.

See also **imagery.**

setting

The time and place of the action. Elements of setting include location, historical period (past, present, or future), season, time of day, and culture.

short story
A brief work of fiction that centers on a single idea. Generally, a short story has one main conflict that involves the characters and keeps the story moving.

See also **fiction.**

simile
A way of describing something by comparing it with something else, using the words *like* or *as*. For example, "This pillow is as light as a snowflake."

See also **figurative language; metaphor.**

sound devices
Words used to appeal to the sense of hearing. Some common sound devices include *alliteration, assonance, consonance, meter, onomatopoeia, repetition, rhyme,* and *rhythm.*

speaker
The voice an author uses to tell a story or present a poem to the reader.

speech
A talk or public address given to a group of people.

stage directions
The instructions to the actors, director, and stage crew in the script of a play. Stage directions often appear in parentheses and in italic type.

stanza
One of the groups of lines into which a poem or song is divided.

static character
See **character.**

style
A way of writing. It involves how something is said, rather than what is said. For example, a writer may use sentence fragments, repetition, and unusual words, or may prefer long sentences and poetic language.

surprise ending
An unexpected plot twist at the end of a story. The surprise may be a sudden turn in the action or a new piece of information.

suspense
The growing tension and excitement felt by a reader. A writer creates suspense by raising questions in the reader's mind. The use of foreshadowing is one way that writers create suspense.

See also **foreshadowing.**

symbol
A person, a place, an object, or an activity that stands for something beyond itself. For example, a white dove is a bird that represents peace.

tall tale
A humorous, exaggerated story about impossible events. Stories about folk heroes such as Pecos Bill and Paul Bunyan are typical tall tales.

theme
The main subject or idea of a piece of writing. For example, the theme of *Barrio Boy* is finding pride in one's heritage and culture.

third-person point of view
See **point of view.**

tone
The writer's attitude toward his or her subject. *Angry, sad,* and *humorous* are examples of different tones.

See also **author's perspective; mood.**

traits
See **character traits.**

turning point
See **climax.**

voice
The writer's unique use of language that allows a reader to "hear" his or her personality.

word choice
The use of clear, specific, and strong words by an author to create certain effects for the reader.

Traits of Writing Scoring Guide

Traits of Writing is a model for assessing and teaching. The traits work within the writing process to support revision and editing. Each puzzle piece below represents one of the traits that define good writing.

▶ **Use the scoring guides on the following pages to assess your own work against these traits.**

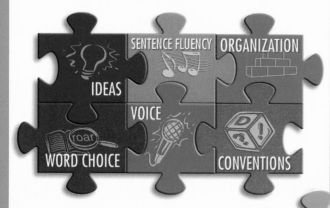

Ideas: The content of the piece, its central message and the details that support it.

Organization: The internal structure of the piece—the thread of the logic, the pattern of meaning.

Voice: The personal stamp of the writer, which includes tone, is achieved through a strong understanding of purpose and audience.

Word Choice: The specific vocabulary the writer uses to convey meaning and enlighten the reader.

Sentence Fluency: The way words and phrases flow through the piece. It is an auditory trait, and is therefore "read" with the ear as much as the eye.

Conventions: The mechanical correctness of the piece. Correct use of conventions (spelling, capitalization, punctuation, paragraphing, and grammar and usage) guides the reader through text easily.

Presentation: This trait addresses how the writing looks to the reader. This includes spacing, handwriting or font, formatting, and images.

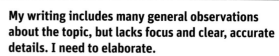

IDEAS

SCORE 6 — EXPERT
SCORE 5 — WELL DONE

My topic is well-developed and focused. My piece contains specific, interesting, and accurate details, and new thinking about this topic.

- I have a clear, central theme or a simple, original story line.
- I've narrowed my theme or story line to create a piece that is focused and a pleasure to read.
- I've included original information to support my main idea.
- I've included clear, accurate details that will create pictures in the reader's mind.

SCORE 4 — ALMOST THERE
SCORE 3 — MAKING STRIDES

My writing includes many general observations about the topic, but lacks focus and clear, accurate details. I need to elaborate.

- I've stayed on the topic, but my theme or story line is fairly general.
- I haven't dug into the topic in a logical, focused way.
- My unique perspective on this topic is not coming through as clearly as it could.
- The reader may have questions after reading this draft because my details don't provide answers.

SCORE 2 — ON THE WAY
SCORE 1 — GETTING STARTED

I'm still thinking about my theme or story line for this piece. So far, I've only explored possibilities.

- I've jotted down some ideas for topics, but it's a hodgepodge.
- Nothing in particular stands out as important in my piece.
- I've not written much. I may have just restated the assignment.
- My details are thin and need to be checked for accuracy.

ORGANIZATION

SCORE 6 EXPERT

SCORE 5 WELL DONE

My details unfold in a logical order. The structure makes reading my piece a breeze.

- My beginning grabs the reader's attention.
- I've used sequence and transition words to guide the reader.
- All of my details fit logically and my pacing is smooth.
- My ending gives the reader a sense of closure and something to think about.

SCORE 4 ALMOST THERE

SCORE 3 MAKING STRIDES

My piece's organization is pretty basic and predictable. I have the essential ingredients: beginning, middle, and end, but that's about it.

- My beginning is clear, but too obvious. I've used a technique that writers use all too often.
- I've used simple sequence and transition words that stand out too much.
- A few details need to be moved around to create a more logical flow of ideas.
- My ending needs work; it's pretty canned.

SCORE 2 ON THE WAY

SCORE 1 GETTING STARTED

My piece doesn't make much sense because I haven't figured out a way to organize it. My details are jumbled together at this point.

- My beginning doesn't indicate where I'm going next.
- I've not grouped ideas nor connected them using sequence and transition words.
- With no sense of order, it will be a challenge for the reader to sort out how ideas relate.
- I haven't figured out how to end this piece.

VOICE

SCORE 6 EXPERT

SCORE 5 WELL DONE

I've come up with my own "take" on the topic. I had my audience and purpose clearly in mind as I wrote and presented my ideas in an original way.

- My piece is expressive, which shows how much I care about my topic.
- The purpose for this piece is clear, and I've used a tone and tenor that is appropriate for that purpose.
- There is no doubt in my mind that the reader will understand how I think and feel about my topic.
- I've expressed myself in some new, original ways.

SCORE 4 ALMOST THERE

SCORE 3 MAKING STRIDES

My feelings about the topic seem obvious and predictable. The piece is not all that expressive, nor does it reveal a commitment to the topic.

- In a few places, my authentic voice comes through, but only in a few.
- My purpose for writing this piece is unclear to me, so the tone feels off.
- I've made little effort to connect with the reader; I'm playing it safe.
- This piece sounds like lots of others on this topic. It's not very original.

SCORE 2 ON THE WAY

SCORE 1 GETTING STARTED

I've not thought at all about my purpose and audience for the piece and, therefore, my voice falls flat. I'm pretty indifferent to the topic and it shows.

- I've put no energy into this piece.
- My purpose for writing this piece is a mystery to me, so I'm casting around aimlessly.
- Since my topic isn't interesting to me, chances are, my piece won't be interesting to the reader. I haven't thought about my audience.
- I have taken no risks. There is no evidence of my feeling about or interest in this topic.

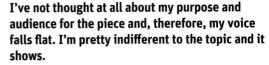

WORD CHOICE

SCORE 6 EXPERT

SCORE 5 WELL DONE

The words and phrases I've selected are accurate, specific, and natural-sounding. My piece conveys precisely what I want to say because I use powerful language.

- My piece contains strong verbs, which bring it alive.
- I stretched by using the perfect words and phrases to convey my ideas.
- I've used content words and phrases with accuracy and precision.
- I've picked the best words and phrases, not just the first ones that came to mind.

SCORE 4 ALMOST THERE

SCORE 3 MAKING STRIDES

My words and phrases make sense but aren't very accurate, specific, or natural-sounding. The reader won't have trouble understanding them, but may find them uninspiring, except perhaps for one or two.

- I've used passive voice. I should rethink those passages that contain it and add "action words."
- I haven't come up with new ways to say obvious things.
- My content words and phrases are accurate, but general. I might have used too much jargon. I need to choose more precise words.
- I need to revise this draft by replacing many of the words and phrases with stronger ones.

SCORE 2 ON THE WAY

SCORE 1 GETTING STARTED

My words and phrases are so unclear the reader may wind up more confused than entertained, informed, or persuaded. I might need to expand writing vocabulary to improve my piece.

- My verbs are not strong. I've used passive voice throughout this piece.
- I've used bland words and phrases throughout—or the same words and phrases over and over.
- My content words are not specific or accurate enough to make the meaning clear.
- My words and phrases are not working; they distract the reader rather than help him or her.

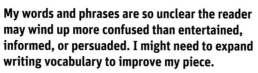

SENTENCE FLUENCY

SCORE 6 EXPERT

SCORE 5 WELL DONE

My piece is strong because I've written a variety of well-built sentences. I've woven those sentences together to create a smooth-sounding piece.

- I've constructed my sentences for maximum impact and used transitions effectively.
- I've varied my sentence lengths and types—short and long, complex and simple.
- When I read my sentences aloud, they are pleasing to the ear.
- I've broken the "rules" at points to create impact and interest.

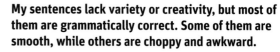

SCORE 4 ALMOST THERE

SCORE 3 MAKING STRIDES

My sentences lack variety or creativity, but most of them are grammatically correct. Some of them are smooth, while others are choppy and awkward.

- I've written solid shorter sentences. Now I need to try some longer ones.
- I've created different kinds of sentences, but the result is uneven.
- When my sentences are read aloud, the reader will stumble in only a few places.
- Any sentences that break the "rules" are accidental and don't work well.

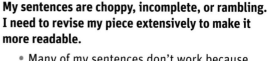

SCORE 2 ON THE WAY

SCORE 1 GETTING STARTED

My sentences are choppy, incomplete, or rambling. I need to revise my piece extensively to make it more readable.

- Many of my sentences don't work because they're poorly constructed.
- I've used the same sentence lengths and types over and over again.
- When I try to read my piece aloud, I stumble in many places.
- If I've broken any "rules," it's not for stylistic reasons. It's because I may not understand those rules.

CONVENTIONS

SCORE 6 EXPERT

SCORE 5 WELL DONE

My piece proves I can use a range of conventions with skill and creativity. It is ready for its intended audience.

- My spelling is strong. I've spelled almost all the words accurately.
- I've used punctuation creatively and correctly, and begun new paragraphs in the right places.
- I've used capitals in the right places throughout my piece, even in tricky places.
- I've taken care to apply standard English grammar and usage.

SCORE 4 ALMOST THERE

SCORE 3 MAKING STRIDES

My writing still needs editing for many problems in one convention or a variety of smaller problems in several conventions. I've stuck to the basics and haven't tried anything challenging.

- I've misspelled some words that I use all the time, as well as complex words that I don't use as often.
- My punctuation is basically strong. I should review it one more time. I indented the piece's first paragraph, but not others.
- I've used capitals in obvious places, but not in others.
- Even though my grammar and usage are not 100 percent correct, my audience should be able to read my piece.

SCORE 2 ON THE WAY

SCORE 1 GETTING STARTED

The problems I'm having in conventions make this piece challenging to read, even for me! I've got lots and lots of work to do before it's ready for its intended audience.

- Extensive spelling errors make my piece a challenge to read and understand.
- I haven't punctuated or paragraphed the piece well, which is necessary to guide the reader.
- My use of capitals is so inconsistent it's distracting.
- I need to clean up the piece considerably for grammar and usage.

PRESENTATION

SCORE 6 EXPERT

SCORE 5 WELL DONE

My piece's appearance makes it easy to read and enjoy. I've taken care to create a piece that is pleasing to my reader's eye.

- I've written very clearly and legibly. My letters, words, and spaces between them are uniform.
- My choice of font style, size, and/or color make my piece a breeze to read.
- My margins frame the text nicely. There are no tears, smudges, or cross-outs.
- Text features such as bulleted lists, charts, pictures, and headers are working well.

SCORE 4 ALMOST THERE

SCORE 3 MAKING STRIDES

My piece still looks like a draft. Many visual elements should be cleaned up and handled with more care.

- My handwriting is readable, but my letters, words, and the spaces between them should be treated more consistently.
- My choice of font style, size, and/or color seem off—inappropriate for my intended audience.
- My margins are uneven. There are some tears, smudges, or cross-outs.
- I've handled simple text features well, but am struggling with the more complex ones.

SCORE 2 ON THE WAY

SCORE 1 GETTING STARTED

My piece is almost unreadable because of its appearance. It's not ready for anyone but me to read.

- My handwriting is so hard to read it creates a visual barrier.
- All the font styles, sizes, and/or colors I've used are dizzying. They're not working.
- My margins are uneven or nonexistent throughout, making the piece difficult to read.
- I haven't used text features well, even simple ones.

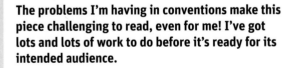

Author and Title Index

CHAIM POTOK [1929 – 2002]   MARGARET PETERSON HADDIX [1964 –]   MARY SHELLEY [1797 – 1851]   NEIL DEGRASSE TYSON [1958 –]   KATHERINE PATERSON [1932 –]   RAY BRADBURY [1920 –]   SUZANNE FISHER STAPLES [1945 –]

ARTHUR C. CLARKE [1917 – 2008]

ANNE FRANK [1929 – 1945]

JACK LONDON [1876 – 1916]

LOUNG UNG [1970 –]

WALTER DEAN MYERS [1937 –]

O. HENRY [1862 – 1910]

Acknowledgments

Grateful acknowledgment is made to the following sources for permission to reprint from previously published material. The publisher has made diligent efforts to trace the ownership of all copyrighted material in this volume and believes that all necessary permissions have been secured. If any errors or omissions have inadvertently been made, proper corrections will gladly be made in future editions.

Caldecott Medal and Newbery Medal seals reprinted by permission of the American Library Association. All rights reserved.

WORKSHOP 1
COLLEGE 101

"Playing the Game" from THE GAME by Walter Dean Myers. Copyright © 2008 by Walter Dean Myers. Reprinted by permission of HarperTeen, an imprint of HarperCollins Publishers.

"How to Survive, Thrive, and Prepare for What's Next" from THE REAL HIGH SCHOOL HANDBOOK by Susan Abel Lieberman. Copyright © 1997 by Susan Abel Lieberman. Reprinted by permission of Houghton Mifflin Harcourt Publishing Company. All rights reserved.

"My People" by Margaret Peterson Haddix from DESTINATION UNEXPECTED edited by Donald R. Gallo. Copyright © 2003 by Margaret Peterson Haddix. Published by Candlewick Press. Reprinted by permission of Adams Literary as agents for the author.

"I Couldn't Imagine Wanting to Dye My Hair Blonde" by Christina Mendoza from REAL COLLEGE ESSAYS THAT WORK by Edward B. Fiske and Bruce G. Hammond. Copyright © 2006 by Christina Mendoza. Published by Sourcebooks, Inc. All rights reserved.

"Chunky Peanut Butter" from "Essay" by James Gregory from COLLEGE ESSAYS THAT MADE A DIFFERENCE: SECOND EDITION edited by Erica Magrey. Copyright © 2006 by Princeton Review Publishing, LLC. Published by Random House, Inc. Reprinted by permission of Princeton Review Publishing, LLC. All rights reserved.

Adapted from "Essay 3A" by Hugh Gallagher. Copyright © 1990 by Hugh Gallagher. All rights reserved.

"On the Cutting Edge" adapted from "10 Radically Innovative College Programs" by Jonathan Gromer and Alex Hutchinson from Popular Mechanics, September 2006. Copyright © 2006 by Hearst Communications, Inc. Reprinted by permission of Hearst Communications, Inc.

WORKSHOP 2
DESIGNING THE FUTURE

"The Last Dog" by Katherine Paterson from TOMORROWLAND: STORIES ABOUT THE FUTURE compiled by Michael Cart. Copyright © 1999 by Minna Murra, Inc. Reprinted by permission of Scholastic Inc.

"Exposed to the Max" by Leah Paulos from Scholastic Choices magazine, September 2008. Copyright © 2008 by Scholastic Inc. All rights reserved.

"Cyberbullies" from READ 180 rBOOK®, FLEX. Copyright © 2006 by Scholastic Inc. All rights reserved.

"Virus" from SMOKE AND MIRRORS: SHORT FICTIONS AND ILLUSIONS by Neil Gaiman. Copyright © 1998 by Neil Gaiman. Published by HarperCollins Publishers. Reprinted by permission of Writers House, Inc. All rights reserved.

"Welcome to the Future" from DK EYEWITNESS BOOKS: FUTURE by Michael Tambini. Copyright © 1998, 2004 by Dorling Kindersley Ltd. Reprinted by permission of Dorling Kindersley Ltd.

"La Vida Robot" by Joshua Davis from Wired magazine, April 2005. Copyright © 2005 by Joshua Davis. Reprinted by permission of the author.

Adapted from "Robo-Legs" by Michael Marriott from New York Times Upfront, October 10, 2005. Copyright © 2005 by Scholastic Inc. All rights reserved.

"Futuristic Fashion Gets Smart" by Mark Tutton from the CNN Web site (www.CNN.com). Copyright © 2008 by Cable News Network. Reprinted by permission of Turner Broadcasting System, Inc. All rights reserved.

WORKSHOP 3
LIFE AT THE EDGES

"The Story of Keesh" by Jack London.

"Blue People of the Sahara" by Sean McCollum from Junior Scholastic magazine, May 8, 2000. Copyright © 2000 by Scholastic Inc. All rights reserved.

From SHABANU: DAUGHTER OF THE WIND by Suzanne Fisher Staples. Copyright © 1989 by Suzanne Fisher Staples. Cover photo © Jim Zuckerman/CORBIS. Reprinted by permission of Laurel Leaf, an imprint of Random House, Inc. All rights reserved.

"Extreme Athletes Run Length of Sahara" by David S. Morgan from the CBS Sports Web site (www.cbssports.com). Copyright © 2009 by The Associated Press. Reprinted by permission of The Associated Press.

"The Science of the Run" from the Running the Sahara Web site (www.runningthesahara.com). Copyright © 2007 by NEHST Studios, LLC. Reprinted by permission of NEHST Studios, LLC.

From HOW TO SURVIVE IN ANTARCTICA by Lucy Jane Bledsoe. Copyright © 2006 by Lucy Jane Bledsoe. Reprinted by permission of Holiday House, Inc.

WORKSHOP 4
1960s: STAND UP, BE HEARD

"I Have a Dream" speech by Martin Luther King, Jr.

Mike Kelley essay from "Coming Home" by Mike Kelley from The Vietnam Veterans Home Page Web site. Copyright © 1998 by Mike Kelley. Reprinted by permission of the author.

Thomas Bird letter from EVERYTHING WE HAD: AN ORAL HISTORY OF THE VIETNAM WAR BY THIRTY-THREE AMERICAN SOLDIERS WHO FOUGHT IN IT by Al Santoli. Copyright © 1981 by Al Santoli and Vietnam Veterans of America. Reprinted by permission of Random House, Inc.

George Williams, Salvator Gonzales, Kenneth Peeples, and Hector Ramos letters from DEAR AMERICA: LETTERS HOME FROM VIETNAM edited by Bernard Edelman. Copyright © 1985 by The New York Vietnam Veterans Memorial Commission. Published by W.W. Norton & Company, Inc. Reprinted by permission of Bernard Edelman. All rights reserved.

From AMERICA DREAMING: HOW YOUTH CHANGED AMERICA IN THE '60S by Laban Carrick Hill. Copyright © 2007 by Laban Carrick Hill. Reprinted by permission of Hachette Book Group USA.

"The Times They Are A-Changin'" lyrics by Bob Dylan. Copyright © 1963, renewed 1991 by Special Rider Music. Reprinted by permission of Special Rider Music.

"The Football Player and the Student Council President" from "Neto Villareal and Andy Percifield" from IT'S OUR WORLD, TOO! by Phillip Hoose. Copyright © 1993 by Phillip Hoose. Reprinted by permission of Farrar, Straus and Giroux, LLC. All rights reserved.

Credits

Credits